D

Takeover Madness

TAKEOVER MADNESS

Corporate America
Fights Back

Allen Michel

Israel Shaked

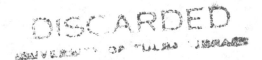
John Wiley & Sons

New York · Chichester · Brisbane · Toronto · Singapore

Library of Congress Cataloging in Publication Data:

Michel, Allen, 1945-

   Takeover madness. Corporate America fights back.

   Includes indexes.
   1. Consolidation and merger of corporations—United
States —Prevention—Cases studies. 2. Tender offers
(Securities)—Case studies. I. Shaked, Israel,
1948-   . II. Title. III. Title: Takeover madness.

HD2746.5.M53   1986   658.1′8   85-32315
ISBN 0-471-01079-0

Printed in the United States of America

10 9 8 7 6 5 4 3 2 1

To Our Families

Preface

The growth of hostile mergers has been staggering. No major corporation is immune from the threat of takeover. Both individuals and corporations have initiated well-publicized hostile raids. Indeed, the well-crafted invasions of corporate turf have often caught their targets off guard. In response, business executives, with the aid of the investment banking and legal community, have developed a wide variety of antitakeover measures. The deployment of such measures has often evolved into intense and exciting battles between management and the hostile aggressor.

The media report such takeover struggles on a daily basis, turning names such as T. Boone Pickens and Carl Icahn into household words. Yet many interested observers are overwhelmed by the wide variety of takeover defense strategies employed. This book is the first to fully describe the defensive arsenal available to corporate management. It also presents the colorful array of characters who are the combatants in these unfriendly battles to control corporate America.

Obviously, to gather the data and portray the details of the defensive struggles presented in the book was a significant effort. In particular, we would like to thank the following individuals: Christine Adamow, Charles Albert, Lorrey Bianchi, Gary Birnberg, Ricardo Bitran, Burton Buffington, Kathryn Cohen, Roseanna Creager, Carolyn Curry, John Cusson, John Dalton, Larry Dominey, Debbie Dorhamer, David Fisher, Richard Flood, Hill Grimmett, Frank Horohoe, Diane Mathurin, June Matte, Christopher McKinney, Clare Morris, Paul Mulligan, Kathy Murphy, Sarah Palmer, Ian Ried, Patricia Rogacz, Larry Smith, Chris Staszak, Edith Sturm, Gerry Yurko, and Michael Zwolinski. We are especially grateful to Ritchie Vener and T. J. Laskaris for their many contributions.

In addition, we would like to thank Vince Mahler, Emily Phillips, and David Cosseboom for their excellent word processing and editorial assistance, and Alice Briggs for her entertaining cartoons depicting each strategy.

In gathering data for this book, we have relied on publicly available information and data sources. We have striven to ensure accuracy in our depiction of the players, organizations, and actions in the merger arena. Any misinterpretation or misstatement is greatly regretted.

Last, but not least, we thank our families for suffering through dinner conversations of poison pills, sharks, and kamikazes instead of ordinary English.

ALLEN MICHEL
ISRAEL SHAKED

Boston, Massachusetts
March 1986

Contents

Takeover Madness

1
The Pac-Man Defense

"Gotcha!"

T. Boone Pickens Plays Pac-Man
MESA vs. CITIES SERVICE

The oil and gas industry has touched everyone's lives. The enormous influence of OPEC has prompted attention from the man in the street all the way to board chairmen around the country. There is another group of men, though, for whom the oil industry is a high stakes game to which Las Vegas pales in comparison. It is a world in which digging wells and selecting leases is no more than a mere crap shoot. But as in the casinos of the world, some play poker at the two dollar table and others at the hundred dollar table. The same holds true in the oil industry. In recent years takeover has been the big game and it has been played hard.

This story focuses on two players in a David and Goliath type battle. What makes this a more than unusual story, though some may dispute it, is the fact that David, not Goliath, picked the fight. Why there is some question as to who started the fight is because "David" is T. Boone Pickens and his Mesa Petroleum Company. Pickens exemplifies the American dream in many ways. After learning the ropes of the exploration business, he founded his own company. That firm eventually grew to be Mesa, with 1981 revenues approaching half a billion dollars. Pickens also habitually sought acquisition targets. Some people would not hesitate to call him a ruthless greenmailer, sapping the lifeblood out of healthy companies and leaving debt ridden, wounded companies in his wake. Pickens, on the other hand, would say he looks for companies where the management is giving the shareholders a raw deal, simply interested in maintaining their jobs, or because they lack the competence to maximize value for the shareholders. Pickens then proceeds to take actions that raise the companies' stock prices.

The other firm involved, Goliath in this case, was Cities Service. Cities dwarfed Mesa in almost all aspects. Its 1981 revenues were $8.56 billion compared to Mesa's $407.7 million. Cities was also a vast company in terms of undeveloped acreage, with roughly 35 million undeveloped net acres worldwide, ranking it among industry leaders.

Preventive Measures

On Thursday, May 28, 1982 Cities Service issued a one paragraph press release. In this brief bit of copy Cities leveled a heavy accusation in no uncertain terms. It said it believed a consortium, led by Mesa, was "conspiring" to force "dismemberment or liquidation" of Cities. It went on to say Cities would take "all appropriate action [to ensure] maintenance of its independence." Cities believed Mesa was trying to obtain financing and determined that any further involvement with Mesa would be "inconsistent with the interests" of its shareholders.

Considering that no tender offer or other proposal of business combination had taken place, such a release might seem a little paranoid. Knowing Pickens's nature and the fact that in August 1981 Mesa had disclosed that it owned 3,244,800 shares of Cities made the announcement more justifiable. Mesa's stake was only 4 percent of the roughly 80 million shares outstanding. However, on Wall Street, such a 4 percent announcement is enough to cause speculation, pushing share prices higher, making any takeover more expensive and difficult. Cities closed at $35.50 a share on Thursday the 28th, the day of its press release, making the cost of an acquisition $2.84 billion.

During the past several years, Cities had been the subject of many rumors about a possible takeover. A popular one focused on Mesa. It said that not only did Pickens buy his shares of Cities at a price $10 per share higher than the current market price, but he did so on margin. Pickens was said to be eager to put Cities up for sale so that he could recoup at least some of his sizable investment.

Cities apparently had been paying close attention to these rumors. During this time it repeatedly indicated an extreme lack of interest in unwelcome business combinations. At one point it went so far as to arrange a $3 billion line of credit to make its point. Since that time it had been trimmed to a mere $500 million. The previous August, after Mesa disclosed it had acquired a 4 percent stake in Cities, Cities' CEO said, "We're telling anyone who comes along with an offer to buzz off."

A Tale of Two Offers: Cities and T. Boone Play Pac-Man

The tone had been set and both players were ready for action. On May 31, 1982 both companies simultaneously made a play for each other. Mesa decided to put Cities "in play" by making a friendly offer and a threat. The friendly offer, subject to a positive vote by Cities' board, would be at $50 per share, well above a recent closing price of $35.50. The alternative would be for Mesa to acquire majority voting power via purchases at $50 a share and then force a combination. The remaining shares would be exchanged for Mesa common stock or a combination of common and senior debt worth $50 per share. The total value of the deal would be $4 billion. T. Boone Pickens said the offer was made "in the mutual interest of our respective shareholders and to avoid the expense and disruption of a protracted dispute." It was disclosed that Mesa's stake in Cities had been upped to 5.3 percent.

A Mesa spokesman declined to comment on how their small company would finance the acquisition of enormous Cities. There was much talk on the street about potential partners Pickens might be looking at to assist him. Among those said to be considered were: Southland Corporation, a Dallas-based operation that owned the 7-Eleven chain and 2,500 gas stations, Davis Oil Company of Denver, the Damson Oil Corporation, and Madison Fund, both of New York.

Though Pickens claimed the offer was made in the mutual interest of both companies' shareholders, it would be hard to ignore the fact that it was also made in light of a Cities tender offer for Mesa.

From its home office in Tulsa, Cities announced it would be launching a tender offer for Mesa starting June 1. The offer was at a surprisingly low $17 per share. That price was just $0.25 above the previous Friday's market price, though sources said the price was not final. The offer was seeking 51 percent of Mesa's shares on a fully diluted basis, or roughly 37 million shares. Moreover, the offer was contingent on at least half of those, or 18.5 million shares being tendered.

Cities kept the conditions on the tender offer very vague. It said it might waive the condition on a minimum number of shares, and also retain the right to purchase more than 37 million pending oversubscription. Cities also did not reveal any form of payment for a second step of the action, saying, "There is no assurance that any such transaction will be proposed or, if proposed, consummated." The offer was to expire at 12:01 A.M. on June 22, with the withdrawal deadline set at 12:01 A.M. June 27, and the proration deadline at 12:01 A.M. June 11. If more than the desired number of shares were tendered to Cities prior to the proration deadline, Cities would take a pro rata number of shares from all those who tendered so the sum would equal the desired number. This would happen only if Cities decided not to buy any shares beyond the number sought. The withdrawal deadline signified the date beyond which a share tendered to Cities was irrevocably committed. Prior to that date a shareholder had the right to ask for his/her shares to be given back. These rules are not specific to Cities, but to all tender offers. For advice Cities was using both First Boston and Lehman Brothers.

Cities' tender offer, while outwardly appearing offensive, was said by sources close to Cities to be defensive. Cities would have liked Mesa to go away, and its offer was meant to achieve this objective in three possible ways. Cities could draw enough stock to effect a swap for Mesa's stock, it could attract other suitors to Mesa, or, according to Cities, "We could always go through with acquiring Mesa." Another Cities advisor said, "We've lit a match in the powder room and Pickens better find a fire extinguisher quickly."

Some Reaction, Some More Information

The next day Cities called Mesa's friendly merger proposal a "rather weak tactical maneuver." However, they stopped short of outright rejection of the bid. This drew speculation from many Wall Street professionals but was flatly denied by Cities' financial and legal help. Cities described the Mesa proposal as "unclear" and thought it "unlikely" Mesa could obtain the roughly $1.8 billion needed to buy 51 percent of Cities in a hostile takeover.

Even though many banks limit lending in hostile takeover bids, Mesa seemed confident the financing could be raised if needed. According to Mesa, the current offer prompted inquiries from many companies interested in joining a takeover effort to acquire Cities.

A Mesa source said, "Pickens says we've more fish than we can string."

In addition to public announcements, Cities' offering circular became available, disclosing some interesting information. Even though the current offer for Mesa would only entail $635 million, Cities lined up $1.7 billion for the purpose of the acquisition. Also of interest, the circular disclosed that acquisitive Mesa already had in place several antitakeover measures. One was a limited partnership agreement that, upon takeover, would give away almost all of Mesa's undeveloped acreage to the limited partners. Another was an enormous golden parachute for Pickens. In the event of a tender offer or other transaction not approved by the board, Pickens could quit his job and receive twice his annual pay plus consulting fees equal to his annual compensation until December 31, 1989. In 1981, Pickens earned $575,008.

Market action was heavy for the stocks of both companies on June 1, the first day of the offer. In NYSE composite action, Cities Service rose $1.25 per share on a volume of 1,004,300 shares traded. Mesa's stock encountered even more heated action. On a volume of 1,156,300 shares traded, the price rose $2.75, leaving it at $19.50 when the closing bell rang.

Litigation and Accusations

Even though no hostile moves had yet been taken by Mesa, Cities took the opportunity to sue them. The suit, alleging fraud and stock manipulation, stated that Pickens fraudulently tried to convince the investing public "that it is feasible or practical for Mesa to acquire the [95 percent] of Cities Service stock which Mesa doesn't presently own." Cities went on to allege Mesa's interest costs to finance its 5 percent holdings of Cities stock was over $30 million a year, and that "Mesa could not pay the carrying costs of the debt it would . . . incur [in a takeover of Cities]."

In an even more unusual move, that Wednesday, June 3, Cities' law firm, Wachtell, Lipton, Rosen, and Katz, applied pressure to the leading bank from which Mesa hoped to obtain financing for the acquisition. The lawyers put Continental Illinois on notice that they planned to take sworn testimony from bank officials in connection with legal action against Mesa. That sort of thing is usually not done. Takeover specialists took this as a warning to Continental to back off.

Pickens called the suit "legal folderol." He went on to say, "We aren't hicks . . . . We didn't ride into town on a load of watermelons." About the carrying costs associated with holding Cities' stock, he said it was "closer to $20 million, and we can handle that easily out of cash flow." Pickens also gave some insight into the motive behind taking on Cities. "We had a feeling we needed to do something about our investment, because Cities Service's management was depleting the company's reserves and not replacing them . . . . [Finally Mesa] decided to make an acquisition proposal . . . to stop this process."

Mesa quickly countersued. It alleged "a long pattern of manipulative and deceptive actions" had been designed to keep management in their jobs. The suit also mentioned one of the press releases issued by Cities, calling it "a deliberate attempt to manipulate the market." Another allegation contained in the suit was that Cities issued 2.1 million new shares of common stock the previous month "for no business purpose" other than to dilute Mesa's holdings. The lawsuit also contained the first mention by Mesa that Southland Corporation and the Madison Fund were Mesa's potential partners.

Separately, Mesa said that Lehman Brothers had informed George Gould, president of the Madison Fund, that Cities was prepared to "play dirty and adopt a scorched earth policy" to defend itself. They also hinted that Cities would not be adverse to making a tender offer for the Madison Fund if it did not back down. The Madison Fund, indeed, had a track record of backing down from deals. It gave up trying to reach agreement with ACF Industries, Inc. and sold its 15 percent stake back to the company at a $5 million loss. It was also repulsed by Dorchester Gas Corp. in its attempt to buy 25 percent of the firm. Other failed attempts were in its history as well, so Cities smelled blood and aimed for the jugular.

Officially Hostile

Even though all parties concerned were acting as if Mesa had made a hostile bid for Cities, up until this point it had been termed a friendly offer. That changed on Monday, June 7. Mesa announced it would begin a tender offer of $45 per share for as many as 12.1 million shares of Cities. The $544.5 million bid was for only 15 percent of Cities, all that Mesa seemed financially capable of buying at the time. The offer was set to expire at midnight July 2. Even as Mesa announced a hostile offer, it repeated its friendly $50 per share offer, which had yet to be rejected by Cities' board. Like Cities Service, Mesa reserved the right to cancel the offer if the two reached a settlement. Donaldson, Lufkin and Jenrette (DLJ) was retained as Mesa's financial advisor.

In response to the offer, a Cities advisor called it "weak." According to sources, Pickens realized the offer was not impressive on the surface. However, there was more to it than met the eye. Mesa strategists felt a proration pool containing more than half of Cities stock would prove to be a very powerful aid in reaching a financing agreement to acquire Cities. "He'd be able to tell bankers and prospective partners, 'Look, there it is, control of Cities just lying there. All you've got to do is provide the money to pick up that stock,' " said a source familiar with the Mesa offer.

So there were two bids by Mesa in play at the same time. One was a friendly offer, subject to the approval of Cities' board, to buy all outstanding shares for $50 each. The second, and most recent, was a hostile offer to buy 15 percent of Cities for $45 per share. No approval was needed from the Cities' board on the hostile bid. Simultaneously, Cities' bid for Mesa was still on the table.

The Two Sides Reject Each Other

The following day, on the advice of DLJ, Mesa rejected Cities' bid, calling it inadequate. While the directors were together they also voted a supermajority provision into the bylaws. Under the provision, a 75 percent vote would be needed to change Mesa's leadership. Such an action could be challenged in court, but would serve to buy Mesa valuable time. Time was important, because with the timing of competing tender offers, Cities could acquire 51 percent of Mesa well before Mesa could do the same to Cities.

Separately, but on the same day, a Cities shareholder sued "to force [Cities] to consider the offer before them." William Clark, the plaintiff, said, "My stock is valued at about $36 a share and I think the [Cities] board of directors has more fiduciary duty to its shareholders to consider that offer and not solely to act in their personal interest and protect their jobs . . . . It appears they've rebuffed not only Mesa's offer in advance of it being made, but any and all future offers."

The day after Mesa rejected Cities' bid for Mesa, Cities rejected both of Mesa's bids for Cities. In a press release, Cities said both of its financial advisors "advised that the offers were inadequate from a financial point of view." At a press conference following the board meeting that led to the rejections, Cities Chairman Charles J. Waidelich said he might consider an offer higher than Mesa's, though he "will not put a price on Cities Service." Waidelich also disclosed that "I have had a call or two" from other oil companies interested in becoming white knights, but "I haven't followed up on them."

A Friendly Offer

In an unusual move on Cities' part, it offered a friendly bid to Mesa on the same day it rejected Mesa's bids. The move was unusual because a friendly offer usually precedes a hostile offer, not the other way around. In a letter sent to Pickens on Tuesday, Cities said that if Mesa supported the proposal, Cities would acquire all of Mesa for cash and stock. The new proposal would have Cities buy 51 percent of Mesa for $21 per share and exchange 0.45 Cities' common stock for each remaining share of Mesa's 73 million shares. The cash portion would be worth around $780 million and the share exchange, based on recent prices, an additional $588.8 million. The total package would be valued at $1.37 billion, or a per-share average of $18.50.

Commenting on the new offer, Pickens said, "The $21 part is easy enough to understand, but what about the 0.45 of a Cities Service share. Some of my analyst friends tell me that if this deal goes through, Cities' stock price will fall to the low 20s or high teens. In that case, 0.45 of a Cities Service share would only be worth about $9 and the total deal only about $15 per Mesa share." Pickens continued to say that Cities' latest move "reflects a weakness of intelligence."

Wall Street analysts did not all share that view, though they could only speculate as to why Cities made what seemed like a futile move. The popular theory was a little complicated, but went as follows. Essentially the move was done to attract greater attention and a response to its hostile bid of $17 per share. If Cities had simply changed its hostile bid to $21 per share, tender offer rules would have forced Cities to extend its proration and withdrawal deadlines. The key is that such deadlines cannot be extended once they have been passed. At $17 per share, it was widely speculated that Cities' offer would be undersubscribed. It was felt that once shareholders tendered prior to a proration date and the offer was undersubscribed, they tended to stand firm. That would then become an advantage for the bidder, who could then incrementally raise its offer price and accept stock on a first-come, first-served basis until the target number of shares was met. In this case it was 37 million shares. Cities' announcement of a "friendly" merger proposal could very likely have been a signal to tell of a price boost ahead of time to prevent its $17 offer from being a flop and not having to extend deadlines at this time.

At the same press conference, when Waidelich was asked if Pickens would be kept on after a Cities-dominated combination of the two firms, he replied, "Mr. Pickens could make a valuable contribution if he chose to stay." Later, Pickens jokingly replied, "I understand Chuck [Waidelich] has a job all lined up for me — regional geologist for southwest Kansas."

You Can't Always Count on Your Friends

On Wednesday, June 9, Mesa announced it had lined up a $75 million loan from Credit Suisse as the final piece in a $1.05 billion bank credit line. About $600 million of that credit line was to be used to fund Mesa's $45 per share offer. What made the transaction noteworthy, despite its small size compared to the total loan package, was that Credit Suisse was a business partner of First Boston, one of Cities' two financial advisors. A spokesman for Credit Suisse in New York denied any conflict of interest. "We're involved in commercial lending in the United States and First Boston is an investment bank. [The two companies' U.S. operations are] essentially distinct. There is nothing unusual about this loan."

Meanwhile, in market action on June 9, Mesa shares fell $1.50 to close at $17.75. Mesa was the most actively traded issue on the big board, registering a volume of 1.5 million shares. Cities common also declined, falling $1.00 per share in very active trading to $34.50. The activity and decline reflected a growing public confusion over the mix of friendly and hostile offers.

The proration deadline for Cities' offer, Thursday at midnight, was drawing near. In the interim, talking about the PR involved in the battle, Waidelich said of Pickens, "Sometimes I feel like I'm doing battle with P.T. Barnum."

When the deadline passed, it was undersubscribed as many had predicted. Cities offer drew only 41 percent of Mesa's shares. The following day, Friday, June 11, Cities raised its offer to $21. For the boosted offer, a junior proration pool had been set up, with a midnight, Sunday, June 20 deadline. Though this was viewed as a setback by some, others felt this may have been Cities' intention.

Money Problems

On the same Friday that Cities was forced to raise its offer, Mesa concluded the final agreements on its $1.05 billion credit line. A spokesman for Mesa said, "It is gratifying that the litigation and other pressure tactics exerted by Cities' management to interfere with Mesa's bank financing for its cash tender offer to Cities' shareholders have been unsuccessful . . . . Cities seems to be running out of bullets in its desperate attempt to protect management jobs." It would soon be seen how well that cash tender offer was received. The proration deadline for Mesa's offer was to be coming Wednesday at midnight.

It seemed Cities was not going to let the financing issue just be laid to rest. On Tuesday, June 15, Cities sued Continental Illinois, Mesa's chief lender. The suit, called "bizarre" by one takeover specialist, charged Continental with violations of securities and margin laws set by the Federal Reserve system, when it was arranging financing of Mesa's offer. Cities alleged Continental "attributed inflated values" to Mesa's collateral, and hence "improperly collateralized" the loan agreement behind Mesa's tender offer. The suit sought to enjoin Continental from "arranging, administering, maintaining, or otherwise effectuating" the financing of Mesa's tender offer.

A Surprise Ending

Seemingly out of nowhere a major player entered and changed the balance of the fight. While Mesa was still tallying the number of Cities shares tendered to it, Gulf Oil Corporation agreed to a friendly merger with Cities Services. On Thursday, June 17, the approval of the offer by the boards of both companies was announced. Gulf would buy 51 percent of Cities for $63 per share, compared to Mesa's $45 or $50 bids, and then swap a fixed income security with a face value of $63 for each of the remaining Cities shares.

Gulf Chairman James E. Lee called the agreement a "unique opportunity" for Gulf to "realize long-term strategic goals." Experts said that it was difficult to predict if such a merger could clear antitrust hurdles. It also seemed Cities never actively sought a white knight and even rebuffed an offer of talks with Occidental Petroleum. Cities talked to no other companies besides Gulf.

In related news, it turned out that Mesa's tender offer drew only 43 percent of Cities' common stock. That amount was short of what was widely speculated to be the amount needed by Mesa to obtain additional financing. Mesa was also not in a good position to challenge Gulf. Though it felt it could take on the very sizable Cities with 1981 revenues of $8 billion, Gulf would prove to be a much more formidable opponent, with 1981 revenues of $30 billion, 75 times greater than the revenues of Mesa.

Peace for Some, Problems for Others

Cities and Mesa signed a peace agreement at 9 P.M. that Friday. In the agreement both would drop their tender offers and Cities would buy back all of its shares previously owned by Mesa for $55 per share. This was not to include any shares tendered to Mesa during the takeover fight. The main reason speculated as to why Mesa would settle for a price below the $63 offered by Gulf was its concern for itself. It seemed that Cities, after midnight that coming

Monday, would have enough shares tendered to it to buy majority control of Mesa. That would be a very powerful bargaining lever.

A source close to Cities said the $55 per share price was decided on "because that's what they told us their total cost per share was, and while we didn't want to hurt them, we made it clear we didn't want them walking away from this with a profit to crow about." Mesa was also barred from making an unfriendly offer for Cities for five years.

Regardless, the voluble Pickens did "crow" and said he was delighted at the outcome. "We helped Cities' shareholders get a better price for their shares than management ever could have done alone."

The Gulf deal turned out not to be as good as it seemed. Gulf stock price plummeted $3.75 on the news of the takeover that Friday. Many felt the $63 price was too high. Lee said the big jump from $45 to $63 was intended to prevent a bidding contest with potential competitors for Cities. However, it was also noted that many analysts felt the "break-up" value, based on Cities reserves, was well in excess of $63 per share.

It turned out the Gulf deal was not meant to be. On August 9, Gulf called off the merger, citing antitrust action. As a result, Cities sued Gulf for $3 billion alleging fraudulent misconduct in its merger bid. So the last act of this oil Pac-Man drama ended with the oil giants pumping money into their lawyers' pockets and the raider running to the bank.

As an epilogue, one year later Cities was acquired by Occidental Petroleum for $4.05 billion. Ironically, this amount was very close to Mesa's bid.

Corporate World War III
BENDIX vs. MARTIN MARIETTA

One of the most celebrated cases in merger and acquisition history is the attempted takeover of Martin Marietta by Bendix. It has gained notoriety for many reasons, among them the fact that both were billion dollar companies. Moreover, not only did these huge companies participate, they also drew in two of the giants of the business world, Allied Corporation and United Technologies. Each of these firms dwarfed both Bendix and Martin Marietta, and both were far from being strangers to the merger game. The case also received much publicity because to many it seemed a struggle between strong willed men (and a woman), not merely a financial transaction. Because of this, the story drew widespread attention from the national news media instead of just the financial world. Some writers use the metaphor of battle to describe mergers and acquisitions. Using such language, this was an epic struggle.

By August 1982 Bendix was a cash-rich company. In late 1980 the company began selling off portions of itself that were involved in basic industries, amassing over $760 million. It began to search for a sizable investment in the high-tech industry. Believing that most potential targets were overpriced, Bendix's excess cash was placed in a profitable short-term portfolio. In 1982 this portfolio was one of the most successful parts of the company. At one point Bendix acquired a 7 percent stake in RCA, but acquired no more when RCA reacted angrily to its initial overtures. Bendix was expected by most knowledgeable investors to try for another acquisition. The only question was who would it be.

On August 26, 1982 the target was revealed. In a surprise announcement, Bendix said they would file with the SEC that day. It announced a tender offer for as much as 45 percent of Martin Marietta at $43 per share. Bendix already owned 4.5 percent of Martin Marietta stock, just under the amount that would require public disclosure. Following the tender offer, Bendix planned to swap stock for the remainder of Martin Marietta's approximately 35.8 million shares outstanding. Bendix said the deadline for the cash portion of its offer would be September 23, with a proration deadline of September 4. Martin Marietta was informed the day before the public announcement. The news came in a hand-delivered letter from Bendix's chairman, William M. Agee.

The timing of the offer may have been heavily influenced by a decline in interest rates at the time. The decline reduced the earning power of Bendix's sizable portfolio, so it wanted to use its money quickly. As a result, it said it would fund the offer from internal resources in addition to making use of existing credit arrangements. Outside observers estimated that Bendix had arranged $800 million of credit.

Bendix immediately sought to offer assurances that it wanted the takeover to be friendly. It pointed out that it was offering a substantial premium for Martin Marietta's stock and that it did not foresee any legal complications that might block such a merger. In the weeks prior to the tender offer, Martin Marietta's common stock traded at close to $33 per share. The previous year Martin Marietta had traded above $50. More recently, it had traded at $39. Some analysts did not think Martin Marietta would view the offer favorably. Francis L. Carey, an analyst at Fahnestock & Co., said he thought the bid was too low. "I don't think the Martin Marietta management will roll over and play dead," was his comment. On news of the takeover bid, Martin Marietta shares rose $3 to close at $42.25 per share. The market also reacted favorably to Bendix, its stock closing up 1⅛ at $51.

Martin Marietta's comments were few. It announced a special meeting of its board on the coming Monday to review the offer and revealed that Kidder, Peabody had been retained as its financial advisor.

For many reasons, Martin Marietta was an attractive company to Bendix, one of the reasons being its aerospace and defense operations. At an analysts' meeting the previous year in New York, Agee stated he would like Bendix to eventually become a prime contractor in the missile industry. Martin Marietta's operations would significantly expand the size of Bendix's aerospace division and the merger would almost surely raise Bendix's status with the Defense Department from subcontractor to prime contractor.

Bendix Seeks a Friendly Transaction

"Everybody on the Bendix team hopes this is going to be a friendly deal," said one source working on the Bendix side. "So far there hasn't been any indication from Martin Marietta that they are going to react with hostility."

The seeds of dissatisfaction were already sown in the form of an offering circular printed on Thursday, August 26. In it Bendix said it had "analyzed the possibility of divesting one or more of the non-aerospace divisions" of Martin Marietta. Bendix went on to say it had not decided whether it would take such a step if its $1.5 billion offer was successful. This disclosure surely added to any management concern already existing at Martin Marietta. On the street the speculation was growing that Martin Marietta might fight Bendix.

Selling off pieces of Martin Marietta would help Bendix significantly in financing the transaction. The offering circular estimated that the cash portion of the offer would exceed $690 million. At the time Bendix had $350 million in cash and marketable securities it could use for the acquisiton. In addition to the cash, it had a $400 million revolving line of credit with 19 banks, plus short-term lines of credit of $275 million with 11 other banks.

However, all signs seemed to indicate that Bendix was not looking for a fight. Not only had Bendix stated that it wished to consummate a friendly transaction, it seemed to be an unspoken policy within the company. According to *The Wall Street Journal*, "It would be unusual for Bendix, a conservative company, to pursue anything other than a friendly acquisition. William Agee, Bendix's chairman, has long expressed a desire to avoid hostile situations — a policy he is frequently kidded about by business associates and securities analysts."

This statement by *The Wall Street Journal* seems to have been borne out by the facts. Earlier in the year, Bendix had started to accumulate stock in RCA. When RCA's management was angered by the open market purchases, Bill Agee quickly sought to pacify them. Bendix struck a deal to stop buying shares and to give RCA notice prior to the acquisition of any future purchases. Bendix was left holding a 7 percent stake in RCA.

"Bill [Agee] always felt a hostile takeover would just lead to trouble," a former associate said. The reason behind this was more than a desire to avoid confrontation. Bendix was a conglomerate with a highly decentralized management system. Each of the general managers heading up the company's divisions had relative autonomy in running his/her operations. Lacking a more structured management system, Bendix could encounter difficulty in "taming" an acquired company against its will.

Martin Marietta Plays Pac-Man

The speed, relative to the size and implications of Martin Marietta's response, was amazing. That is to say nothing of the bewilderment with which the response was received. At a special meeting of Martin Marietta's board on Monday, August 30, Bendix's offer was termed "inadequate." At this stage of the game most companies in Martin Marietta's position would have issued a statement saying "alternative possibilities are being taken under advisement." However, this was not the case. After an eight-hour board meeting, not only did Martin Marietta reject Bendix's offer, but it announced its own tender offer for Bendix.

Martin Marietta's president and CEO, Thomas G. Pownall, said the board "concluded that if these two corporations are going to be combined, the interests of the shareholders will best be served by combining the two corporations on the terms contemplated by the Martin Marietta offer, rather than the Bendix offer." That offer would consist of a two-part bid. The first part was to be a tender offer for 11.9 million of Bendix's 23.7 million shares (just over 50 percent), at $75 per share. The second step would be a stock swap for Martin Marietta shares, an amount which would give Bendix shareholders approximately $55 for each of their shares. The average price over the two steps would be $65 per share, giving the entire transaction a value of roughly $1.5 billion. At the time of the announcement, Martin Marietta expected the proration deadline to be September 9 and the tender offer to expire on September 28.

A Wall Street source close to Martin Marietta rejected the idea that Martin Marietta's offer was just a defensive ploy to drive Bendix away. "You'll note there won't be any condition to let Martin Marietta drop [the tender offer] if Bendix acquires Martin Marietta shares. We mean business . . . [William Agee] is going to be very sorry he started this." Martin Marietta also said its offer would not be conditioned on getting a minimum number of Bendix shares. This is a factor closely watched by arbitrageurs to see how serious a firm is about its offer. An offer conditioned on a large number of shares being tendered is seen as a way out for a company not truly committed to an offer.

Other actions by Martin Marietta included filing a suit against

Bendix alleging "various violations of securities laws in connection with the Bendix offer." Martin Marietta also arranged bank credit of over $1 billion to back its tender offer. The amount of credit was enough to allow Martin Marietta to offer as much as $80 per share for the cash portion of its offer. No comment was immediately forthcoming from Bendix.

The Companies Dig In: Is Peace Possible?

The next day Bendix's board met for three hours. Upon adjournment it was announced that they rejected Martin Marietta's tender offer and in no way would alter their own offer for Martin Marietta shares. "We are determined to push our transaction through to completion," Agee said. He went on to say Bendix had taken additional steps to support its tender offer. Arrangements were made to amend the original offer to allow Bendix to purchase more than 50 percent of Martin Marietta stock. Bendix also filed suit in federal court in Michigan seeking to block Martin Marietta's tender offer.

Martin Marietta issued a statement in response to Bendix's rejection of its offer, saying it would stand by its original offer. It went on to say that long-term employment contracts, golden parachutes, had been arranged. The parachutes were set up to protect the income and benefits of 27 of their top employees in case Martin Marietta was acquired.

Both companies seemed willing to enter into some sort of negotiation, but their positions diverged. Agee of Bendix said, "We repeat our willingness to negotiate any and all terms of our offer with Martin Marietta." On the other hand, Thomas Pownall of Martin Marietta said, "The interests of the shareholders will best be served by combining [the companies] on the terms contemplated by the Martin Marietta offer rather than the Bendix offer. Our position is that any negotiation must be in that context." However, Martin Marietta's SEC filings indicated that the possibility of seeking a white knight had not been ruled out. Both companies retained their right to drop their bids if a satisfactory agreement could be reached.

In lieu of a peaceful settlement between the two, the alternative could end up being a race to get voting control over each other. State securities laws would then play an interesting and perhaps decisive role. In terms of the tender offers themselves, Bendix had a head start. Its tender offer expired five days prior to Martin Marietta's. However, state law in Maryland, where Martin Marietta was incorporated, required a 10-day waiting period prior to the calling of a special shareholder meeting to vote on a change in directors. Under the laws of Delaware, where Bendix was incorporated, Martin Marietta could call such a meeting immediately after acquiring control of Bendix. A Bendix source, however, said, "We'd have an army of lawyers out there fighting like hell before a bunch of silly state laws settled this thing."

The timing of state laws seemed to favor Martin Marietta, but the possibility of winning such a race might not produce a clear victory. According to Martin Marietta's tender offer circular, "It is possible that Martin Marietta and [Bendix] each could become a substantial stockholder in each other [and that the use of funds by the two companies to acquire each other's shares] would limit Martin Marietta's ability to affect substantial future debt financings and would cause a reduction in the credit ratings of Martin Marietta [whether it goes on to acquire Bendix or not.]"

As the proration deadline of September 4 for Bendix's offer approached, the two companies continued to dig in. On September 2, Bendix filed a new suit in Baltimore, alleging that Martin Marietta's offering circular violated federal securities laws by giving inadequate and misleading information about several aspects of the $75 per share offer for Bendix stock. Bendix went on to allege that Martin Marietta's contention that it would be able to take control of Bendix before Bendix could take control of Martin Marietta was "simply wrong." Also, Bendix alleged that Martin Marietta did not adequately disclose the negative impact that the addition of $900 million in debt to acquire Bendix would have on the company.

In an event possibly related to the impending proration deadline, Martin Marietta held a marathon meeting late into that evening with the firm's legal counsel, Wachtell, Lipton, Rosen, and Katz. Takeover observers speculated that the meeting represented an attempt on Martin Marietta's part to reach an agreement with a potential ally. The reason observers placed importance on an effort to reach an alliance was more subtle than merely getting a white knight. If an ally launched a tender offer for as little as 10 percent of Martin Marietta's stock, an extension to the withdrawal deadline under the Bendix offer would be forced. That would change a potential five-day disadvantage in Martin Marietta's offer into a five-day advantage over Bendix's.

In addition to the corporate infighting, it is interesting to note that other law suits were being filed. Richard A. Ash, a lawyer from Philadelphia, filed suit in federal court to try to block Martin Marietta's planned takeover of Bendix. The suit said, "The Bendix plan would be in the better interest of the shareholders of Martin Marietta who would sell their shares at a premium, but would be to the detriment of management, who would lose corporate control." The suit charged that Martin Marietta's directors violated their fiduciary responsibility in rejecting Bendix's bid and authorizing a counter offer.

Bendix Takes the Lead

The clock kept ticking and Bendix smelled victory. In an announcement made on Labor Day, September 6, Bendix said that by its proration deadline, roughly 58 percent of Martin Marietta stock had been tendered to it. Quickly taking the media initiative, Bendix called the results a "clear referendum" supporting its $43 per share offer.

A spokesman for Martin Marietta called the announcement "not meaningful, since Bendix won't be in a position to buy any shares of Martin Marietta stock until after the September 16 withdrawal deadline under the Bendix offer . . . . As we've noted before, we expect to be in a position to take control of Bendix before Bendix can take control of us."

Of course, as Bendix had previously mentioned, it would not sit idly by and let state securities laws settle the dispute. To try to turn around the potential disadvantage, Bendix was trying to call a special Martin Marietta shareholder meeting for September 21, the day before Martin Marietta could legally buy any Bendix shares. The purpose of the meeting would be to amend the company's charter to retard or stop any unilateral assumption of control over Bendix, even though it was allowed under Delaware state law. Proxy materials were to be mailed that week.

When questioned about possible forthcoming counter measures to Bendix's actions, Martin Marietta's strategists alluded to something in the works. "All I can tell you is that we're working on a lay down hand," said one. What the strategist was referring to was the situation in the game of bridge, where one player's hand is so powerful that all other players merely lay down their cards rather than attempt to play.

Lay Down Hand?

The next day Martin Marietta went on the offensive. It did not seek a white knight as had been speculated. Rather, it sought a partner. In a surprise announcement, United Technologies, in alliance with Martin Marietta, launched its own $75 per share bid for 50.3 percent of Bendix. In a two-step merger, United Technologies sought 11.9 million Bendix shares at $75 each. The second step would be a one-for-one stock swap. The total value of the deal would be approximately $1.5 billion. The tender offer was conditioned on, among other things, "Bendix terminating its offer for Martin Marietta without having purchased any shares." It also required that Bendix not adopt several amendments to its charter aimed at frustrating hostile takeovers. United Technologies' investment advisor, Lazard Freres & Company, would coordinate with Martin Marietta's Kidder, Peabody.

The joint strategy, worked out in lengthy meetings that had started in the middle of the previous week, presented Bendix with the constant threat of takeover by one ally or the other. The two companies worked out a deal to carve up Bendix if either of their offers was successful. United Technologies would get Bendix's sizable automotive and industrial products divisions and over $500 million in cash and marketable securities, including approximately $100 million of RCA stock. Martin Marietta, in return for $600 million in cash, would get certain aerospace and electronics businesses that would present antitrust problems for United Technologies. In addition to adding pressure on Bendix to back off, the alliance would end speculation about whether Martin Marietta could handle the debt that would have accompanied their original offer. Rather than a $1.5 billion offer, Martin Marietta now had only to come up with $600 million.

A special part of the deal between the two companies was that Martin Marietta would not look for a white knight. If it did so, United Technologies could be stuck in a very untenable position. Without Martin Marietta taking control of certain Bendix divisions, it would be very unlikely for United Technologies to be able to clear antitrust proceedings. Besides protecting United Technologies, such an agreement made the alliance seem to have a greater resolve.

United Technologies

United Technologies at the time was engaged primarily in aerospace, electronics, and automotive supply. Through its Pratt & Whitney unit it was the largest supplier of civilian and military aircraft engines in the world with total 1981 sales of $13.7 billion.

The bid for Bendix was United Technologies' first major takeover attempt since it acquired Carrier Corporation in July 1979. Harry Grey, United Technologies' chairman, president, and CEO, had a proven record as an aggressive acquirer.

Bendix reacted to the move by sweetening its offer for 45 percent of Martin Marietta from $43 per share to $48 per share. In its second step, it would trade 0.82 Bendix shares for each remaining share of Martin Marietta. All other conditions would remain the same. At that time, Bendix already owned 4.5 percent of Martin Marietta but even a successful tender offer would give it less than majority control.

Agee also sent a letter to Martin Marietta's president, Thomas G. Pownall. In it he asked for a meeting "with a view to achieving a sensible, businesslike solution in the best interests of the shareholders of both companies." Agee also said that his board would consider United Technologies' bid, but based on published reports the offer seemed "even less than that proposed by Martin Marietta." That bid was rejected as inadequate.

Pownall turned down Agee's invitation to meet. He also said Martin Marietta's directors had unanimously rejected Bendix's sweetened bid as "inadequate."

In a related action, United Technologies sued Bendix in Baltimore federal court, seeking an injunction against the proposed changes to its charter on which Bendix stockholders were expected to vote on September 21. The suit alleged that the proposed amendments were aimed to "chill any bidding for Bendix by any prospective acquirer, entrench incumbent management," and prevent Bendix shareholders from receiving a premium price for their shares.

Following the announcement, United Technologies' stock fell 2⅞ to 47⅜. The next day, Wednesday, September 8, it recovered 1⅛ to close at $48.50 on the NYSE. The same day the price of Bendix's stock leaped $6.25 to close at $62.75. Even with Bendix's $5 per share boost in its offer for Martin Marietta, Martin Marietta's shares closed down $.25 to close at 35⅞.

Back to the Trenches

Though obviously not pleased with the most recent development, Bendix was not ready to yield. On Thursday, September 9, the board gave golden parachutes to 16 officers of the corporation. The agreements gave each of the executives his current base salary plus incentive compensation payments for three years from the date of a change in control. For Agee, the deal was for five years. Agee's most recent salary and bonus totaled $805,000. Bendix could also purchase the executives' stock options outright after a control change. At the time, 867,650 shares were under option. The parachute, worth $15.7 million, secured the safe landing for all 16 officers.

Company spokesmen explained the golden parachute provisions as a method of ensuring that top executives would stay with the company during the battle. They enabled executives to act "in the best interest of the corporation and its stockholders with respect to [the takeover offers] without concern for income security."

The next day Bendix dug in even further. After officially rejecting United Technologies' bid as "inadequate" and "unfair", it ordered an antitrust suit to be filed in Baltimore federal court to try to block United Technologies. It then voted to pursue Martin Marietta, even though opposition was now tougher. To help do this, two additional actions were taken. First, Bendix raised the target number of Martin Marietta shares it sought from 15.8 million to 18.5 million. This move would give Bendix a majority when added to its present holdings. It also added First Boston to its list of advisors. Many felt this showed a lack of confidence in its present financial advisor, Salomon Brothers, whose chief merger specialist, Ira Harris, had not been handling Bendix.

Later that same day, over 75 percent of Bendix's shares were tendered to Martin Marietta. To continue the pressure, the following Monday, Martin Marietta's directors voted to drop all but two conditions in their offer for Bendix. The conditions dropped included: unforeseen government or legal opposition to the acquisition, major deterioration in Bendix's financial condition or prospects, materially adverse developments in the litigation between Bendix and Martin Marietta, limitations in the trading of Bendix shares, and issuance of new securities by Bendix or its payment of any extraordinary dividend or a new tender offer for all or part of Bendix's stock.

The remaining conditions included Martin Marietta dropping its offer if Bendix did the same, presuming no shares had been purchased. They also required that Martin Marietta not be obligated to buy Bendix shares if Bendix shareholders voted in favor of the previously mentioned amendments to help block hostile takeovers.

According to Pownall, Martin Marietta wanted it "explicitly understood" that it would go ahead and buy Bendix shares "even if Bendix may have earlier purchased Martin Marietta shares under the terms of its tender offer." Bendix had not yet purchased shares of Martin Marietta beyond its original stake. Under the terms of its offer it could purchase tendered shares three days later, at midnight on Thursday. As one investment banker stated, "Martin Marietta is now committed to buy control of Bendix at $75 per share whether or not the current directors, or Bendix nominees, may be sitting on the board two weeks hence." "We are on course," was Bill Agee's response to these actions.

"A Three-Ring Circus"

At this time, the national news media, not just the financial press, began to take an intense interest in the fight. Its elements of intrigue, color, and suspense placed the story on the pages of *Time* and *Newsweek*. Even *The Wall Street Journal* which is usually objective and sedate, began "color" reporting, beyond their usual crisp synopsis of the facts. In one article, they called the battle a "three-ring circus." To many it was unusual because, as a partner at one of the investment banking firms involved said, "This one could be the only deal I've seen where the raider becomes the white knight's target." Another article described Martin Marietta's inexperience in takeovers and their heavy reliance on Kidder, Peabody and outside directors. For the nonfinancial press a 44-year-old chairman of the board, William Agee, and his now renowned wife, Mary Cunningham, seemed to make good news.

On the same day that *The Wall Street Journal* called the fight a game of "financial chicken," United Technologies sweetened its bid for Bendix. On Wednesday, September 16, it was announced that the first step of its tender offer was being revised upward, from $75 per share to $85 per share. The second step would remain a one-for-one stock swap. Based on a 49.25 price for United Technologies, the new deal implied a blended value of roughly $67 per share for a total of $1.59 billion. All agreements between United Technologies and Martin Marietta stood the same. This was needed because as expected, the previous day the Justice Department gave antitrust clearance to a Bendix–Martin Marietta merger, but still had not given the same to a Bendix–United Technologies merger. The deal was contingent on acceptance by Bendix's board. Analysts perceived the pressure as "You'll get $85 per share on the front-end of the deal if you're nice, and you'll have to take $75 if you still want to fight." It also assumed Bendix felt its own takeover was a fait accompli.

Meanwhile, speculation ran rampant on the street that a new bidder would appear for Martin Marietta. If a bid were made for as little as 10 percent of the outstanding stock, a postponement of the existing withdrawal deadline would be forced for 10 days under SEC rules. That would prevent Bendix from buying shares the following evening and help Martin Marietta's side of the fight.

Bendix Buys

On Friday, September 17, Bendix announced that at midnight the previous evening it had bought all the Martin Marietta shares that had been tendered to it under its $48 offer. It also announced that it was expanding the number of shares it sought for the third time. Bendix sought 70 percent of Martin Marietta and starting that morning would begin purchasing shares for cash on a first-come, first-served basis. Bendix then called on Martin Marietta to convene a special shareholder meeting at which new Martin Marietta directors would be elected.

Some observers called the move bold, while others called it reckless. Interestingly, it was almost prevented from taking place. Judge Young of the federal court in Baltimore postponed the date on which shares could be purchased to September 26. This was done because "grave and irreparable harm [might be suffered by Bendix, Martin Marietta, United Technologies] or two or more of them, or the investing public." The judge continued by saying it was "necessary to maintain the status quo to all parties so that a meaningful decision on the merits pending litigation wouldn't be put in jeopardy." Judge Young was overturned that same evening in federal appeals court.

Another sidelight to that day's action was another suit brought against Bendix and its directors by its shareholders. It alleged that they illegally conspired to block the takeover of Bendix and made misleading disclosures about the offers for it.

The following Monday, Bendix continued to buy shares, with an eye toward the coming Wednesday. On that day, at midnight, Martin Marietta could begin to purchase shares of Bendix. Bendix felt it held the advantage by holding more stock than Martin Marietta. "It is one thing if we own 50 percent and their board votes to buy control of us to protect a near majority . . . . But how do you base such an action on serving shareholders when we hold 70 percent [of the shares]," said a takeover specialist for Bendix.

Enter the Twilight Zone

The next day, the takeover battle moved a step closer to the bizarre. Bendix held a "Unity Day Rally" for its employees. Included in the day's festivities were an airplane flying overhead carrying an "I love Bendix" banner and a squad of company pom-pom girls, wearing the company colors and leading cheers. The same day, *The Wall*

Street Journal carried a column four, front page article entitled, "Dirty Tricks Abound in Takeover Business as Well as in Politics — Bendix, Martin Marietta, and United Technologies Step Up Their Struggle and Drag Down Its Tone." The article contained a number of allegations including one suggesting Bendix's law firm, Hughes, Hubbard & Reed, hired a private investigator to check out both United Technologies and its chairman, Harry Grey.

On the same day, Judge Young of the Baltimore federal court spoke about the fight, referring to the potential harm investors might suffer. "My concern is that the individual stockholder, the guy on the street, is standing by without much to say and he may be harmed." He continued later, saying, "I suspect Shakespeare had something like this in mind when he said in *Romeo and Juliet*: 'A pox on both your houses.' "

According to Bill Agee, a last ditch effort was made to try to avert a Pac-Man situation from being carried out to its conclusion. After considerable effort, he finally arranged a meeting between himself and Martin Marietta's board. In the meeting he planned to make the situation a more friendly one by informing them that Bendix would accept the full legal responsibility if Martin Marietta would give up its tender offer at this point. This was not to be. Agee went to Bethesda and rented a room in a roadside motel to wait for the call to come before the board. He was forced to "cool his heels" for hours, while the call was repeatedly delayed. When he was finally instructed to appear, he arrived at Martin Marietta headquarters only to find the board meeting was adjourned.

Martin Marietta Buys; Enter Allied Corporation

Firmly placing both feet into the annals of takeover history, Martin Marietta purchased 42.4 percent of the Bendix shares just after midnight early in the morning of Thursday, September 23. The purchase of 10,060,000 shares cost Martin Marietta $754.5 million. The company said it would immediately begin buying an additional 1.9 million shares on a first-come, first-served basis. These actions came following a decision by a U.S. appellate judge to allow the purchase, and a Delaware court saying Martin Marietta could not vote those shares to change current Bendix management.

Meanwhile, a new player burst onto the scene. Allied Corporation, a chemical, oil and gas, fiber, plastics, and electronics firm, based in Morris Township, New Jersey, announced it had reached an agreement in principal to merge with Bendix. Starting that day, it would begin a tender offer at $85 per share for 55 percent of Bendix's shares. In a second step, Allied would complete the merger by swapping stock and fixed income securities for each Bendix share. The value for the second step was slated to be roughly $73 a share, giving a blended value of $79.53 a share for a total of approximately $1.9 billion.

Other provisions of the agreement would have Allied buy Bendix's crown jewel, its aerospace division, for $800 million, even if it was outbid by another acquirer. The lock-up deal was designed to discourage either Martin Marietta or United Technologies. In addition, Bill Agee would become president of Allied and retain his posts of chairman and CEO at Bendix. Allied would also acquire 39 percent of Martin Marietta. Unhappy with the deal, four Bendix directors resigned in protest. Interestingly, if Allied had been given the go ahead to file merger papers with the SEC by Bendix's board and its own, the Martin Marietta purchase could never have taken place. Pending a new offer, SEC rules would have forced an extension of withdrawal rights for 10 days. However, the deal did get board approval. This left Agee and Cunningham free to fly home to Detroit and have dinner with Jimmy Carter.

Cash Just Circles Back

The following Monday the deal became clearer. More specifically, Allied would acquire all of Bendix stock and 39 percent of Martin Marietta for $1.9 billion. Allied would then swap the remaining Martin Marietta stock held by Bendix for Martin Marietta's holdings of Bendix, roughly 50 percent. It then had to structure a deal to acquire the remaining Bendix shares. In the deal it struck, Allied traded 1.3 newly issued shares plus a fixed income security valued at $38.50 for each Bendix share. It would retain Bendix's remaining 39 percent sake in Martin Marietta and agree not to take over Martin Marietta for ten years. In return, Martin Marietta would allow Allied to keep a stake 10 percent larger than its second largest shareholder. If Allied should choose to sell its stake, it would first have to offer it to Martin Marietta, or otherwise sell it piecemeal on the open market.

The stock swap between the three companies would work as follows: Allied would pay Martin Marietta $892 million for its Bendix shares. Martin Marietta would then turn around and pay that $892 million to Bendix for the 31 percent of Martin Marietta it would get back. This would then be given back to Allied, which would give Bendix a note for it. "The cash just circles back to us," said Allied senior vice-president Harold W. Buirkle.

The victory took Allied a "quantum leap" forward in its efforts to transform itself into a high tech company, said Edward L. Hennessy, Allied's chairman. The combined companies' assets were roughly $8.5 billion and projected 1983 sales were to be $12 billion.

Mary Cunningham

Behind the scenes, but central to the drama in this entangled web of corporate warfare was Mary Cunningham. Most people are familiar with her name. Or more accurately, most people are familiar with Cunningham's name being dragged through the mud. She gained notoriety not for being the intelligent, skilled executive she was, but more for her meteoric rise through the Bendix organization under the guidance of Bill Agee. Dirty rumors abounded and perhaps seemed justified by the eventual marriage of Cunningham and Agee. In the midst of the rumors, Cunningham left her position as chief strategic planner for Bendix and joined Seagram as vice-president for strategic planning. Either out of habit or for pure human interest, the media began to insinuate that Cunningham was playing a disruptive role in negotiations between the contending firms.

Toward the end of the takeover battle, a takeover advisor said, "[Mr.] Agee depends on her counsel to a really remarkable degree." During the entire battle it was disclosed that she was one of Agee's principal advisors. The others were lawyer Arthur Fleischer Jr., Bruce Wasserstein of First Boston, and Bendix president Alonzo McDonald Jr. The popular gossip was that Cunningham's presence upset Martin Marietta and therefore contributed to the failure of successful negotiations. Agee denied this. Moreover, after the conclusion of the battle, a Martin Marietta spokesman said that Cunningham's "presence definitely wasn't an obstacle."

Speaking to *Fortune* after the battle, Cunningham had the following to say: "People have a tendency, particularly with women advisors, to fall prey to the Garden of Eden psychology that they somehow have undue influence over the man. At the other end of the spectrum, there is the stereotype of the chairman's wife who quietly defers to anything he has to say." Speaking on resentment of her influence on Agee, she said, "I think it has been used as a tactic in the acquisition picture to undermine Bill."

Epilogue

On September 27, United Technologies announced the withdrawal of its tender offer. Martin Marietta stock plunged 8⅜ per share to 35⅛ and it was estimated it would take them seven years to straighten out their balance sheet. In early October both Moody's and Standard & Poor's lowered their credit ratings of Martin Marietta.

At one point, say insiders, business became secondary. "The underlying story," says one businessman, a former Bendix director, "is that this epic struggle involving four big companies and more than four investment bankers and hordes of lawyers is not about economics, is not about using assets wisely, is not about economic growth. It's a struggle between a few ambitious men."

Movies, Vodka, And Fried Chicken — Pac-Man Entertainment
GENERAL CINEMA vs. HEUBLEIN

This is a story of a mild case of Pac-Man, if there can be such a thing. The two adversaries are General Cinema Corporation and Heublein. The story takes place over the months of February to October 1982. Interestingly, at the same time, American General and NLT Corporation in the insurance arena and Cities Service and Mesa Petroleum in the oil industry were involved in bitterly contested Pac-Man battles. The term mild is used here, not because the dispute was not bitter, for it was. It is termed so because each company's purchase of the other's stock was made in the open market rather than with a hostile counter tender offer. Also, unlike most merger stories, which take place on the front pages of *The Wall Street Journal*, this one was recorded in the back pages. Nevertheless, this Pac-Man situation became a classic in the annals of takeover history. While these two companies were in different industries, family influence characterized both of them. It is useful to review the background of the players before taking a closer look at the battle.

The Companies

Heublein is a spirits and food manufacturer. It may not be well known by name but certainly is by product. Heublein sells Smirnoff and Popov vodkas, Harvey's Bristol Creme Sherry, Don Q rum, and Jose Cuervo tequila. Its wines include both Inglenook and Colony brands. The foods Heublein owns include Kentucky Fried Chicken Corporation, A-1 Steak Sauce, Ortega Mexican Foods, and Grey Poupon Dijon Mustard. As can be seen, the company produces a variety of products with very high brand recognition. Based in Farmington, Connecticut, Heublein had 1981 revenues of $2.1 billion and earnings of $88.4 million. The Heublein family owned roughly 10 percent of the outstanding common shares.

General Cinema is the biggest at what it does. Based in Boston, it is the largest U.S. theater chain and the largest independent bottler of soft drinks. It is in many ways, as is Heublein, a family business. Both have first generation descendants of their founders in present management and both own sizable, though noncontrolling, amounts of their respective stocks. The families of General Cinema's chairman and president, Richard A. Smith, his sister, Nancy L. Marks, and Vice-Chairman Sidney Stoneman own a combined stake amounting to 35 percent of the company's stock. General Cinema was founded by Smith's father and had 1981 revenues of $823 million and earnings of $44.3 million.

The First Shot

In an SEC filing on Wednesday, February 2, 1982, General Cinema stated it had acquired 2.1 million shares of Heublein. This translated into a stake of roughly 9.7 percent. The purchases were made in the open market and in private transactions for prices ranging from 30½ to 40⅛. The median price was near $36.25 and the total cost of the purchase to General Cinema was about $74 million. The buy, made for "investment purposes," took place from early December to the Monday just preceding the filing.

Followers of General Cinema were quick to speculate that General Cinema might buy more than 20 percent of Heublein and perhaps all of it. It was noted that prior to the announcement General Cinema had over $100 million in cash and "vast" borrowing power. For some time General Cinema had been talking about making a big investment in the consumer products field. However, General Cinema said it had no "current intention to increase its investment" in Heublein to any specific amount. It did make clear that it intended to exceed the 15 percent level. Analysts noted that with its strong cash flow, General Cinema could easily take on additional long-term debt to help fund such a purchase.

Heublein officials had no comment at the time. They said they were reviewing General Cinema's SEC filing. On circulation of the news on that Wednesday, Heublein shares closed up ¼ at $37.25 on the NYSE. General Cinema closed at $36.25, unchanged.

More than two weeks passed before any further action took place. On Friday, February 19, Heublein replied to General Cinema's purchase by filing suit in federal court, asking it to declare "null and void" General Cinema's purchase of 9.7 percent of Heublein common stock. Heublein alleged "manipulative and deceptive practices [and] misleading and incomplete disclosures." The suit sought to block General Cinema's "illegal attempt to gain control" of Heublein. Heublein also claimed that General Cinema violated the Hart-Scott-Rodino Antitrust Act by not disclosing the purchases until it had accumulated 9.7 percent of the outstanding shares. This would have allowed it time to buy shares at a price lower than if it had announced its intent to the market.

In the suit Heublein was asking the court to enjoin General Cinema from "acquiring additional Heublein shares, voting the stock it now owns, transferring its shares to anyone but Heublein without court approval, or exercising influence on Heublein management." The suit also sought to force General Cinema to sell all of its Heublein holdings in a manner that would not "disrupt the market for Heublein securities."

On the following Sunday, February 21, General Cinema's senior vice-president and general counsel, Samuel Frankenheim, said that his company "believes the litigation is frivolous."

The Hunted Becomes the Hunter: Heublein Plays Pac-Man

Several days later, on February 26, Heublein disclosed that over the previous week it had purchased 380,000 shares of General Cinema common stock on the open market. This amount was equal to roughly a 3.5 percent stake. It paid $14.1 million for the stock, nearly $37 per share. The following Monday, Heublein announced that as required by antitrust law, it had filed with federal authorities to clear a purchase of an additional $15 million of General Cinema stock. Wasting no time in making its intentions clear, on Tuesday Heublein announced it would increase its stake in General Cinema to more than 15 percent and possibly more than 25 percent, but certainly less than 50 percent. Many followers of the fight thought Heublein's actions were undertaken with a defensive intent. Some speculated Heublein would try to negotiate a stock swap. Others disagreed and were calling the situation "Wall Street's dogfight." Neither company would give specific comments.

On the same day, General Cinema announced that it had not yet increased its holdings of Heublein beyond the 9.7 percent level. About this time, observers were beginning to voice their speculation on what General Cinema might want. Some felt that General Cinema would seek to increase its holdings in Heublein to 20 percent. Under the equity method of financial accounting, with an equity holding of at least 20 percent but less than 50 percent the investing company is deemed to have "significant influence" in the company it has invested in. Because of this, the investing company can recognize its proportionate amount of the net income of the company it invested in on its own income statement. The implications are that dividends are consequently not recognized as revenue. They are actually subtracted from the investment account on the balance sheet. An alternate theory was that General Cinema might try to swap the stock for part of Heublein's operations, such as wine or other consumer brands.

Share Repurchase, or Some People Take Threats Poorly

Another week passed before the two feuding companies made the news again. On Monday, March 19, General Cinema announced that it intended to acquire as many as 3 million of its own shares. By reducing the number of shares outstanding, such a move would increase the percent of stock owned by family members from 35 to 47.5 percent. Obviously, this would decrease the likelihood of a successful hostile takeover.

The move came after a meeting between the two companies went sour. They met to discuss the implications of each other's actions and to try to reach some resolution. During the talks Heublein threatened General Cinema with a tender offer for 51 percent of its outstanding common if it rejected Heublein's offer to buy back its own stock. Apparently General Cinema's management did not take the threat well and reacted in a way Heublein did not count on. It was after that meeting that General Cinema decided to repurchase some of its own shares.

For the repurchase, General Cinema said it could buy approximately a million shares without the consent of its lenders. Beyond that amount approval would be needed. General Cinema also mentioned that it was talking to "third parties" about selling certain assets. Most analysts believed those assets to be General Cinema's Heublein shares. On this news, shares of General Cinema closed at 39¼, up 1⅝ from the previous trading day and Heublein shares closed down ⅞, at 34⅜.

On Thursday, March 11, General Cinema proved its counter-threat was not an idle one. It purchased 1,080,800 of its own shares on the open market at $37 per share. On top of all its defensive measures, to be prepared for the unexpected, it also doubled its line of credit.

The Game Is in Full Play

When one company begins buying the stock of another, federal authorities have the right to impose a 30-day waiting period for further purchases. This gives them time to investigate antitrust implications. This waiting period expired for General Cinema on March 12, giving it the right to buy more Heublein stock, if it so desired. No purchases were made immediately. On March 16, a federal court waived the Federal Trade Commission mandated waiting period for Heublein, freeing it to buy General Cinema stock. The FTC announced it would not appeal the court's decision. Normally, the waiting period would have expired April 2.

Both Heublein and General Cinema, gave the appearance of readying themselves for stock purchases of each other. General Cinema announced on the day it received clearance that it would begin buying again. On the same day Heublein demanded a stockholder list from General Cinema to inform the stockholders "about the propriety of General Cinema buying its own stock and the stock of Heublein." Heublein said the list would also enable it to determine whether or not to purchase General Cinema stock directly from its holders.

No action took place until April 15. In an SEC filing, General Cinema announced it had raised its stake to 12.8 percent in open market purchases. From then until June 1, General Cinema added to its holdings of Heublein in small increments via open market purchases. On April 26 it held 14.3 percent. The stake increased to 16 percent on April 29, to 18 percent on May 26, and to 18.9 percent on May 31. With the last purchase, General Cinema announced that it had decided to stop buying shares of Heublein. But it would resume purchases if the two companies could not reach an agreement. It did not say what such an agreement would be. As it stood at that point, 4,092,000 shares of Heublein's 21.7 million shares had been purchased. General Cinema paid $159.6 million for them, or around $39 per share on average. Many analysts were surprised that General Cinema stopped short of the 20 percent needed to consolidate a proportionate amount of Heublein's earnings on its financial statements. Strangely, little action was taken by Heublein during the following month.

Bickering

When General Cinema announced it had decided to stop buying Heublein for the time being, it also said it had "several meetings with Heublein [and it] intends to have several additional meetings." Heublein, however, said it did not plan to have any more meetings with General Cinema. It went on to say it had not had "several meetings," but only two and they were "unproductive." J. Atwood Ives, General Cinema senior vice-president, finance, called Heublein's statement "false," contending that several meetings had been held and that more were planned.

The next day Gwain H. Gillespie, Heublein's vice-president, finance and administration, talked to a meeting of securities analysts regarding the disagreement over the number of meetings held and plans for future ones. Gillespie said, "They must be talking to themselves." He also stated that Heublein would actively oppose any attempt by General Cinema to get representation on Heublein's board. "I don't see any situation where we'd want to and that's the answer we told them," Gillespie said. Talking about General Cinema's decision to stop buying Heublein's stock, he said, "We don't know why they stopped buying our stock, but we're glad they have."

A Conclusion, Almost

Again, in the midst of battle, almost a month passed before anything but words were exchanged. Then on July 29, R.J. Reynolds Incorporated entered the scene. It announced that it had agreed to buy Heublein for $1.3 billion in a two-step merger. This offer was a significant premium over what General Cinema had been paying in the open market, an average of $39 per share. In the first step, Reynolds' offer was to be $63 per share for 11,350,000 shares, over 50 percent of Heublein's stock. It was scheduled to begin the next day. On its conclusion, in the second step, Reynolds planned to issue fractional shares of its common and preferred stock to give a combined value of $56.83 for each of Heublein's remaining 10 million shares. This second step was designed to be tax free.

Reynolds, based in Winston-Salem, North Carolina, was a $12 billion-a-year tobacco, energy, food, and shipping concern. Its worldwide tobacco operations accounted for approximately half of its business. Reynolds also owned Del Monte Corporation, the largest canner of fruits and vegetables in the country. The acquisition would double its food business. Heublein would be combined with Del Monte to form a new food and beverage group, headed by Hicks B. Waldron, Heublein's CEO. He would report directly to J. Paul Stricht, Reynolds' CEO.

Interestingly, Reynolds' interest in acquiring Heublein was initiated by a series of unfounded rumors. As early as the week of January 25, 1982 rumors began to circulate in the financial community that Heublein was discussing a possible merger and that Reynolds was its possible merger partner. However, according to Reynolds, "At the time, the managers of [Heublein] had not had any such discussions and Reynolds management contacted [Heublein] to deny it was the source of such rumors." From that time, until June, there were only "intermittent, informal social contacts between senior officers of [Heublein] and Reynolds, but no negotiations took place." The statement went on to say that the talks started June 13. On July 30, Reynolds made its tender offer.

General Cinema would not comment on the offer until it had time to study it. However, Richard Smith, chairman and CEO of General Cinema, said his firm had not purchased Heublein stock with a possible takeover in mind. "We saw the stock as a good value, with a very strong future, and a line of top quality brands . . . we weren't interested in short-term gains."

General Cinema Doesn't Tender; More Bickering

On Tuesday, August 3 General Cinema announced it would not tender its stock under Reynolds' tender offer. Because it owned the stock for less than six months, it said it would not be allowed to profit on such a tender offer under federal securities laws. The rule implied that because General Cinema owned more than 10 percent of Heublein's stock and was considered an insider, it was not allowed to profit on "short swing" trading that occurred within six months of taking a position in that company's securities. According to the rule, any profit that is made must be turned over to the company on whose securities the profit was made.

According to General Cinema, based on its interpretation of the law, it would be allowed to receive the Reynolds stock in the second step of the merger, because it would not have any control of Heublein after the merger had been approved. General Cinema said it had not decided if it would vote for the merger. A spokesman for Reynolds said, "We expected them to do this all along. We don't expect this to have an effect on the merger." General Cinema planned to realize about a $75 million paper profit on the stock swap. That amount was $23 million less than the $93 million it could have made if it could have tendered under the cash offer. The swap was to be tax-free, though, allowing General Cinema to hold the stock until it qualified for the lower tax rate on long-term capital gains.

Though the war was over, General Cinema and Heublein continued to battle. On October 12, 1982, Heublein asked a federal court to force General Cinema to turn over $30 million allegedly gained on Heublein stock. Heublein was challenging General Cinema's right to exchange its Heublein holdings for the stock of Reynolds. It claimed that such action would be a violation of the same securities law that General Cinema cited as the reason for not taking part in the cash offer.

General Cinema called the suit "frivolous and totally without merit." It went on to say that it voted against the merger and that the Heublein shares it bought still remained in its treasury.

The suit was laid to rest with a ruling against Heublein, then a unit of Reynolds. On February 27, 1984, after losing in both federal district court and federal appeals court, the Supreme Court refused to hear the case, giving a de facto victory to General Cinema.

The Common Thread

We have just seen three examples of a takeover strategy typically referred to as Pac-Man. Yet, what exactly constitutes a Pac-Man situation? Like the popular video game, it occurs when a company turns around and tries to swallow its pursuer. There are really two variations. The first is the counter tender offer. As both an offensive and defensive move, a firm makes a tender offer for some portion of the shares of a firm that is simultaneously trying to acquire it. It is a response to a real or perceived threat from an unsolicited acquirer. This can be seen in the case of Bendix—Martin Marietta and also T. Boone Pickens's battle against Cities Service. The other variation of the Pac-Man theme is called counter accumulation. Using this strategy, the target purchases the acquirer's shares in the open market. This was Heublein's strategy in its attempt to acquire General Cinema. The reasons for undertaking a counter tender offer and the effects of its use are substantially the same as counter accumulation. We will examine the nature of the Pac-Man strategy, including the difference between counter tender offer and a counter accumulation, why they are used, and what governs their use.

Pac-Man: A Child's Game with Adult Consequences

Without a doubt, mergers and acquisitions have been a hot topic, not only on Wall Street, but also in the general news media and in Congress. In terms of the economy as a whole, there are divergent opinions on whether such activity is healthy. Some people view the consummation of an acquisition in a neutral light. If a firm chooses to grow via acquisition, so be it. The shareholders of the acquired firm are free to reinvest that money in different, and perhaps more productive assets. There are many others, however, who do not hold such a nonjudgmental view of the subject. They view mergers and acquisitions as games played by powerful men, without regard for the possible consequences. If this is the case, Pac-Man must be viewed as a twisted variation of that game.

Prior to 1982, Pac-Man was not a widely accepted strategy alternative. Then in 1982 a quick flurry of activity took place, including all three cases discussed in this chapter. Immediately following this period, Pac-Man played a somewhat less prominent role in takeovers, partially due to the negative publicity and ill feeling generated by the Bendix–Martin Marietta case. Yet, rumored use of Pac-Man as a viable defense strategy has again started to surface.

Accumulating in Silence.　The major difference between the use of the counter tender offer and counter accumulation is that the latter can be undertaken with less commitment than a tender offer. No offering circular with legally binding statements has to be distributed, though intentions must be filed with the SEC to get anti-trust clearance and to avoid charges of market manipulation. In the case of Heublein's battle against General Cinema, shares were purchased by the potential counter acquirer, not tendered to them. The actual ownership of the stock, purchased in this manner, can introduce securities trading problems involving regulations guiding insider trading. These regulations hampered a quick and profitable disposal of General Cinema's Heublein holdings. As it turned out, the court ruled that an insider had to have access and opportunity to use material inside information to have violated rule 16(b) of the 1934 Securities Act. Clearly, this was not the case in the General Cinema–Heublein battle and it is unlikely to be the case in most Pac-Man situations.

There are other factors that are also important. A counter accumulation avoids the cost of paying a price premium that is usually associated with a tender offer. This effect may prove to be short-lived because when market participants see the increased demand for a company's stock resulting from this strategy, they are sure to bid up the price. The money "saved" by purchasing an initial block in the open market can be applied to a subsequent tender offer, if the firm chooses to make one later in the fight. A higher tender offer price can be given for the remaining shares desired, one that would have a greater likelihood of success than one that could have been offered right from the start. The final benefit to counter accumulation is such that if a position of over 20 percent is acquired, it is possible to use the equity method of accounting. This would let the firm report a proportional part of the other company's earnings on its income statement, offsetting some of the acquisition costs.

Have They Gone Mad?　Just as one would expect, conventional mergers and acquisitions can lead to extreme behavior on the part of the target firm. Though we often like to think of corporations as rational entities, we can expect them to react to a hostile stimulus as one would expect an animal to react when cornered. Pac-Man seems to push this one step further when both the initial acquirer and the firm to be acquired become targets. This gives the potential for both to lose their rationality and can also make the fight more ruthless. For these reasons, behavior that is more extreme than usual frequently occurs.

A few of the proceeding cases illustrate this. In T. Boone Pickens–Cities Service, Cities sued Mesa's lead lender, Continental Illinois. Such activity was so unorthodox that one takeover specialist involved called the action "bizarre." In the case of Bendix–Martin Marietta, the players came close to the line of making it a personal struggle. Many people felt business judgment was thrown to the wind. Private eyes were rumored to have been hired, a plane was flown with an "I love Bendix" banner, and a federal judge said of the situation, "A pox on both your houses." Pac-Man also gave rise to one of the only cases of the raider becoming a white knight's target, as United Technologies tried to help Martin Marietta acquire Bendix.

The Pac-Man Gamble. Another interesting observation that can be drawn about Pac-Man is the fact that it generates considerable uncertainty in the marketplace. Primarily, this is for two reasons. First, it is not necessarily easy to discern who the winner will be. Speculators, who play a significant role in accumulating shares so they will be tendered, do not know who to bet on. Second, one counter offer seems to beget another. In both Cities Service–Mesa and the simultaneously occurring insurance industry Pac-Man war between American General and NLT there were a total of four offers outstanding at different points in time. Bendix–Martin Marietta not only had multiple offers outstanding for each other, there were other firms involved, making separate bids. Greater uncertainty means greater risk. If there is really greater risk, greater reward would be needed to compensate any new investor buying into the game at the time. This appears to be borne out by the facts.

A tangible effect of the uncertainty is that price movement toward the offer price is less in a Pac-Man situation than in a more conventional tender offer. This can be observed in all three cases. For now, however, let us look at a conventional tender offer. Firm A announces a desire to acquire a substantial number of firm B's shares. On this news, the market price of a share of stock in firm B increases from its present level to one nearer the offering price. It may even go beyond the offering price if market participants expect a higher bid to be forthcoming. The price is usually below what is perceived to be the price that will actually be paid. This is because a speculator sees that there is a chance that the merger may not take place until firm A actually buys the shares. If it would take place with certainty, the speculator would be willing to pay an amount up to the tender offer price. Since it may not, the speculator is willing to pay some amount less than the offer price. Any price appreciation the speculator may get is reward for taking on risk.

In Pac-Man there is even greater risk, so one would expect a speculator to be willing to pay less than he ordinarily would. In the two tender offer Pac-Man cases examined in this chapter, immediately following B's counter offer, the market price of a share of B's stock dropped from the level to which it had appreciated as a result of A's initial offer. After the Pac-Man offer, there was greater risk that the speculator in B's stock would not realize his/her sought after gain. Thus, the price must decline in order to compensate for this additional risk. The same phenomenon also occurs in the case of counter accumulation. For example, General Cinema's announcement that it was planning to acquire more shares of Heublein caused Heublein's stock price to move up. When Heublein announced it would counter accumulate, its share price retreated.

A separate effect on the uncertainty raised by the use of the Pac-Man strategy is seen in the debt market. Both firms usually open up substantial lines of credit to back up tender offers, the outcome of which is uncertain in the marketplace. For example, in Martin Marietta's battle with Bendix, both the aggressor and the initial target had their credit ratings lowered by Standard & Poor's and Moody's during the battle.

Regulation and Speed.   One interesting characteristic of Pac-Man is the time frame in which it takes place. A classic case of Pac-Man takes approximately one month. The reason is fairly obvious. Pac-Man is literally a race between two companies. The winner is the firm that acquires the other first. Both Mesa–Cities Service and

Bendix–Martin Marietta took place in one month's time. A notable exception can be seen in the case of Nashville-based insurer, NLT's defense against American General. This was a protracted dispute in which the counter offer was not made for three weeks after the initial offer. The reason was that both were insurance companies and insurance is a heavily regulated environment. The same would hold true for other regulated industries, such as banking and communications. Regulation slows down the battle and gives both sides more time to garner greater forces or to rethink their strategies. A longer period of time to deal with the situation may take a great deal of the menace out of a Pac-Man defense. While on the subject of speed, it should be mentioned that counter accumulation does not always move as quickly as a counter tender offer, though it may. In counter accumulation no deadlines are set for share purchases and purchases can be made along a wide range of increments. This means the opponents are not locked into a time frame.

The Lonely Pac-Man Needs Friends. A big question is whether or not Pac-Man is a successful strategy. If the evidence at hand is looked at, mixed outcomes can be seen. In both Mesa–Cities Service and General Cinema–Heublein the target goes to a white knight for a higher price than that offered by the aggressor. In Bendix–Martin Marietta, the aggressor gets taken over by a white knight. In this case, although it is not clear if the target won, it is clear that the aggressor lost. A factor that one must keep in mind is that a company rarely relies on a single defensive technique. Usually a combination of several is used.

As previously mentioned, a defensive strategy is rarely set up to stand alone. In almost all cases a golden parachute scheme is added. In the case of Cities Service's counter offense to control Mesa, Mesa's chairman, T. Boone Pickens, would have received compensation worth $10.5 million at the time. When the same is done for other executives, it can easily be seen how such a move would raise the cost of a takeover. Because in Pac-Man the initial aggressor becomes the target, it, too, must develop a defense. For example, shares were repurchased by General Cinema in its battle with Heublein. This is especially interesting because share repurchase is also used by many companies as the major thrust of their defense. Raising the money needed to finance a Pac-Man strategy may result in the depletion of assets or substantial increase in leverage. These effects may cause the target to adopt a scorched earth defense. In this defense, a company liquidates a significant portion of its assets so as to make itself less attractive. Antitakeover measures, like those attempted by Bendix, are often voted in special shareholder meetings. Legal maneuvering is always present, but an antitrust defense is no longer feasible. While the list of multiple defenses continues, the point is that a company rarely relies on a single defense. Pac-Man is no exception.

Why Is Pac-Man Used?

Theoretically, the reason behind using the Pac-Man defense is the same as any other defense—to serve the best interests of the stockholders. Having said this, there are a variety of reasons why such a defense should be undertaken. These could include the desire to remain independent, or if sold, at least at a higher price than that being currently offered. The overall strategic reasons for using Pac-Man may seem valid or dubious, depending on one's point of view. The reasons have stood the legal test of the business judgment rule. However, there are more important tactical reasons why a company, having decided to "defend" itself, would adopt the Pac-Man defense or look for other remedies for rescue.

Sorry, No Antitrust. A starting point for this discussion is to take a look at why Pac-Man is called an offense/defense, not merely a defense. One fact that completely separates Pac-Man as a "defensive" strategy from others is that by choosing it, the management of the target company has implicitly said that a business combination of the two entities makes sense in and of itself. It is merely an academic question of whose management is better qualified to bring out the maximum value of the assets to be combined. This automatically closes off a common avenue of defense, the antitrust suit. In the case of American General–NLT, NLT initiated antitrust proceedings against American General when it first perceived a takeover threat. In deciding to undertake a Pac-Man defense, the suit had to be dropped and NLT was forced to tacitly say it was frivolous. Because each of the three cases under study did not end up in some form of business combination between the initial players, there are obviously other reasons why Pac-Man might be utilized.

In Play.   Clearly, another objective of a Pac-Man defense is to get the aggressor to end its efforts. Pac-Man offers several unique ways to cause this end. One way in which this outcome may occur is to make a tender offer for the suitor's stock. The other way results from ownership of some portion of the aggressor's stock. Having an outstanding tender offer for a company's stock affects a firm in the following manner: There are many companies looking for potential acquisitions. The publicity surrounding a defense against a hostile tender offer makes a firm more visible to others. The novelty of Pac-Man increases this effect by its intense coverage in the media. It stands to reason that a firm making a good acquisition candidate for one firm might be an equally good or better acquisition for another. As a result, a firm that is defending against a hostile tender offer may find other suitors knocking at its door. Takeover specialists call this putting a firm "in play." By instituting a Pac-Man defense, the initial target has put the aggressor in play. If this causes the aggressor to be acquired by a third party, Pac-Man has achieved its objective. Martin Marietta put Bendix in play and even though Bendix was the initial aggressor, it was acquired by a third party.

The initial target can also gain tactical advantage through ownership of a portion of the aggressor's stock. The first purpose this could serve is to effect a stock swap. Neither party may want to carry a fight as far as Bendix and Martin Marietta and thus, rather than force potential disaster on itself, the aggressor may agree to swap the shares each has accumulated in the other. The second reason deals with the voting power inherent in common stock. Takeovers of considerable size usually must be approved by the stockholders of the acquiring company. The target could plan to use its accumulated shares in the aggressor to vote against the proposed takeover at the aggressor's shareholder meeting. This reason and the preceding one were speculated as reasons behind Heublein's counter accumulation of General Cinema shares. Carried to a further extreme, enough stock could be sought to take control of the aggressor's board if majority control is desired. The first company to gain control has a possibility of remaining independent. This last statement is qualified due to the timing of board changes governed by securities laws in different states.

Less Attractive.   Last, but not least, is the "kamikaze effect" a Pac-Man defense may have on the firm that applies it. In order for the initial target to purchase shares of the aggressor, it may have to sell off key assets. Alternatively, the initial target may incur substantial debt to raise funds, which are then expended in the purchase of the aggressor's shares. Such action makes the initial target a less attractive acquisition prospect. The effect on the target, should it succeed in driving the aggressor away, can be unfortunate. Martin Marietta, for example, was saddled with substantial debt long after its bout with Bendix.

The Pac-Man Time Bomb: What Makes It Tick?

As with the rest of our lives, conscience and law are the guiding forces. In Pac-Man, law has the dominant position. Pac-Man raises two important legal questions: (1) Should it be allowed at all? and (2) if it is allowed what happens when the two firms acquire majority control in each other? Let us deal with the second question first.

State of Pac-Man.   The question is a little more complicated than it seems on the surface. By the nature of Pac-Man, except in the most unusual of coincidences, one firm will issue its tender offer prior to the other firm issuing its offer. A problem arises, however, with state laws. In the Bendix–Martin Marietta case, Bendix was incorporated in Delaware and Martin Marietta was incorporated in Maryland. Because of a difference in state laws, even though Bendix would have majority control of Martin Marietta five days before the reverse was true, Bendix would be prevented from exercising its rights until five days after Martin Marietta took control. Martin Marietta having acquired majority control of Bendix, a Delaware corporation, in the interim, would be allowed to exercise its rights immediately. The situation seems absurd. Bendix would be the majority shareholder in Martin Marietta, so on whose behalf would and should Martin Marietta be acting if it tried to dislodge Bendix's board? Recognizing this as a problem, the court temporarily restrained Martin Marietta from voting its Bendix shares. This question was left unresolved, though, because the two parties disengaged prior to the issue being settled.

In response to a related question, an opinion of sorts was given by the court. Martin Marietta asked a Delaware court to enjoin a Bendix special shareholder meeting, where provisions would be voted which could negate Martin Marietta's timing advantage. Both the Chancery Court and the Delaware Supreme Court refused to enjoin. The court said, "If the Martin board so acts after September 16, 1982 to gain control of the Bendix board, it will do so in violation of a moral duty to its majority stockholder, Bendix. While this may be an enforcable duty under Maryland law, even it if is not, it is a proper consideration as to whether a Delaware equity court will intervene on Martin's behalf." The court let the issue rest with this far from crystal clear statement. So it is not a settled issue. It seems, though, that the company which is the first to buy a majority of the other company's shares is most likely to win.

In addition, an aggressor having a staggered board might signal to the target the futility of instituting a Pac-Man defense. For a firm that fears it may be a potential target, staggering the board would raise the level of danger for any aggressor. The possibility is present that a firm could defend itself using Pac-Man and win, even though the aggressor's offer came first.

The Pac-Man Game, the Judge, and the Judgment.   The question of whether or not Pac-Man should be allowed at all is also an interesting one. A person such as T. Boone Pickens of Mesa Petroleum is likely to say that it is clearly a strategy to entrench current management in their jobs. In all three cases discussed in this chapter, suit was brought for this or a related reason. The directors of the corporation being sued are held up against what is called the business judgment rule. The rule requires directors to make their decisions in good faith and in accordance with what they reasonably believe to be in the best interest of stockholders. The law implies that without fraud, self-dealing, or bad faith, the directors operate under the presumption of good faith. Thus, the burden of proof is on the party seeking to establish failure of the management to meet the business judgment standard. The mere allegation that a tender offer may have been rejected to keep directors in office has not proven to be enough. As mentioned earlier, present management could easily claim Pac-Man was undertaken because they could better manage the combined assets or to get their shareholders a more favorable return.

In almost all cases of Pac-Man a suit is brought by one side, or both, dealing with the business judgment rule. To see what the courts actually have to say, all one has to do is check the transcripts. A good example occurred when Bendix filed a motion for a preliminary injunction against Martin Marietta's counter offer based on the business judgment rule. The court found "no credible evidence in the record that in proceeding with its tender offer Martin Marietta's board was not acting in good faith and in furtherance of what they reasonably believed to be a good corporate purpose."

Big Brother Watches — The SEC.   In response to Pac-Man and the rest of the considerable merger activity taking place in the late 1970s and the 1980s, in 1983 the SEC appointed an 18-member Advisory Committee on Tender Offers. In its final report, issued in early July 1983, the committee said that in many cases Pac-Man could be used to benefit the target company's shareholders. Because of this it recommended the following:

> There should be no general restrictions on the counter tender offer as a defense. The employment of the counter tender offer should be prohibited, however, where a bidder has made a cash tender offer for 100% of the target company.

The reason given for recommending restrictions on cash tender offers for 100 percent was that "the counter tender offer is not appropriate because there will be no remaining shareholders on whose behalf the target management is acting."

Credit must be given to the committee for all the hard work they must have put into the report. However, the proposed 100 percent rule is not soundly constructed. For a 100 percent cash tender offer to result in no remaining shareholders on whose behalf the target company's management would act, it has to be assumed the tender offer will be totally successful. Without knowing the adequacy of the price, in relation to what could be considered fair, it is very difficult to assume the offer will be completely successful. In addition, why should the duty of present management to seek the best offer be diminished because the offer is for 100 percent, rather than 95 percent or any other level? As of this date, this particular recommendation has not been made into law.

Any-and-All.   Another important consideration dealing with the timing issue is the "any-and-all" tender offer. Let us take the position that the first firm to acquire majority control will be the winner. Though this may or may not be the case, if the choice were offered of being first or second, it would seem more advantageous to be first. Most conventional tender offers are only partial offers. Firm A bids for 51 percent of firm B's stock. Such two-step mergers are typically advantageous to A because once it controls 51 percent it can dictate the merger terms. This saves A because it can vote that the remaining shareholders receive less, and win. Offers of this sort are strictly regulated and have to have proration and withdrawal deadlines. The SEC dictates the minimum number of days that can pass prior to these deadlines. Because of this, there is no way for the target, short of a preemptive strike, to get control first under a partial offer. Legally, it must wait the same time period as the aggressor, but the aggressor has a head start.

However, the disadvantage of being second can be turned into an advantage with an any-and-all counter offer. In such an offer, the issuing firm is saying just what the name implies. It will buy any and all shares of the firm whose shares it is seeking to obtain. Because all shares are offered for purchase, no proration deadline is needed. This time-saving device turns the aggressor's headstart around. On the other hand, if an aggressor fears a Pac-Man defense, it may want its initial volley to be an any-and-all offer.

Pac-Man: What Next?

There are certain salient aspects of Pac-Man that must be kept in mind if its use is considered. One must have a solid understanding of the many tedious rules that surround its use. This means not only the rules that are known with certainty, such as the greater importance of proration and withdrawal deadlines. One must also be cognizant of the undecided issues surrounding state laws and other provisions related to the replacement of boards. These issues inject an air of uncertainty into the outcome if Pac-Man is played to its ultimate conclusion. As with most defensive strategies, Pac-Man should not be played by itself. Rather, it should be used in conjunction with several other strategies. However, by its nature, it is used to the exclusion of antitrust. Pac-Man also seems to generate extreme behavior; this should be expected and not be met with surprise.

The Pac-Man strategy is clearly one of the most exciting defenses against hostile takeover attempts. It has all the ingredients of both Shakespearian tragedy and comedy. It also has the action of an Agatha Christie thriller. These attributes led to the public uproar following the Bendix–Martin Marietta case, causing the strategy to lie dormant for a while. Nevertheless, it remains powerful and workable. Indeed, it was redeployed in January 1984 when Houston Natural Gas used Pac-Man to successfully defend itself against Coastal Corporation. It was also speculated as a possible defense in Union Carbide's 1985-86 battle against GAF. Only time will tell whether Pac-Man will increase or decrease in importance. In any event, it is one of the most shocking defenses a firm can deploy.

2

The Lock-Up
Defense

The Halloween Surprise: Mobil's Trick Or Treat

MOBIL vs. MARATHON

In the summer of 1981 Mobil lost to duPont in its well-publicized bid to acquire Conoco. Mobil's strategy in pursuing Conoco was revealed in one of its reports filed with the SEC:

> The board has . . . concluded that the purchase of existing reserves where they are available at costs comparable to or preferably below those incurred in discovering new reserves will in the long run be financially beneficial to the Corporation and its stockholders . . . .

In the three years preceding the loss to duPont, Mobil had spent nearly $1.5 billion to acquire General Crude Oil and TransOcean Co. and had bid unsuccessfully for both Belridge Oil and Texas Pacific Oil.

Given its determination to buy crude oil reserves in order to save exploration and drilling costs, and its failure to acquire Conoco, many analysts expected Mobil to attempt a takeover of another reserve-rich oil company. They did not have to wait long.

"I Slammed on My Brakes when I Heard the News"

On Halloween Eve, 1981, the black knight attacked. That Friday, Mobil announced a two-tier bid to acquire Marathon Oil Co. of Findlay, Ohio. The announcement terrified a significant part of the population of small Findlay, Marathon's headquarters for the past 96 years. One sad resident said, "Things will probably never be the same again." A more upset woman, the wife of a top Marathon executive, told a reporter, "I slammed on my brakes when I heard the news on the car radio. I was flabbergasted."

Findlay had about 40,000 residents and Marathon was its largest employer. The oil company employed 2100 people, or 10 percent of the town's workforce, and generated 20 percent of the town's tax revenues. With 1980 sales of $8.7 billion, Marathon was the nation's sixteenth largest integrated petroleum producer.

In its offer, Mobil announced it planned to buy up to 40 million Marathon common shares, or approximately 67 percent of its stock, for $85 cash per share. It conditioned its offer on receiving at least 30 million shares by the November 11 proration date. The proration date is the day on which the proportion of tendered shares that are purchased is determined. For example, in this case, proration will be required if more than 40 million shares are tendered to Mobil. As a practical matter, holders expecting a cash payment would be unwilling to withdraw from this pool unless a significantly higher offer were received. The proration date, therefore, marks the day a competing bidder must offer substantially more in order to lure a shareholder from his "sure thing."

If the 40 million shares Mobil sought were not tendered by November 11, then under the second half of its bid, Mobil would buy any shortfall by exchanging a 30-year Mobil debenture to be valued at $85 for each Marathon share. At that time Marathon stock was traded at $67.50. If concluded, the merger would cost nearly $5.1 billion, and it would be the most expensive corporate takeover on record.

Mobil was undoubtedly attracted to Marathon's most prized possession, its 49.5 percent interest in the Yates field in Texas. This field was the nation's second-largest oil field after Prudhoe Bay, Alaska. Considering Marathon's other reserves, including its interest in the Brae Field in the North Sea, acquisition of Marathon would have increased Mobil's net undeveloped domestic acreage to 12.6 million acres, an increase of 26 percent. The acquisition would also have greatly increased Mobil's refining and marketing capacity, giving it the largest pipeline network in the United States.

Marathon was particularly attractive as a target because its shares had recently been trading very low relative to their intrinsic value. The cost of drilling for and finding oil was $12 to $15 per barrel. By buying Marathon's vast reserves for $85 per share, Mobil would be buying oil at $3 to $3.50 per barrel.

The Yates Field's Sex Appeal: 50 Years Old with Another 90 Years to Live

Marathon possessed a source of vast earnings in the Yates field, a resource almost without equal in the industry. Much of the oil in this field was located in natural reservoirs only a few thousand feet below ground. The surrounding limestone was highly porous and easily permeable so that the oil flowed freely. Moreover, water pressure from beneath the reservoirs pushed oil to the surface without the need for expensive pumping operations.

Not only was the field easily accessible, but it was also incredibly fertile. It had between 3 and 3.5 billion barrels of oil in place, and even though it had been producing for over 50 years, petroleum engineers considered it to be only in the intermediate stage of depletion. At the time of Mobil's bid, the field was producing 125,000 barrels a day, and at that rate was expected to continue producing for another 90 years. In fact, Marathon had applied to Texas authorities for permission to increase production to 150,000 barrels per day.

Other minority-interest oil companies who shared the cost of developing the field were Standard Oil of California, with 15.5 percent, Gulf Oil, with 10.5 percent, and Amoco, Shell, Getty, Exxon, and Conoco, with 2 to 5 percent each. Marathon possessed its 49.5 percent interest because its predecessor, Ohio Oil Co., agreed to do the original wildcat exploratory drilling for the owner of the field, Ira Yates, along with Transcontinental Oil. After the first gusher in 1926, Ohio Oil bought out Transcontinental's interest.

Warning Signs

Many analysts believe that Marathon should have anticipated the attack. At the time of its bid, Mobil owned 178,000 Marathon shares, bought mostly in the month preceding its bid. Additionally, the low price of Marathon stock relative to its intrinsic value should have alerted management to the fact that the company was highly ranked as a potential target. Management, though, took no steps to defend itself.

Marathon's only preparation was to obtain a $5 billion line of credit in July 1981, when some observers believe speculation in its shares began. This fund was apparently to be used for defense. However, by failing to draw down the money for affirmative defensive measures, Marathon's unleveraged position made it an appealing target. According to one oil industry analyst, management's response amounted to reacting "by the seat of their pants."

Marathon's Reaction

Although Marathon did little to defend itself prior to Mobil's announcement, within hours of the news, Marathon put into action its now-classic takeover defense. Marathon president Harold D. Hoopman assembled a power-packed group of advisors to direct its maneuvers. The advisors included such heavy weights as investment bankers Bruce Wasserstein and Joseph Perella from First Boston, attorney Joseph Flom from Skadden, Arps, Slate, Meagher & Flom, and public relations expert Richard Cheney of Hill & Knowlton. Hoopman often wore a red baseball cap to strategy meetings with these advisors and was reported during this period to have been overheard daydreaming aloud "about his desire to run his own little drilling company." With these players, Marathon's defensive strategy was formulated. In a hasty series of weekend meetings following Mobil's offer, it was determined that the offer was "grossly inadequate." Marathon's board unamimously rejected the bid. Observers felt that the possibility of Mobil displacing Marathon's management and employees was at least as important as the inadequacy of the $85 offer. The defense was about to begin.

The alternatives considered included the sale of certain assets, the takeover of another company, a liquidation plan, a tender offer for Marathon's own stock, and legal action. As expected from a target fighting back, its first move was on the legal front. On the Sunday following the bid, Marathon filed an antitrust suit against Mobil in federal district court in Cleveland, alleging that Mobil's proposed merger would violate Section 7 of the Clayton Act. Marathon obtained a temporary restraining order preventing Mobil from proceeding with its offer. It alleged that the merger, if carried out, would substantially reduce competition in gasoline marketing in areas where the companies' markets overlapped. It also argued that Marathon, as the nation's leading supplier to independent gasoline retailers, must remain viable in order to supply these dealers. This, they claimed, was necessary to maintain needed price checks on the large oil companies.

The restraining order as originally drafted was to expire November 10, thirty-six hours before the proration date under Mobil's offer. Preventing Mobil from soliciting shares or accepting tendered shares afforded Marathon a chance to seek a friendlier buyer while Mobil's hands were tied. In response to Mobil's predicament, on November 10, the court amended the order to allow Mobil to solicit shares and accept tendered shares without actually purchasing them, pending a ruling on Marathon's application for a preliminary injunction. The proration date was also moved back to November 21, which was both good and bad news for Mobil. It gave Mobil additional time to secure commitments for shares, but it also allowed Marathon more time to find a competing bidder before shares tendered to Mobil were committed to it.

Will the Battle Get Wild and Woolly?

After Mobil announced its bid, Marathon began discussions with a number of possible buyers. Other oil companies received Marathon's advances with reservations. For example, Standard Oil of California declined to bid, explaining that most bidding wars result in prices that can't be justified. Gulf Oil considered making an offer, conditioned on Marathon's granting it an option to purchase 10 million shares, a condition which Marathon would not accept. One can question Marathon's reasoning in trying to find help among the oil companies when its primary argument against Mobil was that the merger would violate antitrust laws.

In fact, many of the other integrated oil companies approached the situation cautiously, precisely because of the yet to be decided Marathon application for a preliminary injunction, scheduled for hearing November 17. As one oil analyst explained, "If Mobil clears the antitrust hurdles, look for the Marathon battle to get wild and woolly. You could see Texaco, Gulf Oil, Shell, maybe even Exxon get involved."

Outside of oil companies, Allied Corporation, and even a group composed of Marathon's two largest shareholders, considered entering the battle. An analyst commented that "there are five investment banks in Wall Street with potential suitors for Marathon and we've only seen two suitors surface so far."

Another prong of Marathon's defense was based on the media's ability to influence policymakers and sway public policy. On November 11, Marathon mailgrammed a statement outlining the company's position to 550 newspaper editorial writers throughout the country. Marathon president Hoopman attacked Mobil's "high-handed arrogance" in its takeover attempt, saying that Mobil "seems to be trying to set back public attitudes to the days of the Standard Oil Trust."

Coincidentally, at this same time *The Wall Street Journal* reported frequent appearances of U.S. Steel Corporation aircraft at Marathon's home in Findlay.

"Straight Out of a James Bond Adventure"

On Saturday morning, November 14, Marathon's strategy team held its first meeting with representatives of U.S. Steel, including its chairman, Charles Corry, and its president, David M. Roderick. The security measures taken by U.S. Steel were described as "straight out of a James Bond adventure." When the Marathon plane landed at the Pittsburgh airport, it taxied directly into the U.S. Steel hangar and the hangar doors were closed immediately after it. Then, the Marathon officials were hurried to an adjacent helicopter pad for the flight to the roof of U.S. Steel's downtown headquarters. They were ushered from the roof directly into Roderick's office.

U.S. Steel's initial offer was $100 per share for all of Marathon's common stock. This offer bolstered the Marathon team's confidence that they could find a better deal than that offered by Mobil. They rejected the U.S. Steel offer, hoping that Allied Industries, which had shown interest in acquiring Marathon, might be willing to pay more than $100 per share. Yet Marathon only received a series of complex and tentative telephone proposals from Allied. Marathon directors spent nine futile hours on Sunday pondering their options. Unable to come to a decision, the board adjourned at 1:00 A.M. on Monday, November 16.

Then Hoopman took the initiative. By dawn on that day, he was on the telephone, assembling his overworked directors both to elicit the best possible deal from U.S. Steel and to solicit competitive offers from other companies, such as Gulf Oil. That morning, they

hastily flew to Pittsburgh and met with Gulf officials at 8 A.M.
"chiefly to see if Gulf was interested enough to give us some leverage in talking with Steel again." Before morning's end, Hoopman
and U.S. Steel's Roderick were meeting tete-à-tete while the other
Marathon team members scurried to a nearby Brooks Brothers store
to pick up fresh shirts and underwear. Roderick was firm in his
$100 per share offer. Yet Hoopman and his newly freshened team
pressed for $110. The Marathon team was asked to leave the room
while U.S. Steel's management discussed the transaction. After
more than an hour, the Marathon team was advised that U.S. Steel's
final offer would be for $125 per share for 30 million shares of Mar-
athon stock. It would then be followed by a second step in which
U.S. Steel notes valued at $86 each would be exchanged for the rest
of the Marathon shares. This offer constituted an average of $106
per Marathon share.

The Lock-Up

U.S. Steel obtained two options from Marathon as a condition to
making its offer. The first was a stock lock-up. It allowed U.S. Steel
to purchase up to 10 million authorized but unissued shares for $90
per share. This amounted to approximately 17 percent of Marathon's outstanding stock.

The second, and most significant, was an asset lock-up which
allowed U.S. Steel to buy Marathon's interest in the Yates field for
$2.8 billion, but only if Marathon were acquired by a third party.
This amounted to about $5 per barrel for proven reserves, far below
market value.

Why U.S. Steel?

U.S. Steel's move was part of a major reorganization, started in response to deteriorating returns, already below those earned by the
rest of the steel industry. Several years earlier, it had closed all or
part of 16 plants, eliminating 13,000 steel-related jobs. Its plan was
to modernize its remaining steel operations, and simultaneously
improve profitability by significant diversification.

Although company officials had announced earlier that it would begin negotiating an acquisition by year's end, the size of the proposed deal, nearly $6.4 billion, was a landmark in steel company diversification, and astounded many steel analysts. Though playing the role of a white knight, U.S. Steel was expected to be a player in a major acquisition. This was evidenced by the fact that it acquired its financial muscle early on. It had obtained a $3 billion line of credit in mid-summer, and it also had $2 billion in cash at its disposal, obtained from selling various assets including coal properties.

At the time of U.S. Steel's offer, analysts estimated that the more profitable Marathon, with sales about two-thirds of U.S. Steel's, would add between 40 and 80 cents per share to the potential parent's depressed earnings.

Mobil's Response

Meanwhile, Mobil failed to amass the required 30 million shares by the new proration date of November 21. As shareholders still had time to withdraw from this pool to tender to U.S. Steel, Mobil was expected to increase its bid.

Before doing so, Mobil filed suit against Marathon and U.S. Steel in federal district court in Columbus, claiming that the oil field option granted to U.S. Steel served to inhibit competitive bidding for Marathon by making the Yates Field unavailable to third parties. It also argued that the stock option made Marathon stock more easily available to U.S. Steel than its competition. Mobil claimed that granting the options was thus a "manipulative act or practice" in violation of the Williams Act.

On November 24, Mobil obtained a temporary restraining order from Judge Joseph Kinneary, who had been assigned to the case. The order prohibited Marathon and U.S. Steel from taking any action in connection with the tender offer or the Yates field option, pending a ruling on Mobil's application for a preliminary injunction. At the same time, Judge Kinneary extended U.S. Steel's proration date to December 8, affording shareholders additional time to decide between U.S. Steel and Mobil, but giving them the unenviable task of anticipating the rulings in both federal court actions. The same day, in an action that some analysts interpreted as aimed to intimidate U.S. Steel, Mobil announced that it had purchased $15 million of the steelmaker's stock. The acquisition, however, represented less than 1 percent of U.S. Steel's 90 million total shares.

The following day, Mobil amended its bid for Marathon. It offered to buy at least 30 million shares for $126 per share and to buy the rest of Marathon common by swapping debentures valued at $90 for each Marathon share. The offer had a proration date of December 7 and was conditioned on the court's finding that the options granted to U.S. Steel were invalid.

At this point, Mobil's position was uncertain. If its application for a preliminary injunction were to fail, presumably Mobil would no longer pursue Marathon. However, if the application were ultimately to succeed, then Mobil still faced a review of possible antitrust problems by the FTC.

The Litigation Continues

On November 29, Judge Kinneary amended the restraining order to allow U.S. Steel to solicit shares. He also moved forward the proration date under U.S. Steel's offer to December 7, the same day as Mobil's.

Meanwhile, hearings had started on Mobil's request for an injunction, centering on the propriety of the valuations reflected in the options granted to U.S. Steel.

Judge Kinneary interpreted the Williams Act to require only that the disclosures made to Marathon shareholders about the actual terms of the options be accurate and not misleading. The substantive fairness or reasonableness of the valuations assigned to the Yates field and Marathon stock were not relevant to Mobil's Williams Act claim. They were, however, relevant to its claim that, under state law, Marathon directors had, in approving the options, violated their fiduciary duty to the corporation and its shareholders.

Mobil introduced a report prepared by First Boston valuing the discounted cash flows expected from the Yates field at a maximum of $3.7 billion. However, testimony revealed that this figure was computed under an assumption out of favor in the oil industry, that is, the windfall profits tax would be phased out over a period of several years beginning in the late 1980s. Ignoring this assumption, the cash flows had a much lower present value, between $2.5 and $2.7 billion. As in any economic analysis, the bottom line critically depended on the assumptions.

U.S. Steel Chairman David Roderick testified that the $2.8 billion figure agreed to by Marathon was intensely negotiated at arm's length. He testified that U.S. Steel and Goldman, Sachs appraised the field at $2 to $2.2 billion, but that Harold Hoopman, Marathon's President and CEO, insisted that $2.8 billion was "the lowest number he'd [take] for the Yates Field, even if it was a deal-breaker."

Further testimony revealed that Allied Corporation made an offer to buy Marathon conditioned on the receipt of an option similar to U.S. Steel's for $3 billion. This offer was ultimately rejected.

Edwin Wells, managing director of Warburg, Paribas Becker, Allied's financial counsel, was "amazed" to see the option granted to U.S. Steel: "We offered $3 billion for openers and we were willing to increase that offer. It's crystal clear to me that Marathon's Yates interest is worth at least $4 billion, and possibly as much as $5 billion."

On November 30, Marathon's application for an injunction in the antitrust action was allowed, prohibiting Mobil from taking further action on its offer. Mobil asked for an expedited hearing in the court of appeals. It argued that if U.S. Steel defeated the injunction in the other action, it would be free to buy shares while Mobil was still held up on appeal. Marathon argued in turn that it needed more time to prepare its case for appeal. Marathon won the timing skirmish with the hearing set for December 17.

Possibly in response to Mobil's predicament, on December 2, Judge Kinneary entered an order prohibiting both U.S. Steel and Mobil from buying shares until five business days after his own ruling on Mobil's request for an injunction. At this stage in the proceedings, Mobil was prohibited from taking any action on its offer. On the other hand, U.S. Steel, although unable to buy shares, was free to advertise and accept tendered shares.

On December 6, Mobil announced that it had reached an agreement with the petroleum refiner and marketer Amerada Hess Corporation (Hess). Under the agreement, Mobil would sell Hess all of Marathon's marketing, refining, and transportation assets if it gained control of Marathon. Mobil said that such an agreement was intended to find a solution to the antitrust violation found by the district court.

On December 7, Judge Kinneary denied Mobil's request for a preliminary injunction against Marathon and U.S. Steel. The judge held that the disclosures made to Marathon shareholders about the terms of the options were not misleading, and so were not "manipulative" under the Williams Act. As for Mobil's state law claims, Judge Kinneary held that despite conflicting evidence on the value of the Yates field, the $2.8 billion accepted by Marathon's directors "was not unreasonable" in view of much of the evidence presented. Finally, he held that granting the stock option was also not a breach of the directors' fiduciary duty to Marathon and its shareholders. He came to this conclusion in light of the fact that the price at which U.S. Steel could buy Marathon stock under the option was greater than both Mobil's initial offer and the market price of Marathon stock at the time the option was granted.

The following day, December 8, Mobil requested the court to consider its preliminary injunction in view of the arrangement with Hess. The next day, the application was denied. The Mobil–Hess agreement, however, received an unusual amount of press coverage, since the assets that Mobil was expected to sell to Hess for $400 million carried a book value of $1.4 billion on Marathon's balance sheet. Mobil was also willing to finance the sale to Hess with an extremely generous financing deal.

As a result of the district court ruling, U.S. Steel was free to begin buying shares on December 15, five business days after the Judge Kinneary's decision. U.S. Steel reported that its transfer agent, Bankers Trust, had been tendered nearly 54 million Marathon shares by the proration date, December 7. In contrast, Mobil's pool, once estimated at nearly 28 million shares, had been all but depleted by withdrawals favoring the U.S. Steel offer.

Mobil appealed Judge Kinneary's rulings, and a hearing was scheduled for December 17, the same day as the hearing on Mobil's appeal in the antitrust action. To protect Mobil in the event Judge Kinneary's rulings were overturned, the court of appeals prohibited

U.S. Steel from buying shares until five business days after its decision on Mobil's two appeals.

Mobil's Fate Is Decided

On December 23, the court of appeals issued separate decisions on the two appeals brought by Mobil. The court effectively put an end to Mobil's chances by upholding the issuance of the injunction in the antitrust case. Because Marathon had demonstrated a strong likelihood that a merger with Mobil would have violated the Clayton Act, issuance of an injunction pending a trial was determined to be proper.

Although the issue was not arguably moot, the court also invalidated the two options granted to U.S. Steel. This appeared to be the first appellate court ruling in which the validity of such options was specifically addressed.

The court disagreed with Judge Kinneary's interpretation of the Williams Act. Although the term "manipulative" is not defined in the statute, the court noted, in typically burdensome legal jargon, that

> The Supreme Court has recently indicated that manipulation is an affecting of the market for, or price of, securities by artificial means, i.e., means unrelated to the natural forces of supply and demand. . . . In our view, it is difficult to conceive of a more effective and manipulative device than the "lock-up" options employed here, options which not only artificially affect, but for all practical purposes, completely block normal healthy market activity and, in fact, could be construed as expressly designed solely for that purpose.

The court reasoned that because the Yates field was a significant asset for any potential acquirer, there would be no reason for a competitor to bid over U.S. Steel's $125 offer if the options were valid. The competitor would only lose the field to U.S. Steel in this event. Referring to the evidence on valuation introduced before Judge Kinneary, the court refused to conjecture "that Mobil and other potential bidders for control of Marathon would not be willing to make tender offers reflecting a Yates field valuation far greater than $2.8 billion, were it not for the Yates Field option which U.S. Steel possesses." The court concluded that U.S. Steel's $125 was in effect a "ceiling" on the price for Marathon shares resulting only from the "artifice" of granting the option to U.S. Steel.

The stock option, as well, was invalidated, as the court felt that it artificially discouraged competitive bidding by making it decidedly easier for U.S. Steel to buy stock at a price unavailable to potential competitors.

Thus, the court determined that the Williams Act is concerned primarily with the protection of competitive bidding, and not simply with the adequacy of disclosures. Although the value assigned to the Yates field and to Marathon stock may have been reasonable, the possibility of higher offers from other bidders prompted the court to rule that the options constituted "artificial" impediments to the competitive bidding process.

In invalidating the options, the court ordered that U.S. Steel's offer be kept open for a period sufficient to allow acceptance of new competing bids by Marathon shareholders. The case was remanded back to Judge Kinneary for his determination of a new timetable consistent with the ruling.

Mobil's Last-Ditch Attempt

On receiving the case, Judge Kinneary set midnight, January 6, 1982 as the time after which U.S. Steel could begin buying Marathon stock. New bidders for Marathon were not expected to surface at that late date, given the resolution of the antitrust issues and the fact that a new bidder would have had to offer substantially more than $125 to lure shares from U.S. Steel's pool. In fact, no new bids appeared.

However, Mobil did make one last-ditch attempt to stop U.S. Steel. In appearances before the district court, court of appeals, and ultimately the Supreme Court, Mobil requested an order blocking U.S. Steel's purchase of shares. It argued that it should have been given an opportunity to amend its merger offer in that the merger was found objectionable on antitrust grounds. With the Supreme Court's denial of Mobil's request on January 6, the battle for Marathon ended.

Early Winners

Fortune called them "The Big Winners from Texas." One was Sedco, Inc., a Dallas-based offshore oil-drilling contractor that owned 7.7 percent of Marathon's stock, and was therefore the biggest shareholder of the Ohio company. Sedco began buying stock in December 1980, and had already made, but not yet realized, a $206 million gain on a $274 million investment. When Mobil announced its offer in late November 1981, Marathon stock jumped from $67 a share to $90 on the NYSE. The day after the U.S. Steel bid, it reached $106.75 a share.

Another big winner was the Bass family. As usual, knowing where the action is, they accumulated enough shares to become the second largest shareholder of Marathon. In fact, Bass Brothers Enterprises, a Fort Worth company, owned 5.5 percent of Marathon's stock and made $160 million on a $165 million investment.

A third winner, although not from Texas, was First Boston, which was paid $17 million for advising Marathon.

Completing the Deal Despite Grass Roots Disapproval

Under the second half of U.S. Steel's plan, the company would begin exchanging Marathon shares for 12-year, 12.5 percent U.S. Steel notes. In order to formally complete the merger, U.S. Steel needed the approval of two-thirds of Marathon shareholders. However, almost immediately after completing the purchases under the first half of its offer, U.S. Steel encountered a groundswell of shareholder opposition.

A number of class action suits were filed against U.S. Steel and Marathon. In one, plaintiffs claimed that the notes to be exchanged for the remaining stock were unfairly low in value, compared to the $125 offered under the first part of the plan. At the time the suit was filed, the notes were worth between $80 and $85.

Another action alleged that even the $125 cash offer was unfair in view of values attributed to Marathon stock by an internal company evaluation and a report prepared by First Boston.

The Marathon internal report estimated that, based strictly on asset value, the stock was worth between $276 and $323 per share, while the First Boston report, also using asset values, assessed the stock at between $189 and $226.

Marathon countered by asserting that these values, liquidation values, could not realistically have been realized by shareholders in a sale of Marathon as a going concern. In other words, Marathon argued that cash flows, not asset values, are used to value stock in an acquisition. Moreover, as a managing director of First Boston commented, "You must realize that, at the time, the directors' choice wasn't between the liquidation value estimates and the U.S. Steel offer, but between the U.S. Steel offer and one from Mobil, which was then only $85 a share."

A third suit alleged that U.S. Steel and Bankers Trust failed to accurately report the number of shares tendered, thereby preventing people who tendered into an already oversubscribed pool from selling in the open market instead of receiving the lower valued U.S. Steel notes.

Although litigation against U.S. Steel and Marathon was ultimately resolved in their favor, the litigation was important in that it highlighted individual shareholder or "grass roots" disapproval of the merger going into the shareholder meeting. Many of Marathon's largest shareholders, such as Morgan Guaranty and Dreyfus Fund, indicated that they might vote against the merger at the meeting scheduled for March 11. Marathon had reason to worry. Under Ohio law, a shareholder who fails to approve a merger proposal can institute an appraisal proceeding and request that the court assess the fair value of his/her shares. After the votes were counted, holders of 110,000 shares sought appraisal. This type of action had never been attempted before on a grand scale. As a result, the shareholder meeting was raucous. But in the end, the merger was approved by 78 percent of the shares, and U.S. Steel's acquisition of Marathon was completed.

Within a year, Mobil had lost two major merger battles. The first, concluded in August 1981, marked a low point in Mobil's corporate history. In its battle with duPont, Mobil had been outmaneuvered by a much less powerful adversary in its attempt to take over Conoco. Now, it was outfoxed again. This time, it was beaten by U.S. Steel, a company a fraction of Mobil's size. Although Goliath met David only once, Mobil had been beaten twice in a one year period by smaller, less wealthy opponents in colossal corporate battles. David won again, and the giant tasted bitter defeat.

The Carriage Trade Defense: Racketeering Charges And Lock-Ups

CARL ICAHN vs. MARSHALL FIELD

The Grande Dame

Marshall Field and Company began with a single dry-goods store in frontier Chicago 130 years ago. The flagship store, occupying a full block of State Street, became a Chicago landmark with its two famous clocks to guide the carriage trade. Marshall Field developed into an elegant emporium with a special staff of craftsmen to reweave oriental carpets and restore antique furniture. They catered to the affluent, fashion-conscious shopper.

In the 1970s, Marshall Field began to lose its retail market share. When skillful fashion merchants like Lord and Taylor and I. Magnin invaded their Chicago turf, Field's lost many once-loyal customers. One former Marshall Field customer complained, "They're [Marshall Field] trying to become a store for everyman. It's trendy, but cheap."

"I Wonder What Kind of Grass They've Been Smoking"

Back in 1970, Marshall Field, fearing a takeover by Associated Dry Goods, retained the services of renowned New York lawyer Joseph Flom. Known as a specialist in counseling companies in thwarting unwanted suitors, Flom advised Marshall Field to make itself big enough to be unaffordable and to create antitrust obstacles by moving into markets where potential acquirers do business. Associated had stores in Cleveland and nearby Erie, Pennsylvania. As a result of Flom's advice, Marshall Field soon acquired the Halle Brothers department store chain in Cleveland. The strategy worked. Associated no longer pursued Marshall Field.

The pace of Field's acquisitions stepped up significantly when Angelo Arena, former chairman of Neiman Marcus, joined Marshall Field as president in 1977. Arena was in office for less than a week when his former boss, Philip Hawley, approached him with a $42 per share buyout bid. Following the strategy of his predecessors, Arena soon broke ground for a new Marshall Field store on Neiman Marcus's home turf in Houston. Arena successfully fought the Hawley bid on antitrust grounds. It seemed that people on the street did not welcome that development. The stock dropped from a high of $36 per share in 1977 prior to the Hawley bid to $13 after the bid was blocked. Subsequently, many angry stockholders filed suit against Arena and the company directors. These suits were finally dismissed in 1978.

In the wake of this action, Arena embarked on an expensive, and somewhat questionable, shopping spree. In all, he tripled the number of stores in the Marshall Field domain. Among the purchases were a large California furniture chain, 11 department stores in Oregon and Washington, and 23 J.B. Ivey department stores in Florida and the Carolinas. Unfortunately, many of the stores that Arena acquired were mediocre performers. The company's acquisitions were not only geographically scattered, but different in style and merchandise, prompting one retailing executive to remark: "I wonder what kind of grass they've been smoking."

The company defended its strategy, stating that it wanted to reduce its dependence on the Chicago stores. Arena claimed that the decision to move to Texas had nothing to do with Philip Hawley's bid. He stated that "the reason we went to the Sunbelt is the same reason our competitors went there—it's a better place for growth. Certainly the conclusion shouldn't be that we did it to create antitrust obstacles."

The acquisitions in the South and West put a heavy drain on Marshall Field's balance sheet. Although revenues doubled, profits bounced up and down since the 1972 peak of $21.5 million. In the fiscal year ending January 31, 1981, the company earned $20.7 million on sales of $1 billion. Sagging earnings, valuable real estate assets, and shareholder wrath over the Hawley bid left Marshall Field vulnerable to takeover bids.

Arrival of a Corporate Robin Hood

Carl Icahn began buying shares of Marshall Field in November 1981 at $15 a share. He described himself as a corporate Robin Hood, working on behalf of the shareholders. Other people on Wall Street gave him less complimentary labels. Analysts maintain that for management in a strong position, with loyal support of stockholders, Icahn did not pose a threat. He says of himself, "I'm not a gambler. I'm a risk-taker and I always go about these things in a very calculated way." Indeed, many people believe in Icahn and believe he plays a fair game. As one New York investment banker says, "He certainly has made fools of many Wall Street geniuses, but he acted fairly during our fights." Another arbitrageur, Ivan Boesky, admiringly stated that "Icahn has a keen eye for identifying undervalued opportunities, and this has been borne out by his financial success in almost every deal he has gotten into." Many wonder how this Princeton philosophy major has been able to identify opportunities overlooked by Wall Street's troops of highly compensated Harvard MBAs.

Carl Icahn's presence made Marshall Field executives anxious and angry. His basic mode of operation was to buy a substantial stake in a company and then threaten a proxy fight. As a last resort, management could succumb to the practice of greenmail and repurchase his shares for more than he paid.

Sewer Tactics: A Novel Racketeering Charge

Icahn's purchases of Marshall Field stock were publicly revealed on January 15, 1982. He confirmed that he owned "some" Marshall Field stock, but declined to say how many shares or to comment about his intentions. However, two weeks later, on February 1, the Icahn Group reported to the SEC. It disclosed that if it owned 9.5 percent of the total shares outstanding and that it intended to increase its holdings of Marshall Field's stock. Two days later, on

February 3, Icahn met personally with Arena and revealed his intentions to acquire 35 percent of the company, to become a director, and to cause Marshall Field to sell its real estate holdings.

On February 8, Field sued Icahn in Manhattan federal court, charging that his SEC report was false and misleading and failed to state material facts. In addition, Marshall Field charged Icahn with "racketeering," a novel legal claim in corporate takeovers. It charged that Icahn was a "notorious corporate opportunist who intends to gain control of Marshall Field and sell off its real estate and other assets solely for personal profit." The legal claim was based on an interpretation of the federal Racketeering Influenced and Corrupt Organizations Act of 1970 (RICO). The act outlaws the use of income received from a "pattern of racketeering." A pattern of racketeering is defined as any two violations of different laws, including the securities laws, in a 10-year period. Some corporate lawyers condemn the use of RICO in takeover suits as "sewer tactics" and "silly." However, others believe that since the charge causes legitimate businesses considerable embarrassment, it may work to deter professional investors from making hostile offers. Severe sanctions are provided by RICO, allowing treble damages and an injunction that could prevent an investor from attempting a future takeover for as long as 10 years.

Federal Judge Pierre Leval granted a 10-day restraining order in favor of Field, barring Icahn from acquiring additional Marshall Field shares. Separately, Marshall Field retained Goldman, Sachs to search for a white knight that would counter Icahn's bid. The restraining order was lifted February 22, after Icahn amended his SEC report to disclose that, as of February 5, 1982, he owned 15 percent of Marshall Field's shares. Icahn continued to buy and by mid-March he owned about 30 percent of the firm's shares.

White Knight Locked In–Carl Icahn Locked Out

Sir Peter Macadam, knighted in June 1980 and chairman of B.A.T. Industries, had long favored diversifying the world's largest tobacco manufacturer. B.A.T. Industries, the parent company of Batus, Inc. was Britain's third largest industrial enterprise. In the 1960s, as people became concerned about the health risks of smoking, B.A.T. began searching for more fertile fields. It set a corporate goal to generate 40 percent of its profit from nontobacco operations. As of 1981, nontobacco businesses provided only 26 percent of B.A.T.'s $693 million net income and 43 percent of its $17.7 billion in sales. Batus, headquartered in Louisville, Kentucky, operated three divisions—tobacco, retail, and paper. The Batus retail division was located in New York City.

On March 15, 1982, Marshall Field accepted a merger agreement with Batus. The terms provided for a tender offer of $25.50 a share for 65 percent of the Marshall Field common stock and $45.90 for each preferred share. This was to be followed by a merger offering the same terms in cash for the remaining shares. In addition, to coax the friendly bid, Marshall Field entered a stock purchase agreement with Batus granting Batus the right to buy 2 million new Marshall Field shares at $25.50 each. The lock-up agreement further granted Batus the right of first refusal in any sale of Marshall Field Chicago area assets during the following year if the Batus merger plan was not successful. Icahn called the terms "grossly inadequate." On March 18, in order to attract more shares, the merger agreement was amended to be a two-step offer with a lower price for those not tendering in the first step. The terms of the offer were increased to $30 for each common share and $54 for each preferred share. For the shares not tendered in the first step, the offer remained at $25.50 and $45.90. Icahn criticized this offer as "still inadequate."

Icahn Files Suit

On March 19, Icahn filed suit claiming that Marshall Field's arrangements with Batus were "manipulative." The Icahn Group attacked the legality of the arrangements based on a precedent decision rendered earlier that year in Cincinnati in a case involving Mobil, Marathon, and U.S. Steel. In that case, Marathon had granted U.S. Steel an exclusive option to buy Marathon's 49.5 percent interest in a rich Texas oil field. Mobil successfully argued that the option sharply restricted interest in Marathon by companies other than U.S. Steel and thus effectively deprived Marathon's shareholders from getting a price their shares might get in an open auction. However, in the case of Marshall Field, Judge Leval, in a surprise move, rejected the Icahn argument that Marshall Field and Batus worked out similar arrangements, thus tacitly endorsing the use of lock-up options. Judge Leval reasoned that rather than executing the agreements as options, Batus and Marshall Field executed them as firm "contracts." The judge further stated that Icahn's argument

> relies solely on the Marathon precedent and I doubt that decision represents the law in this circuit. In my view, the reasoning of that decision could unduly interfere with the right of company management to combat a takeover attempt that it believes in good faith to be harmful to its shareholders.

Shortly after the ruling, Icahn announced plans to tender his shares to Batus, claiming that the decision "was forced by the terms of the Batus offer." In the Batus offer, the proposed second step merger was less lucrative than the $30 a share tender offer.

The Battlefield Is Cleared

On March 30, Batus increased its offer for the remaining 34 percent of shares it did not obtain in the initial purchase. It offered $30 for each common share and $54 for each preferred share remaining. Carl Icahn then signed an agreement with Marshall Field prohibiting him from buying any more Marshall Field shares. In addition, Icahn agreed not to encourage alternatives to the pending merger of Batus. Icahn withdrew his suit attempting to block the merger, and all pending litigation was dropped. The racketeering charge against Icahn was never decided.

Given that Batus was the largest retailer in Milwaukee and Marshall Field the eighth largest in that city, the FTC required Batus to sign an agreement to divest some stores in Milwaukee. The agreement also precluded Batus from acquiring equity interest or assets of another department store, general merchandise organization, or furniture store in the Milwaukee area for 10 years without FTC approval.

On June 14, 1982, Batus completed the purchase for a total of $365 million. Now that the financial war was over, Batus could concentrate on operations. It hoped that its new acquisition would open up new markets and raise B.A.T.'s U.S. profile. The job of fixing up Marshall Field went to Robert Suslow, chairman and CEO of Batus's retail division. Angelo Arena was named vice chairman of the retail group, prompting an analyst to comment, "It looks like they're moving him to where he can't do much trouble."

Icahn Attempts to Vindicate Himself

On May 22, 1983, Carl Icahn published a *New York Times* editorial entitled "To American Management: Stop the Oppression of Shareholders." In it he described the events of this merger. He recounted that when he began buying Marshall Field it was selling at $15 a share and that several months after these initial purchases Marshall Field sold out to Batus at $30 a share. He stated that the shareholders obviously benefited from the 100 percent return made in only several months. Based on that, he claimed, shareholder activism is an important check to keep management answerable. He concluded that the shareholder activist "can be a catalyst for the flow of funds into essentially solid, though undervalued companies with mediocre managements."

The Treasury Lock-Up: Putting The Aggressor In Handcuffs

AMPCO-PITTSBURGH vs. BUFFALO FORGE

Buffalo Forge Corporation was notified by Ampco-Pittsburgh Corporation of its tender offer just prior to its Monday press release announcing the proposed takeover. Not surprisingly, the short notice and abrupt nature of the offer led Buffalo Forge to call the takeover bid unfriendly. So began the Ampco-Pittsburgh tender offer for all of Buffalo Forge's 2,141,322 outstanding shares. The $25 offer announced Monday, January 5, 1981, extended nearly one month through February 3 and was for $7 more than Buffalo Forge stock had traded the Friday before the announcement.

A surprised Buffalo Forge board of directors instructed top management and their investment banking and legal counsel "to carefully scrutinize the tender offer . . . from a business, financial and legal point of view and to promptly report back to the board."

Two Healthy Warriors

Management at Ampco-Pittsburgh was working to expand and diversify the firm's product base by acquisition. In 1979, it implemented this policy in full force by either initiating or completing three strategic acquisitions. These additions gave Ampco-Pittsburgh a product line ranging from steel pipe thread protectors and railroad freight cars to tractor-drawn tillage equipment. The acquisition trend continued in 1980 as Ampco-Pittsburgh attempted to take over Beldon Corporation and subsequently Crouse-Hinde Company. While both takeover attempts were unsuccessful, they both generated funds for Ampco-Pittsburgh, with the "unsuccessful" Beldon attempt netting them a cool $8 million.

As a result of its acquisitions and attempts, Ampco-Pittsburgh's sales and earnings increased dramatically in 1980. Its net sales were $430 million, an increase of 58 percent over 1979, and earnings were 61 percent over 1979.

The other warrior, Buffalo Forge, was an engineering and manufacturing firm that sold fabricated metal equipment for both industrial and commercial use. Founded in 1878, its first product was a portable forge with a lever-operated, gear-driven blower that made conventional blacksmith bellows obsolete. By 1981, Buffalo Forge's product line was greatly expanded and included gas handling and control equipment and fluid pumps. It also produced machinery to bend, punch, shear, and drill metal. Buffalo Forge had eight plants in North America: five in the United States, two in Canada, and one in Mexico.

In 1980 sales were $121 million, 16 percent more than 1979, and earnings were $6.2 million, up 31 percent from the year before. This growth was well above the industry average. With an order backlog totaling some $89 million, Buffalo Forge was confident its stellar 1980 performance would continue in 1981.

Testing the Water

On Thursday, January 8, Buffalo Forge directors gathered to design a response to Ampco-Pittsburgh's tender offer. They urged their shareholders to refrain from any action until the board had a chance to carefully review the offer. Buffalo Forge's stock, which sold at $18 per share before Ampco-Pittsburgh's announcement, responded strongly to the offer and jumped 7¼ points to $25.25 per share.

Ampco-Pittsburgh geared up for its attempt at Buffalo Forge. To raise cash, it tendered to Inter-North Corp. 390,000 Crouse-Hinde shares it had accquired. It thereby ended its acquisition attempt for Crouse-Hinde. The sale increased Ampco-Pittsburgh's cash position by some $15 million.

Four days later, on January 12, the Buffalo Forge directors announced that the $25 per share tender offer "isn't in the best interest of our shareholders." Buffalo Forge hired Kidder, Peabody as an independent investment advisor and with its counsel quickly submitted a filing with the SEC. In this filing, it rejected the offer, saying that "Buffalo Forge is worth more than $25 a share." A raging two-month war began. Buffalo Forge lawyers promptly proceeded with an injunction against Ampco-Pittsburgh and requested a hearing under the New York Act, to look at Takeover Disclosure Act violations. Buffalo Forge alleged Ampco-Pittsburgh did not adequately explain the ramifications of its tender offer to Buffalo Forge shareholders. In addition, Buffalo Forge continued its scramble to avoid the takeover attempt by considering some other possibilities. It planned to look for a white knight, or alternatively, to acquire a privately held company. It hoped the result of the latter strategy would be to make Buffalo Forge a more expensive target for Ampco-Pittsburgh.

Despite all this commotion at Buffalo Forge, Ampco-Pittsburgh's president, Marshall Berkman, proposed no changes. "At this time we are continuing the offer." Indeed, not backing off for a minute, Ampco-Pittsburgh promptly sent out tender offer materials to Buffalo Forge stockholders. By January 16, it had established a $75 million revolving credit loan agreement to finance its acquisition attempt. This increased its available acquisition fund to $90 million.

Continuing the legal battle, on January 19 Ampco-Pittsburgh filed a countersuit against Buffalo Forge, charging that it failed to disclose its compensation arrangement with Kidder, Peabody.

In the first two weeks of the takeover attempt, Buffalo Forge gained precious time to organize an interim defense strategy with an assortment of injunctions, hearings, and suits. Ampco-Pittsburgh, not easily put off, had continued to gear up financially for the tender offer and had entered the legal fray offensively with a countersuit of its own.

Can Buffalo Forge Buy Time?

Buffalo Forge, ready to wage a battle against the $53.5 million tender offer, entered a second phase of defense, using a persuasion campaign. Under this strategy, Buffalo Forge hoped to pad the stock price enough to make the tender offer less appealing to its stockholders compared with the alternative of just holding the shares. In this manner, more time could be gained while it continued to scramble looking for a white knight.

On January 13, a timely Buffalo Forge announcement conveyed that 1980 sales and earnings had grown significantly over 1979's. Following the announcement, top management sent a letter to the shareholders informing them of a pending change in Buffalo Forge's dividend policy. President Newcomb stated in the letter that "management intends to recommend that the board of directors consider and approve an increase in the dividend rate effective the next dividend." Newcomb also outlined that the dividends have been increased by 67 percent over the last six years. He inferred that no officer or director of Buffalo Forge planned to tender his shares under an offer as inadequate as Ampco-Pittsburgh's. Continuing with this persuasive approach, Newcomb urged shareholders not to tender shares to Ampco-Pittsburgh. He again mentioned that he was engaged in closed discussions with potential suitors to achieve either a sale or a merger. All of this banter had its effect. By January 26, Buffalo Forge stock was selling on the NYSE at $26.50, well above the $25 tender offer.

Despite the poor outlook, Ampco-Pittsburgh continued with its $25 per share tender offer. By January 26, the mandatory waiting period under federal antitrust laws had expired, and the next day Ampco-Pittsburgh began accepting shares tendered under the offer. That same day, Judge Curtin refused Buffalo Forge's injunction request based on alleged antitrust violations. He announced that without any additional legal delays Ampco-Pittsburgh would be free to offer $25 per share for Buffalo Forge stock. Ampco-Pittsburgh, upset with Buffalo Forge's persuasive assault, added fuel to the fire by saying it would significantly change the makeup of Buffalo Forge's board upon gaining control. However, it planned to keep the same management and maintain Buffalo Forge's operations in its three present locations.

Just when the legal debris finally started to clear and Ampco-Pittsburgh began to take action on its offer, more road blocks hampered its progress. On Tuesday, January 28, New York State Attorney General Robert Abrams temporarily blocked the tender offer while investigating whether it violated any takeover disclosure laws. The investigation was to conclude no later than the first week in March. However, the courts did provide Ampco-Pittsburgh with a list of Buffalo Forge stockholders.

Two days later, Buffalo Forge appealed the antitrust ruling and in compliance with the Judge's request, submitted more information. After reviewing the information over the weekend, the U.S. appeals court backed the lower court's decision in refusing to block Ampco-Pittsburgh's takeover attempt on the basis of antitrust violations.

At any rate, by Tuesday, February 3, only 9200 shares had been tendered. The next day, Attorney General Abrams found that Ampco-Pittsburgh failed to meet the New York Security Takeover Disclosure Act requirements. Ampco-Pittsburgh's chairman, Marshall Berkman, responded by stating that Ampco-Pittsburgh would "promptly" comply with Abrams's order and prepared a mailing that satisfied all requirements. The tender offer was then extended to February 11. On Friday, Abrams stated he would lift the holding order on Ampco-Pittsburgh. By the following Wednesday, after mailing the security takeover disclosure information, Ampco-Pittsburgh was expected to be allowed to continue purchasing the tendered Buffalo Forge stock.

Back and forth it went. Buffalo Forge appealed the injunction ruling and the courts again put a hold on Ampco-Pittsburgh's purchase of tendered shares. However, Buffalo Forge was rapidly running out of legal avenues. But the persuasive technique, Buffalo Forge's major successful defensive move, had kept the stock price above the $25 tender offer. It seemed that the next move for Ampco-Pittsburgh would be to raise its offering price to entice more shareholders to tender their stock.

A Surprise Lock-Up

Buffalo Forge's management kept telling the media about closed door discussions with an undisclosed firm. This might have been the prime driving force behind the relatively high stock price. Indeed, it proved to be more than just a smoke screen. On February 10, Buffalo Forge agreed to merge with Ogden Corporation. Ogden was a $2.2 billion conglomerate, primarily involved in marine transportation, aluminum recycling, and the manufacturing of machine tools. The merger agreement between Buffalo Forge and Ogden included several shrewd elements. Above and beyond the merger deal, Ogden purchased 425,000 shares of Buffalo Forge treasury stock at $32.50 per share. It paid for the stock with a 9 percent note having a face value of $13.9 million. In addition, it received a one year option to buy an additional 143,400 shares under a similar agreement. This gave Ogden a 16.6 percent share of Buffalo Forge with the option to increase their ownership to 21 percent. It was agreed that the remaining outstanding stock would be exchanged for Ogden stock on a share-for-share basis. With Ogden's shares trading at $32.50, the merger was valued at $69.6 million. Buffalo Forge's board agreed to submit the offer to shareholders and to vote their shares for the deal.

Under this carefully crafted lock-up agreement, Ogden effectively received a gift of all the treasury shares, an $18.5 million bonus. If Ogden and Buffalo Forge merged, then Ogden would regain ownership of its own 9 percent note, cancel it, and thereby would gain 21 percent of Buffalo Forge for free. Ampco-Pittsburgh, on the other hand, was facing a far worse prospect. In order to be competitive it had to bid up its offer. If they eventually succeeded in acquiring Buffalo Forge, they would have to essentially purchase the treasury shares sold to Ogden and in return receive a 9 percent note. Under these conditions, the acquisition would be $18.5 million more expensive for Ampco-Pittsburgh than for Ogden. This treasury stock sale guaranteed an advantage for Ogden in a merger with Buffalo Forge and put Ampco-Pittsburgh at a great disadvantage, practically locking it out of the takeover opportunity.

Ampco-Pittsburgh's chairman was furious when he found out about the lock-up agreement. The firm quickly became more aggressive in its approach. Its response was twofold. First, it increased the offer to $34 a share, or $87 million in total, and extended the offer until February 26. Second, Ampco-Pittsburgh intended to sue Buffalo Forge, its directors, and Ogden to rescind the Buffalo Forge sale of the 424,000 treasury stock to Ogden, and also sought to rescind Ogden's option to buy the additional 143,400 shares of Buffalo Forge treasury stock.

The Last Shots Before the Silence

Still taking advantage of its opportunistic deal and its white knight position, Ogden improved its bid. Under the new deal, Ogden began a tender offer at $37 per share for 850,000 shares. The remaining shares would be exchanged at a one-for-one rate to complete the merger. The 850,000 shares from the tender offer plus those they already held would give Ogden about 50.5 percent of Buffalo Forge. Both the Buffalo Forge and Ogden boards approved the merger plan.

Under the new offer, with Ogden's stock trading at $31.25, the merger was valued at $71.8 million. Although the overall nominal value of the two-tier offer was less than Ampco-Pittsburgh's, Ogden saw some distinct benefits in its offer for stockholders. Since both boards had approved the deal, it was more likely to take place than the Ampco-Pittsburgh deal. In addition, the stock exchange would be tax-free and wouldn't subject the holders to capital gain taxes.

Ampco-Pittsburgh didn't have any intention of giving up. On March 2, a week after Ogden presented its new deal, Ampco-Pittsburgh raised its tender offer to $37.50 per share or $97.3 million, and extended the deadline to March 12. Initially, the offer was conditioned on receiving a minimum of 900,000 shares, but that was waived just three days after the new offer began. Alleging security law violations, Ampco-Pittsburgh asked the court to halt the competing friendly offer for Buffalo Forge by Ogden and accused Ogden of "unlawful conduct" in its effort to thwart Ampco-Pittsburgh's takeover attempt.

Despite Ogden's distinct financial advantage, the aggressive bidding by Ampco-Pittsburgh proved too much for Ogden. By March 10 it withdrew its offer. Ogden executive vice-president Donald Krenz commented, "at that price [Buffalo Forge] wasn't worth it." Shortly after Ogden ended its bid for Buffalo Forge, Krenz announced that Ogden would tender all its shares to Ampco-Pittsburgh. It also planned to exercise its option to buy the remaining 143,400 treasury shares for $22.75 per share with a 9 percent note.

The new $97.3 million tender offer, not including the 143,000 shares Ogden had yet to buy, was near double the initial Ampco-Pittsburgh offer. It was unanimously accepted by the Buffalo Forge board. Ampco-Pittsburgh, however, was still enraged by Buffalo Forge's treasury stock sale to Ogden and refused to purchase the stock Ogden owned. Ampco-Pittsburgh stated it would not buy the Ogden owned shares unless the court decision on its suit required that it does so.

The wheels of justice turned very slowly. A year later, the court handed down an unpleasant decision for Ampco-Pittsburgh. It decided that the lock-up deal between Buffalo Forge and Ogden did not hamper the free market bidding process, but rather had enhanced it. So the suit charging Ogden with obtaining a lock-up option on Buffalo Forge fell through, possibly in part, due to the zealous bidding by Ampco-Pittsburgh.

Realizing that Ampco-Pittsburgh financed much of the purchase with bank loans, it would be a long time before Ampco-Pittsburgh reached a breakeven point on this investment. Buffalo Forge's predicted annual income of $8.1 million was not even close to covering Ampco-Pittsburgh's projected interest expense.

Ampco-Pittsburgh's chairman, Marshall Berkman, felt the importance of Buffalo Forge to Ampco-Pittsburgh should not be measured in the short run. "It's a mistake to value an acquisition on the near term. Three to five years from now, we'll find that [Buffalo Forge] is a meaningful addition to our company."

Ogden came out a hefty $2.8 million ahead in what, to them, seemed like a risk-free transaction. Ampco-Pittsburgh, on the other hand, ended up paying with blood for an investment with a dubious rate of return.

The Common Thread

Lock-up options have gained popularity as a defense and were used in a number of recent hostile takeover attempts. While the lock-up strategy is generally not used to prevent a takeover, it is used by the target to influence its choice of acquirer. The underlying principle of the lock-up strategy is to block a black knight from gaining sufficient shareholder control to consummate a takeover. The strategy can be designed to deprive a hostile bidder of the primary reason for its offer by promising the target's prized asset to a white knight. It also can be designed to make it much more expensive for the hostile bidder to acquire control. Use of the lock-up is often thought by the target to deter competing bidders and as a result increase the white knight's assurance of success. It is frequently argued that such a defense reduces shareholder returns by reducing the number of competitors. It is also argued that when lock-ups grant a bargain purchase option enabling a white knight to acquire company assets below market value, the potential bidder is unfairly restricted and the shareholder harmed. Such was the 1985 Revlon lock-up agreement with Forstmann Little and Co., which was struck down by the Delaware Supreme Court. Yet other cases to date suggest that the appropriate use of a lock-up may indeed increase rather than decrease returns to stockholders.

Lock-Up Strategies

Basically, three lock-up strategies can be employed. The first is called target company stock lock-up. In this scenario, the white knight has the right to purchase authorized but unissued shares or treasury shares of the target company. This forces the cost of the acquisition to any hostile acquirer to increase sharply. It requires the raider to purchase the newly issued shares in addition to those already outstanding. Subsequently, this tactic is a strong deterrent to a hostile bidder, even if the shares do not constitute a controlling interest. Buffalo Forge used this strategy in battling Ampco-Pittsburgh, as did Marshall Field against Icahn. In Marshall Field's defense, it gave Batus the right to two million authorized but unissued shares of Marshall Field in the event of Icahn's success. If Icahn's tender offer had succeeded, then the shares sold to Batus would have given it roughly a 17 percent interest in the company. Batus would then have sold its shares back to Icahn at a profit or possibly attempt to prevent Icahn from taking control. Three years later, in mid-1985, Carl Icahn again faced the same lock-up defense. TWA, in its battle to fend him off, gave white knight Texas Air an option to buy more than $120 million of TWA shares. To balance the scales, TWA pilots, fearing the white knight's union busting activities, expressed their support for the raider. In fact, their support was important in gaining the directors' approval for his takeover even though his bid was $2 less than Texas Air's.

In some cases the stock lock-up option is used to insulate the winning bidder against unexpected newcomers. Even though a merger agreement has been signed, in many cases several months may pass before the merger is formally completed. The lock-up is used to protect both parties during this window of uncertainty. In a straightforward use of the stock lock-up to insulate a white knight, Avco, in 1984, granted Textron an option to purchase 4.3 million newly issued shares amounting to 18.5 percent of Avco's stock. The amount was no doubt influenced by the fact that, under NYSE rules, this is the largest percentage of shares which can be granted in such an option without obtaining shareholder approval. The option was given to Textron to ensure that Leucadia, the New York-based consumer finance and insurance concern which made an offer for Avco, would not gain control of the firm. The option also had the intent of simultaneously repulsing another hostile raider. Another unusual story involving such a lock-up is that of Scovill, Inc., the manufacturer of Yale locks, and its 1985 attempt to fend off the powerful Belzberg family. Initially, the Belzbergs' offer was rejected by Scovill management. The target probably realized that it eventually would be taken over by someone. To manage its inevitable fate, it responded by soliciting sealed white knight offers. As it turned out, the winner of the sealed bidding process was the original bidder, the Belzberg family. To prevent other even less desirable surprise bidders before the deal was formally completed, Scovill granted the Belzbergs an option to buy several million authorized, but unissued shares. The option was structured such that, should an unwelcome raider take over Scovill, the Belzberg brothers, Samuel, William, and Hyman, would hold 20.7 percent of Scovill's shares.

A second lock-up scenario often used is referred to as an asset lock-up. When it is used, the white knight has the right to purchase a specific asset of the target if the target falls prey to a hostile raider. The asset, which often is dealt in the heat of battle, is typically the key element of interest to a hostile bidder. Such a lock-up arrangement generally leaves the target a far less profitable prospect to a hostile acquirer than prior to the lock-up arrangement. For example, the Yates field lock-up was designed to make Marathon a much less desirable target for Mobil than for U.S. Steel. Similarly, this type of option was used as a second lock-up strategy in the takeover battle between Marshall Field and Icahn. In this case, Marshall Field's Chicago properties accounted for almost two thirds of its profits. Moreover, it was these properties that probably tempted Icahn to bid for the Chicago-based department store. In structuring its defense, Marshall Field gave Batus the first right of refusal on these properties if the Marshall Field–Batus merger failed. In St. Regis's 1984 attempt to fight off the advances of Rupert Murdoch, St. Regis gave a combination of stock and asset lock-ups to its white knight, Champion International. The asset lock-up included an option to sell its desirable printing paper division to Champion in the event that another bidder acquired more than 50 percent of the company. It also gave Champion the option to buy a significant fraction of its common stock. In another 1984 case, white knight David Murdock and his partner Peter Kiewit & Sons, received both asset and stock options from a beleaguered target, the Continental Group. They had been stalked by hungry takeover pro Sir James Goldsmith. Only at the last minute did Murdock and friends appear on the scene. To entice them, Continental gave the white knights an option on its crown jewel, Florida Gas Transmission, as well as an option on close to 8 million of Continental's common shares.

A third, less common scenario, is the shareholder stock lock-up. It involves the option to purchase a block of the target's shares from one or more of the target's major shareholders. This purchase is often large enough to block a potential acquirer from gaining a controlling percentage of stock. Thus, the acquirer is "locked out" of the opportunity to take control of the target and to force the merger.

The lock-up is often borne out of preventive motives. While a cash tender offer is frequently the easiest way to gain control of a corporation, SEC rules state that tendered shares cannot be purchased until 15 business days after the tender offer has commenced. This gives a competing bidder sufficient time to evaluate the target company, arrange financing, and make a bid. Once the competing tender offer is made, the initial bidder cannot purchase any target shares until 10 business days after the commencement of the competing offer. If the initial bidder obtains a lock-up agreement with the target, the value of the target to the initial bidder is possibly greater than it is to competing bidders. This may discourage competing bidders which, it is often argued in court, results in a lower offer price than the target could have received. Even if the initial bid is from a hostile raider and the lock-up is granted to a white knight, there is a possible dollar loss to the shareholder. Competing bids, it is often argued, mean profit to shareholders. Moreover, the hostile aggressor generally argues that a measure such as a lock-up arrangement shows the lack of fulfillment of the fiduciary duties of the target's board.

Mobil and the Law: Is a Lock-Up Manipulative?

Lock-up provisions have come under attack on both legal and public policy grounds. Legally, the 1968 Williams Act (specifically

Section 14(e)) which prohibits "manipulative practices in connection with tender offers," has been used to try and strike down lock-up provisions. There are, however, difficulties in defining what is manipulative.

The current state of the law with regard to lock-up options is unclear. The federal court system and the courts of appeals are divided. The Court of Appeals for the Sixth Circuit sided with Mobil in striking down the arrangement between Marathon Oil and U.S. Steel because it violated Section 14(e) of the Williams Act. Yet, no other circuit has followed this lead. In fact, the Mobil decision has been severely criticized by the courts of appeals for both the second and the third circuits. Some of the lock-up cases in which the Mobil decision has been criticized include the 1983 battles of Buffalo Forge vs. Ogden Corporation, Data Probe Acquisition vs. Datatab and the 1984 case of Schreiber vs. Burlington Northern.

The following quote from Section 14(e) of the Williams Act describes in "legalese" what has become the key legal issue surrounding lock-ups, namely stock manipulation:

> It shall be unlawful for any person to make any untrue statement of a material fact or omit to state any material fact necessary in order to make the statements made, in the light of the circumstances under which they are made, not misleading, or to engage in any fraudulent, deceptive, or manipulative acts or practices, in connection with any tender offer or request or invitation for tenders, or any solicitation of security holders in opposition to or in favor of any such offer, request, or invitation.

In assessing the lock-up case before it, the Mobil court rejected Marathon's claim that Section 14(e) required nothing more than full disclosure, stating that to do so would be to read the term "manipulative" completely out of the statute. The court observed that full disclosure would have little effect in that case, since Marathon shareholders would be powerless regardless of their knowledge of how these options could deter higher offers.

The real effect of the options given to U.S. Steel on the outcome of its battle with Mobil is debatable. Arguably, the contest was decided by the antitrust rules. But did the options dampen competition?

Mobil and the Law: Can a Lock-Up Enhance the Bidding?

The court of appeals might have been correct in holding that granting the options inhibited competitive bidding. As the testimony in district court pointed out, several interested parties placed the value of Marathon's stock at more than $125 per share.

But the court was simply speculating as to whether any other parties would have made bids for Marathon. In view of the ruling in the antitrust case, no other oil company could be expected to fight U.S. Steel successfully. And no other companies had stepped forward indicating an intention to bid. In short, since no other bidders were likely to bid anyway, granting the options was not demonstrated to have inhibited bidding. If it had any effect, it was to inspire U.S. Steel to enter the race in the first place, as it would not have bid for Marathon without obtaining the options. As Bruce Wasserstein, then a co-director of the mergers and acquisitions group at First Boston, has commented:

> How in this case are you protecting the public shareholders if they now have the chance to get $125 a share instead of $85? A hostile bidder shouldn't have the right to low-ball. The next time around, a Mobil might win at $85.

As U.S. Steel was induced to bid because of the options, and Mobil's second bid was obviated by the court of appeals' first ruling, granting the options most likely served to improve shareholder returns, not diminish them.

The one undeniable effect of the options was the uncertainty introduced into the fight by the litigation challenging them. Shareholders had a difficult time as it was, anticipating the outcome of the antitrust litigation. With the lock-up issue to be decided by the court of appeals, and the possibility that Mobil's amended offer could have lapsed by its terms, a shareholder's decision about whom to tender became even more agonizing.

Conversely, other courts have refused to read Section 14(e) and, in particular, the term "manipulative," in as broad a manner as did the Mobil court. Among the courts rejecting the Mobil court's interpretation was the respected U.S. District Court for the Southern District of New York. In the legal battle between Marshall Field and Icahn, it stated that application of the reasoning in Mobil would unduly interfere with management's right to combat takeover attempts that are contrary to the interests of the shareholders. The Court of Appeals for the Second Circuit declared that Section 14(e) cannot be applied literally to a lock-up situation. It stated that the Williams Act "was designed solely to get needed information to the investor." An essential ingredient of a Section 14(e) cause of action, therefore, was misrepresentation. It further stated that this was equivalent to "omission or misstatement of material facts." The court went on to say that "Congress's concern was more with the procedural provisions of the Act than with the substantive terms of the takeover bids . . . . Congress's ban on 'manipulative acts and practices' was directed only at rigged transactions that might mislead investors in the making of these decisions." The Court of Appeals for the Second Circuit refused to apply Section 14(e) in the lock-up cases before it because there was no allegation that there had been a lack of full and honest disclosure.

Moreover, in the Buffalo Forge lock-up arrangement with Ogden, the court determined that the treasury stock lock-up enhanced, rather than hampered the bidding for Buffalo Forge. Indeed, while the lock-up defense did not prevent a takeover, or assure a white knight of Buffalo Forge's own choosing, it did force hostile Ampco–Pittsburgh to increase the value of its bid. If the goal of the Buffalo Forge–Ogden deal was to increase shareholder's return, the lock-up must be considered a success. As a postscript, if Ampco–Pittsburgh had withdrawn its bid, Buffalo Forge stockholders would still have been better off than with the original Ampco–Pittsburgh deal.

Indeed, it is frequently debated whether the board of directors abdicates its responsibility to the shareholders when it enters into a lock-up agreement? Often shareholders are hopping mad when the board turns down a tender offer as was the case when Angelo Arena turned down the $42 per share offer made by Carter Hawley Hale stores for Marshall Field in 1979. Numerous suits were filed by shareholders afterward. T. Boone Pickens, the "company hunter," has reportedly received many letters from disgruntled shareholders of potential targets asking, "Have you thought about our company, Mr. Pickens?" In the case of Marshall Field, a company that had poor earnings and a questionable expansion strategy, shareholders were ready for a raider's offer. On the other hand, is it possible that management might have had a better idea of the worth of the company and its future earnings capacity than anyone else and therefore be justified in structuring a lock-up?

The Directors and the Business Judgment Rule

Lock-up options have also been challenged in state courts on the theory that granting such options violates the fiduciary duty of the target company's directors to their shareholders. This approach recognizes that there is an inherent conflict of interest between the shareholders and directors of a target company. Although a raider may provide shareholders with adequate compensation for their shares, it is likely that the directors will lose their positions if the takeover is successful. Therefore, they are likely to act with mixed motives.

The business judgment rule has been applied by the influential Delaware Chancery Court in evaluating whether the use of a lock-up option constituted a violation of the fiduciary duty of corporate directors. This rule presumes that directors have acted properly in all matters requiring the exercise of business judgment. Only once there has been a showing of fraud, self-dealing, or bad faith, must the directors justify their actions to avoid the provisions being struck down.

In the 1984 case of Thompson vs. Enstar, the court criticized the arrangement as epitomizing the undesirable aspects of lock-up deal options. Under the lock-up, Enstar, the takeover target, transferred voting control of its Indonesian subsidiary to a white knight, Unimar, for a period of 10 years. The transfer of voting rights was to take place regardless of whether the Unimar tender offer was successful. While the lock-up agreement did not transfer Enstar's ownership in its Indonesian joint venture to Unimar, it did transfer effective control. As a result, an ultimate buyer of Enstar would find itself in a precarious position. Without control over the subsidiary's voting rights, the buyer could be forced to sell its interest, not necessarily to the highest bidder. Because of the lock-up, Tesoro Petroleum and other potential bidders quickly backed off and Enstar merged with its white knight. The court pointed out that the lock-up provision chilled the possible offers of other potential acquirers, infringed on the voting rights of shareholders, and constituted a waste of corporate assets. Amazingly, the court also held that the Enstar arrangement did not violate the business judgment rule. The court reasoned that "the plaintiffs [had] not sustained their burden of showing a reasonable probability that the approval of the lock-up agreements is not fair to the shareholders or that the directors acted unreasonably in adopting them."

The court did not define what would be unreasonable. It simply stated that the arrangement immediately in question was not unreasonable. However, the court did set forth and support the challenger's criticisms of the Enstar lock-up provision as constituting representative aspects of undesirable lock-ups. Although the court seemed to emphasize the provision's effect on encouraging or discouraging bidding for the target company as being the most important factor in determining its validity, it failed to quantify precisely what would be unreasonable.

While there may be negative effects to granting a lock-up option, there is a formidably high standard of proof required by the business judgment rule in order to conclude that corporate directors violated their fiduciary duty. The best interpretation of the Enstar decision is that, although it is not clear precisely what actions will violate the business judgment rule and, as a result, invalidate a lock-up option, it is obvious that those actions must be flagrant.

The 1985 Revlon case may well have been sufficiently flagrant to be the straw that broke the Delaware court's back. Revlon agreed to sell two choice units to Forstmann Little for a price estimated by the investment bank Lazard Freres to be at least $100 million below an arm's-length market price. As a result, the court decided in favor of Pantry Pride, the hostile acquirer, and voided the lock-up.

However, within weeks of the Revlon decision, New York Federal Court Judge Shirley Kram validated a similar option. It was granted by SCM Corporation to Merrill Lynch in order to thwart a takeover attempt by British conglomerate Hanson Trust PLC. Judge Kram emphasized that 9 of the 12 members of SCM's board were outside directors and therefore not "dominated or unduly influenced" by SCM management. She contrasted this to the Revlon case where most of the board either were members of management or did business with Revlon.

Since the SCM lock-up decision, other lock-ups have appeared on the merger scene. For example, in MidCon's early 1986 attempt to escape the clutches of WB Partners, it granted both an asset and a stock lock-up to white knight, Occidental Petroleum. The asset lock-up was an option to purchase a controlling interest in one of its most valuable assets, its Natural Gas Pipeline Co. of America. Interestingly, within a week of MidCon granting its lock-ups, the federal court of appeals blocked Merrill Lynch from exercising its bargain purchase lock-up option with SCM.

Review of the decisions regarding lock-up options leaves one with no clear legal doctrine upon which their validity rests. Although they have been declared illegally manipulative by one circuit and unfairly restrictive by another, the weight of authority suggests that properly constructed lock-ups are not violative of federal law. While lock-ups appear vulnerable to attack under state law, a different standard of proof must be met in order for a lock-up challenge to succeed. As such, it is not unlikely that appropriately constructed lock-ups will continue to withstand challenge in both federal and state courts.

The Defense Cocktail–Mixing the Strategies

The lock-up strategy is frequently not used alone. Its power can often be increased by additional use of complementary or multiple defenses. For example, in Marshall Field's battle with Icahn, not one but two lock-up options were granted to Batus. They followed Marshall Field's implementation of an antitrust defense to ward off both Philip Hawley and Associated Dry Goods. Each of the lock-ups was powerful in its own right, but together, they packed a knockout punch. One lock-up was a stock purchase agreement giving Batus the right to buy 2 million new Marshall Field shares and the second was an asset lock-up giving Batus the right of first refusal on Marshall Field's prized Chicago area assets. These combined lock-ups tipped the scales against Icahn. Soon after the court decision allowing their use, Icahn threw in the towel.

Buffalo Forge used creative financing along with its Ogden lock-up arrangement. Ogden was allowed to purchase approximately $18.5 million of treasury shares with a nine percent note. If Ogden and Buffalo Forge merged, Ogden would regain the note, destroy it, and as a result, receive the $18.5 million for free. While the lock-up was not successful in warding off Ampco–Pittsburgh, it was found to stimulate the bidding, with the resulting purchase price generating sizable returns to Buffalo Forge shareholders.

In another case in which lock-ups played a major role with other defenses, Jewel Companies, the giant supermarket and drugstore operator, provided its suitor, American Stores, a lock-up option to buy more than $150 million of authorized but unissued shares. The lock-up was provided only after American Stores made a run at shark repellent-laden Jewel. Jewel had instituted staggered terms for its directors and amended its bylaws to make takeover more difficult. Yet, in May 1984, American Stores made Jewel an offer. It was initially rejected, but in the end, both sides gained via the lock-up. Jewel gained by negotiating the lock-up as part of a deal to up the ante from $70 a share to $75. In addition, it assured itself that a desired suitor, as opposed to an unknown raider, would become its partner. From American Stores' perspective, it was assured that no other firm would steal its target from them.

Marathon, in battling Mobil, also used several strategies. The Yates field option to Marathon was one of the two key defenses. The other was its antitrust argument. While the lock-up fell victim to the courts, Marathon prevailed on antitrust grounds. The case demonstrates the advantage of relying on more than a single defense. A prudent approach is to develop a set of joint strategies mounted simultaneously. At a minimum, the resolve shown by the target may well reduce the efforts and momentum of the hostile aggressor.

Lock-Ups and the Future

While a cloud hangs over the bargain price purchase option as a result of the Revlon case, the future of appropriately constructed lock-ups looks bright. In nonbargain purchase situations, lock-ups have only been stricken by the courts in one case, Marathon's battle against Mobil. In fact, in virtually all other cases the reasoning of the Mobil decision has been chastized.

Directors and management wish to control the fate of their organizations. While a lock-up strategy does not enable directors to exert unbridled control over their firm's fate, an appropriately constructed lock-up enables them to significantly affect the probabilities of alternative outcomes. Although many call the lock-up manipulative and not in the shareholders' best interests, most court decisions have sided with the directors' business judgments in structuring the agreements. Yet, not all legally constructed lock-ups result in the recipient of the lock-up winning the battle. Indeed, even in such situations, evidence such as the Buffalo Forge lock-up with Ogden suggests that lock-ups may enhance rather than hinder returns to shareholders.

3

The Leveraged
Buyout Defense

It All Started With "Young Lady, Everything Has A Price"

WESTERN PACIFIC INDUSTRIES vs. CONE MILLS

An Extraordinary Plum Ready to Be Plucked

By late 1983 Cone Mills was clearly not qualified to be a beauty contest winner. Founded in 1895 by two German immigrants, Moses and Caesar Cone, it originally made fabric for farmers' bib overalls. In time it grew to become the country's leading manufacturer of denim and corduroy with some of the industry's most modernized plants. Unfortunately, its being the leader and having brand new machines was not reflected in Cone Mills's bottom line. In 1982 it earned 2 percent on $608.2 million. While such results would ordinarily be poor for textiles, in 1982 they were not unusual. The chief cause of the textile industry's disappointing performance was the industry-wide erosion of domestic sales by cheaper imports.

Corporate raiders and other scholars of the "expansion school" don't miss an opportunity to attack the weak. Indeed, in light of the textiles' weakness there were a number of takeovers and attempted raids in the industry. These included the 1982 purchase of Cannon Mills, maker of linen and towels, by David Murdock, and the 1983 bid for Dan River by Carl Icahn. This wave of new landlords was described by Merrill Lynch analyst Pamela Singleton, who said that "many have been vulnerable due to poor earnings. There is a clear pattern."

Like Cone Mills, the other party in this story would most likely not be found as the first choice on graduating MBAs' employment list. Western Pacific Industries had been primarily a railroad company. It was formed in 1971 to acquire the Western Pacific Railroad. However, eight years later in 1979, it sold the railroad and focused its attention on industrial counting machinery, precision parts, socket screws, and thermoplastics. Headed by Howard Newman, the former chief of the Philadelphia and Reading Corporation, Western Pacific's 1982 sales were $184.2 million, and it seemed that its appetite for external expansion was in a high gear. In November 1983 it attempted a takeover of Cone Mills, which was four times larger than Western Pacific.

One might wonder what Western Pacific saw in a "2 percent bottom line," such as Cone Mills's. As is often the case, beauty is in the eye of the beholder. Beside the industry-wide factors which weakened most textile firms and made them takeover targets, in 1983 Cone Mills was a classic prospect. It had a strong balance sheet with little debt. This was enhanced by the fact that it owned a good deal of undeveloped property in the Greensboro, North Carolina area, acquired in the first decades of its existence. Since the property was carried on its books at acquisition cost, Cone's actual market value was significantly higher than its balance sheet value. Jay Meltzer, an analyst for Goldman, Sachs, summed it up: "Cone is a very fine company. It is asset-rich. They have real estate on the books at acquisition cost, very, very low prices." Similarly, as another analyst described it, Cone Mills was "an extraordinary plum ready to be plucked."

In fact, Western Pacific began buying Cone stock in the open market as early as October 1982, accumulating 333,000 shares. In addition, it obtained an agreement to buy the 600,000 shares owned by Caesar Cone II, the son of one of Cone's founders and its former chairman. This agreement, which was disclosed to Cone on October 31, was executed on November 30. The two deals gave Western Pacific a combined stake of 16.9 percent.

Lest one think that Cone harbored some grudge against the firm founded by his father and his uncle, it should be said that he did not know the identity of the purchaser at the time of the agreement to sell. That deal was the work of a broker at Jeffries & Company named Jill Delaney. Ms. Delaney had talked earlier with Mr. Cone about his willingness to sell his shares and although he claimed not to be interested, he is reported to have said, "Young lady, everything has a price." Ms. Delaney apparently had his price in hand when she returned with the Western Pacific offer to buy Mr. Cone's stock at $50 a share. Cone Mills stock was trading at approximately $46 per share when Cone accepted the offer. It meant that he would receive a premium of approximately $2.4 million over the prevailing market price of his shares.

On November 3, Western Pacific reported to the SEC that it had acquired the 333,000 shares of Cone Mills, had an agreement to purchase 600,000 shares from Cone, and that it would further seek a majority stake in the target. Cone was paid by Western Pacific $50 per share, or $30 million, and about $13 million for the other shares, at prices ranging from $43.75 to $46. Shortly after Western Pacific's announcement, the price jumped to $52. Moreover, by the day Cone completed the sale of his stock to Western Pacific, the price had further climbed to $66.75. At this point, the price paid to Cone looked like a bargain. In all, Western Pacific paid $43,352,556 for 933,000 shares of stock, an average of $46.50 per share.

The Defense: Let's Buy It Out

On November 7, Cone Mills made its first move. It filed suit in federal court, seeking an injunction against Western Pacific on the grounds that Western Pacific was an unregistered investment company. Since Western Pacific had $143 million in cash and marketable securities at the time, this no doubt seemed plausible. Two days later, Western Pacific replied that Cone's lawsuit was entirely without merit. It then went on to say that it might acquire enough additional common stock of Cone Mills to boost its total holding in the company to more than 50 percent. In fact, on November 7, it had already notified federal antitrust regulators of the possibility of such a move.

Cone also announced that it had secured a $300 million line of credit from a group of banks. Although it did not say so explicitly, there was no doubt about what Cone Mills intended to do with its credit line—resist.

A meeting of Cone's board was held November 8. The agenda was an exploration of available alternatives other than being acquired by Western Pacific. According to the proxy prepared by Cone Mills for its shareholders, it stated that it had contemplated a wide variety of options, including

an acquisition of Cone by a third party, a business combination between Cone and a third party, negotiation with Western Pacific, a leveraged buyout of Cone by members of management, sale of addi-

tional securities of Cone to a third party, an acquisition by Cone, a tender offer by Cone for stock of Western Pacific and a repurchase of outstanding shares of Cone.

Since 1977 Cone had used Salomon Brothers as its investment banker. It now instructed Salomon to explore a possible merger with a firm other than Western Pacific. With this goal in mind, Salomon contacted 12 companies and also responded to two unsolicited offers. None of these contacts produced any firm offers or resulted in concrete negotiations. At the same time, the chairman of Western Pacific was seeking meetings with Dewey L. Trogdon, Cone Mills's chairman. These attempts produced no results, as Newman indicated when he said, "I thought at least we'd talk. I should have known better." Cone was determined to resist the unwelcome bid.

During this same period, Trogdon and some other senior Cone executives were seriously exploring a leveraged buyout. They began to arrange for financing with several banks. Naturally, they kept in close contact with Salomon Brothers and the other members of the board. Trogdon also talked with two firms engaged in organizing and investing in leveraged buyouts but reached no agreement with either. Salomon Brothers expressed the opinion that considering Cone's business and cash flow, a leveraged buyout at a price up to $72 per share was reasonable.

On November 28, a meeting of the board convened and began to consider a proposal from the management group led by Trogdon for a leveraged buyout at $68 per share. Because of the conflict of interest of those board members who were also members of the management team proposing the buyout, a special committee was formed consisting of six outside directors. This committee met that same day, holding discussions with Salomon and Cone's attorneys, and also with Trogdon and others in his management group.

In addition to management's proposed buyout, the special committee had to consider another proposal for a leveraged buyout. This was submitted by one of the two firms Trogdon had approached earlier, but with which no deal had been arranged. Whether by coincidence or not, this bid was also for $68 per share.

In the end, Cone decided on the leveraged buyout by management. It rejected the offer from the other firm since "a leveraged buyout was not likely to be successfully effected without the co-operation of the management of Cone." No doubt this was true. At the same time, the management group recognized that its offer might be topped by another investor not yet involved, and it increased its bid to $70 per share.

The terms of the leveraged buyout called for the merger of Cone Mills with a new corporation to be formed by a group of 47 managers and a group of banks. If approved, the new firm would pay $70 per share for Cone's common stock in a transaction valued at $385 million. At the meeting, when the board of Cone Mills voted to accept the buyout offer, the board also approved in principle a somewhat novel plan. An employee stock ownership plan (ESOP) was established and it was expected to become a major holder in Cone's equity.

The news of the leveraged buyout did not sit well with Standard & Poor's. Within a few weeks of the announcement, the bond rating agency had put Cone's debt securities on their credit watch list for a possible rating change from the present single A-. Referring to the leveraged buyout, Standard & Poor's said, "Such a step has negative credit implications since considerable debt financing may be required."

Western Pacific Backs Off

However, in a report filed with the SEC a few days later, Western Pacific indicated that while it still desired to acquire control of Cone, it decided not to take any immediate steps. But, to be on the safe side, Western Pacific stated that despite its latest position, it may from time to time purchase additional Cone shares, either in the open market or privately. Alternatively, it might consider the disposition of some or all of its shares.

The company based its decision to back off on several factors including the current $66.75 price level of Cone stock. This price, which the company felt reflected the effect of the buyout proposal, was well above the $50 a share that Western Pacific had paid for its most recent purchase of 600,000 Cone shares, but below the $70 per share offered in the buyout. Also, Western Pacific expressed the feeling that Cone's management was in "a better position to evaluate the common stock because it had information about the assets, business, and prospects of Cone that isn't available to Western Pacific." Finally, Western Pacific said that until the required proxy information with details of the buyout was available to stockholders, it could make no further decisions.

At Last the Details!

Finally, on January 5, 1984 in a filing with the SEC, further details about the proposed leveraged buyout were provided. As mentioned previously, the management group organized to purchase Cone Mills was offering $70 per share or $385 million in total. Spokesmen for Cone said it would cost about $465 million to finance the transaction, including the purchase price, interest, and the refinancing of part of Cone's debt. About $420 million of the cost would be financed through bank borrowing. Financial institutions were expected to purchase preferred stock to provide the bulk of the remaining purchase price.

The management group had 47 members including all the top officers of current management, led by Dewey Trogdon, chairman and CEO, and Benjamin O. Sampson, president. A large part of the management group's investment was expected to be financed by cashing in stock options held by Cone's managers.

In proxy material sent to stockholders in early March 1984, Cone management provided an annual projection of both sales and operating profits over the next five years. Because of both economic upturns and possible slowdowns, the road was expected to be bumpy, with the net sales forecast for 1988 a modest $741 million as compared with actual sales of $687.8 million five years earlier, in 1983.

The projections disclosed in the proxy material were originally drawn up for Salomon Brothers to help determine the feasibility of the buyout. They were also provided to the lead banks involved in the financing of the deal. Accompanying the projections was the statement that management believed its forecast to be conservative and that it would be reasonable to expect Cone's future performance to exceed its projections.

The proxy material also stated that Salomon Brothers had determined the value of Cone shares to be $83.64 compared with the stated January 2, 1983 book value of $60.95 a share. The value determined by Salomon Brothers resulted from changing the inventory valuation, adding $8 million in excess pension fund assets, and increasing the estimated replacement cost of property and equipment.

Cone's board and the special committee assigned to review the buyout, termed Salomon Brothers' valuation "hypothetical" and not representative of amounts that could be realized in liquidation.

However, Salomon Brothers, the financial advisor for the management group, provided a letter attesting to the fairness of the $70 offer to the stockholders. Interestingly, at about the same time it was reported that Salomon Brothers would receive a $4 million fee if the transaction were completed.

The Outcome

On March 26, 1984, Cone Mills held a special meeting of its stockholders at which it sought approval of the proposed leveraged buyout. At the meeting, more than 70 percent of the shares were voted in favor of the buyout.

The buyout was completed by merging Cone Mills Incorporated into the new firm, Cone Mills Acquisition Corporation (CMA). CMA was 70 percent owned by the 47 Cone Mills managers, and 30 percent by the banks which provided the financing. It paid $70 per share for the 5.5 million outstanding shares. The payment of $385 million for Cone Mills stock marked the successful completion of the leveraged buyout.

Although Western Pacific did not achieve its initial goal of acquiring Cone, it did succeed in precipitating a defensive reaction that would net the company a tidy profit. At $70 a share, Western Pacific earned a profit of close to $22 million—a 50 percent return on investment in less than a year!

The Bass Family, The Belzbergs, And A Surprise Guest

THE BASS BROTHERS AND THE BELZBERGS vs. SUBURBAN PROPANE

The New Rockefellers

In a deal that pitted the Belzbergs against the Bass family one should expect excitement. Both families had wealth, power, and the ability to spot a takeover situation ripe for picking. The Belzbergs are widely believed to be cheapskates. Indeed, one investment banker complained that "they want to buy a dollar for eighty cents." Their sense of value is so certain that their investments virtually always attract the attention of arbitrageurs and competing bidders. This story follows the same pattern.

The three Belzberg brothers are also known as greenmailers. They don't seem to mind asking for greenmail from management seeking independence—at any price. While in the past they practiced greenmail on others, in 1982 an unsavory form of greenmail, usually called blackmail, was used on them. The quiet life of the eldest and least visible brother, Hy, was interrupted when three armed kidnappers threw him into a van, and kept him blindfolded and handcuffed until a $2 million ransom was paid.

The art of corporate greenmailing is not the sole property of the Belzbergs. Hardly a month goes by without the Bass brothers reporting to the SEC on more than a 5 percent interest in a potential target. Like the Belzbergs, they can smell a bargain. As described by a Fort Worth businessman, "The Basses like to buy at fire sales. They're looking for someone at the gravesite who's ready to put the first shovel in the ground." Indeed, the Bass brothers are equipped for the merger game with wealth and appropriate education. All four are Yale graduates, two with MBAs from Stanford and Wharton. Although family acquaintances gossiped that the brothers don't always live side by side in peace, when it comes to chasing a deal, they become a well-oiled machine.

As frequently happens in the takeover world, one bidder begets another. Suburban Propane proved to be no exception. Prior to the

Belzbergs and the Bass brothers entering the story, former Treasury secretary Bill Simon's Wesray Corporation and a giant oil developer, Petro-Lewis, were already on the scene. One might wonder what kind of company would draw the attention of these firms and takeover pros such as the Belzbergs and the Bass family.

Primed for Takeover

Suburban Propane was established in 1945 to acquire businesses and properties for the distribution and sale of liquefied petroleum gas on the east coast of the United States. By 1982 Suburban expanded its business into 41 states. About 64 percent of the company's revenue came from sales related to liquified petroleum-gas. The remainder of its revenue came from various petroleum products and the exploration and development of gas and oil producing properties. In addition, the company produced gas burning appliances and solid fuel heaters.

Suburban had an impressive track record prior to 1982. Sales, earnings per share, and dividends per share all increased in each of the years from 1972 to 1981. The only blot on its record occurred in 1982 when sales dropped to $828 million, a slight decrease from 1981's record. The sales slowdown mainly reflected consumer conservation efforts. Yet, Suburban anticipated sales would turn around as a result of its exploration operations and an intensive propane marketing program.

Many analysts believed Suburban was primed for a takeover attempt because its stock price was grossly undervalued. They felt that Suburban's future looked strong due to "the government decontrol of propane in January 1981, and the economies of using propane as an ethylene feedstock and as a motor vehicle fuel have brightened the long-term prospects of propane companies."

The Word Has Spread: A Flood of Offers

First Offer—The Petro-Lewis Affair. Robert Rosenkranz, president of Petro-Lewis, contacted Suburban to "discuss a possible acquisition of the company." Mark Anton, chairman, president, and

CEO of Suburban, advised Rosenkranz that "the company did not wish to pursue acquisition discussions." However, later, Rosenkranz advised Anton that Petro-Lewis had accumulated 225,000 shares of Suburban, a little over 4 percent of the shares outstanding. While the actual percentage was small, 4 percent was large enough to prompt Suburban's board to retain E.F. Hutton for "the purpose of providing certain financial advisory services in connection with unsoliciated proposals for the acquisition of the company."

On March 24, 1982, E.F. Hutton, representing Suburban, met with Rosenkranz to discuss the formation of a joint-venture corporation that would be 40 percent owned by Petro-Lewis and 60 percent owned by a group formed by Rosenkranz. It consisted of at least a limited participation by Suburban's management. Even though the price offered was $37.50, the proposal was rejected as "not being in the long-term best interests of the company's shareholders." Following these initial discussions, there was no significant contact between Suburban and Rosenkranz.

Second Offer—The Wesray Affair. In May 1982, Suburban received a letter from Wesray Corp., a firm with experience in structuring leveraged buyouts. Wesray, whose name is a combination of William E. Simon's initials and his partner, Ray Chambers's first name, was a new and aggressive player in the leveraged buyout field. This aggressiveness is a result of Bill Simon's boundless energy through which he gained the reputation for demanding that his subordinates match his 18 hour work days. If they didn't, "Bad Bill" was known to throw temper tantrums. Wesray suggested a proposal for a new corporation to be equally owned by Wesray and Suburban's management. Shareholders would receive $45 per share in the merger agreement. Management also rejected this proposal because it still felt "the best interests of the company would be continuing as owners of a public corporation." No steps were taken to implement the proposal.

Third and Fourth Offers—The Offers Start Coming in Groups (The Bass Family and The Belzbergs). On October 26, 1982, Suburban received two reports from the SEC. The first of the two informed Suburban that Texas Partners, a group in which the Bass family had a substantial interest, owned 5.01 percent of the outstanding shares of Suburban. The report indicated that the purchase was to be held by the Bass family only as an investment. As many investors do, to keep their options open, they said that "depending on market conditions and other factors that they deem material to their respective investment decision, they may purchase additional shares of the stock in the open market, or in private transactions, or they may dispose all or a portion of their shares that they now own or may hereafter acquire."

The other report was filed jointly by First City Trust Company and First City Financial Corporation, both entities controlled by the Belzbergs. The report stated that the Belzbergs purchased 8.9 percent of Suburban's shares for "the purpose of obtaining an equity interest in the company." The report further indicated that they "have not at this time determined to seek to acquire all or substantially all of the equity." They would first like to meet with Suburban management to "learn more about the company, and to explore possibilities with management for structuring such an acquisition that would be beneficial to all parties involved." Anton responded with the well-worn words that "the long-term interests of its shareholders are best served by the company continuing as an independent energy company." On October 29, Suburban met with Sid Bass regarding a possible acquisition of the company for cash, conditioned on the support and involvement of management. Suburban also met with the Belzbergs who expressed a desire to obtain more information about the company and to pursue further discussions with management. Playing tough, the Belzbergs also made it clear that their pursuit of an acquisition was not dependent on the support of management.

A few days later, on November 4, E.F. Hutton, representing Suburban, met with Salomon Brothers, financial advisor to the Belzbergs. Belzbergs' goal was the "acquisition of the company as a wholly owned subsidiary of First City for cash or cash-like consideration in the low 40 dollar range." They desired cooperation but kept other options available. It was also revealed that the Belzbergs' ownership of Suburban increased to 11.7 percent of the outstanding shares.

Fifth Offer—The Bride and the Bass Family May Get Married. After concluding that it was unlikely that Suburban could continue as a publicly held corporation, company management met with Sid Bass to structure a leveraged buyout designed to "assure fair value to all of the company's shareholders." Following a series of negotiations, a merger agreement was proposed where the Bass family would own 80 percent of the stock and 20 percent would be owned by members of company management. Suburban's shareholders would receive $45 in cash in exchange for their shares. The board determined that the terms of the agreement were fair to Suburban's shareholders, and on December 7, 1982 they approved the merger agreement. The Belzbergs planned to reduce their holdings to below 5 percent before Suburban's shareholders voted on the acquisition. The planned reduction in the Belzberg's holdings did not reflect their disinterest in the target but rather was aimed to disarm Suburban of one of its shark repellents. More specifically, Suburban's charter included a supermajority provision whereby a merger intitiated by a holder of more than 5 percent required a 75 percent approval by shareholders.

Sixth Offer—The Belzbergs' Challenge. On December 17, the Belzbergs sent a letter to Suburban stating that the $45 price offered by the Bass family was inadequate. The Belzbergs proposed to enter into a merger agreement at $48.50 per share, and they "were prepared to make available as much as 20 percent of the equity of the company surviving the merger to Suburban's management." The letter suggested that if Suburban provided the Belzbergs "with certian necessary and relevant information, they would be likely to offer more than $48.50 per share." The Belzbergs were also prepared to take alternative action if the company did not enter into an agreement with them. The possible actions included "a direct offer to shareholders" or "voting [possibly seeking proxies] against the merger agreement" with the Bass family. A meeting was held on December 20, but Suburban stated it was not prepared to consider the requests set forth unless First City (1) made a cash tender offer of at least $50, (2) produced a satisfactory commitment for the financing of the tender offer, and (3) stated exactly what percentage of ownership management would receive under the agreement. The

Belzbergs countered that they would first have to "review certain nonpublic information concerning the company." The meeting ended in a stalemate.

Seventh Offer—A New Player Enters the Bidding.   On December 17, representatives from a major industrial corporation contacted Suburban management regarding a possible acquisition of the company for approximately $51 per share. However, Suburban did not disclose the identity of the new bidder. The conditions required that Suburban grant an option to the proposed acquirer to purchase as yet unissued common stock amounting to about 18 percent of its outstanding shares. They also required that the continuity of Suburban senior management following the acquisition be assured. In addition, any acquisition "would be deemed an unapproved acquisition for purposes of the employment agreements." This would entitle each of the top officers to resign at any time within a year after the acquisition and enable them to redeem their golden parachutes. The undisclosed bidder, however, was not willing to agree to Suburban terms, and management was unwilling to accept the bidder's terms, so discussions terminated.

Five days later, on December 23, Steven Goldman, a Suburban shareholder, filed suit against Suburban because it "breached [its] fiduciary obligation to the company and the minority stockholders by assenting to a proposed transaction which is not in the best interests of the company." His complaint against the merger agreement between Suburban and the Bass family claimed it to be "grossly inadequate." This was in contrast to the offers subsequently made after the agreement. He also stated that it was "designed solely to eliminate the minority stockholders' equity in the Company." Management responded to the litigation by saying "the claims are totally without merit" and that it intended "to defend the action vigorously."

Eighth Offer—The Belzbergs Make a Final Effort.   On December 30, the Belzbergs contacted E. F. Hutton to outline an additional proposal. Its principal elements were (1) the breach or termination of the merger agreement, (2) the purchase of the 18 percent authorized but as yet unissued common stock, (3) a cash tender offer to purchase 75 percent of the common stock at $52 per share, and (4) an exchange of the remaining stock for securities designed to have a value equal to $52 per share. The proposal had to be accepted by that evening. Despite being the highest price offered, Suburban indicated that it could not possibly make a decision that quickly and, as a result, rejected the offer.

Ninth Offer—The Outcome. In a surprise move, the new player originally making the seventh offer, revealed itself as National Distillers & Chemical Corporation. In an overnight deal, National Distillers bought out all of the Suburban shares for $52 per share including the 8.2 percent of Suburban owned by the Belzbergs. Their agreement was reached only after Suburban compromised on its executive severance plans and after National Distillers agreed to pay Suburban holders their regular 40-cent dividend even though the tender offer expired before the dividend was due.

As in any marriage, this one included the elements of give and take. Both sides saw gain from the relationship. Much of National Distiller's business overlapped with that of Suburban. It had a propane and natural gas division and also sold distilled alcohol and a variety of chemicals. Because of this overlap, the marriage proposal offered the possibility of enhancing the value of both partners.

Is The Winner A Victim Of "The Winner's Curse"?

WILLIAMS COS. vs. NORTHWEST ENERGY

Too Many Sharks: Get Allen to Buy Us Out

This case cannot be viewed in isolation. The natural gas industry was experiencing a rash of takeovers. In the summer of 1983 CSX bought Texas Gas Resources for $1 billion and MidCon agreed to purchase Union Pacific's pipeline subsidiary. At the same time, Burlington Northern bought El Paso and Goodyear Tire & Rubber bought Celeron Corporation. When Northwest Energy asked the NYSE not to open trading in the firm's stock on August 5, 1983 because of an announcement it was going to make, this set the stage.

Beginning in late July, rumors were rampant that Northwest Energy would be taken over. The stock of the company had risen from 19⅞ on July 22 to 27¾ by August 4. Companies thought most likely to attempt a takeover included MidCon, Mobil, Coastal, and Standard Oil of California. On Friday, August 5, the company asked the NYSE to suspend trading of its stock, and on Monday it announced that it had reached an agreement to be bought out by Allen & Co. for $31 per share. This was to be a friendly takeover with Northwest management expected to remain in control. The facts indicated that this was to be another dull financial transaction. However, on the Street the unexpected often occurs, and when it does, it brings surprises.

The Investment Banker Smells Gas

Northwest Energy was a major supplier of natural gas in the midwest, south, and northwest United States. In 1982, when it acquired Central Pipeline from Cities Service, its capacity was more than doubled.

Analysts generally felt that this undertaking was in the best interest of Northwest. The $350 million cost, however, gave Northwest more debt than many thought prudent. John G. McMillian, Northwest's chairman, engineered the Central Pipeline acquisition, even though it appeared as if Cities Service and Williams Cos. had already reached a purchase agreement for Central Pipeline.

In a prior move, McMillian was "successful" in winning a project to construct a gas pipeline from Alaska to the 48 continental states. However, surplus gas conditions in the United States left the project up in the air. Although $440 million was spent on design and engineering work, not one foot of pipeline was laid. This was not expected to change in the foreseeable future.

The addition of Central Pipeline, with its 9700 miles of pipeline, gave Northwest about 16,000 total miles. It made it the sixth largest supplier in terms of total mileage. Central became the crown jewel of Northwest. Northwest also had over 6 trillion cubic feet of natural gas under contract, a 19-year supply. With such reserves, the company was considered an attractive takeover candidate. On the other hand, its debt of over $1 billion made further borrowing questionable. The debt service was already potentially burdensome. The annual interest expense just from the debt arising as a result of the Central purchase was over $40 million. In addition, the company produced coal which generated $26 million in losses from discontinued operations in the third quarter of 1982. The company as a whole for fiscal 1982 earned only $63.6 million on sales of $2 billion. This represented a decline from earnings of $71.5 million on sales of $1.5 billion for the same period a year earlier, and the latest quarterly earnings were insufficient to cover the preferred dividend payments. To further cloud the picture, Northwest's independent auditor, Arthur Andersen, gave the company a qualified opinion due to uncertainties surrounding the Alaska pipeline project.

The backgrounds of the main characters of the New York-based dealmaker, Allen & Co., were unrelated to oil. Paul Gould, 38, received his undergraduate degree in biochemistry from Cornell. He joined Allen a few years later, since "life in a lab can mean not making much money." Enrique F. Senior, 41, earned three degrees from Yale in six years: engineering and architecture, industrial administration, and behavioral psychology. He followed these with an MBA from Harvard, and joined Allen at age 30. Gould and Senior were credited by Allen with putting the acquisition together. Leading this investment banking firm was its president, Herbert A. Allen. Under his leadership the firm became known for its investments in both new and established companies. For example, in 1973 he purchased a 6.7 percent share of Columbia Pictures for $2.4 million. In 1982, the firm sold its shares to Coca-Cola, cashing out with $42 million.

Events passed quickly. Rumors of hungry sharks caused Northwest's management to rush and plan its defense. Indeed, the dealmakers were under such time pressure that on the day of the announcement, the list of Allen's partners was still incomplete. In addition to speed, the deal required secrecy. "As a public company, the whole thing had to be very secret," said Senior. "I was concerned that word would get out of the office."

In fact, the emergence of Allen was a surprise to the market. Financing of the deal required $650 million, at that time one of the largest LBO transactions. Allen planned on using Northwest's assets as collateral for loans to buy the outstanding shares.

In order to discourage other entities from entering the bidding arena, two additional options were granted to Allen. First, Allen was given the option of purchasing approximately 3.3 million additional unissued shares for $31 each. Second, Allen was given an option to purchase the crown jewel, Central Pipeline, for book value, which was $382 million. The defensive nature of the two options ensured that should another buyout come along, Allen would be guaranteed a healthy profit. Allen would generate this profit by exercising its option and selling its shares to the new buyer at the higher price. Furthermore, any new buyer would be faced with the necessity of purchasing an additional 3.3 million shares, thus making the acquisition more costly. The second option had the effect of allowing Allen to purchase the most valuable assets of Northwest at a price substantially lower than their true value. If this happened, the resulting value of Northwest would be significantly reduced.

It was also expected that the management team at Northwest would continue in place. "Mr. McMillian and his management team are the key to any decision here," said Mr. Allen. It should be noted that McMillian and Allen were not strangers. Allen's firm acted as a consultant to Northwest several years earlier, and the two men had become friends. Allen named McMillian to the board of Columbia Pictures when he, Allen, was chairman of that company.

Almost immediately, class action suits were filed to stop the Allen acquisition. The suits alleged that the friendly takeover was an attempt by the management and the board to solidify their control by allowing a buyout at a price substantially below equity value. Also, on August 12, Standard & Poor's added Northwest debt issues to its credit watch list.

Meanwhile, rumors persisted that the deal was far from locked up. On August 18, the stock was trading at $30, or only $1 below the agreed price. An analyst who wished to remain anonymous said, "something's cooking. The stock wouldn't close at this level because of a deal that's months down the road unless there's another buyer out there."

The Bad Guys Arrive

The long-awaited second bidder surfaced. Williams Cos. offered $39 per share for all of Northwest's shares. Williams stated that if it gained control it would move as quickly as possible to replace the Northwest board. The stock rose to $37, which was an indication that the professionals on Wall Street felt that the Williams's attempt would be successful. However, the Williams's offer was contingent on the termination of Allen's option to buy Central Pipeline. In addition, if Allen exercised its option to purchase the 3.3 million shares, Williams stated that it would not purchase those shares unless ordered to do so by the court. For its part, Northwest indicated that it would have an answer to the Williams offer by September 23. One Northwest director, L.P. Himmelman, when told of the $39 offer, said, "Oh, gosh. It'll be a difficult decision because we've already accepted the $31. The directors will have to do a lot of soul searching." Allen, in response, indicated it would not increase its offered price. The following days were anything but dull.

On September 16, Northwest said that its directors voted to defend the legality of the option to sell Central Pipeline to Allen. This decision was a setback to Williams and outraged arbitrageurs who had been accumulating shares at prices greater than the $31 Allen offer in anticipation of a higher bid, such as the one made by Williams. One arbitrageur complained, "the exercise of the option would strip the company of its assets. How the directors can allow this is beyond me." On September 16, Standard & Poor's added Williams to its credit watch list. The reason given was that the debt to be incurred by Williams to finance the acquisition of Northwest, when added to the heavy burden already existing at Northwest, would substantially weaken Williams's capital structure.

On September 20, Northwest asked the NYSE to delay the opening of its stock, pending an announcement. It was rumored that the company was seeking peace with the high-bidding but hostile suitor, Williams. As one arbitrageur saw it, "We hear that Williams will get Northwest and that Allen & Co. will go away without exercising their option in return for a pile of dough."

On September 21, Williams announced that it had signed an

agreement with Northwest allowing it to proceed with the takeover. Williams would pay $39 per share for the outstanding shares and pay $26.7 million to Allen & Co. for its stock option. Allen would also give Williams its option to buy Central Pipeline. A third significant provision in the agreement was that Williams agreed to allow Northwest to satisfy its golden parachute obligations which had been provided to some of the senior management, including McMillian.

The Winner's Curse

Williams was the winning bidder. It acquired Northwest at a cost of $875 million. Given that Williams had only $150 million in cash and marketable securities, they had to rely almost entirely on borrowed funds to complete the transaction. Although the purchase price was $875 million, Williams mobilized seven banks to obtain a combined credit line of $900 million. Allen lost Northwest but received $26.7 million for surrendering its option to purchase 3.3 million Northwest shares. Allen's investment was essentially limited to the 170,000 shares it actually bought. Its estimated cost per share was $20, so that it made $19 per share, or about $3.2 million. Although the original plan for a leveraged buyout failed, for its activities Allen & Co. walked away with a total gain of approximately $30 million.

The agreement certainly benefited the holders of Northwest common stock. Since the stock was trading below $20 in July and was purchased by Williams for $39 in September, holders, prior to the merger speculation, had the distinction of realizing a gain of 92.5 percent during the third quarter of 1983. This was the largest percentage appreciation of any NYSE stock during this quarter.

What about the Northwest management? In a report filed with the SEC outlining the terms of the acquisition, Williams said it would pay McMillian about $15.8 million and give him an office and a secretary in Salt Lake City for two years. Thomas W. DiZerenze, Northwest president, would receive about $9 million, and Albert N. Porter, vice-president, would receive about $5 million. Several other employees were to receive payments as well. The parachutes were indeed golden.

On November 22, Standard & Poor's lowered its rating on Williams debentures from BB + to BB − , due to the financing needs of the Northwest acquisition. In addition, the debentures of Northwest Pipeline, a subsidiary of Northwest Energy, were lowered to BB from BBB. The rating on Northwest Pipeline preferred was reduced from BBB − to BB − , and ratings of the debentures and preferred of the Central subsidiary were also lowered from A to BB + . Standard & Poor's stated that although Northwest Energy should help stabilize Williams' cyclical earnings pattern, there is concern that "pro forma debt leverage is extremely aggressive and pre-tax fixed charge coverage is poor." Not unexpectedly, Williams had no comment. Indeed, it seemed like the winner's curse grabbed another victim.

The Common Thread

"Five years ago, you never heard of anyone going private as a defensive measure. Now it's the first option that comes up in conversation." Those were the words of Fred Joseph, head of corporate finance at Drexel Burnham Lambert. The three cases just presented illustrate the diverse approaches to using a leveraged buyout (LBO) as a defense in hostile takeover battles. In the case of Cone Mills, the company's management bought out the firm in the face of an attempted acquisition by Western Pacific Industries. Suburban Propane was also the target of an unwanted takeover attempt, and sought a white knight, which happened to be one of the two initial suitors. In the end Suburban was acquired by a third party, National Distillers. Northwest Energy felt it was a likely takeover target and sought to preclude such an attempt by allowing a friendly buyout by the investment banking firm of Allen & Co. After competitive bidding, Northwest was finally acquired by Williams, which structured its acquisition as a leveraged buyout as well. Indeed, many players realize the advantages of leveraged buyouts. Let's consider some of the reasons for their popularity.

Leveraged Buyouts: Managing and Borrowing under One Umbrella

Leveraged buyouts are often referred to as management buyouts because the purchaser usually consists of a group of investors including existing management. When an LBO is used as a defensive strategy, the target is typically a public company or a subsidiary of a public company that is taken private with a significant portion of the cash purchase price being financed by debt. This debt is secured not by the credit status of the purchaser, but by the assets of the target firm. As Michael Brown, Drexel Burnham Lambert's West Coast merger captain, said, "We take a minnow, identify a whale, then look to its assets to finance the transaction." Often the assets are mortgaged; if they aren't, the lenders are likely to encumber the company with various restrictive covenants, such as a pledge not to mortgage the assets elsewhere. The debt-equity ratio of the firm after it has gone private can often range from 4-to-1 up to 12-to-1, a much higher debt level than is typically acceptable for a public firm.

One element that fanned the popularity of LBOs was the existence of high and ever-increasing inflation rates which allowed the heavy debt load to be repaid in ever cheaper dollars. Even when inflation subsided, the wave of enthusiasm for LBOs was maintained by the appearance of new high yield securities, commonly referred to as junk bonds. The bonds permitted the acquirer to borrow massive amounts and take over a company with virtually no down payment. Typically, the credit worthiness of such bonds is extremely low, certainly below investment grade. Although in December 1985 the Fed proposed a limit to the use of junk bonds to finance takeovers, many observers felt that even if implemented, such a rule would not diminish corporate America's thirst for acquisitions. Another reason for the popularity of LBOs is the enormous increase in cash flow that can arise. Once the company is bought out, management speeds up inflows in order to retire the debt as quickly as possible. For tax purposes the purchasers will usually write up the company's assets to the present market value. Doing so, they are able to obtain larger depreciation deductions. However, if prior to the buyout the company has used accelerated depreciation, the sale of the company would result in substantial tax liability for the seller. In such a case the seller's asking price could be increased to compensate for the resulting tax recapture, thus making the buyout less attractive. Other methods used to step up cash flows include paring down inventories, accelerating collection of receivables, and, whenever possible, delaying bill payments.

One of the biggest attractions of LBOs is familiar to any homeowner charging off large mortgage payments on his/her tax return. For the highly leveraged firm, operating profits not already sheltered by stepped-up depreciation deductions can be offset by huge interest deductions. In the early years after a buyout, many companies pay little or no corporate tax. Uncle Sam is subsidizing the deal!

"We're After Dull and Ugly Companies"

An important criterion for an LBO is a gap between existing market value of the firm and real value as determined either by the underlying appraised value of the assets or by capitalization of expected cash flows. In recent years the economic environment has caused the stocks of many diversified companies to trade at what some analysts believe to be a discount from their underlying "real" value. The purchasers in an LBO believe they can exploit this gap between underlying and market value by offering shareholders a substantial premium over market value. In particular, each of the target companies in the three cases reviewed in this chapter were solid performers, yet were caught at a time of temporary weakness. For example, while Cone Mills's earnings were generally strong, its 1982 earnings followed the depressed condition of the industry. Similarly, the troubles faced by Suburban Propane in 1982 were an exception to its consistent profitability in the 10 prior years.

Usually the firms purchased through an LBO are mature companies with a demonstrated record of stable, consistent performance. These firms have well-developed product lines and production facilities, enjoy substantial market share, and have highly experienced, in-place management. Manufacturing and retailing businesses are popular because they provide a substantial basis for asset-secured loans or stable income for unsecured or subordinated loans. Service companies do not fit the mold because of their narrow asset base. On occasion, however, a service company does become the target of an LBO. Such was the case of the giant broadcasting and cable television company, Storer Communications. Following a threat of liquidation by investor Coniston Partners, they were bought out in a mid-1985 deal worth $1.64 billion by a firm formed by leveraged buyout specialists Kohlberg, Kravis, Roberts & Co. (KKR). Similarly, developing companies are not suitable because they usually require substantial reinvestment of their cash flows. "What's appealing about LBOs is that they don't depend on fancy products or brilliant growth prospects. We're after dull and ugly companies," explains Gilbert Butler, a former Morgan Guaranty vice-president who now heads Butler Capital Corporation, a firm that provides funding for LBOs.

The LBO Arena: The Actors

Leveraged buyouts are said to benefit everyone involved. A typical scenario is for members of the target's top management to approach an investment banker with the LBO proposal. The investment banker would evaluate the target and put together a package of financing. It can involve a team of investment bankers, commercial banks, insurance and finance companies, venture capitalists, pension funds, and even the target firm's employee stock ownership plan (ESOP).

The buying group, consisting of the principal lending partner and the management group, begins negotiations with the target via the board of directors, who are supposed to represent the shareholders. To understand the role of the LBO participants, let's discuss the various players, and what each gets from the deal.

The Buyers.   Typically the buying group consists of three or four different categories of investor, identified by the type of financing they provide.

First, there is the lender. The lender, usually a commercial bank, supplies the senior or secured debt. Given the stable nature of the firm's operations and high proportion of fixed assets, from the lender's perspective an LBO represents significant financial risk but low business risk. In order to absorb the high financial risk, lenders typically charge interest at rates up to three percent above prime.

Lenders also benefit from "point" equivalents, upfront charges, and prepayment penalties. In addition, they often receive equity "kickers" in the form of warrants or stock available free or at bargain prices.

At the other end of the financing spectrum is senior management, and frequently a broader group of management, who purchase common stock of the new firm. The high leverage in an LBO provides management with the opportunity to obtain an ownership interest far larger than their individual resources would normally permit, provided they are successful in paying off the debt. The management group's investment is funded in part from the proceeds of the sale of securities it held in the target firm. Another source of funds for management is cash settlement of various stock option and bonus plans that are terminated in connection with the acquisition. This source was used in the Cone Mills case.

Since success of the LBO will depend on the hard work of management, both lenders and independent investors realize that they will benefit if management has a significant personal financial stake in the business. Therefore, management may be permitted to acquire a stock interest partially paid with notes written at below market interest rates. Managers may also receive warrants entitling them to expand their stock holdings at a set price once the acquisition debt is repaid.

In all, for management the LBO provides the chance to become entrepreneurs and the opportunity to realize hefty financial gains assuming the debt can be paid back. Usually the management group's resources are stretched at only a small percentage of the initial investment, typically in the range of 5 to 25 percent. Often lenders want more equity protection than corporate management can provide. This equity gap has led to the creation of the new growth industry referred to as mezzanine-level financing. Mezzanine lenders are often limited partnerships with wealthy investors, venture capital pools, or pension funds as the limited partners and an investment banking firm as the general partner. In addition to investing in common equity, mezzanine lenders also usually hold securities senior to management equity, such as preferred stock or subordinated debt. LBOs are becoming so popular that by 1986 a number of investment banking and venture capital firms had set up units to promote and participate in them.

Kohlberg, Kravis, Roberts is one of the most well known investment banking firms involved in LBOs. In fact, in order to play an even larger role in leveraged buyouts, they announced in July 1985 that they were seeking a $2 billion war chest to aid embattled managements facing hostile tender offers. KKR typically collects a one percent investment banking fee for putting a deal together and usually invests that fee in the stock of the acquired firm. Traditionally, KKR receives consulting fees of $150,000 to $300,000 per year from each of the companies in its portfolio. Usually two or three KKR partners are placed on the boards of KKR's buyout firms, collecting directors' fees and representing the limited partners that KKR brought into the deal. In addition, as general partner, KKR usually received 20 percent of the appreciation its equity partners realize. That 20 percent, which is only paper profit until the gain is actually realized, is a standard in the LBO business. Is it any wonder that buyouts became a hot investment vehicle? Prudential Insurance, which has been financing LBOs since the early 1960s, estimates that its $2 billion leveraged buyout portfolio earns 4 percent more per year than single-A corporate bonds bought at the same time.

Most mezzanine investors are short-to-intermediate term investors. Usually their goal is to resell their share of the firm a few years after its purchase and realize a large return on their investment. This expectation is well within the realm of reality. Several years ago, Norris Industries of Long Beach, California traveled full circle from public to private to public in 22 months. In December 1981 KKR took the company private by paying $420 million for this manufacturer of auto, household, and defense products. Renamed NI Industries, the company went public again in October 1983. Right after it was taken private Norris had a debt/equity ratio of nearly 9 to 1. In spite of slowdowns in the auto and home-building industries, the company was able to reduce its long-term debt substantially. When it went public again it was able to issue the stock at $20 per share—a sevenfold increase from the $2.75 per share paid when the company went private.

One of the LBO deals which fanned their popularity was the 1982 buyout of Gibson Greetings by former treasury secretary and energy czar William E. Simon's Wesray Corp. Wesray put up $1 million to buy the company for $80 million, leveraging the rest. Within 18 months the firm was taken public at a valuation of $250 million. Simon's personal investment of $330,000 became worth $66 million. Not a bad return for someone who in 1952 was a stockbroker trainee at $75 per week.

Bill Simon didn't wait long before deploying his newfound wealth. The new deal had all the elements of a corporate soap opera. The target was Atlas Van Lines. Its former president, Edward Bland, who resigned in December 1983, was charged with running several businesses on the side while serving as Atlas's president. He was also charged with purchasing art and furniture at inflated prices from companies in which he or his wife had an interest. In 1984 Contrans Acquisition Inc. made a takeover bid for the company. A key element of its strategy was to reinstall Bland as president. To escape from Bland and Contrans, Atlas agreed to be rescued with a $72 million leveraged buyout by Simon's Wesray. Wesray played the role of dealmaker, while much of the money was put up by subsidiaries of Merrill Lynch and a unit of General Electric Credit Corporation that specializes in acquisition financing.

One of the major problems from the financiers' point of view is that too many dollars have been chasing too few deals, thus bidding up the prices. As an alternative to traditional financing by an outside institutional investor, the target company's ESOP can become a major equity investor in an LBO. In the Cone Mills case a newly established ESOP was expected to play a significant role in financing the purchase. This strategy provided a tax-advantaged way of transferring a substantial economic stake in the company to employees and may even be accompanied by wage concessions and increased productivity. With a qualified plan an employer can make federally tax deductible contributions to the ESOP. At the same time the plan is not subject to taxation. A leveraged ESOP is one which borrows money to purchase employer stock. If such a plan becomes a participant in a leveraged buyout, both the interest payments and the principal repayment are tax deductible because the principal is repaid from tax deductible annual employer contributions.

The Sellers.   The appeal of an LBO for shareholders is that they get to cash in their shares at a significant premium over market value. In one study of 72 going-private transactions, the average premium offered was 56 percent above the market price. This extra value arises from expected savings of registration and other public ownership expenses, improved incentives for decision makers under private ownership, and the expectation of increased interest and depreciation tax shields. In addition to obtaining this premium, sellers are also able to realize the value of cash balances held by the company at capital gain tax rates rather than the ordinary income tax rate which would apply to a dividend. Occasionally sellers are offered notes or debentures for their shares. But these must equally be of high quality and readily marketable or the LBO will not be approved by the shareholders.

There Is No Free Lunch: Some Actors Might Lose Some Sleep

The use of the LBO defense is not riskless. The first risk is that the LBO offer may serve to attract more bidders. However, this should not be a major concern if the goal of management is truly to get the best deal for the shareholders. In 1982 the management of a food giant, Stokely Van Camp, initiated a $50 per share LBO bid. Eight months later, in July 1983, Quaker Oats outbid Stokely management by offering $77 per share—an increase of more than 50 percent above the initial $50 per share LBO offer.

The second risk is much more significant. This is the risk of insolvency. By far the most common financing tool used in large buyouts is the revolving-credit bank loan at two or three points above prime. If interest rates shoot up or the economy goes sour, there could be serious pressure on many of the newly private, highly leveraged companies. Back in 1981, KKR paid $425 million for Bendix Forest Products. Shortly thereafter, business plummeted because of the housing construction slowdown. KKR had to return part of the forest land to Bendix in exchange for canceling $65 million of debt. In total KKR and its partners lost $5 million of their $95 million equity position.

The first major LBO failure occurred in December 1984 when Thatcher Glass Corporation filed Chapter 11. It was "rescued" by a

Canadian packaging company which bought most of its assets at liquidation prices. It paid $40 million compared with the $140 million paid to former owner, Dart & Kraft, in a 1982 management buyout.

Bankruptcy risk in an LBO is increased by several major factors. The firms bought out are often so burdened with debt that they are unable to make needed capital investments to compete effectively. Furthermore, the amount of management time spent dealing with the typically burdensome debt has often created anxiety about the ability of the firm to survive. In another glass company, managers at Dorsey's glass division took on $35 million in debt to take it private, then borrowed an additional $80 million to acquire Norton Simon's glass division. The resulting firm neglected its plants and barely managed to cover interest costs. It was then saved by a 1985 offer from Diamond Bathurst. It seems, according to an investment banker, that "managements are trying to buy themselves out and looking for greater fools."

Because most of the companies thought to be ideal for a leveraged buyout are in mature, single product industries, diversification risk becomes a significant element for the LBO management and their bankers as well. The fact that they become private adds to the risk, particularly for the bankers. Because private firms do not report their financial results, lenders often become understandably nervous about debt repayment. James Needham, director of mergers and acquisitions at Arthur Young & Co., suggests, according to *Business Week*, that many LBOs which are on the verge of collapse stay in business because creditors are afraid to call their loans when there is so little equity to recover.

One example of an extremely highly leveraged LBO is Twentieth Century-Fox, which oil baron Marvin Davis took private in 1981. By pulling $539 million out of Fox, Davis at least partially paid for the company. It is reported that he also needed to raise an estimated $400 million just to keep going. A rival film executive puts it bluntly, saying, "Davis has just raped this company."

So far, most of the bankruptcies of buyout companies in recent years have involved relatively modest transactions. But during an economic slowdown, larger ones are certain to loom on the horizon. Prudential reports that to date 5 to 15 percent of its $2 billion

LBO portfolio may be in trouble at any point in time, but the profitability of the portfolio as a whole remains robust.

Portfolio investors, such as Prudential, face considerably reduced risk because of diversification. In contrast, management investors are putting their life savings on the line. For them the risk is high, but so are the rewards. Finally, lest one think that the former shareholders are sure winners, consider this "caveat venditor": there is a little-known provision in the Federal Bankruptcy Code which may require former shareholders to return the money they received for their shares. If the cash paid for stock causes the firm's liabilities to exceed its assets and the firm goes under, the transaction can be reversed. Stephen Diamond, chairman of First Chicago Credit Corp., stated, "Very few investment bankers, or stockholders either, seem aware of this."

Another major risk also involves bankruptcy. Presently, unless fraud is involved, the recourse for the shareholders who felt management had been unfair in setting the LBO price was to obtain an independent appraisal and negotiate a higher price for their shares. If too many shareholders opted for the appraisal proceeding, the lender would pull out, and the deal would fall through. However, there is some legislative sentiment that the burden of proof in the fairness issue should be shifted from the shareholders to management. Such a move could open the door to successful class action suits on the part of shareholders. A class action judgment against the LBO purchasers after the transaction has occurred could seriously impair an already highly leveraged company.

Strategy and Structure: The Effects on Investors and Uncle Sam

Although there are many variations on the theme, there are basically three acquisition methods that can be used for leveraged buyouts — merger, sale of assets and liquidation, or tender offer and freeze-out. The difference between these structures is not just technical. Investors care because of different liquidity and tax consequences, Uncle Sam cares because of the revenue implications, and management cares because both investors and the government care. The different structures also provide management varied degrees of flexibility in controlling their businesses. Let's take a closer look at the types of possible acquisitions.

Structuring the LBO as a Merger.   The acquisition group consisting of management and investors can form either a one-tier corporation, or a two-tier corporation (parent and subsidiary) to be used as the acquisition vehicle. The acquiring corporation in the one-tier structure or the subsidiary of the acquiring corporation in a two-tier structure is then merged into the company being acquired. Shareholders of the target firm receive cash for their shares and the acquiring firm receives the shares of the target.

The one-tier structure assures tax-free status for management's stock in the acquired company because the transaction will be treated as a recapitalization under the Internal Revenue Code. Under the two-tier structure, tax-free treatment for management shares is less certain. However, the two-tier structure is required if the new owners intend to step up the basis of the acquired company's assets. But, in the case that the acquisition group's investors owned 20 percent or more of the acquired company prior to the LBO, a step-up in asset basis is not permitted. Additionally, the holding company structure provides flexibility in future operations. For instance, it can facilitate disposition of unwanted portions of the business. It can also protect assets in the holding company from the creditors of the acquired business. Another advantage of the holding company structure permits the separation of acquisition debt from operating debt.

Structuring the LBO as a merger can result in possible tax advantages. However, because a merger requires shareholder approval, a great deal of time can be lost in preparing and distributing proxy information and setting up a shareholder meeting. Thus, a proposed LBO using a merger as the initial acquisition vehicle would not provide a timely response to a competing acquisition offer. Nevertheless, if the target's management acts promptly early in the battle, this technique might prove adequate. For example, when Dan River battled against Carl Icahn, the threat from the aggressor was not immediate takeover but rather an increasing stock accumulation program. Cone Mills also used a cash merger LBO successfully, but here again it initiated its buyout offer when Western Pacific was only threatening to launch a tender offer. There was no explicit tender offer already on the table.

Structuring the LBO as an Asset Purchase.   In this case the investor group forms a corporation which purchases all the assets for cash and assumes all the liabilities of the target company. The target company, on receipt of the cash will formally liquidate and distribute its assets to the acquirer and distribute the cash received to the target's shareholders. Setting up this formal liquidation of the target avoids a corporate tax on the sale of the assets. One should note that a "forward merger" in which the target merges into the acquirer, rather than vice versa, is also considered to be a sale and liquidation for tax purposes. Because sale of assets and liquidation requires shareholder approval, this method suffers from the same time-lag difficulties as in the case of an LBO structured as a merger.

Structuring the LBO as a Tender Offer and "Freeze-Out" Merger.   This technique has been used only recently in leveraged buyouts and is responsible in large part for the rapid rise in popularity of the LBO as a defensive technique. Because it does not require a vote of the shareholders, it can be implemented much more quickly than either an initial-merger or a sale of assets.

The general format is that the acquiring company, typically owned by the target's management plus independent investors, makes a tender offer for the target company's shares. Generally the tender offer will specify that the share purchase will occur only if a predetermined percentage of the target's shares, say 80 percent, are tendered. Once the acquiring company owns a majority of the target's shares, it then votes in favor of a cash merger of the acquiring firm into the target. This last move forces any remaining shareholders of the target to surrender their shares for cash. Either the acquirer or the acquired firm then borrows the amount necessary to fund the payments to the target's old shareholders.

LBO as Part of the Defensive Portfolio. One factor that we should keep in mind is that companies rarely rely on a single defensive technique. Often a combination of several techniques is used. Golden parachutes are one of the most common combination techniques. There seems to be a general public perception that golden parachutes hurt shareholders. Those detractors fail to realize that these parachutes can protect both managers and stockholders. If the acquisition alternative which provides the greatest value to stockholders is the sale of the company resulting in the retirement of the current management team, stockholders don't want their managers to block a bid out of fear of losing their own jobs. Golden parachutes alleviate this self-interest bias.

Another common defensive tactic used in combination with LBOs is the lawsuit. If it cannot be based on antitrust considerations, another reason is generally found. For instance, Cone Mills filed a lawsuit against Western Pacific because, in its filing of intent with the SEC, Western Pacific had failed to disclose that it was an investment company. The outcome was that Western Pacific had to amend its filing. Anything to buy time is fair game.

A less common combination tactic is locking up the crown jewel in an option deal with a white knight. Northwest Energy attempted to do this when it granted to Allen & Co. an option to purchase all the shares of Central, Northwest's crown jewel, for a price equal to Central's book value. This option became exercisable once any person or group had acquired 45 percent of Northwest.

Another version of the lock-up combination involves the stock lock-up agreement. For example, in 1983 a mini-conglomerate, HMW Industries, defending against Clabir Corporation, tried to use this gimmick when it granted its LBO partner KKR the option to purchase 300,000 unissued shares of HMW for $40 each. However, this option was subsequently canceled as soon as an HMW shareholder filed a class action suit against management. One of the complaints in the suit was that management was discouraging other potential bidders from bettering the LBO offer by increasing the number of shares that any potential rival must buy to gain control.

While this list of combination techniques is not exhaustive, it should convey the idea that creativity is a definite plus in a takeover defense.

Why Are Leveraged Buyouts Used?

A leveraged buyout defense can have either of two successful outcomes from the shareholders' perspective. If the LBO actually occurs, it is likely that the shareholders have received a hefty premium for their stock. If the LBO is not consummated, it is probably the result of being outbid either by the original raider or by someone else. In either case, the LBO defense has succeeded in bidding up the price of the shareholders' stock above the initial offering price of the raider. In both cases, the shareholder has won.

As long as management plays fairly, a leveraged buyout attempt is an excellent defensive tactic against a hostile takeover. In many situations it has a good chance of succeeding in thwarting the takeover. It can increase the value for the shareholders regardless of the outcome. Another advantage of the LBO is that it allows managers to become entrepreneurs. It thereby encourages greater efficiency and productivity and tends to produce improved returns for lenders and outside partners. The big question mark in any LBO transaction is, "Is it fair?"

If a hostile bidder is a public company of approximately the same size as the target company, a management-led investor group has an excellent chance of outbidding the hostile bidder. The private investor group, by leveraging the company's assets, may well be willing and capable of paying more than the public company bidder because of the large tax shelter cash flows associated with heavy debt. As the size of a proposed leveraged buyout increases, there are fewer companies that can finance a competitive bid. Public companies can use debt to finance the transaction, but they are required by shareholders and credit rating agencies to use much more equity than a private investor group. A public company might be able to stretch its debt/equity ratio to 2 to 1 or possibly 3 to 1 while private investor groups are sometimes willing to tolerate a 12 to 1 debt/equity ratio. In addition, public companies must consider the effect of the potential acquisition on reported earnings, while the potential for short-term dilution in reported income is not a factor for a private investor group. Of course, if the public company is much larger than the target company, debt and earnings dilution considerations become much less significant.

An LBO Has Advantages, But Beware of the Limits

Fairness.　Because management is on both sides of the transaction in a leveraged buyout, fairness is a very sensitive issue. There are a number of ways that management or major stockholders of the target firm can violate their fiduciary responsibilities to the general stockholders in favor of the LBO. For example, there were shareholder allegations of such violations in the Suburban Propane case. In this case, a shareholder filed a class action suit alleging that the LBO offer of $45 per share was grossly inadequate, thus putting pressure on management to favor a third bidder, National Distillers, when it came forward with a higher offer.

Fairness of price is particularly sensitive. Management has the power through unnecessarily conservative accounting assumptions to adversely affect the market price of the company's stock and thereby lower the price paid to shareholders in a management-led LBO. Management also is in a better position than anyone else to forecast future profitability of the firm. If it was to deliberately understate potential earnings, the value of the firm based on capitalization of income could be significantly understated, thus reducing the price received by shareholders in an LBO.

Some people have expressed the opinion that if a leveraged buyout is used as a defensive measure and the offer is higher than that of the hostile bidder, there is no longer a question of fairness because it gives the shareholders a better deal. However, in the case of Suburban Propane, the company rejected an offer higher than that of the LBO, because they would have had to break their existing merger agreement with the Bass family. The recommendation for management buyouts is that negotiation of price be an arm's length transaction. Suburban Propane attempted to satisfy this objective. Its board set up a special committee consisting solely of nonemployee directors for the purpose of evaluating the LBO offer. Based on a recommendation from E.F. Hutton, this special committee voted unanimously to approve the terms of the LBO merger and to recommend that shareholders vote for its approval. Even after engaging in this arm's length transaction, the company was sued for breach of fiduciary responsibility because it rejected a higher offer that came in after earlier approval of another merger. In order to minimize conflict of interest allegations, the selling firm should reserve the right to terminate the acquisition agreement if a higher offer for the business is received.

In the HMW defense against Clabir mentioned earlier, a stockholder filed a class action suit alleging that lock-up options granted to KKR were intended to discourage potential bidders from bettering the KKR offer. It would do so by increasing the number of shares a potential rival must buy to gain control of HMW. Lock-up options were also a litigation issue in the case of Northwest and Williams. In both cases a settlement was reached before the matter was decided in court. There is an inherent conflict of interest in granting such options to ensure the management buyout and to preclude higher bidders. Such an act could potentially lead a court to rule that the self-dealing nature of this action violates the business judgment rule and puts the burden of proof on the board of directors.

Another fairness issue relates to a company stock repurchase plan. As we mentioned earlier, Norton Simon repurchased 50 percent of its own stock over a period of a year and a half at normal market prices. This repurchase program reduced the number of shares that the LBO had to purchase at a premium. One has to question whether stock repurchase was the best use of the company's cash or whether management had ulterior motives. This is an issue which regulators are starting to consider.

There are other potential areas involving conflict of interest for management. One has to do with their fiduciary responsibility for the company's ESOP. Is investment in the LBO the best decision for the ESOP, or are managers possibly jeopardizing the ESOP to further their own self-interest? Another is the granting of golden parachutes. As mentioned earlier, golden parachutes can benefit shareholders as well as management by minimizing management's self-interest bias when it is considering an acquisition. However, Congress has not taken kindly to golden parachutes. The Deficit Reduction Act of 1984 denies companies a tax deduction for golden parachute payments in excess of an executive's average compensation over the preceding five years. Other changes may also be on the horizon. For example, Representative Timothy Wirth has submitted legislation that would outlaw golden parachutes for management if approved after a tender offer has begun.

Some regulations relating to fairness are already in place, but the body of regulation is most certainly on the increase as LBOs become more popular.

Going Private Rule. When the target company is a public corporation and shareholder approval of a merger or sale of assets is required, normal proxy rules will apply. In the case that the transaction would reduce the number of shareholders to the point where the firm would no longer be considered a public corporation, the SEC's special Going Private Rule would apply. The rule insists on very detailed disclosure related to the financing of the LBO, plans for the company after it is taken private, purpose of the transaction, alternative means that were considered for achieving the purpose, and reasons that the transaction was structured as it was. The rule also requires the company to state whether it reasonably believes the transaction to be fair or unfair to stockholders. Dissenting or abstaining directors must be identified and their reasons disclosed. To back up this statement of fairness, very detailed valuation and appraisal data is required.

In addition, if the LBO is structured as a sale of assets, proxy material must contain even more disclosures, including additional information on valuation of assets and the requirement that any actual or potential conflict of interest on the part of management be disclosed. Unfortunately, some fairly watered-down disclosures have been used with impunity in past LBO transactions.

State Law Considerations. The SEC disclosure requirement facilitates a challenge. Frequently, the challenge revolves around the fairness rules defined by various states. In 1983, a Delaware court found that the fairness test had been violated because of failure to disclose a feasibility study that would have supported a higher buyout price. The court ruled that the fair value of the shares must be determined in an appraisal proceeding. This ruling actually made it easier for LBOs to obtain financing. This is because LBOs are heavily dependent on lender confidence that there will be no material contingent liabilities. In an appraisal proceeding, dissenting shareholders as a group can have an independent appraisal done on the company. If the appraisal value is higher than the offered price, these individual shareholders will receive the additional amount for their shares. Since the lender can contractually specify that it can back out of the deal if more than 5 to 10 percent of the outstanding shares seek appraisal, it is not afraid to enter the deal. On the other hand, if class action suits became the remedy of choice for the fairness issue, the fear that all shareholders might be entitled to an additional payment in the future would keep many lenders out of LBOs.

At present, specific going-private regulation as well as the business judgment rule still tend to favor management. But as more abuses are identified in the acquisition arena, especially with the self-interest element inherent in LBOs, we can expect to see a lot more regulation in the future.

A Few Things to Keep in Mind

If a tender offer has already been placed for the target's shares, there is no time to waste. First, the group considering the LBO should arrange for financing as quickly as possible. With the recent popularity of LBOs this is much easier than it used to be. However, the funding source will likely condition its commitment on a satisfactory examination of the company. Therefore, in the package offered by the LBO's group it will be tempting to condition the offer on the absence of any significantly adverse findings by the lender. On the other hand, this escape clause could be tactically unwise, since it would discourage shareholders from tendering to the LBO group if they could make a certain sale to the hostile bidder. Ideally, the group should attach no strings to the offer, and the target should try to achieve a definitive financing arrangement with its lenders and investors prior to the expiration date of the hostile acquisition offer.

Since ordinarily the management group using an LBO as a defensive measure offers a higher price, it has a definite advantage. But the higher price implies higher cost. One could save money by considering a partial offer with a clean-up merger later. But in such a two-step offer the SEC dictates a minimum number of days that must pass prior to the proration and withdrawal deadlines. Since the hostile bidder typically has a timing advantage over an LBO group, the group often mitigates that advantage by making an "any and all" offer. With this type of offer the issuing firm is saying that it will buy any and all shares of the target firm, thus saving time because no proration deadline is required.

The leveraged buyout is an increasingly used defense against a corporate raider. If it doesn't succeed in thwarting the takeover, it can at least bid up the price for the shareholders. If structured well, the LBO can provide an excellent return for lenders and outside investors. In addition, it provides management the opportunity to maintain established relationships with employees, suppliers, and customers. If the LBO is handled fairly, everyone involved can be a winner! But the uncertainty associated with the economic environment and burdensome leverage has caused Drexel Burnham Lambert's junk bond king, Frederick Joseph, to say that "because we are playing closer to the edge of the cliff, there is tremendous pressure on us to be right."

4
The Self-Tender Defense

T. Boone Pickens Strikes Again: A Self-Tender Christmas Present

MESA PETROLEUM vs. GENERAL AMERICAN OIL

"Chief executives, who themselves own few shares of their companies, have no more feeling for the average stockholder than they do for baboons in Africa." So summarizes the philosophy of professional corporate raider T. Boone Pickens. While some call him "nothing but a pirate," Pickens estimated that small investors have seen their wealth appreciate by $12 billion as a result of his raids.

This time it all started with an advertisement. The ad said the purpose of the offer was to "acquire control of . . . the company as a step toward [its] acquisition." No stranger to the acquisition game, Pickens led Mesa Petroleum Company was on the prowl again. Earlier in the year, Mesa tried to acquire Cities Service in a hostile takeover bid, only to lose out to Occidental Petroleum. The target now, close to Christmas 1982, was to be General American Oil.

Here Comes Pickens

Mesa's $40 per share offer for 13 million General American shares would give it 51.6 percent of General American's common stock in addition to the 7.5 percent which Mesa already owned. According to a 24 page circular issued by Mesa, General American would then be forced into the second step of the merger with less favorable financial terms than those of the first step. It was also disclosed that, as part of the takeover plan, General American's board could be ousted by mid-January. The offer was structured such that General American shareholders who tendered their shares could withdraw them until midnight, January 11, 1983. Mesa also announced that the offer would expire midnight, January 18, unless extended. Its offer just beat the new SEC rule for extending the proration period from 10 to 20 business days. The proration deadline in this case was set for December 29, just two days before the new rule was to take effect.

General American Oil was a Dallas-based company primarily engaged in the exploration and production of oil and natural gas in the United States, Canada, the Gulf of Mexico, and the North Sea. Through a subsidiary, it also offered consumer and commercial banking services. For the most part, it was rich in oil and gas reserves, and according to one source, it owned leases that were considered prospects for oil and gas production. The tender offer caught General American's officers by surprise. It was such a surprise that, when contacted by reporters, an officer said he couldn't comment about the offer because he hadn't heard about it.

Cheap Oil and Gas

Many analysts on Wall Street believed Pickens's move would signal a new flurry of interest in oil and gas companies as potential takeover targets. The reasoning was that oil and gas stocks had been depressed by a softness in worldwide markets. The $40 per share offer was more than a third less than the $65 per share break-up value some analysts placed on General American. "Nobody believes [they] will get it at $40 per share," said H.B. Juengling, an oil and gas analyst for Schneider, Bernet and Hickman, in Dallas. "I suspect another tender offer within a week." The stock closed up $8.50 per share that Monday, December 20, to $43.50 per share. Trading was extremely heavy with roughly 1.5 million shares changing hands. To many analysts the fact that the market price was $3.50 above Mesa's offer provided evidence that traders expected the tender offer price to be driven up.

T. Boone Pickens, Mesa's well known chairman and president, responded from his temporary headquarters at the Waldorf Towers in New York City. "We believe it to be a fair offer for the company and hope it will be accepted on that basis." According to the tender offer circular sent out by Mesa, the firm had lined up enough financing to pay up to $45 per share.

At this point, with no comment from the board of General American, it could not be discerned if the bid was friendly or hostile. The two firms were not strangers though. During May 1980, Mesa accumulated over 1.8 million shares of General American. Then, in an unusual move, Mesa issued $76.6 million of 8.5 percent debentures exchangeable for most of its General American holdings.

Both firms were similar in terms of revenues, reserves, and undeveloped acreage. In addition, both Mesa and General American had been very profitable despite the oil industry slump at the time. What particularly attracted Pickens's attention was General American's virtually debt-free balance sheet.

Battle Lines Are Drawn: Hiring the Street's Giants

The next two days showed the tender offer to be a hostile one. General American expressed feelings that the offer was too low to be considered and promptly arranged for some "big guns" to help defend itself. For legal help, the firm of Wachtell, Lipton, Rosen, and Katz was lined up. First Boston, which had been involved in the three largest oil and gas industry takeovers, was hired as its financial advisor. Mesa also arranged for some muscle on its side in the ensuing battle. Morgan Stanley, with the largest merger and acquisition department on Wall Street, was brought in as its financial advisor. On the legal front, Skadden, Arps, Slate, Meager, & Flom, the largest and one of the most feared takeover law firms in the country, was hired. Mesa also acquired the services of D.F. King, the financial community's most experienced proxy solicitation and advisory concern in hostile takeover battles. Because of these major league players, arbitrageurs speculated on a higher offer for General American, pushing the share price up to $45.

General American's Self-Tender Counterattack

On December 22, General American took its first defensive move to alter or eliminate the Mesa offer. Catching many off guard, General American announced a self-tender offer set at $50 per share for 8 million of its own shares. It was $10 more than Pickens offered and represented roughly one third of the total common stock outstanding. The firm also reserved the right to purchase up to an additional 5 million shares. The price tag of such a move would be between $400 million and $650 million. The offer was to expire on January 21, with the proration and withdrawal deadline both set at midnight, January 7. In advertisements, General American said the purpose of the offer was to "defeat the takeover attempt by Mesa . . . by making it more difficult for Mesa to gain control of [General American], or, if Mesa does gain control, to provide [General American] shareholders with at least a partial cash alternative to Mesa's acquisition of the remaining shares in exchange for unspecified Mesa securities having a value less than $40 per share."

Wall Street felt the strategy hinged on management controlling 6.7 million General American shares held in a foundation and two trusts, all set up by its late founder, Algur Meadows. Under General Accepted Accounting Principles (GAAP), repurchased shares would be retired or held as treasury shares, giving the block a clear majority. Conveniently positioned, top management officials of General American served as trustees of the trust and directors of the foundation.

In response to General American's self-tender, T. Boone Pickens said:

> It's a classic case of the scorched earth policy; it's obviously a move to keep management on their jobs . . . . I'm not sure that by borrowing the money for the counter offer they haven't materially hurt the company . . . . In fact, it may be worth less now than we offered for it in the first place.

Obviously, Pickens preferred to term the self-tender defense a scorched earth policy, thereby hoping to draw a more negative response to General American's self-tender. In addition, he added that he and other Mesa officials were meeting to determine a response to the move.

Trust Funds and Silver Wheelchairs

The next day an SEC filing by General American disclosed that its defensive strategy was broader than just the self-tender. The defense would also include golden parachutes, a legal assault, and a commitment to seek a white knight. The golden parachutes would give workers at least three months' pay if they were fired or left voluntarily following "adverse" changes in pay or duties. The benefit provided four weeks pay for each year of service and employees who got the minimum "would receive additional amounts not yet determined." The parachutes would be triggered if any other organization besides the Meadows Foundation acquired the firm. The cost of the parachutes to an acquirer was estimated to be between $14 and $15 million. The filing also stated that General American would drop its self-tender if Mesa dropped its offer.

Of interest, General American also disclosed it had not yet completed financial arrangements for its self-tender. It stated that it would have to revalue its assets upward in order to be able to buy 13 million shares without violating the laws of Delaware, its state of incorporation. Legality aside, General American announced that on Sunday, the day after Christmas, it arranged a commitment from Republic Bank Dallas and other banks to lend it $600 million for the self-tender. The company declined to say how it would raise the other $50 million it would need for purchasing a full 13 million shares.

Apparently unhappy about General American's defensive actions, Mesa filed suit in Delaware's U.S. district court. The complaint alleged that General American violated both Delaware state laws and federal securities laws in its tender offer. The suit went on to charge that General American used defensive tactics that deprived General American shareholders of a fair opportunity to consider Mesa's offer. In addition, it was argued that the tactics could lead to the "financial destruction" of General American. The suit also sought to test the legality of the golden parachute provisions, which Pickens called a "silver wheelchair bonanza."

General American responded to Mesa's assertion that its self-tender precludes consideration of Mesa's offer. It called the charges "frivolous." A company spokesman said that "it is hard for us to understand how Mesa has the best interest of General American shareholders at heart when it seeks to block a $50 offer so that only their $40 offer is available."

Turncoat Trust Fund?

For Wall Street observers who had expectations of a wild battle shaping up, their hopes were not to be denied. Surprisingly, on December 28, the Meadows Foundation, whose officials included officers of General American, tendered 6.6 million shares under Mesa's offer. Speculation on Wall Street was rampant, but many analysts saw this move as a bluff. The foundation had until January 11 to withdraw and until January 7 to tender to General American if it decided to do so. The foundation said it tendered to Mesa to be in the proration pool in order to take advantage of a possible sweetened offer after the proration deadline. The move was perceived as a bluff because of the lower dollar value of Mesa's bid. Many professionals felt the move would diminish the appeal of Mesa's bid to others. With 6.6 million shares tendered, professional arbitrageurs stood to have fewer shares taken from the proration pool if the offer would be oversubscribed.

Scorched Earth

In a letter sent to shareholders that Friday and disclosed to the media on Sunday, January 2, General American provided information that proved to make the takeover battle even more noteworthy. In the letter, General American disclosed that its $600 million bank credit could be financially crippling. The credit was to be repaid in full within two and a half years of execution. The sources of repayment were to be internally available cash, refinancing, and asset disposition. By General American's own estimate, the purchase of the 13 million share maximum set under its tender offer would be devastating. For example, it would transform the shareholders' equity on its balance sheet for the year ended the previous June 30, from $465.1 million to a negative $220.6 million. Book value per share would be a negative $18.34 per share rather than a positive $18.30. With interest charges, earnings would have been reduced to $19.4 million compared with the reported $61.5 million.

The letter from General American chairman and president William P. Barnes, dated December 30, stated that the moves "could make [General American] a less attractive takeover target and cause Mesa to terminate its offer." The letter also urged those who "desire to sell shares" to tender them under General American's bid, reminding those who have already tendered to Mesa that their shares could be withdrawn until midnight, January 11.

Several days later, on January 4, General American decided to intensify the battle by dropping several conditions that were originally included in its self-tender. Barnes said:

> [The changes] further enhance the attractiveness of our offer to our shareholders in relation to Mesa's inadequate bid . . . . General American will, unless legally prohibited, purchase shares under its offer unless there is a new offer which the board of directors doesn't oppose, or a merger or other form of business combination agreed to by General American.

The tender offer would proceed even if Mesa withdrew its offer. General American spokesmen added that a definitive agreement had been signed with Republic Bank Dallas and others for up to $600 million at slightly above the prime rate. The loan agreement had covenants requiring consent of the lenders prior to General American merging with another firm or disposing of its mortgage/banking subsidiary.

T. Boone Pickens was well equipped for the battle. The art of gambling was in his blood. In his words, "I was very fortunate in my gene mix. The gambling instincts I inherited from my father were matched by my mother's gift for analysis." The gambler in him said:

> [This move] is just another example of their scorched earth policy. It's like a guy in a poker game bluffing with a busted hand . . . . To date they've had one legitimate offer for their company — ours . . . . Their only hope is finding somebody out there who will be unrealistic.

White Knight

In the early days of January, the battle between Mesa and General American was fought at a fever pitch. Then, on Friday, January 7, a friendly bid of $1.14 billion from Phillips Petroleum was accepted by General American. Just as quickly, a settlement with Mesa was reached. Shareholders were to receive an average of $45 per share.

Part of the deal called for General American to repurchase as many as 10.3 million of its own shares for $50 per share under its existing offer. To encourage more stockholders to tender, the deadline was extended by one week. General American would then retire all the stock repurchased, leaving about 15 million shares outstanding. Phillips would then enter into a stock purchase agreement for 7.5 million shares at $45 each, including those held by the Meadows Foundation. Any shares not purchased would then be purchased by Phillips for $38.17 each on completion of the formal merger process.

The Second Place Trophy or Winning Isn't Everything

To appease Mesa, General American paid its tender offer expenses of $15 million. In return, Mesa dropped the tender offer, agreed to refrain from buying any General American securities for five years, and dropped all litigation stemming from the takeover battle. Mesa also gained in an indirect way because it had convertible debentures based on General American stock, now selling at a substantial premium. Based on its value, Mesa expected to realize a pretax gain of $44.9 million on conversion.

An amazing aspect of this deal was the staggering number of firms actively involved in the battle. Consider General American's defensive effort: Striving to attract suitors, First Boston, General American's financial advisor, had 18 investment bankers working full time on a rescue plan. They contacted approximately 90 firms, sending detailed information about General American to 25 of them. Company technical experts then answered questions from an estimated 25 professionals sent by seven prospective bidders.

Like in any other corporate control battle, the true intentions are never known with certainty. There were, indeed, some who doubted whether Pickens actually wanted to take control of the company or whether he was merely interested in greenmail. However, after the battle was over, in an interview with *The Wall Street Journal*, Pickens said, "Don't get the idea we didn't want General American. We darn sure did and we were very close to getting it too . . . . But at least we got the second place trophy [the gain on the debentures] and that's not bad for three weeks' work."

Battling The Posner Attack

SEPCO vs. GRANITEVILLE

Victor Posner was used to battle. Not only did the grade school dropout strike fear into the hearts of corporate executives, he was used to fighting the government. In 1977, he was nailed by the SEC for neglecting to report that he and his family took money out of his companies. The SEC forced him to repay $1.6 million. The IRS was also on Posner's tail. It charged him with tax fraud, claiming that he inflated the value of land donated to Miami Christian College.

In early January 1983, Victor Posner made his move. His Southeastern Public Service Company (SEPCO) purchased approximately 230,000 shares of Graniteville stock. This, in addition to large purchases over the previous eight months, gave SEPCO 26.1 percent of the 4.3 million shares outstanding. With such a large holding, Posner made arrangements in the ensuing months to place three people on Graniteville's board at the upcoming annual meeting on April 28. They were Posner himself, his son Steven, and Dante Fabiani. As a unit of DWG Corporation, SEPCO was a utility service concern based in Miami Beach, Florida. It was controlled by Victor Posner, a 64-year-old financier from Miami Beach. Graniteville was a textile maker based in Graniteville, South Carolina.

Double Crossed?

If everything had gone as planned this would be a quiet story. However, on Monday, April 25, Graniteville dissolved the firm's two pension plans and committed between $25 to $30 million from them into a newly created ESOP. In addition, plans were announced to issue and sell 781,000 previously authorized shares to the new ESOP. Such a large number of shares represented 15 percent of the total outstanding common and would potentially dilute Vic Posner's holdings from 26.1 to 22.1 percent. This threatened Posner's chances of getting the three members of the Posner team on Graniteville's board. According to press accounts, he felt betrayed. Three months had passed since he and Graniteville's board agreed to appoint himself, his son, and Dante Fabiani. Now, just three days before the annual meeting, Graniteville seemed to be backing out.

Investment Protection

Posner's ingenuity was unquestioned. Even he had no doubts about his ability. His self assurance is best reflected in his own words: "I could have retired at 18 if I'd wanted to . . . . I am a genius." Indeed, his reaction to Graniteville's announcements was swift. Within two days of Graniteville's dissolution of its pension plan, Posner announced a tender offer for Graniteville common at $15 per share. Swearing he didn't want control of the South Carolina textile firm, the tender offer was nonetheless made for 51 percent of the stock. Posner said his hand was forced by the 15 percent stake sold to the ESOP. The diluting effect this had on his holdings caused him to act. Evidently caught off guard by such a quick countermove, Graniteville postponed its annual meeting. Robert B. Timmerman, president and CEO of Graniteville, seemed uninterested in Vic Posner's advice to hold the meeting to "let stockholders see what he's trying to do." Timmerman said Graniteville is "obviously" not in favor of Posner gaining 51 percent, though it did not anticipate such a move in retaliation for issuing diluting shares to the ESOP. Drexel Burnham Lambert was brought in by SEPCO to act as dealer manager for its offer.

In addition to the tender offer, SEPCO filed suit in federal court in Columbia (SC) to "enjoin Graniteville Company from funding a new employee stock ownership plan and to enjoin the plan from buying any Graniteville shares." It alleged that the directors of Graniteville took action as "part of a plan of managerial self-entrenchment [that would] inflict grave and irreparable damage" on holders of Graniteville stock. The damage was alleged to include "diluting existing shareholder interests, wasting corporate assets, preventing potential suitors from making attractive offers for the company or its shares, precluding SEPCO from protecting its investment, and risking Graniteville share's removal from the NYSE for violation of its [bylaws]." This case was eventually lost.

Graniteville Fights Back with a Self-Tender

Roughly one week later, Graniteville took some moves of its own to block the hostile tender offer. Using First Boston as its advisor, Graniteville urged shareholders to turn down the tender offer by SEPCO as unfair and not in their best interests. The reason was that those who owned shares not purchased under the offer for 51 percent may remain minority holders for an extended period of time. This was particularly relevant because SEPCO had given signs it did not intend to consummate a merger. It was felt that the merger's lack of completion stood a good chance of adversely affecting the market value of any stock not purchased by SEPCO. Graniteville also gave indications of a possible self-tender by announcing it was negotiating for up to $30 million to be used for a stock repurchase. In addition to these defenses, Graniteville claimed that one of its directors, Buck Mickel, would have his firm, RSI Corporation, buy shares of Graniteville in an attempt to place a large block in the hands of friendly interests. First Boston was also instructed to explore a self-tender and other possibilities, such as a leveraged buyout or a white knight.

Posner's response to this flurry of activity was, "It looks like they want to steal it for themselves." To stay on top of the situation, his lawyers monitored the events "continuously" and indicated that SEPCO's tender offer would remain in effect until midnight, May 27, unless extended. The next day, apparently to play it safe, SEPCO raised its offer to $17.50 per share from the previous $15.

The next move in the quick and intense battle that was shaping up was not unexpected. On Friday May 13, Graniteville matched SEPCO's tender offer with a $17.50 per share self-tender. The offer was to expire midnight, June 10, with Graniteville retaining the right to extend it. But Graniteville was cautious with its funds. It did not want to spend all this money on a self-tender unless forced. As a result, it reserved the right to terminate its offer if Vic Posner

terminated his offer or if Posner's offer expired without any shares
having been purchased.

SEPCO Is Setback; Punts

Apparently, either SEPCO's offer wasn't good enough or Graniteville's shareholders were following their management's recommendations. As May 27 drew near, not nearly enough of the 1.4 million
shares desired had been tendered to SEPCO. In response, the tender
offer was extended to midnight June 7. The same fate awaited this
extension. On the day it was to expire, SEPCO still came up short.
This is probably the reason Vic Posner chose to modify his strategy.

SEPCO then decided to follow a different course of action. It offered to buy the remaining 3.8 million outstanding shares conditioned on, among other things, at least 1.3 million shares being
tendered. The significant difference between this and the previous
offer to purchase 1.4 million shares was that this offer assured all
present holders of Graniteville stock of getting the maximum value
for their shares. It was designed to allay fears that shares not tendered under the original offer would lose market value.

However, the first prong was contingent on a deal being forged
with the newly formed URSA Corporation, a company jointly
formed by Buck Mickel's RSI and a unit of Citicorp for the purpose
of aiding Graniteville's embattled management. In previous weeks
Mickel had been alluded to as a potential friendly purchaser of a
large block of Graniteville stock. The deal with URSA was complex. In it, SEPCO would sell its 23 percent stake in Graniteville to
URSA for $22 per share. URSA would then try to reach a merger
agreement with Graniteville and planned to buy the remaining
shares for $17.50 each. If URSA could not reach a merger agreement
with Graniteville and obtain financing, or if agreement between
SEPCO and URSA was not reached by July 1, SEPCO would proceed with its tender offer.

As of Monday, June 6, only 201,555 shares of Graniteville common had been tendered to SEPCO. The new offer to buy all the
shares was extended to June 29 or 20 days after SEPCO and URSA
determined they could not reach an agreement.

Victory for Both Sides

This strategy worked. Originally, Graniteville's management was concerned for those whose stock would not be tendered under SEP-CO's initial offer. With the new amended offer, those fears were no longer valid. Based on a tentative agreement with Vic Posner's SEPCO, the self-tender that was blocking the way was withdrawn. All shares that were previously tendered would be promptly returned. SEPCO's tender offer had to be extended once more to midnight on Monday, July 25. The next day SEPCO announced that over two-thirds of the outstanding shares had been tendered, giving it control.

While the self-tender defense caused Posner to improve his offer to Graniteville shareholders, it added to the cash flow difficulties of his empire. Indeed, looking back with hindsight at the four year period through 1985, the empire's cash flow did not even cover its interest obligations. Targets like Graniteville might wonder what fuels Posner's takeover lust. The answer is best summarized by a Wall Street source, who suggested that "the only thing that keeps this [empire] from hitting the wall is that the banks are into him for so much that they might think it easier to just keep playing along."

"My Grand Plan Is To Stay Out Of Trouble"

COASTAL CORP. vs. TEXAS GAS RESOURCES

Oscar Wyatt Jr., founder and chairman of Coastal Corporation, was giving his first interview in over two years. Coastal was engaged primarily in oil and gas production and exploration. "My grand plan," said Mr. Wyatt, "is to stay out of trouble." In the course of an interview quoted in *The Wall Street Journal*, he announced that one of Coastal's primary goals in 1983 was to reduce its leverage. At that time, Coastal's debt-to-total capitalization ratio was a high 62 percent. This reduction was to be accomplished by cutting the workforce, by trimming capital expenditures, and by reducing refinery capacity. One would expect such a firm to keep away from acquisitions. This was not the case. The Coastal chairman said that, in spite of its precarious debt position, the debt level could be maintained, or even increased, if the right acquisition came along. "Now is a fabulous time" to make an acquisition in oil and gas because the prices of such stocks have plummeted due to a slump in the business.

Coastal Makes an Offer

True to his word, one week after announcing these drastic measures to cut costs, Coastal announced a tender offer for the shares of Texas Gas Resources. Formerly Texas Gas Corporation, Texas Gas Resources was a natural gas pipeline, oil and gas exploration and production firm. It also had interest in inland barge traffic, ship building, and trucking. Located in Owensboro, Kentucky, at the time it was planning a move to Houston. The tender offer was announced on June 6, 1983 in both newspaper and radio announcements. Through its Colorado Interstate Corporation unit, Coastal was offering $45 per share for 10 million of the 19 million shares of Texas Gas. Accordingly, the bid for 52 percent was to cost $450 million. The advertisements called the offer the first step towards a complete takeover. At the time, Coastal owned 528,900 shares which it purchased in the open market. The offer was a surprise to Texas Gas; such a surprise that a spokesman for Texas Gas in Owensboro said it was unaware of the offer.

But according to Oscar Wyatt, a letter was sent to the chairman of Texas Gas dated June 5, 1983 stating his intentions. In the letter, Wyatt said that Coastal "would like to accomplish this transaction on a completely amicable basis if possible . . . . There are no serious business or legal impediments to a Coastal takeover . . . . I hope you and your board agree."

The withdrawal deadline for the tender offer was set for June 24. Unless extended, the offer and proration period were to expire midnight July 1. Coastal stated it may buy more than 10 million shares, but indicated it was not obligated to do so. On the other hand, if the offer was poorly subscribed, Coastal would still buy all shares tendered. Coastal's motivations were clear. In 1982, it earned $65.6 million on revenues of $5.8 billion. During the same period Texas Gas earned about twice as much, $113.5 million, on revenues half as great, $2.87 billion. Unfortunately for Coastal, it was not going to be a smooth acquisition.

Enter CSX

The day following its offer, CSX Corporation, of Richmond, Virginia, made a counter offer of $52 per share to overtake what was termed a "hostile" bid by Coastal. A Texas Gas spokesman said, "Ideally, any company as financially strong as ours would rather remain independent . . . . Coastal just wasn't a company we wanted to get involved with." Serious talks between Texas Gas and CSX had not been held until just prior to the CSX offer. However, Hays T. Watkins, chairman and CEO of CSX, said his firm had been talking "in a very preliminary manner with Texas Gas for some time."

Texas Gas agreed to the terms CSX stipulated. The bid for a merger would involve cash, stock, and a note. Its proposal was to proceed as follows: CSX would make a tender offer for 35 percent of Texas Gas at $52 per share. It also retained the right to buy an additional 16 percent of Texas Gas shares for $166 million. In addition, it received the option to buy previously authorized but unissued stock for $194.5 million. The payment would come in the form of $18.7 million in cash and a note due June 30, 1984. Following the tender offer, CSX would exchange .684 shares of its stock for each remaining share of Texas Gas stock. This step, to complete the merger, would be subject to shareholders' approval. The closing price for CSX common stock on the day before the offer was announced as $66 per share, making the stock involved in the proposal worth $224 million. Under the tender offer, Texas Gas shareholders would be able to withdraw their shares through June 20. The proration date and the expiration of the offer were both set to be July 7, unless extended.

Under the offer, Dennis R. Hendrix, Texas Gas's president and chairman, would become one of the three top officers in CSX. His new title was still unknown. He would be joining Hays Watkins and the president of CSX, A. Paul Funkhouser. Seven of Texas Gas's directors would also be added to the 22 member board of CSX.

To help fend off Coastal, Texas Gas filed suit in federal court in Houston to enjoin Coastal from making a tender offer for its shares.

The suit alleged Coastal circulated "misleading" rumors designed to induce arbitrageurs to purchase shares of Texas Gas prior to its offer. It was presumed the arbitrageurs would then tender their holdings to Coastal. The suit also charged that Coastal circulated misleading statements about its ability to acquire Texas Gas. The only way it said Coastal would be able to finance the acquisition would be to hold a "fire sale" for Texas Gas assets.

As part of the proposed merger between CSX and Texas Gas, Texas Gas planned to set up a voting trust for its barge unit. However, the idea was likely to cause problems with the ICC. The problems originated back on November 1, 1980 with the formation of CSX. CSX was created by a merger of Chessie Systems Incorporated and Seaboard Coast Line Industries Incorported, two railroad holding companies. As a result of the merger of the two railroads, the Panama Canal Act required any change of control involving a barge unit to receive ICC approval. Anticipating this and other legal battles, CSX decided to enlist the heavy artillery of the New York law firm of Wachtell, Lipton, Rosen, and Katz.

Texas Gas Fights Back

Over the next several days Texas Gas undertook several more steps to discourage the hostile offer. The board issued golden parachutes to the top nine officials in the firm and accelerated stock options to them and 11 other employees. The golden parachutes were to be employment contracts to provide payments equal to four years' salary plus bonus. These were to be payable if any of the executives left the firm within three years after a change in management not approved by the board. In the case of Hendrix, with a yearly salary of $376,581, this portion of his parachute would be worth more than $1.5 million not including his bonus.

In a surprising move on the part of the management, Texas Gas rejected the offer for golden parachutes made by its board. Filing an amended SEC report on June 8, the firm disclosed that "the company, on further consideration decided not to implement the termination agreements." In a telephone interview with *The Wall Street Journal*, management confirmed the unusual move that they, and not the board, made the decision against the parachutes.

The Bids Go Higher and a Last Ditch Self-Tender

The same day Texas Gas stock closed up 1⅜, fueled by the speculation that Coastal would sweeten its offer. Most analysts felt that in such a move Coastal had to specify the amount it would pay in the second step of the merger plan. As it then stood, it planned to issue securities of undisclosed value for the remaining 48 percent of outstanding common after a successful tender offer. However, the first step of the tender offer could increase significantly in value and still be viewed as inferior to Texas Gas's without providing sufficient explanation regarding the securities to be exchanged in the second step of the merger.

Almost two weeks passed before a sweetened offer was made by Coastal. In newspaper ads on June 20, it raised the price it would pay from $45 to $55 per share. It went on to say that it would offer a package of debt and securities "substantially" equivalent to $48 per share or roughly $650 million for the remaining 48 percent. Coastal also said it would purchase an additional 1.75 million shares of Texas Gas for $96.3 million if Texas Gas went ahead with its plans to sell unissued shares to CSX. This would bring the price paid by Coastal for Texas Gas to $55 per share. Under the new offer, Texas Gas shareholder withdrawal rights were to expire on June 29. Along with the offer, Coastal petitioned the ICC to make the voting trust for Texas Gas's barge subsidiary unlawful under the Panama Canal Act.

Both Texas Gas and CSX declined to comment. A Wall Street advisor close to CSX called the offer a weak one and disputed the value Coastal put on the second step. "Coastal is worsening its debt position so significantly in the first step of the tender offer that the credibility of any securities they wish to issue is strained at best," he said. Coastal confirmed that the new offer would raise their debt-to-equity ratio from 58 to 75 percent. However, its officials claimed that following the first step, a package could be designed to alleviate this problem.

Even though some analysts found Coastal's new offer dubious, CSX and Texas Gas moved in concert the next day to block out Coastal. CSX revised its offer for 7.1 million shares at $52 per share to encompass all 20.6 million shares outstanding. The additional funds needed for such a move would come from internally generated cash and lines of credit. CSX claimed to have "ample" resources.

In a move of at least equal significance, Texas Gas announced a self-tender at $45 per share for up to 10 million shares. The self-tender would be triggered if Coastal bought any Texas Gas shares. If Coastal didn't buy under its offer, Texas Gas would not be obligated to buy under its own offer. This was set up as a threat to destroy the financing arranged by Coastal. Texas Gas would spend up to $450 million of its assets to accomplish its self-tender. It believed Coastal had pledged these assets as security to back its own $550 million cash offer. The contingent nature of the offer was also intended to keep speculators from holding back on CSX's offer of $52 per share that expired midnight, June 29, enabling them to get Coastal's offer of $55 per share at midnight, July 1. However, it was felt, that for an extra $3, speculators would not risk the possible collapse of Coastal's bid.

Coastal Concedes

These two moves were enough to induce a settlement in the take-over battle. Several days later, on Thursday, June 23, Coastal accepted a payment of $18 million from Texas Gas to end the fight. Under the settlement, Coastal agreed not to buy any Texas Gas shares for five years and to withdraw all litigation that resulted from the fight. This ending in no way made Coastal a loser. In addition to the $18 million received from Texas Gas, it could also repurchase 528,900 shares previously sold to CSX. With the bargain purchase price of $36.03 per share, the deal earned Coastal an extra $8.4 million, giving it a total gain of $26.4 million for its efforts. According to Coastal, it felt these earnings were better than any it would have gained had it tried to outbid CSX and won.

As in the days of the knights of the Round Table, the knight in shining armor, CSX in this case, saved the drowning heroine, Texas Gas Resources. Unlike most business wars, the knight, the heroine, and the villain, Coastal, all felt they had come away the victor.

The Common Thread

Self-tender is one of the more important defensive weapons in a company's strategic arsenal. It is important because it has the ability to greatly affect the issuer's balance sheet, provides shareholders with an alternative offer, and helps the target obtain certain strategic objectives. Yet the question arises, why use self-tender as opposed to other defensive strategies? This section will look into what constitutes a self-tender, why it is used, and what rules govern its use.

Self-Tender: The Shape of the Weapon

A self-tender defense occurs when a firm undertakes a tender offer for its own shares as a method of defending against a hostile aggressor. After purchase, the shares are taken off the market and commonly referred to as treasury stock. This is important to note because there are similar tender offers that are not self-tenders. If the shares are to be bought for a third party, such as a management group wishing to gain control for themselves, the offer is simply an ordinary tender offer.

The self-tender is usually employed to defend against a "two-tier" or "front-end loaded" hostile offer. A two tier offer is the type seen in each of the three self-tender cases discussed. After acquiring majority control, the raider often plans to force a merger, giving the remaining shareholders an undisclosed amount of cash and/or securities. It is this second step, the undisclosed amount of cash and/or securities, that makes management and shareholders nervous. Unless the second step is based on a disclosed amount of cash, it is very difficult to affix a value to it, though it usually can be counted on to be less. To keep roughly half of the shareholders from getting a raw deal, a defense is undertaken.

Even though it is most often seen as a defense against two-tier offers, the logic applies equally well to a one-tier offer. If the management of the target company feels that the aggressor's offer is too low in relation to the underlying value of the target's shares, then a defense is warranted.

A self-tender is usually for fewer shares than the offer it is defending against. In most cases it is for 25 to 50 percent of the common stock outstanding. In some cases it is equal to the amount the hostile offer is seeking, but this happens only when the aggressor already holds a significant position so its bid for control involves a tender offer for much less than 50 percent. The reason why self-tenders are usually smaller in magnitude than the hostile offer is that most managements are seeking to defend against the hostile offer; they are not interested in selling assets to raise the cash necessary for a large scale self-tender. Selling such assets is, in some cases, tantamount to liquidation. The size of the offer is also limited by corporate and contractual covenants, and other legal restrictions. But it is clear that even if a firm has outstanding unsecured debt, it does not necessarily have the right to liquidate its assets. To do so would mean the firm was consciously defaulting and thereby introduces the potential for being accused of fraud.

It is also interesting to note the price per share offered in a self-tender. Though in some cases the offering price is higher than that of the hostile bid, in many it is just equal to it. An example is Graniteville's self-tender against Victor Posner. When faced with identical offers in both price and numbers of shares sought, shareholders tendered decisively in favor of management. It is likely to often be the case that when shareholders are faced with identical offers, they are loyal to current management, all other things being equal.

A self-tender puts a time frame on the events surrounding the action. Because tender offers have an expiration date, a self-tender defense ensures that the battle will conclude within approximately a month's time, roughly the time frame of most tender offers. When the target firm announces it will begin buying tendered shares on a specific date, the aggressor must decide on its course of action by that date or be left without a strategy. By definition, fixing the time frame limits the options open to the aggressor. Of course, the same is true for the target. In the cases we have reviewed, it is possible to see the effect of a self-tender on the speed of the transaction. In General American's battle with T. Boone Pickens, the entire battle lasted less than 10 days and in Texas Gas's fight with Coastal, it lasted only two weeks. Interestingly, Graniteville's war with Victor Posner had already been raging five months when the self-tender took place. Only weeks later, the war was over.

A common thread running through most self-tenders is their contingent trigger. The trigger is set such that the offer is conditioned on the aggressor carrying out its tender offer in part or in whole. The motivation for the contingent trigger is to avoid a financial squeeze. When a self-tender is taken to the point of purchasing the shares, the issuer will undoubtedly incur large cash outflows. To facilitate this, either assets will have to be liquidated or a large amount of debt will have to be incurred. For these reasons, many firms prefer not to have to go through with offers for their own shares unless forced. To save themselves from the possible dramatic balance sheet alteration that could take place, the majority of offers are structured with a contingent trigger. For example, Texas Gas tried to avoid an unnecessary $550 million cash outflow in case Coastal withdrew its offer. To do so, it made its offer conditional on Coastal proceeding with its offer. Similarly, General American also made its offer conditional on Pickens not canceling his offer.

Sometimes an offer is not conditional, and a game of financial chicken takes place. The idea behind an offer that isn't conditional goes as follows: picture two drivers playing chicken in cars. The two drive at each other at a high rate of speed. The one who swerves first to avoid the impending crash is chicken. Now imagine that one of the drivers knows he is not going to chicken out. This raises the possibility of a crash that neither would want. To show his commitment, he rips out his steering wheel and throws it out the window, so that the other driver can see he can no longer swerve. In this case, the other driver has the choice of either swerving or crashing. This is the logic behind the unconditional self-tender.

In its battle against T. Boone Pickens, General American removed almost all the conditions that would allow it to drop its self-tender. The only way it left for the self-tender to be called off was if a better offer came along. General American committed itself to go through with the self-tender if Pickens proceeded with his offer as it stood. Just as the other driver was forced to swerve or crash, Pickens had to either amend his offer, drop it, or crash.

In April 1985, Atlantic Richfield Company (ARCO), after watching all the other fish in the sea of oil being chased by the sharks, decided to take preemptive action. In a program revolving around share repurchase, it announced a reduction in equity from $10 to $5 billion, fully financed by a $5 billion increase in borrowing. Different players in the takeover game have radically different views of the effects of such a massive repurchase. T. Boone Pickens said, "What they're doing is maximizing value for their shareholders." In contrast, Sanford Margashes, an analyst with Shearson Lehman/American Express, said that the plan was "ill-timed and excessive." Moody's revealed that it considered downgrading the rating of ARCO's debt. It had good cause. ARCO needed to find a banker who wouldn't lose sleep over such a massive leveraging of a firm that operates in a single business segment. This new breed of risk-taking banker is a far cry from his/her 1970s predecessor.

Most defense strategies are not used alone. They are used in concert with several other defenses. Self-tender is no exception. In many cases, golden parachutes are added or are already in existence. General American Oil set up parachutes worth between $14 and $15 million, which T. Boone Pickens called "Silver Wheelchairs." Antitakeover measures, such as staggering board elections, also help to discourage hostile bids because they often increase by years the time from initial investment by the aggressor to control of the firm. Of course, all parties concerned take action on the legal front, suing for everything from antitrust and manipulation of the market to violation of the business judgment rule. Self-tender has also been used as a secondary strategy in takeover attempts. Heublein and General Cinema, for example, were involved in a Pac-Man counter accumulation when General Cinema enhanced its defense by instituting a self-tender in the midst of the Pac-Man war.

Another common use of the self-tender in a multipronged defense is to restructure the balance sheet to substitute debt for equity and thereby make the company less attractive. In the much publicized 1985 case of CBS against its nemesis, Ted Turner, CBS used all the bullets in its rifle. In a defense engineered by its chief executive, Thomas H. Wyman, CBS reacted swiftly and effectively. Not only did it use standard shark repellents, it used everything available in its successful defense: it argued its antitrust case to the FCC; in the midst of battle, it "coincidentally" bought several large radio stations with the obvious implication of making itself more difficult to be swallowed; it instituted an innovative variant on the poison pill; and it announced its willingness to buy back 21 percent of its stock in a self-tender. The implications were a 2½-fold increase in debt and a drop in equity by a factor of three. But the self-tender was the killer. At a minimum, it caused Ted Turner to rethink his position. Within a week after CBS's announcement, Turner indicated in an appearance before the National Press Club in Washington, D.C. that "for all practical purposes, that particular offer [CBS's], if successful, would make it extremely difficult . . . very, very difficult, if not impossible, for our offer, or any other similar to it, to have any chance whatsoever."

There is a big question that anyone contemplating a self-tender must ask. Will it be a successful strategy? Unfortunately, that is not such an easy question to answer, because success should be measured relative to the goals of the firm employing it. In the case of SEPCO–Graniteville, Graniteville was taken over by Victor Posner, but at a price 16.7 percent higher than the original offer. Texas Gas was rescued from Coastal by a white knight, CSX. Similar fate befell General American Oil. It was rescued from T. Boone Pickens by Phillips Petroleum. But Pickens has a long memory. Two years later, in 1985, he got his revenge by greenmailing the old white knight, Phillips. In general, if the target does not remain independent, at least it realizes a higher per share price for its stockholders. Such a result tends to indicate that self-tender is a viable, workable, results-oriented defense strategy.

Why Pull the Trigger?

The main thrust behind any defense effort is to serve the best interests of the shareholders. Management often feels that shareholder values will be maximized if the firm remains independent. Alternatively, if it is to be sold, it should be at a higher price than the price currently offered by the hostile bidder. This is the reasoning that typically passes the test of the business judgment rule, the requisite legal validation of any defensive strategy. The real question is, why specifically self-tender, as opposed to poison pill or scorched earth?

One reason a management might undertake a self-tender is out of genuine concern for its shareholders. As mentioned previously, in a two-tiered hostile tender offer the shares in the second step will often be paid somewhat less than those tendered in the first step. A self-tender insures that more shareholders receive a fair price. In the case of Graniteville, management issued a self-tender for 34 percent of their shares at a price equal to Posner's offer. Though this would not take care of 100 percent of its shareholders, it ensured that most of them received fair compensation.

Many self-tenders have an offering price just equal to that of the hostile offer and, as described earlier, are conditioned to take place only if the hostile offer proceeds. Sometimes, however, the self-tender is at a higher price if the management feels that the offer, even if it is extended to all shareholders, is still too low. This was the case in General American Oil's offer in response to Pickens. There are also cases where the self-tender was at a level surprisingly lower than other outstanding offers in the market place. At first glance this would not seem to make any sense. Why would anyone tender to an offer lower than existing offers? For example, in the Coastal–Texas Gas case, a Coastal offer of $55 was on the table when Texas Gas announced its $45 self-tender. This unusual bid was explained by Jim Parkman of First Boston, who worked with Texas Gas and CSX. He attributed the viability of the lower bid to a low probability that Coastal would be able to get its financing in place.

As a means to fend off a hostile suitor, self-tender acts to raise the aggressor's cost of a potential acquisition in several ways. The first way is fairly obvious. If the aggressor initiates a two-tier takeover bid, it usually plans to buy the second half of the company for a price lower than the first half. Any increase in the cost of the acquisition lowers its value to the acquirer. If the cost can be increased sufficiently, the raider will cease its efforts unless its judgment becomes clouded by the emotions fired up in battle. Though it is reducing the number of shares the aggressor ultimately has to buy, the self-tender has two major effects. First, it might raise the minimum price shareholders are willing to accept. Second, it reduces the target's cash reserves, making it less valuable.

Another way the cost can be raised by self-tender is to undermine the aggressor's financing. In the situation previously mentioned, Coastal, in its bid for Texas Gas, based its financing plans on the quick disposition of some of Texas Gas's assets. It was on this basis that several hundred million dollars of Coastal's bid was arranged. In setting up the financing for its self-tender, Texas Gas pledged the very same assets as collateral. Obviously, two different parties cannot pledge the same assets and, of course, Texas Gas, owning them, had prior claim. This strategy was pivotal in causing Coastal to end its efforts. If Texas Gas liquidated those assets to pay for its self-tender, Coastal would be forced to not only pay higher finance charges for the now unsecured loan, or perhaps newly issued junk bonds, it would also have to service such debt financing from earnings rather than from the planned sale of Texas Gas assets.

A third way a self-tender makes a hostile acquisition more expensive is related to the first two reasons. A feature that may have attracted the hostile offer in the first place may have been a relatively debt-free balance sheet and/or available surplus. The borrowing plans of the aggressor may have been based on the debt/equity mix of the combined units. If the target takes on debt or reduces its surplus by initiating a self-tender, it lowers its value to the potential acquirer. Such a lowered value makes the aggressor's initial offer more costly relative to its perceived value of what it is getting.

In its winter 1986 battle with GAF, Union Carbide, in order to win a better deal for its shareholders or remain independent, structured a defensive buyback proposal. It initially offered to pay $85 a share in cash and securities in a buyback offer for at least 35 percent of its shares. Furthermore, if GAF acquired more than 30 percent of Union Carbide's shares, Union Carbide would buy back an additional 35 percent of its shares. This second step would exclude GAF and would effectively leave the GAF in control of a company saddled with huge debt obligations. GAF strongly objected to the move and filed suit. In a strongly worded opinion two days before New Year's Day, 1986, Judge Milton Pollack chastized GAF's attempt to upset Union Carbide's defensive strategy. He argued that, "The hostile offerer is not entitled to have boards of directors smooth his path to control. Self-appointed potential acquirers of control are not a protected species in corporate law." Several days after Judge Pollack's decision, Union Carbide upped the number of shares it was willing to buy back in the first step of its buyback offer to 55 percent from 35 percent.

At the same time as Union Carbide was mounting its defense against GAF, MidCon Corporation, a natural gas pipeline company, was battling for its survival with a partnership formed by Wagner & Brown and Freeport-McMoRan, Inc., two big players in the energy business. In fighting off the $62.50 unsolicited offer, MidCon launched a $75 a share cash and securities buyback for 24 percent of its shares. One immediate result of MidCon's defensive effort was a statement by the acquiring partnership that it would enter into a negotiated transaction which would "provide a meaningful increase in the value for each MidCon share."

One objective of the self-tender defense is to make the target less attractive. In fact, the self-tender can be designed as a cousin of two other nasty strategies, the poison pill and kamikaze. The similarity with the poison pill is in the contingent nature of the self-tender. It can be set up so that the target firm dissipates its assets only after the aggressor becomes a major shareholder. In the case of General American defending itself against a hostile Pickens, the self-tender would not merely have made the firm less attractive as in the kamikaze strategies, it would have ruined it. If the self-tender were carried out and all the shares sought were purchased, General American would have been left with stockholders' equity of negative $220.6 million and a book value per share of negative $18.34.

Though General American's offer would have most certainly been challenged in court, it was almost unconditional, leaving only a raised offer or a white knight to keep it from destroying itself. As indicated earlier, most offers are conditioned on the actions of the aggressor. If the aggressor purchases a certain number of the target's shares, the self-tender is triggered, causing the target to increase debt or run down assets. In this way it is a relative of the poison pill and the kamikaze strategies. It is like saying, "If you try to swallow my company, I will poison myself and you in the process."

If a significant block of stock is placed in friendly hands at the time of the hostile takeover attempt, retiring the self-tendered and bought shares increases the voting power of the friendly block. This effect was present in each of the cases looked at in this chapter. Though by itself, this does not take the target out of contention, it does make it easier and cheaper for the friendly hand to become a white knight. To the aggressor, such a possibility should indicate the fight may be more difficult than planned and therefore cause it to consider ceasing its efforts or make a more attractive bid. To the target, it offers the possibility of assisting a friendly firm in a takeover. The self-tender could either help it fend off the aggressor or cause the aggressor to better its current offer.

Another reason that makes self-tender a desirable defensive tool is the timing advantage it currently enjoys over partial tender offers. In 1983, immediately following T. Boone Pickens's tender offer for General American, a rule went into effect. What the rule said was that in the case of a partial tender offer, the proration period had to remain open for a minimum of 20 business days. Prior to the new rule, the proration period had been 10 business days. In contrast to this, another rule sets the minimum proration period for a self-tender at 10 business days. So even if the aggressor has led the battle by several days, the target firm has the ability to take action prior to the aggressor, if it so desires.

The Rules of the Battle

Unlike several other defensive strategies, self-tender rests on fairly solid legal ground. Questions still remain about the extent to which a self-tender can be used. This issue will be explored first and then a look will be taken at the legal ground on which self-tender stands.

When contemplating a self-tender, the first thing a firm must do is check state laws. In many states the dollar size of the self-tender is limited to a certain portion of the firm's equity, legally termed surplus. This means that as a defensive measure, a firm may not be allowed to repurchase as many shares as may be necessary to have a successful self-tender. The definition of surplus also may vary from state to state. There are a large number of states, Delaware included, which permit a revaluation of assets when calculating available surplus for stock repurchase. General American took advantage of this to increase the size of its stock repurchase. It was able to revalue its assets upward, enabling it to purchase more shares than it otherwise would have been able to. Revaluation is based on the current market value of assets, rather than historical cost.

A firm must also check its various indentures and bank credit arrangements associated with its debt instruments and loans outstanding. Many agreements are structured to mandate that the borrowing firm maintain certain asset levels. A self-tender, by drawing down assets and increasing debt, may be prohibited under existing covenants. If it is not prohibited, it is almost certain such outstanding agreements will in some way limit the latitude available to the firm.

An important issue for a firm to consider when deciding on the size of self-tender is the possibility of being delisted. The major stock exchanges have specific rules regarding the number of holders and shares outstanding. Violation of these rules can cause a stock to be dropped from the exchange. Some firms, however, choose to ignore the consequences of delisting at the peril of their ability to raise equity capital in the future. If the target's stock is delisted from a major exchange, it is difficult and costlier for investors to trade in its shares. In general, investors will pay less for a given security when it is less liquid than comparable securities.

The business judgment rule is one of the central guideposts surrounding management action. Typically, the aggressor claims that the management is acting in its own interests in order to save its jobs, not to further the interests of its shareholders. The way the law is interpreted, however, puts the burden of proof on the party seeking to establish failure of the management to meet the business judgment standards.

Not surprisingly, the use of self-tender as a defensive tactic has well met the test of the business judgment standard. In 1982, the Texas oil firm Pogo Producing defended itself against the oil hungry conglomerate, Northwest Industries and its partner, Sedco, a Dallas-based petroleum industry service contractor. A federal judge ruled that using a self-tender as a "deterrent" was justified by the target company's belief that the bidder could not manage the company as well as current management. The court went on to find that it was a permissible means to mitigate the effects of a possibly inadequate second step. For similar reasons, another federal judge upheld the use of self-tender under the business judgment rule in the case of Graniteville's battle with Victor Posner.

In July 1983, the 18 member Advisory Committee on Tender Offers issued a series of recommendations regarding the conduct of mergers and acquisitions. According to the committee, self-tenders are a valid means of defense and should be allowed to continue. They would, however, have liked to take away the timing advantage associated with a self-tender. The most important element of the committee's recommendation read as follows: "Although there may be a perception that a self-tender will decapitalize the target company, the committee does not view the practice as one that is substantively invalid." However, the committee argued that although self-tender is a viable and workable means of defense, there seems to be no valid reason for giving the target firm a timing advantage. A takeover attempt should stand on its own merit. It is only fair to the shareholders that all bidders should have an equal chance.

Facing "Any-and-All" Ammunition

If a company is acquisition minded, it might rightfully worry about a self-tender defense being used against it. As in the Pac-Man defense, one way to mitigate this possibility is to make an "any-and-all" tender offer for the target firm. This helps avoid a self-tender defense in two ways. First, an any-and-all offer has no proration deadline. This serves to mitigate the timing advantage the target would have when employing a self-tender against a two-tier acquisition. Second, it may avoid triggering the self-tender weapon because all shareholders are assured of getting an equal value. Of course, this equal value may be deemed inadequate, prompting defensive measures. Firms may be reluctant, however, to use the any-and-all offense because the purchase typically costs more than a two-tier acquisition. In addition, the raider may be stuck purchasing a sizable stake short of majority.

Self-Tender: Past, Present, and Clouded Future

It appears that self-tender has been a viable, successful strategy. However, in 1985, T. Boone Pickens met his equal, Unocal's Fred Hartley. Pickens, aided by the junk bond specialist Drexel Burnham Lambert, offered $54 a share for 37.7 percent of Unocal. Part of the offer included $3 billion in high-yield junk bonds. Unocal, in response, unveiled a daring, never-attempted exclusionary self-tender defense. It indicated a plan to buy back as much as 49 percent of Unocal at $72 a share, conditioned on Pickens's success with his tender offer. However, Unocal also revealed that it would exclude Pickens's shares from the self-tender. It was the first time such a discriminating exclusionary strategy was used to ward off an attacker. Given that the federal securities laws clearly prohibit any discrimination against specific shareholders, the legal and investment communities were shocked to find that the Delaware Supreme Court ruled that Unocal didn't have to include Pickens's Mesa group in its buyback offer. Three days later, Unocal and Pickens came to terms and ended one of the most hotly contested takeover battles of the 1980s. The agreement looked like Pickens would take his first major defeat in a takeover war. Unocal announced that it would buy back only 7.7 million of the 23.7 million Unocal shares held by the Pickens group, potentially resulting in a Pickens loss estimated to be $115 million. But Pickens had the last laugh. Using a little known tax provision intended to prevent holders of closely held companies from bailing out and getting preferential tax treatment, he turned a multimillion dollar loss into an $83 million gain.

While the Delaware court blessed Unocal's exclusionary self-tender defense, many have suggested this precedent would not stand the test of time. Indeed, by July 1985, the SEC had already proposed a rule that would prevent corporations from excluding certain stockholders in self-tenders. Yet, as a result of the Unocal decision and the legal validation of other corporate defenses against the two-tier bid, the popularity of such offers has declined. However, there is little doubt that future litigation and regulation will play a major role in the continued use of this potentially lethal defense.

5
The Kamikaze Defense

While The San Francisco 49ers Fought Their Way To A Superbowl Victory, A Crown Jewel War Was Kicked Off

WHITTAKER vs. BRUNSWICK

Bringing a Company Back... and Moving It Forth

The roots of the 1982 war between Whittaker and Brunswick were seeded back in 1970. That year was the beginning of a dangerously precarious period in company history for Whittaker. Following a sequence of questionable acquisitions, bankruptcy threatened the historically healthy company. In 1970, the company's debt soared to $331 million of which half was payable within the year. Whittaker was in jeopardy of losing control to its lenders—the banks practically owned the company. Early 1970 stock prices told the story best. The price of Whittaker stock had sunk to $5.50 a share from a high of $73 two years earlier. At this time, a major concern of Joseph Alibrandi, Whittaker's president and CEO, was to bring Whittaker back to a position of strength as a major U.S. conglomerate. Alibrandi recalled that: "Whittaker had a massive indigestion problem and when I arrived, it was a giant mess requiring fast change." He immediately began to clean house and planned to strategically position the company to become an industry giant.

Bogged down by the massive diversification efforts of the 1960s, Alibrandi began to divest Whittaker of all unprofitable and marginal operations. This move boosted the company's capital reserves and gave it breathing space from its creditors. Over the following seven years, he divested 63 percent of Whittaker's holdings. The major focus of his strategy was to capture market share in an area where Whittaker had a competitive advantage. Acquiring market share required Whittaker to seek out a comfortable, natural fitting industry niche. He introduced the company to the life science business early in his tenure, and it became Whittaker's most profitable market segment. Moreover, it later provided the industry battlefield for a hard fought corporate takeover challenge.

Alibrandi's Ace

In 1975, Whittaker's life sciences group was a youngster in a company family which included diversified product lines, such as metals, marine items, and chemical supplies. Its multidivision structure included technology development, medical supplies, marine power, and recreation divisions. Corporate planning efforts directed the company to focus on providing hospital management consultation and supply distribution both in the United States and abroad. Alibrandi regarded health care as "an industry in which technology and the needs are constantly changing and that spells opportunity . . . ." In early 1982, an opportunity to boost the "operating effectiveness of [its] combined entities in domestic manufacturing and distribution activities" in the health care market softly knocked at Whittaker's door.

Super Sunday

As the San Francisco 49ers fought their way to victory in the Superbowl on January 24, 1982, another bruising game was simultaneously kicked off. Brunswick became Whittaker's unwilling takeover target. Brooks Abernathy, the Brunswick chairman, later recalled Superbowl Sunday, 1982, as the "day of infamy." It was on Super Sunday that Alibrandi phoned Abernathy to tell him that on the following Monday Whittaker would make a tender offer for control of Brunswick.

Brunswick Corporation, an Illinois-based producer of recreational and oil rigging equipment, boasted $1 billion in sales in 1981. Although the company focus and the source of its $0.7 billion capital reserve was the recreation division, which concentrated on bowling equipment, Brunswick also manufactured products for the oil refining industry. It was considered by the industry to be a major product distributor to oil drillers and exploration firms. The primary area of interest to Whittaker, however, was Brunswick's

Sherwood Medical Industry Division. Alibrandi perceived that adding Sherwood to Whittaker's existing medical division through an acquisition of Brunswick "would lead to increased opportunities for long-term growth and would enhance the ability of the company to compete in both domestic and overseas markets." The offer to acquire Brunswick with an eye on the Sherwood division would give Whittaker a chance to vertically integrate its own general medical hospital supply division, an incentive attractive enough to begin the siege. Analysts contended that Brunswick was an extremely attractive takeover target. This was due to its low book value, $12.50 per share, relative to its market value of $24.50. Also, Brunswick's low debt-to-equity ratio of .90 contributed to its value as a target for any firm seeking a liquid operation.

The Battle of Brunswick

The day after the 49ers landed their win, Alibrandi initiated his play for victory. On January 25, Whittaker announced a $275.6 million cash tender offer to buy 49 percent of the voting power of Brunswick. It offered to purchase 10.4 million Brunswick common shares for $26.50 a share, including the 400,000 shares already owned by Whittaker. The deal also included an offer to purchase the $20 million principal amount of Brunswick's 10 percent convertible subordinated debentures. For these debentures, Whittaker offered $1234 for each $1000 of principal amount. Its offer was scheduled to expire on February 23. Following the deal, Whittaker planned to acquire the remaining 51 percent of the Brunswick shares in exchange for three-tenths of a share of a new series of Whittaker preferred stock. The value of this stock exchange was estimated at $370.2 million, bringing the combined value of the two steps of the offer to $645.8 million.

News of the potential takeover drove the market value of Brunswick's stock up 5¼ to $24.25 the next day, while Whittaker's stock declined $1 to 31⅜ a share.

Abernathy had shut down any possibility of a friendly merger in early January after a preliminary meeting with Alibrandi, alleging that "not enough matters of common interest [existed] to have further meetings." Not surprisingly, when Whittaker's January 25 offer reached Abernathy, Brunswick immediately filed for a temporary restraining order against Whittaker in federal district court, claiming antitrust violations. Brunswick's claim was unsuccessful in securing a court order to slow Whittaker's momentum. The battle went on and Whittaker successfully counter attacked by securing temporary restraining orders in federal courts in Illinois, Delaware, and Nebraska, preventing Brunswick from invoking those states' takeover statutes. It was a minor victory for Whittaker in a long cold war in which Brunswick intended to generate lots of heat. Alibrandi earlier had tried persuading Abernathy to agree to a friendly merger. "I really think if we had the opportunity to sit down and discuss the merit of this, [they] will see that it's the thing to do. I frankly don't like an unfriendly takeover . . . it's distasteful to me." Although the events subsequent to Whittaker's offer were anything but friendly, Alibrandi still held out the hope that Brunswick's chairman would have a change of heart later on and capitulate. However, he couldn't have been more wrong. Brunswick responded to the takeover bid with such an irascible sale of crown jewel defense that it almost destroyed itself.

It is unclear whether Brunswick's counter attack came as a surprise to Alibrandi. At any rate, a takeover threat to Brunswick management was perceived as a real possibility. It is best evidenced by the fact that in late 1981, Brunswick's directors were persuaded to issue diamond studded golden parachutes to nine members of the Brunswick management team. The multimillion dollar parachutes were designed to price Brunswick out of the target takeover market. Adding fuel to the fire, Whittaker attempted to purchase the interests of one of Brunswick's major stockholders. However, Gulf & Western, which slowly had acquired 15.43 percent of Brunswick's voting shares over several years simply as "an investment," would not play ball. Simultaneously, Brunswick, under relentless hot pursuit by Whittaker, began to fortify itself against defeat by initiating a stronger fortified defensive plan. Brunswick enlisted no fewer than three investment banking firms, Lehman Brothers Kuhn Loeb, Salomon Brothers, and Merrill Lynch, for a down payment of $500,000 to each plus juicy contingency payments if they were victorious in the battle. At the same time, while waging a financially rooted attack, Brunswick packed a solid punch through a well directed public relations campaign.

Seeking the Sheikh

Brunswick assaulted Whittaker by alleging that Whittaker was controlled by Arab sheikhs. Brunswick used the association between Alibrandi and the al-Fassis family, an Arab family notorious for decorating a Beverly Hills mansion with nude, flesh-colored statues, as the basis of a smear campaign. The PR effort was designed to dash the flames of Whittaker's takeover plan. A *Washington Post* article dated February 24, 1980 quoted al-Fassis as saying "This [Whittaker] is one of the biggest companies in the world, and I control it. Joe Alibrandi is my employee." Nevertheless, the "gutter tactics" did little to slow Whittaker's forceful attack. By February 8, Whittaker's offer was heavily oversubscribed, and it certainly looked as if Alibrandi had won the battle.

Crown Jewel Tactic

Brunswick proved to be a competitive opponent and went for the crowning blow. It struck a deal with American Home Products Corporation (AHP) by which AHP acquired 60 percent of Brunswick's common stock at $30 per share, resulting in a $450 million package. Then AHP planned to exchange the shares for Brunswick's Sherwood Medical Division. The crown and the sword had finally met. Alibrandi was caught off guard and later confided "I just couldn't believe that capable and mature managers would ever sell off a prize like that. My advisers said . . . I was naive." Not one to lose, Whittaker increased its cash offer from $26.50 per share to $27 a share for up to 10.4 million shares. Whittaker also offered to pay $1,257 for each $1,000 in face value of Brunswick's convertible debenture, an increase of $23 per $1,000 from its previous offer. The value of the revised offer was now $657.9 million. The extra gunpowder sparked Brunswick's advisors to recommend that it accept Whittaker's revised offer.

The new offer involved new 16 percent debentures instead of new preferred stock. Whittaker was prepared to swap $30 of debentures for each Brunswick common share that it did not own.

The revised second stage was valued at $390 million as compared to the $348 million offer made earlier. The debentures would be redeemable through a sinking fund commencing at the end of the second year. The revised offer for both stages combined was valued at approximately $708 million.

But Brunswick's board dug in and approved AHP's offer. The battlefield was indeed bloody. Afterwards, analysts argued at great lengths as to the board's absolute decision to stop negotiations with Whittaker. All speculation was stamped out by Brunswick's finance chief, Max McGrath, who in an agitated state declared that Brunswick's goal was to remain independent at all costs.

... and What Costs ...

Without Sherwood, the company became mired in a cyclical low-growth business. The management felt heat long afterwards for making a decision that many believe was not in the best interests of Brunswick's shareholders.

In mid-March 1982, a wounded Brunswick was placed on Standard & Poor's credit watch list. The company also announced a layoff of 150 to 470 employees from its headquarters due to "revised needs of the business." Although the "revised needs" involved a loss of well over a quarter of its operating income, all the management pay benefits put through in late 1981 and early 1982 remained intact— including the golden parachutes. The stock continued to sell well below book value and the aftereffects of the battle continued to make Brunswick an attractive takeover target. As a Paine Webber analyst put it, "Brunswick seems to be one dog who, in this dog-fight, seems to have bitten itself badly."

"Marvin Is Burning The House Down": A Fatman Defense

GEARHART INDUSTRIES vs. SMITH INTERNATIONAL

For the year ending January 31, 1983, Gearhart Industries, Inc. reported its twenty-eighth consecutive year of uninterrupted sales growth and was being hailed as one of the nation's fastest growing companies. The performance of the Fort Worth, Texas oil service company had not gone unnoticed on the Street.

In early 1982, General Electric Venture Capital Corporation (GE) began purchasing Gearhart shares. During the summer of 1983, GE, which was then a 20 percent shareholder, approached Gearhart management proposing a $26 a share offer for control of the company. The GE proposal was flatly rejected by company chairman and founder Marvin Gearhart, who termed the talking price "too low." In an effort to cool the GE overtures, Gearhart proceeded to solicit the interest of other suitors, including the Newport Beach, California oil tool company Smith International. GE, however, continued to express interest in Gearhart, reporting to the SEC in late September that it purchased 306,000 shares between September 2 and September 12, increasing its stake to 23 percent.

"We Welcome Them as a Major Shareholder"

On October 24, 1983, in a surprise announcement, Smith made public an agreement to purchase GE's 23 percent stake in Gearhart Industries. The purchase price for the 3.6 million Gearhart shares was announced at $112.9 million, or $31 a share. At the time, Gearhart stock was trading at $22 a share. Smith also outlined its intention to purchase additional Gearhart shares from time to time. In a joint public statement, Gearhart management noted, "We are pleased to have affiliated ourselves with Smith and welcome them as a major stockholder." This professional courtesy could hardly veil Gearhart management's true sentiments. At a December 1983 analysts' meeting, Wayne Banks, Gearhart's senior vice-president of finance, noted Gearhart had not been informed of GE's sale of its Gearhart holdings to Smith by either party until after the deal had been completed. Marvin Gearhart termed the sale "unethical," claiming that "GE and Smith dealt behind my back." Although Smith and Gearhart declared no hostility between the companies and announced plans to discuss possible areas of mutual interest, the battle lines had been drawn.

The Target Propels Itself to Market Prominence

As stated in its 1983 annual report,

> Gearhart Industries, Inc. is a high technology company that performs wireline and other well evaluation services for the oil and gas exploration and production industry. In addition, the company manufactures wireline equipment and supplies both for its own use and sale to independent wireline service companies.

Essentially, wireline services provide drillers with "down-hole" information allowing a constant evaluation of rock content and alerting the drill team when the bit hits oil. The more precise the "down-hole" information, the lower the drilling costs.

Established in 1955 by Marvin Gearhart, the company propelled itself to market prominence in 1977 with a technological innovation using computers to significantly increase wireline accuracy. In 1979 the company introduced a second revolutionary measurement technology known as measurement-while-drilling (MWD). A highly cost-effective drilling service, MWD measures the petroleum content of a rock bed as the drill works. The MWD allows a drill rig to work continuously, eliminating down-time for wireline measurements. These Gearhart innovations vaulted the company into third position in the wireline market with 1982 net income of $15.5 million on total revenues of $345 million. This positioned the firm with an 8 percent market share as compared to roughly 10 percent for Dresser Industries and 65 percent for the market giant, Schlumberger.

Industry analysts attributed the company's new-found success to Gearhart's position as an industry innovator. Much of this success reflected the "inventiveness" and product development skills of Chairman Marvin Gearhart. For his efforts, Gearhart owned 273,364 shares of the company and for the year ended January 31, 1983 earned a salary and personal benefits package worth $294,874.

The Suitor Badly Needs Diversification

The company profile taken from its 1983 annual report reads "Smith International, Inc. is a worldwide supplier of products and services to the oil and gas drilling, ... production, and mining industries." Smith was considered a major factor in the oil field service industry and was a leading manufacturer of domestic drill bits. Revenues in 1983 totaled $697 million as compared with $1.07 billion the previous year. This performance highlighted the need to diversify Smith's revenue base.

The dramatic drop in the domestic rig count in 1983 had severe implications for all oil service companies. For Smith, 1983 was a year for retrenchment and developing a competitive strategy for the future. As outlined in the 1983 annual report, management elected to "invest in some promising opportunities for the development of advanced products and potentials for growth." Smith, under the leadership of Jerry W. Neely, chairman and CEO, intended to bolster the company's technology through acquisition. It would be Neely who would face the responsibility of formulating an acquisition strategy. Neely joined Smith in 1965, moving up the ranks to the position of chairman in 1977. In return for his rise to the top, by December 31, 1983 Neely was the beneficial owner of 381,462 shares which represented 1.7 percent of Smith. For his responsibilities he received annual compensation of $400,000.

The Water Is Tested

In mid-March 1984, Smith entered the market for additional Gearhart shares. By April 6, Smith had raised its holdings to 4.2 million shares, or 26.5 percent of Gearhart's shares. In an SEC filing, Smith outlined its intention to "seek and exert its influence" on Gearhart management, expressing a desire for board representation. The company also revealed its intention to purchase additional shares and made known its contemplation of a tender offer.

Marvin Gearhart publicly expressed surprise at the Smith move, indicating that Smith management had agreed to inform Gearhart in advance of any additional stock purchases. The Gearhart reaction was strong. Gearhart noted, "Obviously Smith doesn't care what we think."

On April 18, Gearhart and certain of its shareholders filed suits in Texas state courts and also in federal courts to block the Smith advances. Gearhart alleged Smith was attempting to seize control over Gearhart through a campaign of misleading public statements which concealed Smith's actual motives. The suits maintained that Smith was attempting to seize control of Gearhart without offering a fair deal to the stockholders. Gearhart also charged that a takeover by Smith would violate antitrust laws as Smith also provided MWD services to the marketplace. A local court enjoined Smith from further purchases or sales of Gearhart shares in order to review the allegations. On Friday, April 27, the court removed certain restrictions. Simultaneously, Smith announced a private transaction with an institutional investor, Kemper Financial Services, for one million Gearhart shares at $30 a share. This purchase raised Smith's stake in Gearhart to 33.2 percent. Marvin Gearhart expressed shock at the announcement, claiming Smith and Gearhart had previously come to a standstill agreement. Gearhart fumed, "He [Neely] had people out buying our stock right while he was talking to me." The day was not over.

Another Man's Poison

On the same day, Friday, April 27, Smith announced a $31 a share cash tender offer for 3.7 million Gearhart shares. This would raise Smith's stake in Gearhart to 56.3 percent. Smith further stated that it did not plan to purchase the remainder of Gearhart stock. Gearhart stock had closed at 28⅝ on April 26. The offer was to begin Monday, April 30, expiring in 25 days. Marvin Gearhart vocally expressed his opposition to a two-tier takeover attempt, stating "it's not fair to all shareholders, so I'll fight it." The counter punch was immediate.

Late that same Friday, Gearhart announced that Drexel Burnham Lambert, whose services were retained to combat a Smith takeover, had arranged a sale of $98.7 million of 10-year senior debentures to various financial institutions. The debentures contained a "springing warrant" provision designed to trigger issuance of approximately 3 million new Gearhart shares under specific conditions. Namely, the "springing warrants" would serve to increase the number of shares outstanding from 16 million to more than 19 million in the event of a proxy contest or unfriendly tender offer. For example, if Smith received the 3.7 million shares it was seeking, thereby increasing its stake in Gearhart to 56 percent, the springing warrants would effectively dilute Smith's interest to the 47 percent range. The debenture sale, according to Gearhart, raised $73 million.

The following Monday, Smith sued Gearhart in a California court in an effort to overturn the debenture sale, alleging that Gearhart's defensive actions violated fiduciary responsibilities and had the single intent of entrenching Gearhart management. The suit requested an injunction against "selling, transferring, exercising or calling the warrants or issuing any further securities of Gearhart." Smith asked the court for general and punitive damages of $60 million.

A California appellate court issued a temporary stay order following Smith's suit, pending further review and action by the federal court. The following day this temporary order was removed.

As the battle began to heat up, Standard & Poor's placed both firms on its credit watch list, citing Smith's purchases of Gearhart stock as having potential negative implications for Smith's debt rating, while Gearhart's defensive measures might have a similar negative impact on its creditworthiness.

Accusations Fly

During the next period of this hostile takeover battle, the lawyers on each side initiated litigious attempts to block the other's actions. In a key move to block the tender offer, Gearhart alleged that Smith had failed to fully disclose to Gearhart stockholders the "potentially disastrous financial impact" of a patent infringement suit brought against Smith by Hughes Tool Corp. The Hughes suit had resulted in a qualified opinion by Arthur Andersen on the 1983 Smith audit. In February 1984, Hughes was granted a large damage award in a similar patent infringement suit brought against Dresser Industries. Given this ruling, analysts estimated Smith's potential exposure under the patent suit at over $100 million. This exposure made the already complicated legal battle between aggressor and target even more complex.

Handcuffed

On Monday, May 28, a federal court in Fort Worth put a temporary court order on both Smith's continuing its hostile takeover attempt of Gearhart and on Gearhart's defensive tactics until after a court hearing scheduled for the following week.

On Tuesday, June 5, the same federal court barred Smith from purchasing any additional Gearhart shares. It ruled that Gearhart was likely to prove its allegations that Smith had misled Gearhart shareholders as to the seriousness of its Hughes litigation. The court further ruled that Smith did in fact breach an oral standstill agreement when it purchased the million shares from Kemper.

As a result of the court ruling, Smith was forced into a waiting game pending a final court hearing. A court date was set for the week of July 16. In order to keep its takeover bid alive, Smith continued to extend the $31 a share tender offer during the waiting period.

Fatman Strategy

During this period of respite, Gearhart began to shore up its defenses for the conflict ahead. Marvin Gearhart was clearly intent on ensuring the independence of his company. As June drew to a close, Gearhart announced it was considering companies for acquisition.

Gearhart's motives for an acquisition were immediately suspect. Industry watchers saw the acquisition strategy as an attempt to leverage up the company, making it less attractive to Smith. Chairman Gearhart denied the defensive connotations, focusing comment on his desire to expand his business. As stated by Gearhart, the acquisition plans "aren't defensive at all — we're just looking for ways to expand our business." On June 26, Marvin Gearhart announced his company was pursuing discussions with the world's leading land-based seismic prospecting company, Geosource, Inc. (Geo), of Houston, Texas.

In 1983, Geo, a unit of Aetna, had piled up $58 million in losses on operating revenues of $285 million. Notwithstanding this abysmal performance, on July 6, Gearhart announced an agreement with Aetna to purchase Geo for $350 million in cash and stock. As pointed out by industry analysts, Gearhart appeared to be offering 80 percent of Geo's book value, although Geo's realizable asset value was estimated at only 60 to 70 percent of book. The agreement called for Gearhart to pay $50 million in cash, issue $10 million in new shares of Gearhart common stock and $110 million in the preferred stock of a new Gearhart subsidiary. Essentially, the deal inflated Gearhart's outstanding common stock from 16 million shares to 26 million shares and gave Aetna a 38.5 percent interest in Gearhart. Under the deal, Smith's 5.3 million Gearhart shares were reduced to a 20 percent stake from 33 percent prior to the issuance of the new common stock. Aetna would not be allowed to purchase Gearhart shares for five years, during which time Gearhart maintained the right to buy back up to 5 million of the common shares it issued to Aetna. In issuing 10 million new shares without seeking prior stockholder approval, Gearhart faced a potential delisting from the NYSE. According to NYSE stockholder protection rules, a company cannot issue more than 18.5 percent of existing shares without prior stockholder approval. The 10 million shares issued to Aetna represented 63 percent of the 16 million shares then outstanding. Industry analysts agreed that Gearhart's purchase of Geo, for all intents and purposes, would serve to thwart Smith's hostile bid.

At the time, it seemed that Marvin Gearhart had apparently saved his job. Few argued against the reasoning that acquiring Geo was intended to block the Smith takeover. Geo was viewed as a "lemon" and expected to be a serious drain on Gearhart earnings. Analysts immediately decreased Gearhart's projected 1985 earnings per share from $1.25 to nothing. A source close to Smith was quoted as snapping, "Marvin is burning the house down." Gearhart's stock reacted strongly to the announced agreement by dropping 20 percent, to $16 a share.

However, the acquisition was not without merit, as long-run synergies were clearly recognized. Some analysts believed that the combination of Geosource's seismic analysis capabilities with Gearhart's wireline technologies would position Gearhart at the head of an emerging technology called "developmental geophysics." This new technology for oil prospecting represented the wave of the future in the industry. With the burden of proof on the Smith side, it would be difficult to press the business judgment issue of the Geo purchase.

Nevertheless, Smith did not plan to give up. It vigorously fought the Geosource purchase, arguing that the transaction mortgaged the shareholders' interest for five years. It also attacked Gearhart's violation of the NYSE stockholder protection rules, arguing that delisting was certainly not in the stockholders' best interests. Marvin Gearhart defended the stock issuance under Texas law. On July 16, a federal judge refused to block Gearhart's purchase of Geo but required the company to hold its annual shareholder meeting by August 20, at which directors would come up for election. Gearhart was off the ropes.

The July 16 court decision virtually killed Smith's takeover chances under the tender offer. The company's final strategy to achieve a takeover was to propose its own slate of directors at the annual meeting. However, in a final blow, the courts determined that Smith could vote only the 3.6 million shares it had acquired before the tender offer, giving the company only 23 percent of the voting shares at the meeting. The judge also barred Aetna from voting its newly issued shares.

No Winners

On March 11, 1985, a full year after Smith originally began purchasing Gearhart shares to increase its 23 percent interest, the two companies announced that they had reached a settlement ending the takeover attempt. Under the terms of the agreement, Gearhart would pay $80 million, or $15.09 a share, for the 5.3 million shares held by Smith. At the time the agreement was announced, Gearhart shares were trading at $11.50 a share, providing Smith with a 30 percent premium over market. However, Smith would record an $80 million loss on the $160 million it paid for the shares a year earlier. As part of the settlement, all litigation between the two firms would be terminated.

Smith International not only took the $80 million loss on its Gearhart effort, but the company incurred significant legal and financial fees in the year-long battle. The battle with Gearhart also served to deprive Smith of other possible diversification alternatives. When it was over, Smith was in no position to attempt a significant acquisition. As a final note, shortly after the settlement agreement was announced, Smith was forced to relocate its headquarters to more modest quarters in a cost-cutting measure. Marvin Gearhart kept his company independent, but at a price.

The NYSE reviewed the events surrounding Gearhart's purchase of Geo and threatened to delist the company. Geo was a significant drain on company earnings, helping to depress the company's stock, which lost over 60 percent of its value during the takeover battle. In the words of one industry analyst, "There were no winners in this."

King Of Spirits And Queen Of Minerals: An All-Canadian Scorched Earth War

JOSEPH E. SEAGRAM & SONS vs. ST. JOE MINERALS

Operations à la FBI: Code-Names and Ammunition

In 1980, rumors surfaced that Seagram was involved in non-spirits activity. Indeed, while speculation on potential Seagram acquisition targets was rampant, the preparations for an attack were thorough but quiet. As a first step, in April 1980, it sold the U.S. holdings of its Texas Pacific Oil Company for $2.3 billion. It collected $500 million in "hard" cash and the rest in long-term notes. Using the notes as security, in December, it borrowed $3 billion from 31 banks. Laying bare its acquisition plan, this equipped Seagram with a much needed takeover weapon: a $3.5 billion cash horde.

During the loan negotiations, several banks, which Seagram requested to provide funds for an unknown end-use, demanded the right to approve any Seagram target as a prerequisite to their participating in the loan. Maintaining its political independence, Seagram refused, causing several banks to withdraw from the deal. Seagram played its cards very close to its vest. As early as September 1980, Seagram's chairman and CEO, Edgar Bronfman, was very vague about the details of Seagram's intentions. He said that Seagram might look for "two or a maximum of three acquisitions" and "except for atomic energy and the steel business," it was prepared to look at any industry. Though the specifics were well locked in the drawer, the strategy was clearly articulated. Arthur D. Little was hired to study possible takeover candidates, guided by the criteria that the target should command a leading position in its industry and should be a price leader. The heavy smokescreen around their search seemed to have some holes. On Tuesday, March 10, 1981, St. Joe stock rose 2³⁄₈ in hectic trading, leading some to speculate that St. Joe was a takeover candidate. However, when queried by the financial press, St. Joe knew nothing to prompt the flurry of trading and was unaware of any other signs of takeover maneuvering, "friendly or unfriendly."

With no doubt in any one's mind, Seagram, in preparing for this attack, adopted some of the FBI's practices. To disguise the identity of its candidate, Seagram's acquisition team code-named St. Joe "April Industries," and called the target's management "our friends" or "the guys on Park Ave." St. Joe's headquarters were at 250 Park Avenue, just down the street from Seagram's executive offices at 575 Park Avenue.

Nevertheless, with all this secrecy, it seemed that someone was able to crack their codes. In fact, St. Joe's price run-up prior to the public announcement of the bid led to an insider trading investigation by the SEC. It was later disclosed that the purchases were for the account of Guiseppe Tome, who Edgar Bronfman described in a court deposition as a friend, personal advisor, and European consultant to Seagram.

The Deal

On Wednesday, March 11, Montreal-based Seagram announced that its chief subsidiary, Joseph E. Seagram & Sons of New York, was making a $2.03 billion tender offer for roughly 52 percent of St. Joe Mineral Corporation's 45.1 million shares. The offer was to run through April 10, with withdrawal rights expiring on April 2. Seagram had already acquired 466,000 St. Joe shares, about one percent, well under the SEC public disclosure threshold of five percent. The $45 a share offer was 50 percent above St. Joe's 30¹⁄₈ closing price on the previous day. Wall Street's response to Seagram's bid was enthusiastic. St. Joe was up 15³⁄₈, closing at $45.50 a share, making it the NYSE's third most active issue. The share price, being 50 cents above the offer price, indicated that the professionals — risk arbitrageurs, and most astute merger speculators — believed that once the merger game began, St. Joe was bound to go to someone, and at a higher price than the original offer. Nonetheless, St. Joe's management, in a press release issued that afternoon, called the Seagram bid "grossly inadequate" and "recommended that the board reject the offer and take all action appropriate to protect the interests of St. Joe's shareholders." Furthermore, John C. Duncan, St. Joe's chairman and CEO, asserted that, "Clearly, if Seagram is willing to pay more than $2 billion for St. Joe in a surprise tender offer, without investigating our properties and without discussions with our management, Seagram must believe that St. Joe is worth far more than $2 billion." In the weeks that followed, "all action appropriate" came to mean legal battles. The propriety of the Bronfman family and Seagram's business practices were questioned, a major stock repurchase plan was instituted, and last ditch tactics which threatened the viability of St. Joe were employed.

The King of Spirits: The Bronfman Family

The Bronfman family held the largest chunk of Seagram stock, estimated to be roughly 40 percent at the time of the takeover attempt, and for the most part controlled the company. Edgar Bronfman was Seagram's chairman and CEO, and his brother Charles was chairman of Seagram's executive committee. Seagram was founded by Sam Bronfman, who left control of the company to his two sons, Charles and Edgar, while barring his two nephews, Peter and Edward, from the management of the company because of a family feud.

Queen of Minerals: St. Joe

The reasons for Seagram's interest in St. Joe were apparent in Edgar Bronfman's glowing description of St. Joe: "superbly managed and . . . [with] major underlying assets, a fine earnings record, and good growth prospects." St. Joe's strong standing in 1981 stemmed in large part from its earnings growth potential. In 1980, St. Joe earned $117.1 million on sales of $1.28 billion, a 51 percent increase over its previous year's earnings. For 1981 earnings growth of over 30 percent was projected. This strong growth could be directly attributed to St. Joe's earlier diversification efforts which had just started to pay off. In the early 1970s, St. Joe was primarily a lead and zinc producer. Its performance was tied to the swings of the lead and zinc markets which like most nonperishable commodities were highly cyclical. To lessen its dependence on these two minerals, St. Joe embarked on a diversification program which targeted the "mineral growth markets" of the 1970s: oil and gas, gold, and coal. In 1972, the company purchased CanDel Oil Ltd., a Canadian oil and gas producer. Two years later, it acquired A.T. Massey Co. and, as a result, secured significant Appalachian reserves of steam coal. Five years later, in 1979, St. Joe increased its stake in the gold and silver markets with an $80 million investment to develop the El Indio mine in the Chilean Andes.

St. Joe's market value was also enhanced by rampant inflation in the commodity markets. Its book value of $16.50 a share, grossly understated the company's true value. Recall that Seagram's offer, which was found by St. Joe to be "grossly inadequate," was almost three times St. Joe's book value. Under GAAP, mineral holdings are carried on the books at cost, whereas in a time of high inflation their actual market value is typically many times higher.

The Roots of Conflict

To assuage St. Joe's fears of a major house cleaning, in its offer announcement, Seagram praised St. Joe's management and indicated that it wanted to keep St. Joe's management team in place. Nonetheless, Seagram did little to develop a relationship with St. Joe's management or to attempt to engineer a friendly takeover. Prior to announcing the offer, Edgar Bronfman tried to reach John Duncan, who was in the Bahamas, and Bronfman ended up speaking with other senior St. Joe executives. This mild overture was not enough to enable Seagram to open a line of communication with St. Joe which could have led to negotiations on a more mutually acceptable basis.

Although the bid promised a share price 50 percent higher than the previous day's closing price, and the offer was almost three times the book value of St. Joe's shares, St. Joe's top management was adamant that the offer was too low. In a press release issued after the March 12 board meeting to discuss the offer, the board reiterated its opposition to the acquisition. The board found that "the Seagram offer fails to recognize the company's underlying asset values and future earnings potential."

The vociferousness of St. Joe's opposition indicated that it would do everything in its power to thwart the bid, thereby promoting speculation of higher offers. On March 12, the day after Seagram's bid, St. Joe's stock price climbed $3.50 a share to close at $49 a share, almost $4 above Seagram's offer.

The Battle: Keeping the Lawyers Busy

Seagram responded to St. Joe's statement of opposition the next day by filing a lawsuit in New York district court which sought to bar St. Joe from making "false and misleading" statements about the tender offer.

St. Joe was caught off guard and had no takeover defense plans immediately available. Rushing to correct this lack of preparation, at the March 12 meeting, St. Joe's directors gave management a broad mandate and authorized them to take "whatever steps it deems necessary" to fend off Seagram. Rumors on Wall Street indicated that the company was considering several "innovative" legal and financial defenses.

Before making its offer, Seagram was aware that the offer did not comply with several state takeover laws. Consequently, on the day it publicly made its offer for St. Joe, Seagram filed suits in federal district courts in New York, Missouri, Nebraska, and Louisiana, challenging the takeover laws of the states where its offer did not comply. This left St. Joe with the traditional legal first line of defense which was often used to hold off raiders until a stronger defense was in place or a more welcome suitor was found.

On March 16, five days after Seagram's bid, St. Joe filed a lawsuit in the Kansas City federal district court, where Seagram had earlier challenged the state's takeover laws. The suit contained mostly rou-

tine takeover defense allegations. St. Joe alleged that Seagram's acquisition plan violated federal antitrust laws and Seagram's offer
violated the Missouri Takeover Bid Disclosure Act. The suit also
claimed that Seagram's disclosures were "false and misleading in
its failure to disclose required information about the integrity of
Seagram's management and about the Bronfman family members
and associates which control Seagrams." More specifically, St. Joe
claimed that the offer disclosure failed to mention "a long history"
of illegal political contributions, federal tax and liquor violations,
"including over 33,000 offenses in Pennsylvania alone."

Although the charges were severe, the tactics were, as a source
close to the St. Joe strategy commented, "standard operating procedure on defense. You pick up their own offer circular and hit 'em
with it in court." For example, Seagram's offer circular devoted five
pages to the results of a Seagram audit committee investigation of
illegal payments and questionable business practices between 1972
and mid-1976. The other allegations were based on legal arguments
considered "unusual" by legal sources.

News of a St. Joe suit increased the uncertainty about the likelihood of the St. Joe deal going through, driving down St. Joe's stock
price 2⅜ to 45⅛ on the day the suit was filed.

Two days after St. Joe filed its suit, the federal district court ruled
that St. Joe's claims should be heard in New York City federal court,
where Seagram had filed another suit to block the enforcement of
the state's antitakeover law and which was also the site of St. Joe's
corporate headquarters and Seagram's executive offices. Consoli-
dating the St. Joe–Seagram legal battle gave St. Joe one less line of
defense, but by no means deterred its management. A St. Joe
spokesman made what was beginning to be a familiar battle cry:
"Their offer is grossly inadequate and isn't in the best interests of
St. Joe and its shareholders. We are determined to be undeterred in
our protection of this company."

However, on March 22, only two days later, St. Joe conceded to
Seagram and agreed not to contest Seagram's offer on the ground
that it violated state takeover laws. St. Joe also agreed to limit its
legal opposition on other grounds to the New York federal district
court.

Scorched Earth Defense

With its legal defense gone, St. Joe had run out of time and now had to deploy a new defense or succumb to Seagram. On March 24, St. Joe unveiled what was promised to be an "innovative strategy."

Its plan consisted of three independent strategies which were intended to provide the company with flexibility and to make it attractive to a wide range of potential bidders. The first component of the plan was stock buyback where the company would purchase from 15.5 to 38 percent of its outstanding stock. To provide cash for this stock repurchase, the company announced its intention to sell its share of CanDel Oil Ltd., a Canadian oil and gas company. In 1980 CanDel's operations accounted for 10 percent of St. Joe's earnings. Canadians were increasingly concerned about foreign ownership of their mineral resources. Selling CanDel would eliminate the possibility of Ottawa opposing any St. Joe merger with a foreign company. Seagram, however, was free from such a barrier, being a Canadian corporation.

Under the second part of the plan, St. Joe was "actively seeking proposals for the merger or acquisition of St. Joe by one or more companies." However, if a "satisfactory" arrangement could not be reached within a "reasonable" time, St. Joe would undertake the third part of the plan. This involved the pursuit of liquidation and the sale of individual pieces to the highest bidder. St. Joe estimated the liquidation value of the company to be more than $60 a share.

Within 24 hours, the New York federal district court prohibited St. Joe from implementing the repurchase and liquidation components of its plan until the plan was formally evaluated by the court. The court's condemnation of St. Joe's liquidation proposal was scathing and illustrates the hurdles that this tactic must overcome if it is to be implemented. The court found that "it is inconceivable that an alleged flourishing enterprise has authorized its board to subject the assets and charter of the company to a scorched earth policy to be accomplished in the name of an exercise of business judgment." At the same time, Seagram's lawyers qualified St. Joe's self-tender as a "rigged" and "illusory" proposal aimed to artificially inflate the price of its shares. They added that the sale of CanDel was an attempt "under the gun to get out from under a legitimate" tender offer from Seagram. The only avenue left open to St. Joe by the court was the potential for a friendly takeover by a white knight.

As to be expected, St. Joe appealed the federal district court's decision. However, the federal appeals court left standing the lower court's decision. At this point, with its position strengthened, Seagram initiated a move to discuss its $45 a share tender offer, opening up the possibility of a higher price for St. Joe and also a board seat for John Duncan, St. Joe's chairman. Meanwhile, intensive negotiations were taking place in St. Joe's offices. The company was not only receiving numerous bids for its CanDel investment, but it was also going through some serious negotiations with a potential acquirer.

St. Joe's best strategic decision was to keep its negotiations secret. John C. Duncan did speak to the press on more than one occasion during the first two weeks following Seagram's tender offer. However, he was extremely selective in releasing information to the press, doing so only when it was likely to enhance St. Joe's value and when it reemphasized the inadequacy of Seagram's offer. For example, one announcement, on March 20, revealed that the company's 80 percent owned gold mine in Chile could increase its gold output fourfold in 1982 because of higher estimates of reserves and ore grade. "This is just a usual corporate release. We would have released it without that situation. [However], it shows that we've got even more assets and reserves than people previously estimated." Bombarding the financial world with another "usual corporate release," St. Joe announced on March 25 that it estimated its 1981 earnings to be $4.31 a share, up from $3.50 predicted earlier. It also predicted that its 1982 profits should reach $7.06 a share, well above most recent estimates.

St. Joe's public relations campaign and intensive negotiations finally yielded tangible results. On March 30, Sulpetro Ltd., a Canadian company based in Calgary, announced that St. Joe had accepted its offer to buy St. Joe's 92 percent interest in CanDel for $545.9 million (Canadian, U.S. $460 million).

A spokesman for Seagram said the company did not take the proposed sale too seriously because it was subject to approval by the federal court in New York. In addition, the credit arrangements had not yet been specified.

The $545.9 million transaction was a massive chunk to swallow for Sulpetro. The company had assets of $197.5 million (Canadian) and earnings of $2.6 million in 1980 compared to CanDel's profit of $15.6 million for the same year. Despite all these doubts, in early April, Sulpetro successfully completed the purchase of CanDel. This, at least removed the possibility of opposition from Ottawa to a St. Joe merger with a non-Canadian firm.

A White Knight Comes to the Rescue

At the same time, intense negotiations were taking place between Fluor Corp., whose investment banker was Lehman Brothers Kuhn Loeb, and St. Joe. On March 30, the two companies worked "practically all night" and concluded negotiations in St. Joe's offices during the afternoon of March 31.

On the same day, Fluor announced its offer to acquire St. Joe in two phases. In the first, Fluor agreed to pay $60 each for 45 percent of St. Joe's 45.3 million shares, for a total of $1.22 billion. In the second phase, a stock exchange, St. Joe shareholders were to receive 1.2 shares of Fluor for each of the remaining 24.9 million shares. The price of Fluor on March 30 was 50⅝, yielding a second phase value of $1.51 billion. Hence, the total value of the two phases combined was expected to be $2.73 billion.

Fluor was the second largest industrial construction company in the United States with 1980 revenues of $4.83 billion and earnings of $132 million. The company serviced heavy industries, such as mining and oil and gas, and was the main engineer for St. Joe's 80 percent owned El Indio mine in Chile. This acquisition was Fluor's first step toward diversification from its main business of designing and building industrial process plants.

The two-step merger of St. Joe and Fluor was approved by the directors of St. Joe and Fluor at the companies' board meetings held April 3 and 4, respectively. At that time, due to weakness in Fluor's stock price, the value of the transaction was reduced to $2.55 billion, or $56.37 a share. Fluor shares that were trading at 50⅝ when the merger was announced had now dropped to $44.50, also bringing St. Joe shares down 1¼ to 54⅜.

Wall Street believed that if the value of the bid continued to drop, it would make it easier for Seagram to propose another offer. Indeed, Seagram indicated that it was prepared to do so. But it considered a $60 price "way out of line."

Do White Knights Gallop to the Rescue Too Quickly?

Then, to the surprise of many Wall Street takeover observers, Seagram withdrew its $2.13 billion hostile offer to acquire St. Joe and conceded victory to Fluor. In Edgar Bronfman's words:

> Our analysis of the values involved do not support an increased offer of the magnitude required to acquire the 100% of St. Joe stock that had been our objective. [Also,] our responsibility, both long term and short term, is to Seagram shareholders. Our action today reflects our assessment of their best interests.

Fluor successfully completed the first step of its tender offer for 20.4 million of St. Joe shares at $60 each in early May 1981. The second step of the offer, however, was not as favorable for St. Joe's shareholders.

When Fluor announced the proposed transaction, its shares, trading at 50⅝, gave the second step stock exchange a value of $41 a share. This was well below the $45 price offered by Seagram. St. Joe shareholders were not the only ones disenchanted by the deal. Terence M. Work, an analyst with Drexel Burnham Lambert, explained that even though "St. Joe's a fine company, it's a mining company and some Fluor holders felt like they would have bought a mining stock if that's what they'd wanted to own."

In hindsight, perhaps some white knights gallop to the rescue too quickly. Indeed, John Duncan called the time spent to reach an agreement with Fluor "so brief it was embarrassing." The deal itself was an embarrassment for Fluor. They rushed into it at the top of the business cycle and paid top dollar. They didn't consider the possibility of a recession or a crash in the price of metals. Maybe minerals and liquors, in fact, don't mix. Not only were the economics of the deal not in Fluor's favor, but their corporate cultures clashed sufficiently to make the likelihood of a success small.

For Seagram executives, life continued to be interesting. Even though Seagram was spurned by St. Joe, Seagram's Edgar Bronfman said it was set to scout the world and study several industries in order to find another target. Indeed, less than three months down the road, Seagram announced its attack on its next target, Conoco.

The Common Thread

The family of the Kamikaze strategies consists of three rather extreme reactions to the appearance of a potential raider. At one extreme is the scorched earth strategy, in which the firm liquidates a significant portion of its assets to prevent its pursuit by another firm. A slightly more modest version, the sale of crown jewels, occurs when a firm liquidates one of its most valuable assets or the one most desired by the raider. On the other extreme we find the fatman defense. In it, the firm, by buying an "ugly duckling," makes itself less attractive. Since these strategies involve the loss of important corporate assets, they are only employed once the firm has been identified as a target and after other less drastic measures have failed.

Scorched Earth: Napoleon Was Thwarted–Will the Raiders Be Stopped?

The scorched earth strategy was most notably practiced in the early nineteenth century when the Russians burned their cities and towns, "scorching the earth," in front of Napoleon's advancing army. Though victorious over the Russian armies, the French were unable to subsist off the devastated countryside and were eventually forced to retreat. In a modern business sense, application of scorched earth results in the target liquidating "all or substantially all" of its assets, leaving nothing for the raider, thereby eliminating its motivation for acquiring the target. Recently, a new variation of the scorched earth defense has appeared where the target significantly alters its attractiveness by leveraging or depleting its earnings base. The SEC Advisory Board Committee defined scorched earth as "actions taken by the directors of the target to sell off the target's assets to destroy the character of the company to circumvent the bidder's tender offer."

Scorched earth tactics are characterized by the sale of all or substantially all of a firm's assets. The phrase "all or substantially all" is the key identifier of this tactic. However, since the definition of this phrase varies from state to state, a strict categorization of scorched earth is difficult. For example, under Delaware law, the sale of assets "quantitatively vital" to the operation of a corporation which "substantially affects the existence and purpose of the corporation" constitutes such a sale. In a Delaware case, the court held that a sale representing 51 percent of total assets, and accounting for 45 percent of sales and 52 percent of pretax operating income constituted a sale of substantially all corporate assets. The court also held that such a sale prevents the firm from continuing in the business for which it was organized. In contrast, a New York court ruled that the sale of 50 percent of a corporation's assets did not constitute disposal of substantially all corporate assets even though the assets sold were the only income producing assets during the two years prior to the sale. Obviously, the vagaries of the law will create legal employment for some time to come.

Scorched earth is usually employed only as a threat or last resort. Such was the case in St. Joe's defense against Seagram where St. Joe threatened to liquidate if it was unable to find a white knight offering a better price, rather than to submit to Seagram's bid.

Sale of the Crown Jewels: The Jewelry Box Is Almost Empty

While the motivation behind the sale of crown jewel strategy is similar to scorched earth, the severity of the strategy is somewhat less. In a sale of a crown jewel defense, the target usually sells the assets which most interest the raider. Such assets are generally considered the most valuable of the corporation. If the sale is substantial, it would lower the value of the target to a point where the raider withdraws its offer, since the offer could then be worth more than the value of the firm. This is particularly true if the proceeds from the sale were distributed to shareholders, or if the assets were liquidated in a fire sale for less than their value to the raider.

This tactic can involve the sale of physical assets or equity. For example, in the British-based Grand Metropolitan's acquisition of Liggett, the U.S. marketer of J&B Scotch and L&M cigarettes, the target sold its lucrative Austin Nichols Liquor subsidiary in an attempt to fend off Grand Metropolitan. In fact, the Delaware judge who reviewed the sale commented:

> I think it fair to say that it is not open to question that Liggett's desire to sell Austin Nichols was motivated by Grand Met's decision to attempt . . . . to gain control of Liggett by means of the tender offer. Also, since Grand Met has been pursuing the possible acquisition of Austin Nichols from Liggett for more than two years, it seems realistic to assume that it was contemplated by Liggett that the practical effect of the sale of its sought-after asset might be to cause . . . . [Grand Metropolitan] to lose interest in its tender offer.

Despite the unquestioned desire by management to remain independent, the courts allowed this sale to proceed since it was convinced that it also benefited the shareholders and thus satisfied the business judgment doctrine.

In another application of the crown jewel defense, Crown Zellerbach, in its 1985 battle to fight off Anglo-French financier Sir James Goldsmith, announced a plan to liquidate its crown jewel, its timber holdings. Its complex plan included a timber liquidating partnership that would own all of its two million acres of timber holdings. The target's intentions were clear. While the plan was not implemented, most analysts felt that the timber assets were the most desirable business segment to Sir James.

In some cases the liquidated asset is not necessarily the crown jewel, but rather a particularly valued part of the company that might draw bidders' attention. For example, in June 1985, United Airlines seemed to be a target ripe for picking. It faced a pilots' strike that temporarily weakened its position and encountered increased attention, focused on the industry as a result of Carl Icahn's simultaneous moves on TWA. In an action perceived by many as defensive, United announced a plan to sell its highly visible chain of Westin hotels to a series of partnerships formed by itself and Merrill Lynch. Formally, management claimed that the proceeds would be used for general corporate purposes and long-range expansion. In contrast, experts suggested that United's intention was to get an immediate realization of the hotel's underlying value, thereby reducing its own attractiveness as a target.

In Union Carbide's winter 1986 battle against GAF, Union Carbide agreed to sell its polymers and composites business for about $230 million. Since raising cash was an important prerequisite to its ambitious share buyback defense, the sale of assets was not unexpected. While the assets in this case were not the firm's crown jewels, the sale was part of the company's defensive restructuring. Many analysts also argued that selling the assets would enable Union Carbide to either increase the number of shares in its buyback program, raise the offering price, or both. The analysts were right. Early in January 1986, Union Carbide made two simultaneous announcements. First, it announced that it was planning to sell its prized consumer products division and second, it expanded its buyback program to increase by $1.3 billion the value of shares it planned to purchase. The consumer products business was indeed Carbide's crown jewel. To keep the value of its shares from plummeting, it announced a special dividend in which holders of the remaining shares after the buyback would receive all proceeds of the sale exceeding the operation's book value. Yet, the net effect of the defense was calculated to increase its debt-to-equity ratio to a burdensome 14 to 1.

Fatman Defense: Gaining a Few Calories to Repulse the Aggressor

As previously defined, scorched earth involves the liquidation of assets in an effort to decrease value to a corporate raider. A variation of the scorched earth defense has emerged whereby a target company acquires assets in an effort to decrease its attractiveness. For sake of identification, we term this the fatman defense.

The fatman defense can be simply defined as the acquisition of assets by a target company which serves to decrease its short-term value. For example, the target attempts to acquire a company which seriously affects its short-term earnings prospects and most likely adds debt to the balance sheet. In doing so, the target makes itself fat and ugly from the raider's perspective, making it less desirable as a target.

Gearhart's purchase of Geo in its defense against Smith International's takeover attempt is a classic example of fatman. Essentially, Gearhart paid a premium for a company which had lost $58 million on revenues of $285 million in the year prior to its purchase. Thus, Gearhart's move served to drastically change both the profitability and equity base of the company, effectively repelling the Smith takeover effort.

The use of fatman seems to be getting popular. Walt Disney, in its 1984 attempt to get fat fast, made two hurried acquisition announcements in its strategy to fend off Saul Steinberg. It completed a $290 million transaction for Arvida, a Florida real estate developer controlled by the Bass family, and also arranged to buy Gibson Greeting for $318 million. Given that Gibson had been priced at $80 million by former Treasury Secretary Bill Simon's Wesray Corporation just two years earlier, the potential detrimental effects of such a generous purchase price in 1984 were clear. However, this turned out to be a fake fatman. Once Steinberg and his investor groups were paid off with $60 million in greenmail profits, Disney called off the Gibson deal, paying what one investment banker called $15 million in "hush money" to Gibson.

In another case of the fatman defense, St. Regis, in July 1984, feared a hostile tender offer from Australian publisher Rupert Murdoch. As a defense, it purchased a 9.9 percent stake in Colonial Penn Group, a Philadelphia-based insurance company. The timing of the purchase was considered defensive. It transferred St. Regis shares into friendly hands and made its acquisition more expensive. Interestingly, in a 1985 study of publicly traded insurance companies published in the *Journal of Risk and Insurance*, Colonial Penn was ranked as the American insurer most likely to face financial distress. Clearly, with such a record, the Colonial Penn purchase deserves to be classified in the fatman category.

The winter 1986 battle of the gas pipeline firm, MidCon Corporation against the energy partnership, WB Partners, saw an attempt to deploy a unique version of fatman. In the midst of battle, prior to white knight Occidental Petroleum arriving on the scene, MidCon made an effort to acquire Monarch Gas, a closely held utility based in St. Elmo, Illinois. WB Partners alleged that MidCon wanted to buy miniscule Monarch with shareholders' equity of only $600,000 "in an attempt to create additional regulatory obstacles" to the MidCon acquisition. If the transaction would have gone through as planned, any bid for MidCon would have required the approval of the Illinois Commerce Commission. A federal judge, however, agreed with WB Partners and issued a temporary restraining order preventing MidCon's Monarch acquisition. A more common use of fatman was also deployed by MidCon. It involved its $1.14 billion acquisition of Houston-based United Energy Resources. Analysts speculated that the purchase was stimulated by MidCon's low debt-to-equity ratio in an unsuccessful attempt to ward off hostile suitors.

What's Folly to Some Is Sound Business Judgment to Others

Indisputably, the most important factor considered by the courts in their review of the legality of these tactics is the business judgment doctrine. To have these tactics blocked by the courts, it is not enough to prove that the target's actions are motivated by the target's desire to fend off the raider. The plaintiff must also prove that the sale is not in the shareholders' interests. Corporate directors are bound to act in the best interests of the shareholders rather than for their own personal benefit. Acting otherwise constitutes a breach of their fiduciary duty and is a cause for a court to block their actions. The courts, however, tend to presume that management is acting in accordance with the shareholders' interests. The burden of proof is on the plaintiff to show otherwise.

The potential of the fatman defense is also limited by the NYSE and AMEX rules. As mentioned in previous chapters, the rules require shareholder approval for an issue of more than 18.5 percent of a listed company's shares for NYSE and 20 percent for AMEX. Obviously, these rules play an important role in structuring other defenses as well.

Do Shareholders Fuel the Kamikaze Planes?

A shareholder's goal is to maximize the value of his/her equity. Perhaps the clearest example of this is the institutional investor who is bound by fiduciary duty to seek the best possible return.

In the case of scorched earth, shareholders will only benefit from the implementation of the strategy if the raider's offer is clearly below the "quick sale value" of the firm. If the raider's offer is adequate, then shareholders will likely be better off to have the merger consummated.

Sale of a crown jewel offers a variety of options. If the raider's offer significantly undervalues the firm, this strategy serves the shareholder's interest, often by demonstrating the value of the firm. When the strategy is used solely to deter the raider, however, it prevents shareholders from securing the best price for their shares and causes them to lose a choice asset.

Fatman can offer shareholders advantages if executed properly. Under fatman, the defending firm's stock will almost certainly lose value, as this tactic is designed to dilute the company's short-term prospects. If, however, the acquired firm has strong prospects and there are long-range synergies, stockholders in the firm using the fatman defense may benefit in the long run. If successful, the raider is deterred, independence is secured, no assets are lost, and assets providing long-range synergy are added. A short-term speculator seeking quick profits or income will not like this action, but a longer-range investor may. Obviously it is crucial that the strategy be skillfully executed. In the Gearhart example, a potential delisting from the NYSE clearly was not in the shareholders' interest.

Incentives and Speed

Management is required by its fiduciary duty to maximize shareholder value. All of management's actions must be viewed from this perspective. However, while management remains obligated by these fiduciary responsibilities, personal interests clearly motivate the use of these tactics. An executive who founded his own company may have a personal motivation in fighting for his independence. If these motivations can be hidden under the guise of protecting shareholder interests and defended under the business judgment rule, these defense measures may pass judicial scrutiny.

Because of the trauma these tactics cause a firm, they are only employed once all other less extreme remedies are exhausted. Once decided upon, executive action is swift. Management's goal is to deter an ongoing acquisition attempt. Negotiations are traditionally conducted quietly, with the proposed deal announced after it is agreed upon. There is often a close link with other defensive strategies. One such strategy is the lock-up option. In it, an asset can be "committed" to a friendly third party in the event the firm is targeted. Care must be taken to avoid charges of manipulation in these arrangements. Legal action should be anticipated, and the target must be prepared to defend the action as a sound move under the business judgment rule. Consummation of the sale must await the expiration of a 30-day waiting period required for antitrust evaluation.

Scorched Earth: Does It Work?

Among the various defense strategies, liquidation of a going concern is a drastic action and is the most difficult to defend under the business judgment test. However, it is not impossible. The scorched earth defense has been upheld by a Maryland court. The court found that "assuming full disclosure, so-called scorched earth defensive tactics are not manipulative and therefore not inconsistent with federal securities laws." Furthermore, scorched earth could be justified in instances where the directors are able to demonstrate that the liquidated value of the assets would exceed the value of the raider's bid. This is more likely to occur in a company, such as St. Joe, where the firm's wealth is based on tangible assets, mineral wealth in St. Joe's case, as opposed to a company where value is based on intangible assets such as management expertise in the firm's markets. Moreover, because individual mines can be sold off easily without affecting other parts of the firm, this strategy might be appealing to such a natural resource company.

To be useful as a defense tactic, however, scorched earth does not have to be legally viable. It is also useful as a threat. For example, a target will make a statement, if only to increase the tender offer, threatening that the firm is worth more dead than alive. Such was the case in St. Joe's defense against Seagram, where the company's scorched earth defense was based on the claim that its liquidated value was $60 a share, 33 percent more than Seagram's offer.

Another possible objective of this strategy is to buy time, since it is bound to be challenged by the raider and thus will require court review which can involve lengthy proceedings. If the target is searching for a white knight, the delay could provide the time necessary to find the right match among the suitors.

The consequences to the firm of applying this strategy are severe. The strategy is best employed where the shareholders will clearly lose value if a raider's bid is successful. A major impediment to successful implementation of scorched earth is the problem of avoiding "fire sale" prices for assets.

Crown Jewel: Does It Work?

Sale of the crown jewels can be an effective deterrent, particularly if the raider is seeking a specific division or asset of the target. Sale of a key asset where the proceeds are distributed to shareholders deprives the raider of the benefits of the sale and gives the shareholders cash. Such a sale could also serve to demonstrate that the company's value is greater than the raider's offer. Proceeds from a sale could also be reinvested by acquiring a firm which is likely to give the raider antitrust or regulatory problems. However, the time required to put together such a deal often prevents this strategy.

On the negative side, a sale under pressure leads to fire sale conditions and reduces the price that might otherwise be obtained. Furthermore, the sale of the crown jewel is likely to generate substantial amounts of cash, attracting raiders seeking a cash horde. In fact, in some instances this cash could be used by the raider to buy out the target firm. In addition, an agreement to sell major assets at low prices, which are likely to be obtained under the rushed sale, could give rise to claims of breach of fiduciary duty.

The Fatman Defense: Does It Work?

Fatman may be the most viable defense. It decreases the firm's short-term attractiveness without shedding any valuable assets. Implemented properly, it can benefit the firm in the long run if the acquisition, a poor earner now, has good long range prospects of offering synergies. The decrease in the target's cash or increase in leverage acts as a further deterrent.

The implementation of a fatman defense must be made with a clear understanding of the business judgment implications. For this reason, fatman acquisition candidates may be difficult to identify and should be selected with care. Since a fatman acquisition is intended to mortgage the short-term performance of a company for the future, consideration must be given to the justification of such a purchase under the business judgment doctrine.

Gearhart's purchase of Geo is an excellent example of a shrewd fatman defense. Gearhart purchased a company that would serve as a severe drain on earnings. Analysts projected a drop in earnings per share from $1.25 to zero in the year following the acquisition. Nevertheless, Gearhart was able to defend the Geo acquisition from the business judgment perspective in both state and federal courts. Gearhart prevailed as long-run synergies were clearly recognizable. Stock analysts agreed that the combination of Geo's seismic analysis capabilities with Gearhart's wireline technologies would position the company as the leader in the emerging field of "developmental geophysics" which represented the wave of the future in the industry.

The fatman defense may have limitations if not structured properly. Under the stock exchange internal rules, the issuance of new shares is limited. As in the Gearhart-Smith battle, some questioned the viability of issuing a substantial percentage of new shares. While in this case the fatman defense was a shrewd and ultimately succesful strategy, it did have an adverse impact on the firm's short-term performance. Marvin Gearhart ensured his company's independence. But in doing so, shareholders lost 60 percent of the value of their Gearhart shares. The ultimate effectiveness of Gearhart's fatman defense will only become apparent when the long-term synergies of the combined Gearhart-Geo are realized.

Hari-Kari: A Summary of the Issues

These tactics are essentially last ditch efforts because of the trauma they impose on the firm. In most instances, sale of crown jewels and fatman allow the firm to continue as viable businesses and, as such, are more easily justified under the business judgment doctrine. However, sale of a crown jewel does deprive a firm of a key asset and thus jeopardizes future earnings potential. Moreover, contrasted to fatman, the crown jewel strategy is irreversible.

Application of scorched earth means the "clinical death" of the firm and, as such, is more difficult to justify from both a business and legal sense. By deciding to use a scorched earth defense, the board signals that it is better to liquidate, and receive the resulting cash, than operate under new control.

Barring their demise through legal restrictions or changes to current laws, each of the strategies will continue to be used as a defense against hostile takeovers.

6
The Poison Pill Defense

A New Course In The Curriculum: "How To Bake A Poison Cake"

NATIONAL EDUCATION vs. BELL & HOWELL

"We're an aggressive, opportunistic company, and wherever the economics dictate, we'll be making acquisitions." The seriousness of these words, by H. David Bright, president and chief operating officer of National Education Corporation (NEC), was demonstrated in July 1983 when he contacted Bell & Howell Co. and suggested that NEC buy some or all of the company.

The Educators

NEC operated the largest network of publicly owned vocational training schools in the nation, with 1982 revenues of $134.5 million. It ran 47 facilities in over a dozen states and taught everything from secretarial skills to computer programming and electronics. Bright felt that the expanding need to train and retrain workers in the United States provided his company with the prospect of continued growth. An aggressive acquisition program began in 1977 and resulted in the purchase of schools which offered programs in the areas of greatest forecasted demand, such as auto repair, real estate, medical assistance, electronics, and computers. This plan paid off. During the four years prior to 1983, NEC's revenues grew an average of 40 percent each year. In order to maintain this growth, Bright considered it necessary to continue the strategy of acquiring like businesses.

The product mix of Bell & Howell, long known as the leader in the camera and home-movie equipment business, changed significantly between 1978 and 1983. In 1978, 20 percent of sales were from the consumer photo market, and five percent from technical schools. However, intense competition from the Japanese as well as other photo-equipment manufacturers with more advanced and less expensive productions, drove Bell & Howell out of this business. In 1979 Bell & Howell sold its photo-products group to a Japanese partner. As a result, by 1983, Bell & Howell's product mix had changed to over 17 percent from the technical schools, and none from the consumer photo business. It was Bell & Howell's network of technical schools, the DeVry Institute of Technology, which NEC found attractive.

DeVry Institute of Technology

In 1983, Donald N. Frey, Bell & Howell's chairman and CEO, felt that the DeVry Institute was the most successful school of its type in the nation. It was difficult to argue with him when one examined the growth in revenues and profits of this business unit. From 1982 to 1983, DeVry's revenues grew about 30 percent to $117.1 million, while earnings grew tenfold from $1.6 million to $16.8 million. DeVry boasted 11 campuses and had, according to NEC's Bright, "an outstanding reputation with potential employers, a very good curriculum, and an excellent faculty."

DeVry's success stemmed from the fact that its seven schools were utilized 12 months a year, two shifts per day. The professors were not paid to publish or engage in research, only to teach, and expensive extracurricular activities were virtually nonexistent. Basically, DeVry's structure greatly reduced the high overhead costs that are typical of most educational institutions. The elimination of these expenses was reflected in DeVry's bottom line, a 1982 return on sales of over 14 percent.

The Overture

During the first few days of July 1983, Bright contacted Frey by telephone, and suggested that NEC purchase from Bell & Howell its nonmanufacturing businesses, specifically DeVry. Although NEC's primary interest was in vocational training schools, Bright expressed the view that he was willing to purchase either DeVry alone, or all of Bell & Howell. Frey refused to discuss the offer.

At the time of the overture, NEC had already acquired over 4.9 percent of Bell & Howell's 4.64 million common shares. NEC had limited its purchase to that level because a disclosure of intent was required by the SEC for any acquisition of 5 percent or more of another company's stock. Furthermore, NEC was careful in that it was pursuing a company much larger than itself. In fact, Bell & Howell's 1982 revenues were five times larger than NEC's.

A Poison Pill

Rumors of the potential takeover began to hit Wall Street on Friday, July 15. Trading in Bell & Howell was delayed, and when trading opened, Bell & Howell shares climbed $5.75 to $53.25. That same day, the company's management announced that it had instituted a two-step plan to discourage takeover attempts.

Although Frey declined to respond to Bright's telephone offer, the spirit of Bell & Howell's reaction became clear when the details of the plan were released. The strategy it adopted was designed to ward off any two-tiered tender offers. To prevent such offers, Bell & Howell's board declared a convertible preferred stock dividend payable at the rate of one share for each 20 shares of common. This dividend was payable August 26 to stock of record July 26.

There were several defense features of the poison pill issued by Bell & Howell. If an organization merged with Bell & Howell, the holders of the convertible preferred could convert their stock into substitute preferred of the acquiring corporation. This newly created convertible preferred could then be converted into the acquirer's common stock based on a specific conversion ratio. The exact ratio could not be computed prior to the acquisition because of the nature of the complex formula on which the conversion was based. The number of common shares into which the preferred was convertible was determined by a fraction. The numerator of this fraction was the highest value of any of three prices: (1) the market value on the day of the merger; (2) the market value on the date that the tender offer was accepted by 50 percent of the common stock; and (3) the highest price paid by the acquirer for any Bell & Howell stock during the previous 12 months. This was divided by either the market price of the acquirer's stock on the date of the merger or on the date of conversion, whichever was lower. The conversion ratio ensured that all shareholders would receive a fair price for their stock, even if a merger was completed and they had not tendered their shares during the initial offer.

Once issued, the convertible preferred stock was not redeemable by either Bell & Howell or an acquiring party for at least 10 years.

This provision was included for two reasons. First, if it was redeemable, then a company could obtain control of Bell & Howell's board, and then remove all of the defensive measures previously established. Second, if NEC was not successful in its attempt to acquire all or part of Bell & Howell, the defense would still be in place in case another company found Bell & Howell attractive. In the event that an acquiring party purchased 40 percent of the voting stock but never attempted to acquire the remaining stock, then a special redemption provision governed. The remaining stockholders could redeem their shares for cash based on a formula that yielded a "fair price." This price used a conversion ratio similar to the one previously described, and included a provision for accumulated but unpaid dividends. This defense tactic was devised for Bell & Howell by the New York law firm of Wachtell, Lipton, Rosen, and Katz. Jon D. Noel, Bell & Howell's vice president for finance and chief financial officer, said, "We're not trying to stop [anyone] from acquiring the company, but [they're] going to pay what it's worth."

Bell & Howell's cash dividend was established so that the combined preferred and common dividends were slightly higher than on the common alone. This provided a disincentive for shareholders to convert the preferred into common. A formula was established so that this relationship would be maintained as long as the two types of stock remained in existence. Additionally, if an acquisition attempt was successful, the acquiring company would be required to continue paying the dividend on the preferred. The minimum cash value of the dividend would be equal to the amount prevailing at the time of the acquisition.

The voting rights of the preferred were similar to those of the common. The only exception would occur if there was an attempt to eliminate one or more of the defensive features of the preferred. In such an instance, 80 percent of the preferred, voting as a class, had to approve such changes. The vote on the defensive features had to be taken before a vote on any merger or other business combination transaction could take place.

Bell & Howell chose to base its defense on the issuance of previously authorized preferred stock rather than alternative defensive tactics which require shareholder involvement. The reason for this was that the company's directors felt it was necessary to establish the defenses quickly. According to some analysts, prior to the NEC bid, Bell & Howell was an underresearched company, and had not been closely watched by analysts during its divestiture program started in the late 1970s. The NEC overtures caught the public's attention and spotlighted a company that had totally changed its business mix and had reached a point where the future looked rosy. It was the possibility of other companies recognizing the Bell & Howell potential that created the need for urgency in the board's actions.

Additional Action with DeVry

Bell & Howell's board also approved the public offering of 20 percent of the shares in its DeVry subsidiary. The company planned on retaining 80 percent of the shares for itself. The motivation behind this action was to establish an independent market value for the schools. According to Bell & Howell's chief financial officer, Jon Noel, stocks of operations such as DeVry are traditionally traded at price/earnings ratios of 25 to 30, much higher than Bell & Howell's P/E ratio of 15. Since the parent company would still control at least 80 percent of DeVry, the subsidiary's high P/E ratio might also affect investors' judgments of the worth of Bell & Howell stock, thereby maximizing shareholder wealth. Noel also stated that officers of the company had been considering this move for at least six months prior to being contacted by NEC.

A Tough Pill to Swallow

In an interview with *The New York Times* on Wednesday, July 20, NEC's President Bright stated that his company had not reached a decision as to whether it would acquire more shares of Bell & Howell, or whether it would continue to pursue only the DeVry subsidiary. It was not until August that NEC's next tactic was made known.

On August 16, NEC filed suit in the Delaware Court of Chancery asking for a preliminary injunction to block the payment of the convertible preferred stock dividend. NEC filed primarily on the grounds that:

1. Bell & Howell's board did not have the authority to alter the voting rights of its shareholders without a shareholder vote;

2. The board was "inequitably manipulating corporate machin-
    ery" in response to the threat by NEC;

3. The issuance of the preferred convertible into shares of an ag-
    gressor unlawfully restricts the action of a future Bell & Howell
    board. This provision, it argued, prevents the board from ex-
    ercising its best judgment on behalf of the company's share-
    holders.

Chancellor Brown, of the Delaware Court of Chancery, felt that
the 48 hours which he was given to rule on the issues was inadequate. Since he was unable to conclude that either party would
probably win at a final hearing, he was not able to grant NEC's
motion for an injunction stopping the issuance of the poison pill.
Thus, on August 25, the court denied NEC's request, at which time
NEC appealed the ruling. On August 26, a three judge panel was
scheduled to meet and decide whether or not to hear the appeal.
The initial ruling by the court, however, allowed Bell & Howell to
proceed with the issuance of approximately 300,000 shares of convertible preferred stock. The dividend was paid that same day to
stock of record August 26.

Securing the Defense

In late October 1983, Bell & Howell filed with the SEC for an initial
public offering of its DeVry subsidiary. When the public offering
came to market, it was for 1.5 million common shares at $13 each.
This represented 15 percent of DeVry's common stock, while Bell
& Howell continued to own the remaining 85 percent.

Further action on the poison pill was also required. In the weeks
preceding the special shareholder meeting, the preferred stock had
traded for as high as $545, and on the day of the meeting it had
closed at $458. The company stated that such a high price was not
convenient for trading. As a result, it announced a 20-for-1 stock
split. The split shares would be payable in a new convertible preferred that would retain the same defense features for which they
were originally issued.

The Final Chapter

The final chapter in the battle between NEC and Bell & Howell was
the settlement of the lawsuit filed in Delaware. In June 1984, the

suit was resolved by Bell & Howell buying back the 4.9 percent of its stock held by NEC, and by paying all legal fees incurred by that company. When asked to comment, NEC stated that it was pleased with the settlement because the price paid by Bell & Howell exceeded the initial purchase price of the shares. From Bell & Howell's perspective, it was able to successfully defend its company against an unfriendly takeover. Although the cost included the litigation fees of the aggressor, the price seemed a small one to pay in order to keep the company intact.

Throughout the acquisition attempt by NEC, the management of Bell & Howell continued to behave as if it was not being offered a fair price for the overhauled company. In fact, looking back, NEC never placed a formal tender offer for Bell & Howell. When Bell & Howell was approached with a business proposition, it immediately responded with the poison pill defense. Nevertheless, it might have had good reason to be upset with the attempted takeover. The company had just successfully completed a painful period of divestiture of old-line businesses and growth of new business segments, and the management was not willing to give up even a portion of the new Bell & Howell. According to Bell & Howell's Chairman, Donald Frey:

> It is a rare occurrence to take an old-line company that was going down the tubes and turn it into a growing, viable business. We're spending our time running our businesses now rather than jettisoning them. All the years of pain and struggling are over. We've made it.

The "Dallas" Stage: Oil Barons, Boardroom Backbiting, And Courtroom Drama

TESORO PETROLEUM vs. ENSTAR

The story of the battle for the control of Enstar Corporation has all the ingredients of a plot line in "Dallas." There are several oil barons who are childhood friends and scheming foreign investors, all involved in boardroom backbiting and courtroom drama. At the center of it all is Enstar's own "J.R. Ewing," Roy M. Huffington, and his long-time friend Robert West, Jr.

Setting the Scene

West, chairman of the Tesoro Petroleum Company of San Antonio, Texas, was having stockholder troubles. With the help of his friend, the chairman of Charter Co., he managed to fend off an angry takeover attempt by the powerful Belzberg family of Canada. But, like the nastiest of soap operas, his friend later turned on him and sold his shares of Tesoro to the Belzbergs. At this point, West had several strategies available to him. He could buy back the Tesoro shares, take his company private through a leveraged buyout, or possibly, as analysts later speculated, undertake the defensive acquisition of a third company. Enstar appeared a suitable target for this last strategy.

From Indonesia to Alaska: The Enstar Universe

West had long been interested in acquiring Enstar, a Houston-based oil and gas producer and engineering company. West, no doubt, was looking to acquire some synergy. Tesoro derived most of its profits from refining and marketing oil and both companies had adjacent operations in Borneo, Indonesia, and Alaska.

Originally, Enstar was a small Alaskan gas utility incorporated in 1966 under the name of the Alaska Interstate Company. In 1971, it embarked on a joint venture to explore for gas in Indonesia. The venture eventually proved successful. Then, in 1982, Alaska Interstate changed its name to Enstar Corporation and moved its state of incorporation from Alaska to Delaware.

Enstar's primary asset was its 23 percent interest in the Indonesian natural gas joint venture. This partnership accounted for 43 percent of its revenues and over 80 percent of its profits. The gas was produced and supplied to a state-owned processing plant in Indonesia and marketed to Japan. The Indonesian operation generated a cash flow for Enstar estimated by analysts at $7 per share. However, Enstar stock traded at half the P/E ratio of other energy concerns because of the political instability surrounding its operations outside the United States.

In 1983 Enstar's earnings were poor. It earned $30 million on revenues of $349 million. Enstar's shareholders were unhappy because the company had been plowing back earnings into its unprofitable domestic operations. At the May 1983 shareholder meeting, several shark repellant proposals were voted down. Two of the proposals rejected were: (1) a required 80 percent holder approval for takeovers and (2) the requirement that any stockholder action be taken at a meeting, rather than by written consent. With the disapproval of the shark repellents, Enstar became a bona fide target.

The Huffington Connection

The major shareholder of Enstar and the operating partner of the Indonesian joint venture was Roy M. Huffington. Huffington, an "oilman's oilman," was one of the nation's richest and most respected oilmen with a net worth exceeding $100 million. After earning his doctorate in geology at Harvard and after a stint at Exxon, he formed his own company, Roy M. Huffington, Inc.

In 1971, while flying a rickety DC-3 over the jungles of eastern Borneo, he discovered his biggest find, the Bandak gas field in Indonesia. How did a boy from Texas end up in Borneo? Huffington recounted that he was attracted to it because its geology "reminded me of the Delta region of Louisiana." In 1971, he set up the joint venture. O. Charles Honig, Enstar's chairman, was a former undergraduate classmate of Huffington's at Southern Methodist University. Enstar became one of the partners in the venture. The venture took several years to get off the ground, and Enstar contributed a great deal of capital to finance it. In return for providing the funds from 1972 to 1974, Enstar received 39 percent of Roy M. Huffington, Inc.

The relationship between Honig and Huffington soured when Honig insisted that Huffington, Inc. pay dividends. Huffington refused, and in the late 1970s, Honig threatened to sell the stock on the open market, thus forcing Huffington's closely held company to go public. In 1980, Huffington agreed to buy back his stock over the next several years for $53 million. In retribution, he also bought a 13 percent share of Enstar. At the time, Enstar said that it sold back its shares of Huffington because it "had never realized a cash flow from its investment." In March 1983, Enstar named Huffington to its board of directors to help quell the animosity. It didn't work.

Another link in the Huffington connection was Robert West, Jr., the chairman of Tesoro. In 1964, West founded Tesoro by combining a small group of oil producing properties. He then spent more than a decade looking for acquisitions in the energy business. After 15 years and several unsuccessful ventures, including a Puerto Rican refining company that went into Chapter 11, Tesoro finally climbed out from under its heavy debt and was considered an attractive takeover candidate itself. In August 1980, Diamond Shamrock made an unsuccessful bid for the firm. Two years later Tesoro was in trouble again. The firm was forced to sell its profitable North Sea holdings to settle the debt resulting from the loss of its Puerto Rican refinery. As one analyst put it, "Tesoro is very much the product of West's magpie acquisitive instincts." As if that weren't enough, there were other troubles hovering around Tesoro: a confrontation with the SEC over alleged bribery payments to agents of foreign governments, an audit by the IRS, and numerous stockholder suits. Enter Mr. Huffington.

Chairman West of Tesoro was well-acquainted with Huffington. The two had been together at Exxon, and their companies, Tesoro and Huffington, Inc., had embarked on joint oil exploration ventures in Turkey. So, on August 8, 1983, after buying up 172,600 shares of Enstar on the open market, West approached his friend Mr. Huffington and asked if he could buy Huffington's shares of Enstar at $31 a share. Huffington owned 1.3 million shares, or 8.4 percent of the company. Huffington agreed to the sale.

Over lunch in a downtown Houston restaurant, West made known his "friendly" intentions to Honig, the chairman of Enstar. He told him of the agreement to buy Huffington's shares and indicated that he was interested in buying the rest of the company for cash and Tesoro securities. Honig balked at the offer.

The Poison Pill

On August 15, 1983, a week after the Tesoro announcement, Enstar's board voted to issue a dividend of poison pill convertible preferred stock. One new convertible preferred share was issued for every 10 shares of common. Since over 15.5 million common shares were outstanding, this meant that over 1.5 million preferred were issued. Each preferred share could be converted into seven common shares, in effect, a 1.7 to 1 stock split. If converted, this would result in more than 26 million shares outstanding.

The stock dividend contained provisions designed to discourage two-tiered takeover attempts. In such attempts, a company acquires a controlling interest, then typically buys the remaining stock at a reduced price. The Enstar poison pill was structured such that if an investing group acquired 30 percent or more of its voting stock, holders of the preferred could make Enstar redeem it for cash. The redemption feature, which was carefully crafted, created the poison pill. It was to be redeemed at the highest price paid by the acquirer in the tender offer or in transactions prior to the tender offer in which this 30 percent ownership was obtained. The preferred stock would become convertible into preferred stock of the acquiring company. Then the new preferred stock would become convertible into the raider's common stock. The conversion formula into common was designed to assure that the holders of the preferred would receive at least as much as the price paid in the first tier of the offer. Such a conversion formula would greatly dilute the common stock of the acquiring company.

Enstar's preferred stock dividend had originally been set to be payable September 22 based on a record date of August 29. But on August 25, Enstar's board voted to postpone the stock dividend so as to have the ability to evaluate the Delaware court's opinion regarding a similar poison pill issued by Bell & Howell to repel an unwanted takeover by the National Education Corporation. National Education had sued to block the stock dividend by questioning its legality and a ruling was expected in 30 days. Three days later, after the court denied the injunction against Bell & Howell's poison pill, Enstar reinstated the dividend, payable September 22 based on a record date of September 9.

The Strategy Appeared Successful

The poison pill worked. On October 10, Tesoro called off the deal. While Tesoro retained the shares it purchased in the open market and the preferred stock issued by Enstar, it was left with only a 1.1 percent ownership of Enstar. It appeared that Enstar's defensive strategy was successful.

Rumors on Wall Street and speculation in Enstar stock started up again on December 1. The Belzberg family of Western Canada, owners of First City Financial Corporation, acquired a 4.9 percent stake in Enstar. They are renowned for their ability to appear in the middle of profitable takeover situations. In fact, not long before, they pocketed $40 million from their attempted 1980 takeover of the brokerage giant Bache Group. Such transactions enabled them to prosper during a time when most Canadian companies suffered from recessions. Rumor had it that Merrill Lynch was offering the Huffington, Inc. block to several aggressive investors, including the Belzbergs. Wall Street decided that something was afoot. Enstar's reaction: "There is no undue reason to be concerned."

The poison pill was not easy for others to swallow. On December 13, 1983 Richard B. Baldwin III, the son of Enstar's founder, and the Belzbergs filed suit in a Delaware federal court to bar enforcement of the preferred stock provisions. The suit against Honig and Enstar accused them of a "scheme . . . . designed to entrench the management of Enstar and to preserve the power, perquisities, and control enjoyed by Enstar's current officers and directors." They also charged that Enstar's alleged purpose in instituting the poison pill was to "deceive, manipulate, and defraud."

The Proxy Fight

On March 19, 1984, Huffington stunned the board of Enstar by filing notice with the SEC that he would solicit proxies to elect a majority of directors at the May 1984 shareholder meeting. The intention was to oust Enstar's board and impose a board "committed to bringing about a sale or merger of Enstar on terms which would maximize shareholder value as promptly as possible." The slate proposed was believed to include a representative of the Belzbergs, whose lawsuit was still pending. Huffington named the Carter Organization as the proxy solicitor and Lehman Brothers Kuhn Loeb as his financial adviser.

Wall Street considered Huffington's chances for success very high. Enstar stock was trading at about $16 per share, well below analysts' estimates of its liquidation value of $23 per share. Institutional investors, who held over 20 percent of the company, were unhappy with this performance and announced plans to back Huffington in this proxy contest. Alan Gaines, a New York money manager with a 5 percent ownership of Enstar, declared: "Huffington's chances are excellent . . . . It's an easy sell. Any shareholder will go along with [the sale of the company]."

The Search for a White Knight

On March 27, at a hastily called board meeting, Enstar announced that it was putting the company up for sale. "Under the circumstances," said Honig, "we recognize that the company must be sold." They voted to delay the annual meeting from May 24 to June 21 to give themselves more time to find a buyer and retained Morgan Stanley to conduct the search. The board first sought to appease Huffington and prevent the proxy fight by agreeing to immediately replace the three directors up for reelection with Huffington's choices. It also offered to let Huffington "participate in the process" of selling the company. Huffington rejected this proposal and insisted on being given immediate control. The board decided that Huffington should not be given control while the sale was going on. The reason given was the "obvious conflict of interest" in dealing with Enstar's Indonesian joint venture, which was considered to be its most important asset. The joint venture was involved in the exploration and production of natural gas jointly with the Indonesian government. The gas was then liquefied and shipped to Japan. Huffington's firm was a joint venturer with Enstar in this pursuit. If Huffington acquired control of Enstar, he would then hold 43 percent of the Indonesian joint venture which would give him veto power over any proposal by other partners and lock in his position as operator.

Huffington declined to give up the proxy fight. Honig remarked on his stubbornness: "Considering the board's decision to sell the company and our proposal to him, we can't understand his motive in continuing the proxy fight." That day, in very heavy trading, Enstar stock rose 3⅛ to 18⅞.

Upon hearing the news, several companies, including Tesoro Petroleum, expressed an interest in buying Enstar. Institutional investors predicted a quick buyout. Gaines, the 5 percent holder of Enstar, suggested that Enstar management might attempt a leveraged buyout: "That way they can keep their jobs." Enstar's spokesman did not rule out this possibility.

On March 28, the day after the board meeting, Huffington filed a lawsuit in a Delaware court to prevent the postponement of the annual shareholder meeting to June 21. He declared the move "an abuse of office" designed to "further the directors' efforts to continue and to entrench themselves in office." The suit was later overruled.

Huffington said that he rejected the offer of the board seats because he wanted immediate control of the company to bring about a sale as quickly as possible. He claimed that he was in a better position to get a good price for the company because, as a partner in the Indonesian liquefied natural gas partnership, "we're the only ones who know what the Indonesian properties are really worth." If Enstar could line up a good buyer quickly, he would not oppose it, but he was afraid it would be a fire sale.

A Watchdog

On April 3, Honig asked Thomas C. Thompson to join the Enstar board as an independent watchdog for the company's shareholders. This move was seen as an attempt to placate angry shareholders. Thomas C. Thompson Interests, Inc., a closely held energy, real estate, and aviation concern, had bought 4 percent of Enstar's shares back in August, shortly after the poison-pill declaration, and at the time had expressed further interest in obtaining Enstar shares. Thompson led an investment group that held 7.13 percent of Enstar. The group included Gulf States Oil and M.H. Whittier Corporation. Enstar took this move to disprove Huffington's claim that management ignored shareholders' interests. "Here's a large shareholder who is independent of management. He would be a valuable addition to our board," stated an Enstar spokesman. Thompson, in an SEC filing, said that his acceptance was conditioned on the addition of another stockholder representative to the board.

Within a week, Thompson rejected the invitation to join the board, calling it "a meaningless sham," and declared his intention to back Huffington's proxy fight if the company were not sold within the following two months. He said that Enstar refused to allow his direct participation in the sale of the company. He also said that Enstar had an obvious conflict of interest in hiring Morgan Stanley to both search for a buyer and ward off a proxy fight.

No Knight in Sight?

By May 4, 1984, the pressure on Enstar was mounting. Six weeks had passed since Enstar had begun searching for a buyer, and none was yet in sight. Twenty companies had inquired, but there were no takers. Analysts estimated a sale price of $22 to $24 per share, while the market price closed at 19⅜. Investor Alan Gaines's group sold half of its holdings, as hopes for a rich buyout diminished, and stockholders feared they would have to settle for the low end of the estimated price.

Finally, on May 22, 1984, Allied Corporation, a New Jersey-based chemical and energy company, and Ultramar PLC, a London-based energy company, formed a partnership called Unimar Company to offer $18 a share to buy 50.4 percent of Enstar for $257.4 million. Both Allied and Ultramar owned separate 26.5 percent interests in Enstar's Indonesian natural gas venture. Combined, the three companies would own 76 percent of the venture. Expiration of the bid was scheduled for midnight, June 20. The relieved Enstar board accepted the offer. Honig, in a letter to shareholders, declared that the offer "is fair to all of our shareholders — it maximizes the value of their investment."

Several conditions came with the agreement. Enstar agreed to another defensive measure, a lock-up agreement with Unimar. It voted to transfer the voting rights in its Indonesian venture to Allied and Ultramar for the following 10 years. The result was that Enstar's most valuable asset would be controlled by Unimar, thereby making Enstar an unattractive target to other bidders. The agreement with Unimar also included a guarantee that, before the merger, Enstar would try to buy back as much of the poison pill preferred stock as possible. The move was estimated to add $2 to each share. As a result, the bid would total $20 per share.

Major shareholders were furious at this low offer by Unimar. Alan Gaines, the New York money manager, said he would not accept any merger agreement without checking first with Huffington. Thompson's group, the 7 percent stakeholder in Enstar, said the bid was too low and was shocked to hear that Enstar's chairman recommended the bid. He invited others interested in the company to make their bids directly to the shareholders. Huffington called the deal "inadequate in terms of value, uncertain with regard to timing, and not in the best interests of Enstar's shareholders."

Tesoro Petroleum disclosed that on May 22 it too had made an offer for Enstar. West's offer was not specific but pledged at least $20 per share, paid with cash and convertible preferred stock. Unfortunately for Tesoro, it was informed that it was only "hours late" by the time the offer was made and that a lock-up agreement had already been reached with Allied and Ultramar. As a result, Tesoro's offer was withdrawn.

Setbacks in the Unimar Offer

On May 30, Thompson filed suit in Enstar's state of incorporation, Delaware, to block the Unimar takeover. He claimed that the lock-up agreement discouraged alternative bids. Thompson asked that the clause be rescinded or eliminated. He also argued that Enstar's chairman distributed misleading information about the offer and did not disclose the second step in Allied and Ultramar's bid. In that step, the companies planned to issue participation certificates in the Indonesian venture valued at between $13 and $15 a share. The following day, Huffington, who was still leading the proxy fight, filed a similar suit in a Delaware Chancery Court.

Part of Enstar's agreement with Unimar was to sell off the Alaskan pipeline and gas distribution business. A setback to the bid occurred on June 8, when the Alaskan Public Utilities Commission denied Enstar's request for speedy approval of the Alaskan spinoff

prior to the tender offer deadline of June 20. The commission indicated that it would consider the request in August at the earliest.
Huffington worked hard to delay this spinoff, flying to Alaska to
speak before the commission and placing advertisements in An-
chorage newspapers denouncing the spinoff. His aides said the ruling "put a bullet through the heart" of the offer. They said "it was
absolutely critical that Enstar gets the values associated with that
spinoff." Thompson said the delay put the bid "into never-never
land."

On June 12, Unimar announced that it offered $2 per share in
cash for the stock previously offered in the Alaskan ventures. Its
bid now stood at $20 per share for the first step of the two-step offer
and $2 plus the addition of an Indonesian certificate for the second
step. Analysts estimated that these certificates would trade at
around $13 to $15. The expiration and proration deadline for the
restructured bid was extended to midnight, June 26.

The Hostile Offer

Later the same day, on June 12, Roy Huffington led a group of four
oil companies, Pennzoil, Tesoro, Pogo Producing and Roy M. Huffington, Inc. in a hostile bid for Enstar. The bid was $19 a share for
100 percent of Enstar's common shares, $17 in cash immediately,
and then an extra $2 when the Alaskan businesses were sold. It
was conditional on the repeal of the lock-up clause with Unimar.
Enstar's board quickly rejected the bid because of this condition.

Huffington's strategy centered on telling shareholders that if they
voted for his slate in the proxy fight, the slate would support his
tender offer. With the June 20 shareholder meeting rapidly approaching, he sought to gain more time. He filed a lawsuit in Enstar's home state, Texas, alleging that the Allied/Ultramar agreement would be illegal under the federal laws governing utility
ownership. One of Enstar's units supplied natural gas to Anchor-
age, Alaska. A ruling was needed to make a company a public utility. Allied said it expected little trouble in obtaining an exemption
that would make it a public utility holding company, but Huffington charged that the exemption could not be granted without a full
hearing that would delay the bid for weeks.

Huffington Sweetens His Offer

On June 18, Huffington's group slightly sweetened its $19 bid by offering to pay shareholders 12.5 percent interest on any portion of their offer that remained unpaid through September 21, if the offer were accepted. However, Huffington was dealt a severe blow when his friend Thompson abandoned his support. "We are still waiting for one of the parties to make a meaningful increase in their offers — this isn't it." Huffington responded, "Thompson is just looking for more cash, as any holder will do."

On June 19, one day before the annual shareholder meeting and the proxy vote, Huffington was dealt another blow. The Delaware Chancery Court upheld the validity of the lock-up agreement and denied the blocking of the Unimar bid. Although the Huffington group's bid was conditioned on the repeal of this clause, it decided against calling off its rival bid. Huffington was unhappy that the judge had found his suit "troublesome," but hoped that separate court challenges in Alaska and Houston would force repeal of the agreement.

The Stormy Meeting and a Popularity Contest

At Enstar's annual shareholder meeting, the proxy contest before the stockholders was to decide whether to vote for or against a Huffington proxy to increase the board from 12 to 18 people and whether to elect Huffington's 10 nominees.

The meeting was stormy, but brief. After spending most of his time trying to talk louder than Huffington's group, Honig adjourned the meeting after only 35 minutes. Huffington's aides quickly produced bullhorns and urged shareholders to remain, even though the board had walked out. They wanted to vote down a new legal clause Enstar adopted in order to strengthen the Allied–Ultramar offer. This new legal clause, a final weapon in Enstar's arsenal, would allow Allied and Ultramar to exercise control immediately over Enstar as soon as they gained a majority of the shares in their tender offer.

Huffington declared victory in the proxy contest held during the meeting, but the final count would not be announced until July.

Also, the fight was not really over. This was a fight for seats on the board, and not a determination of who would get the tendered shares. Surprisingly, some of the holders who supported Huffington said they might tender their shares to Allied–Ultramar, whose offer was to expire June 26 at midnight. Alan Gaines, who was leaning toward Allied–Ultramar, said, "The proxy contest doesn't matter. It's just a popularity contest."

On June 24, Huffington's attempt to block the Unimar bid was again stymied when the Alaska Public Utilities Commission rejected his claim that Enstar was in contempt because it did not seek the Commission's permission before accepting the offer. Also, the Alaskan Superior Court dismissed the request for a temporary restraining order and injunction against the merger. It said the merger was in accordance with the Utilities Commission's regulations and also dismissed Huffington's lawsuit against the commission's endorsement.

What now remained was for the shareholders to decide between tendering their shares to Huffington's group for $19 in cash for 100 percent of the shares or to Unimar and receive $20 for 50.4 percent of the shares. The blended value placed on the latter bid, including its second step, was estimated at $18. However, the lock-up agreement giving Enstar's Indonesian joint venture voting rights to Unimar was an important consideration in deciding whether Huffington could actually control the company if his group won.

The Fight Ends

On June 26, hours before their tender offer expired, Allied and Ultramar claimed victory in their attempt to control Enstar. Their tender offer for 14.3 million shares had drawn 21.8 million shares. Even Huffington conceded, and tendered his company's shares to Allied–Ultramar. However, he said he would still seek to improve the total cash yield for Enstar shareholders. The recourse open was to file suit.

People were very surprised at the odd situation of Huffington's winning the proxy fight but losing in the tender offer. One Wall Street arbitrageur commented, "Everyone I knew voted for him last week and against him this week. Everyone was hoping he could do something in those few days to up the bids. I'm still in Huffington's camp, but if you don't tender now, what will you get?"

At the June 27 annual meeting, Allied and Ultramar took control of Enstar. They doubled the number of directors on the board and filled the new seats with their people. Even though Huffington had won the proxy and could place his people on the board, Unimar now had a majority and Huffington was rendered powerless.

On July 3, Huffington agreed to a $3 million settlement with Unimar. In it, he agreed to terminate all outstanding litigation against the merger, resign from the board, withdraw all resolutions he made at the last shareholder meeting, and not oppose the pending merger. The $3 million was partial reimbursement for expenses incurred in his proxy solicitation. The directors elected on Huffington's slate also resigned. Huffington planned to resign from his company and let his son, R. Michael Huffington, take over.

The transaction was finally completed as planned. The two-tier acquisition of Enstar's common was executed and all that remained was the disposition of the poison pill preferred. Each Enstar convertible preferred was exchanged for $14 in cash plus seven Indonesian participation units.

Allied took over the operation of Enstar's domestic oil and gas operations, with the profit going to the partnership, Unimar. With this final transaction, the boardroom backbiting and courtroom drama came to a close.

In perspective, one stockbroker remarked on the incredible fight that had occurred, "this is a quagmire I'm sorry I ever got into . . . . It's a comedy."

From Woodrow Wilson To Nancy Reagan: The China-Gate And The Poison Pill

BROWN-FORMAN vs. LENOX

In its March 31, 1983 issue, *Financial World* listed Lenox chairman John Chamberlin as one of its finalists in its "CEO of the year pageant." He was cited for his efforts to diversify Lenox's earnings base. Chamberlin's work had led to a steady increase in the price of Lenox's stock in 1982.

1982 was not as kind to W.L. Lyons Brown Jr., president of Brown-Forman Inc. Though it was earning the highest return on sales in the business, Brown was concerned because the company was running out of suitable candidates for acquisition within its own industry. Brown-Forman was also falling victim to the new health and fitness awareness sweeping the country, which was threatening to severely affect its historic 30 percent annual growth rate.

Brown-Forman was controlled by the same family since George Garvin Brown sealed the first bottle of Old Forester bourbon in 1870. It is told that Robinson S. "Robbie" Brown Jr., former chairman and cousin of W.L. Lyons Brown, once suggested to a liquor distributor "If you are on a railroad train and it's moving in the wrong direction don't be afraid to get off." His cousin, great grandson of George Garvin, had trouble following that advice.

Following a meeting of Brown–Forman's board on June 7, Brown called Chamberlin to inform him that his company would announce an offer for Lenox's stock with the intention of merging the two companies. He requested a meeting with Chamberlin to pursue the matter. Chamberlin told Brown that he would call back in the morning.

The following day Chamberlin returned Brown's call and "politely" told him that Lenox would prefer to remain independent. The same afternoon Brown sent a four page letter to Lenox's chairman expressing regret that his offer had not been more enthusiastically received. He stated that he "wanted this to be done on a friendly basis," and that his company intended to pursue the merger.

Though initially unwilling to comment on these events, Chamberlin would later give a different version of this "polite" discussion. "Is it friendly when somebody calls you at a quarter of ten at night at home? Is it friendly if he tells you that, unless you meet him tomorrow morning, there will be a tender offer tomorrow afternoon?" The thin veneer of amicability was soon stripped off and what followed was a street fight pitting Martin Siegel, takeover defense specialist for Kidder, Peabody, against Peter Kellner, a Morgan Stanley managing partner, advisor to Brown–Forman.

The Brand Names

Lenox, Inc., based in Lawrenceville, N.J. has been a symbol of fine American china since 1917, when Woodrow Wilson replaced the imported china used in the White House with Lenox products. This tradition was continued in the infamous "china-gate" incident, when First Lady Nancy Reagan ordered $209,000 worth of the company's presidential china. The company also had recently acquired the Hartman Luggage Company, another prestige brand name. Lenox's growth rate over the 10 year period from 1973 to 1982 exceeded 150 percent, with sales growing from $102 million in 1973 to $255 million in 1982. However, sales in 1982 were down 2 percent from 1981 due to several factors affecting the jewelry industry. Two of their jewelry divisions, Keepsake and Rosenthal, had suffered losses, as did many other companies in the industry. A large drop in gold and diamond prices caused these two divisions to suffer large inventory losses while a slowdown in the economy led them to experience a sharp sales decline. Lenox was also involved with several less glamourous products including candles, soaps, and class rings. With Chamberlin as CEO, the company enjoyed a period of strong growth. Some thought this growth was not fully reflected in its stock price. In mid-1982, E.F. Hutton's capital management unit started to buy Lenox stock at $30 to $40 per share, after its screening technique picked up the stock as undervalued. During the year following June 1982, the price of the stock ranged from $35.25 to $59.75. On April 30, 1983, Lenox announced a 2-for-1 stock split payable July 1 to stockholders of record on Friday, June 3. Mr. Brown would later admit that he had been eyeing Lenox for some time, with the recent strong upsurge in the stock price, determined that he could not afford to wait any longer.

Brown–Forman was a Louisville-based marketer of brands of liquor such as Jack Daniels, Canadian Mist, Southern Comfort, Bolla, and Martell. It gained a reputation as a leader through its ability to spot brands that were poised to take off. While in 1982 the company earned $95.2 million on $885 million in sales, it had been looking to expand further for some time. To do so, it established a department to find suitable candidates which met the companies' criteria. These criteria included proven leadership and the ability to earn a

14 percent return on investment. In the three years since its development, the group was unable to find any such targets.

The Offer

On June 8, 1983, Brown–Forman announced an $87 per share offer for Lenox's 4.5 million shares outstanding. The offer was not preconditioned on a minimum number of shares being tendered and was at a price that was a substantial 21 times Lenox's 1982 earnings. The market responded to the June 8 offer by bidding up the price of Lenox's stock to $86.50. Anticipating maneuvers to block the deal, Brown–Forman instituted proceedings in federal courts in New Jersey and Missouri to stop Lenox from enforcing takeover laws in those states.

At this time Lenox asked its investment banker, Kidder, Peabody, and its outside counsel to review the proposed offer and to report back to the board. Chamberlin asked shareholders to defer any decisions until after a board meeting scheduled for Tuesday, June 14.

The proposed merger struck many analysts as well as Brown–Forman officers as surprising. Joseph Frazzano, an analyst for Oppenheimer & Co., asked, "Why buy a company that grows at half the rate of your own?" Others commented on the apparent dissimilarity of products and marketing style. A competitor remarked, "They [Brown–Forman] don't bring anything to the place-setting." Chamberlin responded to Brown's assertion that both companies "deal in areas that revolve around gracious living and entertainment." He commented that "We sell to the high end customer. I guess they do, too, but so does Mercedes, so do expensive swimming pools. Does that mean I should get into those businesses?" Richard T. Gralton, president of Savin Corporation and a former president of Lenox, foresaw a "natural aggravation between two types of marketing people who will think differently." He saw Brown–Forman as a product line built around distinctive packaging and taste, while Lenox's strength was in product design.

Mr. Brown likened Brown–Forman's selection of Lenox to Lenox's decision to acquire Hartman Luggage earlier that year. In his letter to Chamberlin he wrote, "Your acquisition of Hartman demonstrates the sound rationale behind acquiring a successful company in a different business."

"We Are Going to Remain Independent"

Lenox immediately began consulting with Martin Siegel, who was known for his aggressive tactics in resisting tender offers. It was conceded that this would be a tough fight, made difficult by the high price Brown–Forman was offering. The situation was further complicated by the fact that institutions owned more than 50 percent of Lenox shares, while Lenox insiders owned less than 5 percent. Lenox also did not enjoy a strong enough cash position to be able to buy back its own shares.

Lenox did, however, have some protection in the antitakeover provisions adopted by its holders in 1978. Those supermajority rules required that any merger offer had to win the approval of at least 75 percent of the 4.5 million shares outstanding.

On June 15, the Lenox board voted to reject Brown–Forman's offer. In an interview following the meeting, John Chamberlin announced, "We are going to remain independent." However, other actions agreed on during the meeting seemed to indicate that Chamberlin's bravado was just a front.

The Poison Pill

While the Brown–Forman offer was evaluated by Kidder, Peabody, Martin Siegel devised a poison pill defense to be used by Lenox. Luckily for Lenox, back in 1968, its charter was amended allowing its management to issue a block of "blank check" preferred stock. This provision enabled Lenox's management to move based on Siegel's planned defense. This defense was aimed at diluting the controlling interest of the Brown family in Brown-Forman. At the time of the offer, the Brown family controlled 62.2 percent of the voting common stock of Brown–Forman.

The defensive strategy that had been devised consisted of two steps. The first step in the defense, the declaration of the stock dividend, called for 250,000 shares of convertible preferred stock with a call provision, to be distributed to all existing common stockholders. One share of new preferred stock would be issued for every 40 shares of common stock in existence after a previously approved stock split took place. The new issue would be payable August 1 to holders of record as of June 25. This preferred stock was to have a redemption value of $500 per share if called, but it could not be called for at least 15 years without prior approval of at least 95 percent of the preferred stockholders. The conversion feature allowed the convertible preferred stock to be converted at any time into 40 shares of Lenox common. However, the objective of Lenox's management was to avoid conversion of the preferred stock into its own shares. In order to give its shareholders an incentive to hold the preferred, Lenox upped the dividend from 96 cents per common share to a combined $1.08 for a holder of both the convertible preferred and the common.

The heart of the defense was the conversion provision of the preferred stock. Not only was it convertible to Lenox common, but it also carried a "forced equity" provision as well. This "forced equity" or "flip-over" provision would be triggered if any merger partner with Lenox owned 20 percent or more of Lenox's stock at the time of the merger. The Lenox preferred stock would be convertible into voting stock of the new acquiring company on a pro-rata basis. This convertibility could only be overridden by a supermajority vote of 95 percent of the preferred stockholders. The net effect of these provisions on Brown–Forman was that in the event the poison pill was issued and the merger was completed, the controlling interest of the Brown family could be substantially reduced. For example, if 80 percent of Lenox's shares were tendered, the Brown family's stake would be reduced from its initial 62 percent to about 53 percent.

The second step in the defense, and one that was voiced to the press by Kidder, Peabody and Lenox officials, was that another 250,000 shares of unissued preferred stock could be sold to an outsider. They indicated that this step would be used only if the first part of the defense failed to deter Brown–Forman from completing its tender offer. It was possible, however, that in the second step Lenox would not be legally allowed to place this stock in the hands of an outsider for less than the Brown–Forman offer of $87 per share.

At such a price there were few possible takers, unless Lenox was willing to "sweeten" the deal to an outsider. This could be done by offering an extremely high dividend on the preferred in order to gain shareholders' support for the poison pill. It seemed unlikely that Lenox shareholders would approve such an expenditure. Nevertheless, Herbert M. Wachtel, a lawyer representing Lenox, claimed that Lenox directors had the right to do whatever was necessary to resist any hostile takeover bid once they determined that such an offer was not in the shareholders' best interest. Despite Lenox's blitz of defensive measures, Brown–Forman did not indicate any intention to withdraw.

It reacted to the Lenox defense in two ways. First it reaffirmed its intention to continue with its tender offer and expressed the hope that any merger could be accomplished on a friendly basis. Its second reaction was to announce that any common stock tendered without the accompanying preferred stock would be rejected.

The response to this announcement was mixed. The legality of the maneuver was as yet untested, as the "flip-over" provision had never before been used as an antitakeover defense. Some analysts viewed this as a "smokescreen" meant to "confuse Lenox shareholders who might be considering tendering their shares." They pointed out that Brown–Forman could negate the strategy by insisting that the new preferred shares be tendered along with the common. The high price being offered, $87 a share, was seen as a possible incentive for Lenox shareholders to go along with this provision. At the same time, Lenox prepared for the worst. On June 16, it filed documents with the SEC detailing golden parachute contracts offered to eight of its executives. Under the agreement, Chamberlin would, if terminated, receive five times his salary, or at least $905,000. Other provisions included the purchase of an annuity contract providing benefits equal to the company's retirement plan as well as life and medical insurance. The total value of this generous agreement was $7 million.

Despite Lenox's multipronged defense plan, outside observers felt that Brown–Forman had a number of options open to it in attacking Lenox. They felt that the poison pill's binding effect on an acquiring company would be ruled as unenforceable in any court test. The feeling was that Brown–Forman could go through with the merger and then use the courts to prevent the Lenox preferred from being converted into Brown–Forman voting stock.

Another option open to Brown–Forman was to do nothing about the Lenox preferred, with Brown–Forman hoping that most of it would be tendered along with the common. Some independent estimates were that as much as 80 percent of Lenox's stock would be tendered. As soon as the tender offer was completed, Brown–Foreman could take one of two paths. It could make a second offer for the remaining Lenox preferred or continue with the merger and allow the Lenox preferred to be converted. If the stock was converted it could then buy sufficient shares of its own voting stock on the open market for the Brown family to retain control.

On June 16, Brown–Forman filed suit in federal district court in New Jersey to block Lenox's defensive maneuvers. The suit charged that Lenox's board lacked both the legal authority and stockholder approval to use the preferred stock as a takeover defense. It further charged that issuance of the preferred stock was in violation of Section 14(e) of the Exchange Act and that its sole purpose was to preserve control of Lenox by the current management. Brown–Forman asked the court to order Lenox to refrain from taking any "extraordinary actions," such as the sale of assets beyond that necessary for the conduct of its business and the further issuance of preferred stock.

Four days later, on June 20, U.S. District Judge H. Lee Sarokin denied Brown–Forman's request for a temporary restraining order against Lenox. He suggested that a prior restraint by the court "might unjustly harm the credibility of Lenox's defense" and affect its stock price. "Gains should be won or lost in the marketplace," he added. Because actions already taken by the Lenox board weren't "clearly illegal and contrary to the shareholders' interests," the judge did not feel that such restraint by the court was warranted. Brown–Forman attorneys were not discouraged, however, since the judge did not pass on the legality of Lenox's actions. That decision was scheduled for a hearing on Tuesday, June 27. It was now high noon, the town square had been cleared for the combatants, and the only question was who would pull the trigger first.

I Dare You

Now, it was Lenox's turn to visit the judge. In an effort to force Brown–Forman's hand, Lenox went on the offensive, filing a suit in federal court in Newark, New Jersey. It sought to prohibit Brown–Forman from proceeding with its tender offer on the grounds that it had made misleading statements. Lenox wanted to induce Brown–Forman to state that it would continue with the tender offer under conditions imposed by Lenox's poison pill. Lenox was reacting to the suggestion by Brown–Forman that if the special dividend was upheld, it would force Brown–Forman to "reassess the manner in which the acquisition is completed, including the desirability of its present intention of pursuing the merger."

Brown–Forman responded to the suit by insisting that it would not back out of the offer, but it did suggest that the offer was now contingent upon its receiving an appropriate amount of the preferred stock. It also insisted that any common stock tendered should include the preferred, and if not, it would withhold part of the $87. The company also announced that the proposed merger had been cleared by the FTC.

It became apparent that Brown–Forman was beginning to gain the upper hand. As a result, Lenox scheduled a meeting of its board to discuss further actions. Observers said they expected the meeting would either seek to invite a white knight, "add teeth to the defense," or map out peace negotiations. The meeting was scheduled for the day before the legality of Lenox's poison pill was scheduled to be addressed in federal court. Lenox stock closed at $85.25 with a composite turnover of about 17 percent of the total shares outstanding. The institutions holding Lenox stock had long since sold out, and it was estimated that arbitrageurs were controlling 60 percent of the shares. A group led by Ivan Boesky was holding almost a half million shares. It seemed that the market was displaying little faith in Lenox's efforts.

It was now becoming obvious that Lenox's strategy would be steamrolled by Brown–Forman's high bid. The offer showed every sign of being able to attract 95 percent of the outstanding shares. Siegel recommended to Lenox's Chamberlin that he must now "drop the other shoe." The "shoe" was the placement of convertible preferred into the hands of institutions. Like the first round of the poison pill, this round was designed to be converted at terms extremely unfavorable to the acquirer.

Can We Talk Here?

The night before the scheduled shareholder meeting, Chamberlin called Brown suggesting that some accommodation might be reached. No agreement was reached that night, but during a conference call the following morning at the Lenox board meeting, the battle ended. The armistice called for Brown–Forman to increase its offer to $90 per share. In return, Lenox board members would recommend the deal to the shareholders and cancel the defensive moves it had instituted. Under the terms of the deal Lenox managers would be allowed to keep their golden parachutes, which the company had funded prior to the merger. Brown–Forman also stated its intention of electing John Chamberlin to its board.

It had appeared that Lenox would stop at nothing to avert a takeover. Its poison pill strategy, if fully implemented, would have increased its shares outstanding from 9 million to 36 million in the space of two months. When the dust settled, the principals spoke confidently of their actions. Peter Kellner, the advisor to Brown–Forman, insisted that the distiller's "preemptive pricing strategy" had shut off any defensive measures.

However, on the day the two companies announced their agreement, the price of Brown–Forman stock fell 1⅝ to $43.25 a share. Investors obviously felt Brown–Forman's "preemptive pricing strategy" resulted in its paying too high a premium for its acquisition of Lenox. Though Lenox's effort to poison the distiller's spirits ended in its loss of independence, Lenox's shareholders walked away smiling. Earning a 50 percent return in three weeks, they could now buy plenty of china.

The Common Thread

As might be surmised from its name, the poison pill is designed to be lethal for an aggressor to digest. The pill is created to poison the raider to the extent that the benefits of acquiring the target are out-weighed by the pain of doing so. The primary mechanism for caus-ing this pain is the issuance of a stock dividend to the target's shareholders. The keys to its effectiveness are both the special con-version and redemption features which significantly reduce the ag-gressor's control of the target. The most powerful part of the pill takes place when the stock dividend is converted to shares of the acquirer. This feature is likely to cause severe gastric distress to any raider wishing to swallow the target.

Before going any further, though, let us consider the objectives of using the pill. It is obviously a response to an unfriendly take-over attempt, either imminent or threatened. It is primarily de-signed to lessen the likelihood that the target's shareholders may be "frozen out" in a two-stage acquisition. After an aggressor has obtained majority control in the first stage, the remaining stock-holders could be at the mercy of that aggressor. They are dependent on the aggressor's willingness to pay as much for the stock as the aggressor paid to obtain control initially. Shareholders, aware of freeze-out possibilities, could be stampeded into succumbing to the first stage of the tender offer solely to avoid the loss of the initial offer premium. Raiders are usually aware of this aspect of share-holder psychology, and the poison pill is frequently structured to protect and assuage shareholder concerns. Although it may not protect the target from an eventual takeover, in the cases presented earlier it provided enough threat to at least successfully delay the merger and result in higher offers for the target companies. For ex-ample, in the Lenox battle with Brown–Forman, Lenox stockhold-ers were given a higher price for their stock and were not frozen out in the second half of a two–stage merger.

As was seen in the classic Bell & Howell poison pill defense against National Education Corporation, the strategy can work to keep the aggressor away. The pill as well as the determination of the target company to remain independent were strong enough to fend off the raider. After a preliminary injunction against the poi-son pill was denied, NEC made no further significant takeover at-tempts and eventually sold back its Bell & Howell stock. In this case, the motives of the target company were probably stronger than in the other cases. Bell & Howell had successfully been improving its image and was not at all interested in a merger. Here, the determination of the target company may have been a key factor in the successful deployment of the poison pill.

The poison pill can also be used in conjunction with a lock-up provision. In such a case it can provide further protection against stock accumulation or a merger attempt by a third party. The lock-up provision played a significant role in the Enstar defense against Tesoro.

Concocting the Poison

To better understand the ingredients of the poison, it is important to recognize some of its special characteristics. While the conversion of the convertible preferred is the lethal component, each of the following elements has its own role in the deadly potion.

"Blank Check." In order for the poison pill defense to be most effective, stockholders must have previously authorized a large block of blank check preferred stock. This stock is not issued until the time the defense is required. Although the conversion of the preferred stock into the target's common stock is not the goal of the poison pill, a situation may arise where conversion takes place and common is necessary. To prepare for such a situation, management should also authorize an issue of common stock. Without it, the board cannot institute a poison pill but rather would have to go through the lengthy process of obtaining shareholder approval. This would delay the time necessary to deploy the convertible preferred and could make the defensive measure less effective. The importance of the blank check is not only its preauthorization, but the fact that it has no specific provisions. Later, when the need arises, this allows the board to design an issue that would be most abhorrent to the "enemy" company attempting the acquisition. Once all provisions have been carefully structured, it takes only the approval of the board to establish the deadly potion. In most of the cases examined, the vote by the board was the first hint of the defending company's response. The other components of the convertible preferred issue that make it so unattractive to the acquirer are the conversion feature, dividends, voting rights, call protection, and the redemption feature.

Conversion.   One of the key ingredients in the poison pill recipe is the convertibility feature. The special issue preferred stock can be converted in different ways, depending on how management wishes to tailor its defense. The target's management, in structuring the defense, should determine the most vulnerable area of the raider. The pill should then be structured to attack this vulnerability. In tailoring the conversion features, typically the following alternatives are considered:

- The preferred can be "flipped over" into convertible preferred stock of the raider. This feature poisons the raider in two steps. First, the target's convertible preferred is converted into the raider's convertible preferred. This is often referred to as substitute preferred. The second step involves the conversion of the raider's convertible preferred into its common. This second step contains the lethal poison consisting of the potentially significant dilution to the raider. Usually the conversion is structured to facilitate the flip-over at a most advantageous price to the target's shareholders and a most disadvantageous price to the aggressor.

- The preferred can give the target's shareholders the right to directly convert the stock into common shares of the acquiring company at, for instance, one-half the current market price. This is commonly known as the "forced equity" provision.

- The preferred can be swapped for notes that must be honored by the aggressor. This is particularly effective against corporate raiders that are already highly leveraged.

As can readily be seen, numerous conversion options are available. One can structure the pill according to management's best view of where their opponent's Achilles' heel may be. It is important to know that the conversion of the poison pill is conditional. It will be executed only when an aggressor acquires a certain fraction of the target's voting stock. In formulating the rate at which the convertible preferred will be converted into the raider's common shares, management has several options:

1.   To signal a very clearcut poison pill to the aggressor. In February 1985, Homestake, for example, issued a poison pill in which

its shareholders were able to acquire shares of the aggressor at 50 percent of the aggressor's market price.

2. To make the consequence of a takeover more uncertain and thereby expand the range of possible effects on the raider. As exhibited in the Bell & Howell pill, the number of the raider's shares to be received by Bell & Howell shareholders was based on a complex formula. Given that the formula was predicated on the stock prices of both the raider and target at several different points in time, it was virtually impossible to know the rate of conversion at the time of the raid.

To determine which option to use, management must decide which of the structures is more likely to thwart a possible acquirer—the explicit terms of a potentially devastating pill or the uncertainty associated with market movements and the possible deadly consequences.

Dividends.   These are usually fixed and cumulative and may be structured to be ultra-preferred, that is, senior to all other preferred shares of the company. At any time, however, the dividend will be higher than that on common shares. This provides a disincentive for holders to convert the preferred into the target's common stock. It also allows the poison pill to remain in effect even after an initial raider has been deterred from the acquisition. This is important because the original hostile bid, even though it may fail, serves only to bring attention to the defending company, that is, "put it in play." This may be only the beginning of the drama, many other companies may be waiting in the wings. As a result, a favorable dividend is crucial to avoid conversion.

Since the distribution of a convertible preferred is similar to a stock split, the dividend on each share of common is reduced, but the shareholder also receives the dividend on the preferred. In total, the combined dividend will be greater than the common alone, typically set at 110 to 125 percent of the common.

An additional provision protects the dividend-receiving shareholder. If a certain percentage of the defending company is acquired by a raider, the preferred stock dividend becomes fixed at the level it was prior to the acquisition. This protects the shareholders of an acquired company from losing the dividend income they would have received if their company had successfully defended itself.

Voting Rights. Typically, the preferred stock has voting rights identical to common stock. The provision of voting rights is an especially important defense against a family controlled firm which typically would be more sensitive to the issue of dilution. For example, the Brown family had historically controlled Brown–Forman through two classes of common stock, one voting and the other nonvoting, where the Brown family controlled the voting shares. In this case, Lenox's poison pill was a major concern to the raider. In many situations, each share of preferred is designed such that the number of votes is equal to half the number of the target's common shares into which they can be converted. More specifically, this occurs in cases such as Lenox, where conversion of the convertible preferred results in a two for one split of the common. In certain instances the preferred has special class voting rights. When an equity security with a ranking that jeopardizes the seniority of the preferred is proposed, the preferred voting as a class can block the new security. Additionally, any amendment to the corporate charter that adversely affects the terms of the preferred stock typically requires the approval of at least 80 percent of the preferred holders. The one situation in which this may not hold occurs when an acquirer does not control a sufficient percentage of shares for the pill to take effect. In other words, in the event that a bidder holds less than the threshold percentage of shares required to enact the pill and gets the blessing of the target's board, a friendly takeover can occur. This exception can take place only if the poison pill provision was carefully drafted to allow the board to neutralize the poison pill's effect.

In the event the aggressor fails to honor any of the provisions associated with the preferred, the holders typically have special rights. For example, voting separately as a class, they can elect corporate directors at a special meeting called for that purpose. This is aimed to discipline aggressors such that the poison pill provision will be honored.

Call Protection and Redemption. The preferred stock is not callable for a specific number of years. For example, Lenox, in its battle against Brown–Forman, instituted a poison pill with 15 year redemption protection unless 95 percent of its stockholders consented to its removal. Similarly, Bell & Howell preferred was not redeemable by Bell & Howell for at least 10 years. This was necessary to ensure that the defense would remain in place as a deterrent to other potential raiders. The redemption feature is usually structured to accomplish two goals: provide a redemption price that is higher than the tender offer, and tie the aggressor into a pricing structure that protects the target's shareholders against a second-step freeze-out. The redemption price is usually higher than the value of the hostile offer and serves to provide one more disincentive for shareholders to accept the aggressor's offer. The structure of the redemption is often designed with some special provisions. For example, if a raider obtains a stated percentage of voting power, say 25 to 30 percent, and does not complete a second-step acquisition within 120 days, the preferred is redeemable at any time. The redemption price equals the highest price paid by that raider during the prior 12 months for either the target's common or its preferred. The real kicker is that this price must be paid in cash unless there is a legal reason preventing the target from allowing the completion of the transaction for cash. In this exception, the shareholders have the right to redeem the preferred in exchange for common stock on a more favorable basis than a cash transaction would have been. In particular, the conversion ratio would once again be based on the highest price paid by the raider in the past 12 months. However, in this case it would be divided by 85 percent of the current market price of the acquirer's common. Some raiders do "bootstrap" acquisitions, financing the second-step out of the assets acquired in the first step of the takeover. The 120-day timeframe and the cash requirement may combine to make such tactics difficult to execute. And that, in turn, may serve to discourage those raiders without extensive cash reserves or willingness to take on more debt.

Can the Pill Poison the Preparer?

There are a number of reasons why a poison pill defense should be used with caution. The pill, once it has been enacted, can also act as a deterrent to any white knight or any future merger partner. The existence of a large block of stock that can be converted at any time into voting stock of a surviving company can act the same for white knights as well as unwanted suitors. The art of tailoring the pill requires fitting a set of circumstances without precluding future welcomed mergers or other investment decisions. For example, in the case of Bell & Howell, NEC was repelled but there were no white knights in the wings. In the Enstar–Tesoro fight, it took almost a full year before several potential buyers appeared on the scene.

Planning in advance may avoid the "white knight repellent" problem. For example, in October 1984, Jerrico Inc., the owner of Long John Silver's and Jerry's Restaurants, instituted a pill to repel a hostile suitor. It involved the distribution of warrants to the stockholder enabling him/her to buy an additional share of stock for $32. This warrant provision was to be triggered only if a third party bought 20 percent of the shares or announced a tender offer for more than 40 percent of the stock. However, Jerrico's management was careful enough to include a provision that left the door open for friendly mergers. Specifically, Jerrico could buy back the warrants for 5 cents a share if its board accepted an offer from a welcome white knight.

Several months later, in a battle of major league proportions, Phillips Petroleum announced its poison pill in its fight to repel takeover shark Carl Icahn. Similar to the warrants issued by Jericho, Phillips issued rights enabling its shareholders to convert them to notes in the event a hostile group were to acquire 30 percent or more of Phillips common stock. Keeping the options open for a white knight, the board could disarm itself of the poison pill's effect by redeeming the rights for 25 cents each.

Another giant to take steps to ward off unfriendly advances while maintaining sufficient flexibility to merge with a friendly acquirer was Gillette. During the last week of 1985, the maker of razors, blades and pens set in motion the prerequisites for a poison pill. The board approved a preferred stock purchase right for each share of Gillette common, giving the holder the right to buy shares in the post-merger company at 50 percent of its market price. To preserve its options to engage in a friendly merger, Gillette can redeem the rights for one cent any time before a potential acquirer obtains 20 percent of Gillette or within 10 days after an investor obtains a 20 percent stake.

A "successful" poison pill defense could leave a company in severe financial distress. It would have the additional burden of paying dividends on the newly issued preferred. In making the preferred stock attractive, many companies propose a generous dividend payout which could lead to a situation where it wins the war but cannot afford the victory.

The issuance of large blocks of new stock in a company may cause a change in its capital structure. This could later prove to be a deterrent to the issuance of more stock if the company needed to raise new funds.

"Knowing your enemy" is an old rule for military action. The merger battlefield is not different. If management's primary concern is to remain in power, it should consider the options available to the raider. In one option, the raider can condition the tender offer on a high minimum percentage, say 80 percent, for both the preferred and common of the target. In this case, the raider faces a relatively small number of shares of preferred in the second step of the merger. In another option, the raider can tender only for common, but again sets a high minimum percentage for acceptance. Here, shareholders may be willing to convert their preferred to common in order to take advantage of the premium offered by the raider. In each of these situations, one objective of the pill is achieved; that is, most stockholders will receive a full bid price for their shares rather than a partial or front-end loaded tender offer. While the stockholders' objectives may well be met, management's goal of remaining in power would likely not be achieved.

Fast Acting Poison

Not only is the poison pill defensive measure quickly implemented, it also achieves rapid results. In the cases examined, the preferred dividends were in place three days to a week after the announcement of the takeover attempt. The outcomes of the immediate takeover attempts were decided within two months. NEC never even placed a tender offer for Bell & Howell, and Tesoro withdrew its offer to purchase Enstar stock before the purchase was consummated. As seen in the latter case, imposed waiting periods for acquirers serve as an effective block during which a defense can be enacted. Targets rarely wait long to act. In the mid-1985 case of

Amsted Industries' battle against Texas investor Charles Hurwitz, the poison pill was deployed only one week after the traditional first defensive punch, legal action against the aggressor. In the third week of May 1985, it followed in the footsteps of many other targets, arguing in federal court that Hurwitz filed false documents with the SEC. A few days later, the poison pill concoction was ready.

The Law, the Pill, and the Tax Man

The business judgment rule is the principal legal guide under which lawsuits affecting management's efforts to prevent takeovers are decided. Wide latitude has been given executives under this rule, and poison pills have been deemed acceptable. However, legal challenges have always been part of the pill's history.

The precedent ruling for the cases we have examined is the case of Telvest vs. Olsen in 1978. The Delaware Chancery Court prevented the distribution of the poison pill preferred stock on the grounds that its provisions did not make it truly preferred. However, this ruling did not eliminate the use of poison pills, only signaled caution in setting up their provisions.

In March 1985, the SEC, in an unprecedented move, intervened in a lawsuit against a poison pill provision. It filed a friend-of-the-court brief in Delaware Supreme Court on behalf of a dissident director of Household International. This was the first time the SEC issued such a brief explaining the policy behind the federal securities law. The SEC wanted to see Household International's brand of poison pill ruled unfair. It stated that the poison pill preferred stock "will virtually eliminate hostile tender offers for Household . . . [and] deter proxy contests by persons seeking to oust Household's management." Household had issued warrants that became effective in the event someone bought or controlled voting rights for 20 percent or more of the company or announced a tender offer for 30 percent or more. Household's shareholders were given the right to buy the acquirer's shares at half the market price if there was a merger or other transaction giving more than 50 percent of Household's assets to the hostile bidder.

On November 19, 1985, the Delaware Supreme Court, in a landmark decision, legitimized the use of the pill in the Household case. The court's decision will no doubt open the floodgates to its use in other cases. Indeed, the timing of the decision couldn't have been better for MidCon in its winter 1986 battle with the energy partnership, WB Partners. The directors of the natural gas pipeline company approved a poison pill designed such that in the event of a merger proposal not approved by them, owners of newly issued preferred stock could convert the shares into equity of the surviving company.

As in most other defenses, the potential response of the stock exchanges should be evaluated. The NYSE and AMEX may object to a preferred stock dividend if it contains provisions for disproportionately large voting rights relative to common stock. Furthermore, NYSE requires shareholder approval for the conversion if the preferred stock is convertible into common shares representing over 18.5 percent of the previously outstanding common shares. Similarly, AMEX requires approval if the preferred represents over 20 percent of the previously outstanding shares.

Another important aspect that should be considered by the target is that legal battles can work for it. In each of the cases studied, the legal battles "bought time" for the target company to strengthen its other defenses. Because of the complexity of the poison pill provision, a legal challenge can provide the time needed to prevent an aggressor from taking further action while the court deliberates.

Preferred stock issued as a dividend is "306" stock for income tax purposes. This means that the sale of the preferred stock separately from its associated common stock results in the entire proceeds from the sale being taxed as ordinary income. To be eligible for capital gains treatment, both comon and preferred have to be sold or tendered as a unit. This tax feature makes it easier for the aggressor to convince the target shareholder to tender both the common and preferred.

The Pill and the Future

The salient aspects of a poison-pill preferred stock dividend are the conversion and redemption features. These features enable the pill to be a particularly effective defense against hostile two-tiered takeover attempts. Despite the legal uncertainty surrounding these features, potential trouble for the pill may come not only from the courtroom, but from bottom-line oriented institutional investors. Representative of this school of thought are the words of Arthur Fleischer, a top defense attorney with Fried, Frank, Harris, Shriver & Jacobson: "The key fact now is how inflammatory is the pill? In any situation that borders on the controversial, is it like a match to dry paper? Are you creating a rallying point for institutional opposition?" A more direct opinion was expressed by Wilbur Ross, a managing director at Rothschild Inc., saying "I think the poison pill is an inappropriate response." Phillips Petroleum, in its battle against Carl Icahn, already noticed the institutional dissatisfaction with the pill. Originally, it announced a plan to restructure its balance sheet in order to appease raider T. Boone Pickens. At the last minute, smelling value, Carl Icahn threatened Phillips with a follow-up attack. In response, Phillips added a poison pill provision to the original plan. This extended plan was voted down. It is believed that Phillip's failure to get the shareholders' support resulted from institutional opposition. More specifically, 17 Phillips institutional investors were members of the newly formed Council of Institutional Investors (CII), an organization created to fight takeover abuses. The CII group is composed of 22 public pension funds with estimated 1985 assets of $100 billion. After CII's institutions voted with raider Carl Icahn against Phillip's management, legal king Martin Lipton warned, "If the institutions act together in combination with the raiders, they will have unrestrained power to topple any corporation in America."

So far, however, early successes using this defensive strategy have caused it to become popular. In the months following the January 1985 favorable Household International ruling, a horde of companies lined up at the door of Household's lawyer, Martin Lipton of Wachtell, Lipton, Rosen and Katz, for the poison pill recipe.

The pill has, in fact, become so popular that the poison pill became a generic name. Almost any defense involving convertible preferred is described by the media as a poison pill. An example is the CBS 1985 issuance of convertible preferred stock to fight off raider Ted Turner. Unlike the classic poison pill issues, the successful CBS recipe did not include a provision for its holders to convert their shares into the raider's shares. Nevertheless, it did include a covenent significantly affecting Turner's chances to succeed. The covenent required that CBS debt cannot exceed 75 percent of its capitalization. Given Turner's original plan to finance the entire transaction with junk bonds, the newly imposed limit made life difficult for the Atlanta broadcaster. Though significant, the maximum debt provision clearly was not an ordinary poison pill. Nevertheless, it was reported as such by the press.

The reason for the pill's popularity is its unquestioned potency. This was the case until Sir James Goldsmith exploited a mile-wide loophole in Crown Zellerbach's poison pill defense. Sir James was not intimidated by the fearsome potion. Back in July 1984, Crown instituted a pill which stipulated that, in the event of a takeover, holders of certain rights would be able to buy two shares of the surviving company for the price of one. These rights were to be issued when an acquirer passed the 20 percent threshold in its holdings and then exercised when merger formally takes place. The loophole was that the rights could not be exercised until an acquiring company obtained 100 percent of Crown's common stock. Goldsmith smelled the loophole early on. He slowly and steadily increased his stake, acquiring 8.6 percent by March 1985, and then upping his total to 19.6 percent, near the threshold limit by May 8. A week later, on May 15, Goldsmith crossed the threshold, raising his stake to more than 20 percent, causing the rights to be issued. Several truces were arranged between Sir James and Crown, but each time, Goldsmith broke the truce and continued to increase his holdings. Defying the poison, he stopped his acquisition of Crown shares prior to 100 percent of ownership. At 52 percent, Sir James won control of Crown, becoming chairman and taking control of a new 11-member board. No doubt, as a result of Sir James's victory, lawyers across the country moved to close the "Goldsmith loophole" in the many pills designed to be poison, not candy for the aggressor.

7
The Employee Benefit Plan Defense

The Great Textile Battle: Will Carl Icahn Sew Up Dan River?

CARL ICAHN vs. DAN RIVER

Raiders have been known to shake the foundation of corporate America. Such was the case when Carl Icahn launched his attack on Dan River.

Carl C. Icahn, a 48-year-old financier and arbitrageur, owned 98 percent of Icahn & Co. In the five years ending in 1982, he accumulated an estimated $70 million by engaging in corporate raids about every six months. His "buy me out or face a takeover" strategy involved finding a vulnerable corporation whose stock he believed was undervalued. He and his associates purchased outstanding shares of the company in the market. By intimidating the officers and other shareholders into buying back his shares or into selling the company to a white knight, Icahn usually realized a substantial profit. As a result, the target companies were usually significantly altered. Companies involved in past confrontations with Icahn included the Tappan, Hammermill Paper, Saxon Industries, Simplicity Pattern, American Can, and Marshall Field.

Icahn was not always a feared corporate takeover baron. In fact, he was the son of a synogogue cantor who went on to study philosophy at Princeton. He then spent two years in medical school but quit after he decided he wasn't enjoying it. After the army and barracks poker games he went on to Wall Street. While he made $50,000 in the bull market of 1961, he soon lost it all. To this day he says, "I can't stand it when people try to predict what the market is going to do. It simply can't be done."

Icahn operates under the premise that corporate governance does not measure up to the trust placed in it by investors. He believes that chief executives place too much emphasis on appeasing their boards and not enough effort on improving corporate performance. He represents the constituency of shareholders that are challenging management to increase value.

As a professional shark in the merger and acquisition world, Carl Icahn saw potential profit in the textile business. The next target on his list was Dan River.

The Dan River Blues

In addition to being one of the nation's oldest textile manufacturers, Dan River was one of the largest, employing over 12,000 people. In view of the economic recession from 1980 to 1981, earnings fell from $19.6 to $14.5 million. Furthermore, by 1982 the recession had severely affected sales in the entire textile industry, and Dan River struggled to stay in the black. Weak consumer markets, record imports of foreign textile products, and low prices resulted in deteriorated earnings. In addition, a capital intensive modernization program was depleting the company's cash reserves. As a result, the second quarter dividend was halved to $0.14. It was not surprising that the company's stock was selling at a four-year low of $10.50. This was approximately one-third of its $34.50 book value.

In an effort to improve operating results, Dan River initiated a reorganization and disposition program. This included the relocation and consolidation of corporate headquarters to Danville, Virginia from Greenville, South Carolina. The estimated savings resulting from the move were $5 million per year. The company also planned to eliminate six plants which were consistently experiencing operating losses of up to $4 million. By the end of 1982, Dan River reported an 18 percent decline in sales to $519 million and a loss from operations of $488,000. A heavy debt burden generated interest payments amounting to $13 million. Its poor operating performance led to plant closings costing another $11 million. Only tax credit checks from Uncle Sam made a $24 million bottom line loss appear as a loss of only $8.7 million.

Previous Target Experience

In the past, Dan River had successfully thwarted two takeover bids. In 1979, it sued two Hong Kong-based textile concerns, Unitex Ltd. and its subsidiary Mannip Ltd., for violating federal securities laws. It charged the companies with inaccurate and incomplete disclosures. The companies had acquired an 8.6 percent block of shares which they still owned at the time of Icahn's attack. In 1981, Dan River reached a standstill agreement with these two companies, limiting their holdings through December 1, 1984 to 12 percent.

In January 1982, Dan River prevented a takeover by David H. Murdock, a Los Angeles financier, who controlled International Mining Corporation. To accomplish its defense, Dan River repurchased from Murdock 327,400 shares or 5.6 percent of its common stock for $15.50. Murdock, thwarted by Dan River, subsequently took control of Cannon Mills, another textile company. Commenting on Dan River's successes in preventing these takeovers, a textile industry source said, "These guys have a history of playing pretty tough." The battle between Icahn and Dan River was another test of the company's mettle.

Round One

In September 1982, after having acquired 6.9 percent of Dan River stock, Carl Icahn and his associates filed a Schedule 13D with the SEC. His investment group disclosed its intentions to seek control of Dan River with either an amicable or hostile bid. Leaving their options open, they were alternatively willing to "sell the shares in the open market or in privately negotiated transactions to one or more persons, which [could] include the issuer [Dan River]." The ensuing confrontation between the Icahn group and Dan River continued for eight months and contributed to the most turbulent period of Dan River's 100 year history.

Analysts speculated that Dan River's repurchasing of stock from Murdock sparked Icahn's interest in the company. Through July 15, 1982, Icahn bought 2.6 percent or 150,000 shares for $10.50 to $12.00. From July 15 to September 10, he acquired an additional 248,000 shares at an average price of $12.80, thus increasing his stake to 6.9 percent of Dan River's 5.8 million shares.

Within a few days, the largest single shareholder of Dan River, Unitex Ltd., and its Mannip Ltd. subsidiary, sold an 8.6 percent block of Dan River shares to Icahn, thereby increasing his stake to about 15.5 percent. Armed with more bargaining power, Icahn met with Dan River's chairman and other officers on September 30, and revealed his desire to increase his interest to 50 percent and take control of the company.

Round Two

To avert the takeover, the company amended its profit-sharing plan so that participants could direct the trustee to invest their funds in Dan River securities. The plan had assets of $12.5 million and more than 2500 participants. In addition, October 5, Dan River contributed 1.7 million shares of cumulative convertible voting preferred stock to a stock bonus plan for salaried employees, rewarding them for past efforts. This gave the employees 22 percent of the company's voting shares. Four shares were convertible to one common after five years. At $5 per share, the new stock had a liquidation value of $8.5 million. The shares also carried one vote each. According to Virginia state law, this implied that a takeover proposal or other major transaction would have to be approved by holders of two-thirds of the new preferred shares.

This action effectively diluted Carl Icahn's 15.5 percent stake to 11 percent. Reacting immediately, he filed with the SEC and canceled his plan for a tender offer, but reserved the right for a future offer. He also filed suit in federal court seeking to void the preferred stock issue. Icahn complained:

> *Management has thus secured, at no cost to itself, voting control of Dan River and has done so without obtaining common shareholder approval and at the expense of common shareholders . . . . The aforesaid acts and transactions serve no legitimate business purpose. They are designed solely to perpetuate management in office . . . . and are a clear waste of corporate assets.*

A Left Hook

Dan River countersued seeking to enjoin the Icahn group from acquiring additional shares. In documents filed in federal district court on October 12, Dan River charged Icahn with a "pattern of racketeering." It claimed he acquired Dan River stock with funds "derived through prior acts of extortion, mail fraud, and securities fraud." The Federal Racketeering Influenced and Corrupt Organization Act of 1970 defined a pattern of racketeering as any two violations of a number of different laws during a 10-year period.

The following violations were noted by Dan River. In December

1981, Icahn purportedly failed to disclose tactics used in the attempted takeover of two companies, Saxon Industries and the Hammermill Paper Company. In 1978, Icahn purchased a controlling interest in Bayswater Realty & Capital. Dan River claimed that Icahn sold Bayswater's real estate holdings and used the cash for the purchase of other targets. These charges were the subject of an SEC complaint in 1981, which he settled by agreeing not to violate certain sections of the federal laws. Dan River also claimed that Icahn's tender offer was a "manipulative and deceptive scheme" in violation of the 1934 Securities Act. In addition, it charged the Icahn group with "intentions to loot Dan River" if it obtained control of the company, thus violating Virginia's corporation laws.

Fancy Footwork

Icahn responded with a conditional offer to buy 3.1 million shares or 54 percent of Dan River's common at $18 apiece. It was conditioned on the company agreeing to stop litigation against the group and not attempting any transaction to block the offer. If accepted, Icahn would not interfere with the voting rights of the newly issued stock. If Dan River did not accept these terms, he would offer $15 a share for 700,000 shares. The $18 offer totaled $55.8 million and the $15 offer was worth $10.5 million. The offer was to expire at midnight November 22, 1982, unless it was extended. However, within a week, Dan River directors rejected the tender offer as "unfair and not in the best interests" of the shareholders.

Icahn met this resistance by pressing further. He revised the minimum offering price to $16.50 for 34 percent of the outstanding shares. This would raise his stake to 50 percent. In addition, the conditional tender offer to buy 3.1 million at $18 was left open if Dan River agreed to a takeover. Thus, two offers were outstanding at the same time. The expiration date was still November 22 at midnight. Dan River also rejected this new offer and recommended that its shareholders not tender their shares.

Knockdown

Meanwhile, Dan River acquired some protection. On November 12, the federal court issued a preliminary injunction barring Icahn from exercising voting rights on Dan River shares he had or may acquire. The order also barred him from trying to change Dan River management, engaging in a proxy battle, or from calling a shareholder meeting. Dan River was ordered not to dispose of any assets out of the ordinary course of business, to pay only regular dividends, and not to issue any new stock. The court set the first week of February 1983 for a trial on the merits of all the issues. Icahn responded quickly. On November 19, a U.S. federal appeals court dissolved the preliminary injunction against Icahn. The majority opinion found the fears of Dan River to be premature and Icahn to be only "extraordinarily frank" about the course of action he may take. This court decision cleared the path for Icahn to purchase the shares at midnight November 22 as planned.

White Knight for Dan River?

On November 19, Dan River's price jumped $2.25 to $17. According to analysts, this price suggested traders were speculating that a higher, rescuing bid was being negotiated. The rumor was that the third party each side was pursuing was one and the same.

In another attempt to stave off the hostile tender offer, Dan River filed with the SEC regarding a prospective buyer and was permitted to keep the possible buyer anonymous. Dan River also instructed its financial advisor, Kidder, Peabody, to accelerate negotiations with the unidentified company and to seek additional prospects. It was known that Dan River had discussed a takeover with David Murdock, the Los Angeles financier, who had been interested in them about one year earlier. However, after having recently acquired Cannon Mill, Murdock no longer was interested in Dan River.

Dan River combined another move with the white knight announcement. It planned to purchase its own stock in an effort to reduce the number of shares available for purchase by Icahn. In total, it would spend up to $15 million for approximately 900,000 shares. This represented 15.5 percent of Dan River's 5.8 million outstanding shares. The details of the purchase were all well planned. It would occur both in the open market and in private transactions and would be financed by short-term loans. The shares would be held as treasury stock.

Even citizens of Danville, Virginia joined the struggle against Icahn. Dan River was Danville's largest employer, where it employed about 8000 of its residents. Local businessmen devised a strategy with the theme "Keep Dan River in Danville. Buy Dan River stock." It consisted of a campaign to get the residents to buy stock in the company with hopes of keeping the price of Dan River shares above Icahn's offering price.

Immobilization

On Monday, November 22, the day that Icahn's offer was to expire, 782,000 Dan River shares exchanged hands. The stock made the most active list for one day. But by midnight, only 233,457 shares were tendered to Icahn. It was not even close to the 2 million he wanted. He retaliated by challenging Dan River's stock-buying blitz in court. He charged Dan River's management with "scheming" to sell the shares to a friendly third party who would vote with management. The Icahn group alleged that this, in addition to the 1.7 million share stock-bonus plan, "constituted a conspiracy making it almost impossible for any person to make a takeover attempt." In addition, Icahn extended the $16.50 offer by another week.

The current market price of $17 to $18 was higher than the Icahn group offering. As a result, it was unlikely that many shares would be tendered to them. Furthermore, Icahn's request to enjoin Dan River from further purchases of stock or uses of its treasury stock was denied by a federal judge. It appeared the Icahn group was being outwitted. Icahn would have to develop alternative strategies.

In the following weeks, Carl Icahn extended his offer twice. He then raised the offering price from $16.50 to $18 when the price showed no signs of dropping. This offer was contingent on his receiving at least 2 million shares, at which time he would request a special shareholder meeting in order to elect a majority of directors. He then proposed a merger of Dan River and Icahn Capital and offered a debenture with a value of $15 for each Dan River share still outstanding.

Possible Rescue

Dan River maintained that Icahn's $18 offer was "unfair and not in the best interest" of the shareholders or the company. On December 16, it announced a possible white knight. McDonough Co., a U.S.-based unit of Hanson Trust PLC, a British textile maker, purchased 475,000 shares of treasury stock or 8 percent of Dan River's postre-purchase 5.8 million outstanding shares. This transaction for $18.50 a share totaled $8.8 million and was approved by Dan River's board. The Hanson unit was considering an offer of at least $18.50 for the remainder of the outstanding shares.

To protect itself, Dan River intended to entertain other offers. In addition, it planned to continue the stock repurchasing program for 900,000 shares which began in November. Dan River had already purchased approximately 475,000 shares which it subsequently sold to McDonough. Proceeds from this sale were added to the repurchase fund.

Within a week, in an amendment to the report filed with the SEC, McDonough reported that it might buy more Dan River shares in the open market but had not determined whether to acquire the company. It also disclosed that it was shown statements which revealed substantial earnings projections as well as increasing dividends for Dan River over the next three years.

This disclosure and Dan River's continued stock-buying plan maintained the price of its shares in the open market between $18.50 and $19.25. As a result, through the December 27 expiration date, Carl Icahn had only acquired 821,568 shares with his tender offers. Given that he started the attack with 400,000 shares and the Hong Kong companies sold him approximately 462,000 shares, at this point his total holdings amounted to almost 30 percent of Dan River shares.

Icahn then extended the $18 offer for 2 million shares by another day, to December 28. He also wrote a letter to financial advisor Kidder, Peabody outlining a new offer of $21 for "any and all" of Dan River common. This offer was subject to his obtaining financing within 30 days for as much as 50 percent of the purchases. Icahn would then give those people whose shares were bought for $18 an additional $3 a share.

Attracting no new shares with the one day extension, he again extended the $18 offer to January 5. This date was the day after an important Dan River board meeting. He wanted to maintain his bargaining power until then.

Saved by the ESOP

Unable to abort Icahn's takeover attempt, Dan River management accepted the assistance of Kelso Investment Associates. This investment banking firm originated the concept of the employee stock option plan (ESOP) as a means of executing a leveraged buyout. At the directors meeting January 4, 1983, the board approved, in principle, a plan for the employees to purchase Dan River for $22.50 a share or $135 million. Kelso proposed the formation of a holding company in which the ESOP would be the largest shareholder. Other shareholders would include members of management. The holding company would form a wholly owned subsidiary to buy out current shareholders and merge with Dan River. Shareholders would receive cash for their shares. The holding company would be dissolved, with Dan River remaining intact following the transactions. Negotiation and completion of the merger was estimated to take three to four months. Chemical Bank of New York made a conditional commitment to finance the plan. The commitment was contingent upon two conditions: Dan River shareholders must approve the merger agreement, and holders of not more than 15 percent of voting stock could pursue their rights as dissenting shareholders. To ensure that the Kelso proposal was feasible and fair to shareholders, Dan River's board engaged the services of both Kidder, Peabody and Goldman, Sachs to perform financial studies. The board also announced its rejection of Icahn's tender offer of $21. The next day Dan River common closed at 20⅝.

Despite the new strategy, Carl Icahn persisted in his effort to acquire more stock. By January 5, he accumulated 1.7 million shares or 30 percent of the common. This translates to 22 percent of the voting shares. Icahn also announced the tenth extension of his offer, this time to January 19. He was determined to remain an active player while Dan River arranged the ESOP buyout.

On January 20, Dan River and Carl Icahn agreed to stop fighting at least until September 15. Litigation would halt, pending the settlement and dismissal of lawsuits against each other, including suits by other shareholders. The standstill agreement included provisions governing the conduct of both parties. Icahn let his $18 offer expire. He agreed not to buy or sell any shares, seek board representation, or assist other parties to acquire the company. Dan River agreed not to buy any of its shares, issue any new securities, declare an extraordinary dividend, or change any of its bylaws. The standstill agreement would permit Dan River to proceed with business without the burden and expenses of continued litigation. This allowed the further development of the ESOP if directors and shareholders still desired to do so. If lawsuits were not dismissed by September 15, Icahn and Dan River could resume the fight.

Lady Luck

At the end of April 1983, Dan River announced that on the recommendation of the review committee, the board approved the ESOP buyout. The review committee studied the opinions of their financial advisors. Kidder, Peabody held discussions with 34 companies, but none had an interest in acquiring Dan River. Kidder, Peabody also reported that "liquidation was not a viable alternative to provide value to Dan River shareholders." The directors concluded that going private was the best option: "This was the only way we could pay out to the shareholders at the highest price." The next step was to gain the support of two-thirds of the voting securities of which Carl Icahn had 22 percent. On April 28, proxy statements with details of the proposal were mailed to the shareholders.

At the annual meeting on May 24, 70.2 percent of Dan River's voting shares approved the proposal to sell the company to the employees for $22.50 per share. Icahn did not vote on the merger proposal "because of possible application of federal securities laws" that require large holders to "disgorge profits on sales of shares held less than six months." If he abstained from voting, the provision would not apply.

The next day, the Virginia State Corporation Commission issued the certificate of merger, thereby accomplishing the merger of Dan River into employee-owned Dan River Holding Company.

Details of the Buyout

The entire transaction cost approximately $153.9 million. This included paying $134.2 million to holders of common stock, $7.1 million to holders of preferred stock, $8.3 million to holders of convertible subordinated notes, and $4.3 million for all other expenses.

Financing of the buyout included the following. Through buying a new stock issue of Class B common, the management group acquired 25 percent and Kelso Investment Associates acquired 5 percent of the company. This equity investment contributed $5 million to the financing of the merger. In addition, Dan River's pension plan was terminated, and $16 million in excess pension assets were secured. Uncle Sam also paid his share of approximately $20 million in federal tax refunds. Yet with these contributions of funds, the financing basket was still far from complete. Dan River obtained $13 million through the issuance of new preferred stock to the company's profit-sharing plan. But the major source of financing was from the new ESOP which bought a 70 percent ownership in the company. It received 4.9 million shares of Class A common stock valued at $22.50 per share. The ESOP borrowed $110 million from Dan River which in turn had obtained the loan from Chemical Bank. However, the terms of the buyout were carefully crafted by Dan River management. They did not give the employees the right to vote their shares directly for members of the board.

The Clean-Up

Although Icahn was defeated in his takeover attempt, he made an estimated $8 million on the sale of 1.7 million shares which he started collecting only a year earlier. As an epilogue, to celebrate the victory, Icahn named his new German shepherd attack dog Shiloh, in honor of the Civil War battle in which the North defeated the South.

He was not, however, the only party to partake in this lucrative transaction. Kelso Investment Associates received $900,000, Kidder, Peabody received $1.3 million, and Goldman, Sachs received $350,000 plus expenses. Important but unpublicized winners were all the other shareholders who one year earlier were holding Dan River shares worth less than $12. They also scored significant gains. Unlike the Civil War, this war resulted in all combatants winning.

The Grumman Pension Fund Dilemma: LTV Or Loyalty
LTV vs. GRUMMAN

It all began with a telephone call. Little did LTV Chairman Paul Thayre realize that his call to Grumman President Joseph G. Gavin, Jr. would result in a long court battle that would eventually draw the FTC and SEC into the fray. Grumman's dogged determination to avoid the takeover led them to pursue the questionable practice of using the company's pension fund as a weapon in its battle for control.

The Combatants

To understand the stakes in the ensuing battle, a short description of the two companies is in order. Grumman Corporation, a large Bethpage, Long Island aircraft builder, was the Pentagon's tenth largest supplier in 1981, with $1.3 billion in defense contracts. Grumman provided top fighter planes, such as the F14 and the A6 naval bomber aircraft. In addition, Grumman subsidiary interests included buses, boats, and truck bodies. Of Grumman's 28,000 employees 20,000 lived in the Bethpage area. Grumman employees also owned much of the company's stock.

LTV Corporation, a Dallas-based company, was the third biggest U.S. steel company and a major supplier of American missiles. In addition, LTV operations included energy and food products, and a steamship concern. Vought Corporation was the aerospace subsidiary of LTV and was the Pentagon's twenty-fifth largest supplier, with a backlog of $511 million in defense contracts. Vought was in the $100 million annual sales range, but lagged behind other LTV operations. LTV saw Vought's prime military business revolving around missiles and efforts to become a force in the avionics subsystem arena. Vought's products included the A7 attack plane and the multiple launch rocket system, a mobile battlefield missile.

The Offer and the Response

The initial offer was made by LTV Chairman Paul Thayre, in a telephone call to Grumman President Joseph G. Gavin, Jr. Gavin's negative response did not discourage Thayre. Two days later, a letter was sent to Grumman's Chairman John C. Bierwirth, who was vacationing at the time of the phone call. Bierwirth's "no" was every bit as emphatic as Gavin's had been, and his statement to the press hinted at financial, legal, and other obstacles to the merger. Over the weekend, Grumman officials vowed to fight the LTV takeover. Despite this reaction, Thayre was determined to attempt it, stating "We are in this to stay."

LTV's tender offer was well planned and included the following elements:

$45 per share for Grumman common stock

$45.50 per share for Grumman convertible preferred stock

$1347.71 per $1000 principal amount of Grumman's 4¼ percent convertible subordinated debentures due in 1992

$1838.61 per $1000 principal amount of Grumman's 11 percent convertible subordinated debentures due in 2000

The cash offer started September 24, 1981 and was to end one month later on October 23. The offer represented 10 million of Grumman's 13.8 million shares. The value of the bid, if successful, was estimated at $450 million. A strong effort was made to acquire

70 percent of Grumman's stock, as this was seen as the first step in a plan to acquire 100 percent of the voting equity of Grumman.

LTV next sued to prevent Grumman and state officials from attempting to delay the takeover. A court order was sought to stop Grumman from enforcing the New York Securities Takeover Disclosure Act. LTV felt that this act would subject them to an "unnecessary, unreasonable, and possible indefinite delay" that would increase the possibility of the tender offer failing. The act would also require LTV to set aside a substantial amount of money for an indefinite period, which LTV felt would result in a loss of alternative investment opportunities.

Synergism and Vulnerability

LTV's search for a partner had started a year earlier, when an offer to Pneumo Corporation for its subsidiary, Cleveland Pneumatic, fell through. LTV saw the merger with Grumman as a chance to create a major, well-balanced aerospace defense company. Such a manufacturer would be better able to serve the needs of the nation, the well-being of the employees of the two companies, and the communities in which they operated. The merger would result in a company better able to compete for military contracts with aerospace giants such as McDonnell Douglas and Rockwell International.

LTV felt a merger with Grumman had many positive results to offer. Grumman's strength in tactical aircraft would complement LTV's multiple launch rocket system. Another effect of the merger would be an increased R&D budget. The broadened aerospace product diversification resulting from the merger would aid in offsetting the swings in defense spending and would strengthen LTV's position as a military airframe supplier.

At the time of the offer, Grumman was in a vulnerable position. Its aerospace operations were doing well, but other operations were suffering losses. Grumman stock had been battered in a bear market, and earlier attempts at diversification into the civilian market had failed miserably. However, the Reagan administration's resolve to increase the production of military aircraft made Grumman's aerospace operations an attractive asset to outside firms, such as LTV.

Initial Resistance and a Question of Affordability

Grumman stated that the disclosures in the tender offer were materially false and misleading, and that LTV failed to disclose enough information regarding its finances. Grumman also objected to the merger on the basis of potential antitrust violations. The two companies were competing for a share in a billion dollar Navy program to build training aircraft and equipment. Another objection raised by Grumman was the effect the merger would have on community and labor relations. Grumman employees were nonunion workers at the time and it voiced concern over the future of its 28,000 employees if the merger succeeded.

LTV planned to finance the acquisition with $100 million from internal sources and $300 million from bank loans at the prime rate. At that time, LTV held $1.49 billion in debt, more than six times Grumman's $231.5 million of debt. The bank loans necessary for the merger would raise debt to an extremely high 60 percent of capitalization. However, LTV claimed that the acquisition of Grumman would lower its debt to 50 percent. Yet even that amount of debt was high in an industry where most companies held relatively little debt. LTV contended that since banks were willing to offer it loans at prime, LTV was a good credit risk.

To add to LTV's financial difficulties, its earnings were hurt by the downturn of the steel market. Additionally, LTV's steel subsidiary faced the expense of installing pollution control equipment, and an inadequately funded pension plan placed further cash demands on LTV.

Antitrust or Antimerger?

Grumman contended that the merger with LTV would violate antitrust laws since both companies were major aerospace concerns competing for defense contracts. LTV felt that since Vought accounted for only 8.1 percent of LTV's sales in 1980, the antitrust allegation was irrelevant. The Pentagon, however, stated that it wanted to ensure a large number of qualified suppliers, so it would investigate the merger. It came as no surprise that no Pentagon official was anxious to press the matter. To do so would have meant taking on Chairman John Tower of the Senate Armed Service Committee, who was from LTV's hometown.

Both companies' Navy planes (the A6 and A7) were designed to attack ground or sea targets with missiles and bombs. Grumman held a 37 percent share of this market and Vought had a 32 percent share. LTV claimed that the production of the A7 would be halted, thus lessening the threat of antitrust. LTV also pointed out that Vought would only be a subcontractor to another company for the Navy training program, while Grumman was to be a prime contractor. LTV felt that direct competition between the two was therefore not an issue.

The First Sign of Abuse

Grumman's pension plan held 525,000 of Grumman's shares and the company's employee investment fund held 3.2 million shares. Combined, the plan and the fund controlled 27 percent of Grumman's 13.8 million shares. On October 7, 1981, the trustees of Grumman's plan met and decided not to tender the 525,000 Grumman shares held by the pension plan and to purchase an additional 1,275,000 Grumman shares with the pension plan funds. On October 12 and 13, the trustees did indeed purchase 1.16 million Grumman shares for approximately $38 per share. If the price of Grumman shares dropped from its mid-30s to its pre-tender price of $22, the pension plan could have faced a loss of millions of dollars.

The $45 per share tender offer by LTV was a higher price than Grumman stock had traded for in over two decades. Despite this, LTV's tender offer failed to attract sufficient shareholders, so LTV extended its offer to November 3 and again to November 10. Even with the extensions, LTV succeeded in attracting only $2.1 million in securities. Grumman stock was bid up only 6⅜ points after the announcement of the tender offer and closed at 33⅛ per share, well below LTV's offer. Clearly, investors were wary of the offer.

One reason for this reaction was the 23 percent block of Grumman stock owned by the employee investment plan, the 4 percent owned by the corporation's pension plan, and the 1.7 percent owned by the directors. Employees also held a large part of the remaining shares. Grumman needed to persuade only one fifth of the other shareholders not to tender their shares in order for the acquisition attempt to fail. It stressed to its shareholders the possible negative effects the merger could have on Grumman employees. It was expected that LTV's battle to attract the hoped for number of shares would be a bitter contest.

Battle of the Media and Employment for the Judges

LTV and Grumman participated in a no-holds-barred battle of the media in an attempt to convince stockholders of the merits of their respective companies. Grumman placed spot ads on 18 New York City and Long Island radio stations to urge shareholders to refuse the tender offer. Spot ads were also placed on two cable television networks in the Long Island area, where 20,000 of the 28,000 employees resided. In the ads, President Gavin warned shareholders of the dangers of a merger with a "debt ridden, Texas-based conglomerate."

LTV responded with ads in two major newspapers in the New York metropolitan area "to communicate in a straightforward way with Grumman officials." Grumman declined to give LTV a list of shareholder addresses and so, by law, was required to mail out LTV's tender offer material.

Grumman next launched a two-week telephone campaign to urge shareholders to resist the tender offer. Its chairman, John Bierwirth, claimed that this action alone put one third of the outstanding shares into the hands of Grumman management.

The federal court of the east district of New York enjoined LTV from proceeding with the takeover of Grumman. This action, taken by Justice Jacob Mischler, followed hearings by the New York State attorney general, at which LTV's Thayre accused Grumman pension plan trustees of a conflict of interest. Specifically, Thayre charged Grumman trustees with authorizing the purchase of approximately 1.2 million shares of Grumman common stock at a cost of almost $40 million. One day earlier, LTV officials had filed suit against Grumman's board of directors and pension fund trustees for using pension funds to purchase common shares, an action raising "serious legal, ethical, and conflict of interest questions."

LTV appealed the injunction but was rejected by the U.S. Court of Appeals. Judges Leonard Moore, Jon Newman, and Charles Tenney held that LTV might violate antitrust laws by once again beginning production of the A7 for the Navy. The judges also cited evidence that Grumman and Vought already held sizable shares in the parts market for commercial planes, and that these market shares would continue to grow in the future.

The FTC stepped into the picture by moving to prevent the takeover on the grounds that antitrust laws would be violated. The FTC stated that the purchase would lessen competition in the carrier-based aircraft field. LTV's Thayre disputed the FTC allegation, basing his argument on LTV's discontinuation of the A7 and the significant reduction of aircraft R&D.

Trouble for Grumman

On October 19, 1981, LTV's allegations of Grumman's pension abuse were revealed by the SEC. The SEC's suit against Grumman charged it with filing certain schedules and statements with the commission that contained untrue facts. The SEC also stated that Grumman failed to disclose information related to a repurchase of Grumman stock by Grumman, and a purchase of Grumman stock by the pension plan and the Madison Fund, a publicly owned, closed-end investment company in New York. A third charge accused Grumman of failing to report a change made in the pension trust agreement. A word about these charges helps to understand Grumman's troubles with the SEC.

Grumman had notified the SEC that the company planned to buy 1 million shares and the pension fund planned to purchase 1.3 million shares, but neglected to make the required disclosure that the purpose was to defeat the LTV takeover. Instead, Grumman was quoted as saying that the shares "will be held in the company's treasury for general corporate purposes." The pension fund, in turn, declared that the stock purchase was "an attractive and beneficial investment for the pension trust."

The SEC also charged Grumman with failing to disclose that it asked the Madison Fund to buy Grumman shares so that another large block of stock would be in friendly hands. The fund bought 396,600 shares between September 30 and October 1, 1981, approximately one week after the initial tender offer, but soon after sold the stock. Grumman denied this allegation. It is not necessarily illegal for a pension plan to purchase the stock of its beneficiaries' company. However, the SEC alleged that the people making the decision were the same people who designed the corporate strategy to fight the LTV takeover and it was their decision to make the purchase part of the strategy.

It was also alleged by the SEC that Grumman failed to disclose that the company changed the trust agreement for the pension fund to permit the indemnification of the fund's trustees for any liabilities related to their activities under the trust agreement. The trustees denied this allegation.

Trouble for the Trustees

October 19 was a busy day for the Grumman lawyers. Not only was that the date the SEC filed suit against Grumman, but on that date the U.S. Labor Department also proceeded to sue Grumman, accusing its three trustees of violating pension laws. The law prevents an employee benefit plan's assets from being used for anything but the benefit of the employees. The suit asked that the trustees personally reimburse the plan for any money lost as a result of the stock purchase. The Labor Department claimed that the pension fund paid on average $38 per share for the 1.16 million shares purchased. The fund, therefore, paid $42 to $44 million for the shares, which could represent a paper loss of approximately $10.2 million if the price of the stock fell to its pretakeover level. The suit also asked to have the court appoint an independent individual to temporarily act on behalf of the pension plan and to make any decisions involving Grumman stock. The Department of Labor sought to prevent the trustees from future violations of pension law. LTV requested that the court rescind the pension fund purchases but Justice Mischler denied the request, saying that the Grumman pension fund purchases did not violate any securities law. However, the judge did issue a preliminary injunction on December 3 to block the trustees from buying or selling any Grumman stock without the permission of the Secretary of Labor.

As a result of Judge Mischler's ruling, Raymond J. Donovan, U.S. Secretary of Labor, called for a temporary restraining order for the three Grumman trustees: John C. Bierwirth, chairman and CEO, and Robert Freese and Carl Paladino, both top Grumman officials. The basis of the suit charged the trustees with violating their fiduciary duties to act in the best interest of the Grumman shareholders. Specifically, charges were based on the following points:

The defendants in the suit also served as high-level officials of Grumman Corporation or its subsidiaries.

Prior to LTV's takeover attempt, Grumman stock was selling at $25 per share.

Prior to LTV's takeover attempt, the pension plan owned 525,000 shares and had not made any purchases for 10 years.

The management of Grumman developed a strategy for resisting LTV's moves, using assets of the pension plan to fend off the takeover.

On May 10, 1982, the Second Circuit upheld the district court's temporary injunction pending a trial. The appeals court suggested that the trustees should have recognized the existence of a conflict of interest and should have resigned or hired legal counsel, so that neutral trustees could have been appointed. The court called the action a "no-win" situation. If the LTV offer had succeeded, the pension fund would have been left a minority shareholder in an LTV-controlled Grumman. If the offer failed, the stock price was likely to fall to its pre-tender level.

Who Is the Winner?

At this point in time, Grumman clearly was in trouble. Troops of government and regulatory bodies were on its tail. The FTC, the SEC, and the Labor Department were all pursuing various charges.

Luckily, the sun shone on its defense when LTV dropped its bid for Grumman in May 1982. To the elation of the target, LTV planned to return the 2.1 million shares that were tendered. It felt the decision to drop the bid was wise. As the federal appeals court had ruled that the antitrust violation was significant enough to justify barring LTV from acquiring more shares of Grumman, LTV would have faced a very costly court battle, after already spending approximately $2 million on the merger attempt.

Grumman professed to be happy with LTV's decision, but had little cause for true celebration. Grumman had spent $1.5 million in legal fees and $600,000 in anti-LTV advertising. The SEC was suing the corporation for violating securities law. To add to their burdens, Grumman executives faced a landmark suit charging them with using pension funds to buy up nearly 1.2 million shares of Grumman common stock. Although the suit was later dropped, if found liable, the trustees could have faced personal liabilities of over $15 million. Some people at Grumman probably looked back with nostalgia at LTV's offer of $45, particularly when Grumman's stock fell back to $24 following the end of the fight. Grumman had indeed won the battle, but in doing so, may have lost the war.

The Unfriendly Skies

TEXAS INTERNATIONAL AIRLINES vs. CONTINENTAL AIRLINES

The announcement that Texas International Airlines sought control of the much larger Continental Airlines was the opening salvo in what would prove to be a bitter and costly battle for both sides. The fight for control of Continental would rage on for eight months both in and out of the courtroom with momentum shifting with each judge's ruling and each decision of the Civil Aeronautics Board (CAB). For Continental, the battle would extend far beyond the corporate boardrooms as employees at all levels became involved in a novel attempt to purchase control of their company and thus avert the takeover by Texas International. To better understand the action in this 1981 takeover battle, it is important to meet the warriors.

The Two Jets Collide

Continental Airlines was a medium-sized nationwide carrier based in Los Angeles. Its system stretched from coast to coast, serving 34 cities. The airline also provided service to Hawaii, four cities in Mexico, and several islands in the South Pacific. In 1980, Continental reported losses of $20.7 million on revenues of $769.6 million, while flying 8.12 billion revenue-passenger miles. Each revenue-passenger mile represents one paying passenger flown one mile. Its president and CEO, Alvin L. Feldman, was a veteran of many years in the airline industry. Prior to taking over Continental, he served as chairman of the board of Frontier Airlines for nine years. At the time of the Texas International offer, Continental was in the final stages of completing a merger with Western Airlines. The terms of this agreement called for Continental shareholders to receive 1.165 shares of the new airline for each of their shares. The final CAB ruling on this merger was scheduled for March 2, 1981. A Continental spokesman called the pending merger a "marriage of equals . . . in the best interest of our shareholders, employees, and the flying public."

Houston-based Texas International Airlines, a subsidiary of Texas Air Corporation, was a regional carrier serving 25 cities across 12 states in the U.S. and Mexico. In 1980, it flew 2.24 billion passenger-revenue miles, reporting earnings of $4.7 million on revenues of $291.5 million. The company's president, Francisco A. Lorenzo, a young Harvard Business School trained entrepreneur, was known to be a shrewd, aggressive businessman with a penchant for privacy. He assumed control of the nearly bankrupt Texas International in 1972 and led the company into a period of continued growth and profitability. Battling airlines much larger than his own was not a new experience for Lorenzo. He had failed in two earlier bids to assume control of National Airlines and Trans World Airlines. In his bid for National, Lorenzo touched off a bidding war which led to the selling of Texas International's shares of National to Pan American World Airways for a pretax profit of $46.5 million. Although in 1985 he again bid for TWA, this earlier attempt to assume control of TWA was aborted with no apparent gain or loss for Texas International. On the competitive front, Texas Air Corporation's newly created subsidiary, New York Air, was battling Eastern Airlines in the hotly contested Boston–New York–Washington, D.C. shuttle market. The planned takeover of Continental was an attempt to further capitalize on the freer environment which existed following deregulation.

The Offer

In its February 9, 1981 announcement, Texas International disclosed that it held 1,459,200 shares of Continental stock, roughly 9.5 percent of the total. The Houston-based carrier also divulged plans for a tender offer of $13 per share for an additional 4 million to 6 million shares, which would raise its interests to between 35 and 48 percent. If the tender offer were to be successful, Texas International would then petition the CAB for control of Continental. Approval of the CAB was necessary when any airline acquired a greater than 10 percent interest in another. In fact, one condition of the tender offer was that pending CAB approval, Texas International be permitted to place the shares tendered to it in a voting trust. The trust would be permitted to vote on the proposed Continental-Western merger. Some industry analysts familiar with Lorenzo's tactics felt he might be more interested in making a profit on Continental stock, as he did with National, than in actually assuming control of the airline. However, there did not appear to be any potential for a bidding contest for Continental, which led the majority of experts to believe Lorenzo's true goal was indeed control of Continental.

Continental's Response

The announcement of Texas International's intentions took officials of Continental by complete surprise. Its initial response was that the offer "raised many legal, financial, and regulatory issues that needed to be analyzed." The matter was referred to Continental's independent financial and legal advisors and further comment was withheld until their analysis was complete.

On February 25, Continental released an official statement rejecting the offer, terming it "grossly inadequate." Continental said that the $13 per share offer represented less than half the stock's adjusted net worth of $29.12, citing figures Texas International itself submitted to the CAB. Feldman, Continental's president, noted that the entire offer was less than what Continental had received for the recent sale of four used aircraft. He advised shareholders to reject the bid and to approve the pending merger with Western Airlines.

Continental also filed both a lawsuit and a CAB petition to block Texas International's advances. The lawsuit contended that the offer violated federal law, the Federal Aviation Act, and state law. The CAB petition stated that the offer attempted to circumvent CAB merger regulations and improperly endangered the Continental–Western combination by attracting speculators who would vote against it in hopes of securing larger profits. Continental also objected strongly to the proposed voting trust for the shares tendered to Texas International, approval of which could be fatal to the Western proposal. It argued that the granting of such a trust would allow Texas International to exercise control over Continental before the matter was adjudicated by the CAB.

Some Good News for Texas International

Texas International felt that precedent was on its side in its bid to obtain the limited voting trust. In its earlier attempt to gain control of National Airlines, it had pursued a similar trust which would have empowered it to vote on all matters affecting its ability to take over that airline. The CAB had denied that request but left the door open for future requests for trusts with more limited voting rights.

On March 2, the CAB approved the proposed Continental–Western merger. However, two other rulings were issued which effectively ended any hopes for completion of that merger. Texas International was granted permission to raise its Continental holdings to 48.5 percent and, in addition, was awarded its limited voting trust. With Texas International casting all of its tendered shares against the Continental–Western merger, it would be impossible for Continental to obtain shareholder approval for the proposal.

In response to the unfavorable rulings, Continental announced plans to seek a preliminary injunction against the takeover attempt in the U.S. District Court of Los Angeles. It also petitioned the appeals court of Washington, D.C. to overturn the decision of the CAB on the grounds that it had misinterpreted that section of the Federal Aviation Act which prohibits one airline from controlling another without board approval. Both Continental and Western Airlines announced the indefinite postponement of the scheduled March 12 shareholder vote on the proposed merger. Continental officials explained that the delay would give them additional time "to deal with the complex situation" and explore alternatives to the Texas International takeover. On March 12, 1981, the federal appeals court denied a motion on Continental's behalf to halt the advances. Insiders reported a sense of hopelessness among Continental officials who appeared to have exhausted all available avenues of defense.

On March 13, Texas International reported that it had purchased the maximum 6 million shares it had sought under the tender offer. Following this announcement, it began to soften its approach in dealings with Continental. Sources close to Texas Air Corporation, the holding company owning 100 percent of Texas International, indicated that they wanted to avoid a long fight and were willing to make compromises to promote an early and orderly transfer of control. Rumored among the possible concessions was the granting of powerful positions in the merged company to some of Continental's top managers. Reportedly, Lorenzo greatly admired the talents of Alvin Feldman and was eager to benefit from his experience. An executive close to Feldman indicated that he would only be interested in a position which accorded him complete control of the resulting airline. As the apparent winner in this battle it was unlikely that Lorenzo would be willing to surrender that level of control.

The ESOP Proposal: A Diluting Punch

On April 8, the Continental Employees Association announced plans to buy control of its airline in an attempt to thwart Texas International's advances. The association was headed up by two veteran Continental pilots, Paul Eckel and Chuck Cheeld. Eckel, a 42-year-old 727 pilot, had flown for Continental for 16 years. He had been fired from the management post of chief pilot in 1980 following a disagreement with a superior, but stayed on as an active pilot. His part-time business was real estate syndication and he was accustomed to bringing groups of investors together. Two months earlier he was selected by his fellow pilots to organize a purchase of Continental shares on the open market in an attempt to fend off Texas International and give employees some voting leverage. He collected $110 million in commitments including $40 million from the pilots' retirement fund. Unfortunately, the ploy failed when the CAB granted Texas International's voting trust for the shares tendered to it. Forty-one year old Chuck Cheeld joined Continental one year after Eckel. He was the custodian of the pilots' retirement fund and therefore had some investing background.

The two pilots each conceived of the ESOP separately before conferring on the matter. Both felt the plan was the "ideal response to the loss of control of our destiny." They believed there was a justified fear among their fellow employees that Lorenzo was planning a raid on Continental assets involving the sale of aircraft and substantial worker layoffs. Eckel stated that the airline resulting from this merger would be so fragile that "a hiccup in the economy would put us out of business." The next task at hand was selling the ESOP idea to Continental management and employees.

Cheeld first met with Feldman to outline the details of the plan. The president said he would consider it, but in fairness he had been negotiating with Texas International and felt an obligation to hear what they had to offer. He also expressed some concern as to whether the rest of Continental's 10,400 employees would support the plan. Eckel assumed the task of educating the employees on the fundamentals of the ESOP. He held press conferences and employee rallies to encourage support and found the objections to be very few and limited. He attributed this to his belief that "owning a piece of the action" was the secret dream of all American workers. An employee vote was held and 98 percent of those voting favored the ESOP.

Following the employee vote of confidence, Feldman spoke out strongly in favor of the plan as an alternative to the proposed merger. He had analyzed Texas International's offer thoroughly and believed the resulting airline would be extremely weak with little chance for survival in the highly competitive market. Prior to the tender offer, Texas International held $154 million in debt and only $54 million in equity, exhibiting a debt to equity ratio of 2.85. After the tender offer its debt/equity ratio was expected to be 4.56, a ratio he felt was "intolerable." Based on this information, he agreed with the assessment of his employees that a raid on his company's assets was imminent.

The plan involved a large-scale issue of stock which would double the 15.4 million shares currently outstanding. Continental was authorized to issue up to 50 million shares. Its intentions were clear. The issuance and resulting dilution were expected to be the knock-out punch. The new stock would have full voting rights, reducing Texas International's interest from 48.5 percent to less than 25 percent. The shares would be placed in a tax exempt trust earmarked for employee distribution. The issue of who would hold the voting rights to these shares was, as yet, unresolved. The shares would be controlled by either an independent trustee or the employees who would eventually receive the stock. The total cost of the new issue would be $185 million for which financing would have to be arranged. The debt was scheduled to be repaid by employees sacrificing approximately 15 percent of their gross pay over the following four to seven years. Lawyers for Continental reviewed the plan and were confident that it was entirely legal.

Legal, Financial, and Regulatory Obstacles

The first hurdle for the Continental Employees Association was securing financing for the proposed ESOP. Officials were encouraged by the upbeat response they received following preliminary discussions with several of Continental's current lenders. On April 24, the association announced that it had received commitments from nine banks for the full $185 million required to fund the issue. They did caution that these were verbal commitments, subject to loan-pricing arrangements and satisfactory resolution of legal issues.

On the legal front, Continental officials were aware that the courts generally vetoed the use of ESOPs as a means of merger defense. However, George Vandeman, an attorney for Continental, felt the proposed plan was precedent setting in that it gave control directly to the employees and he expected to receive court approval. Feldman felt the company had a strong case. In his opinion all that was involved was the sale of previously authorized, new equity capital to employees. Continental fully expected a tough legal battle but was confident of its chance for victory.

The largest obstacle for the plan involved the regulations surrounding the issuance of such a large volume of stock. It was highly probable that the NYSE would require a shareholder vote before approving the issue. If the ESOP came to a shareholder vote, Texas International was certain to use its 48.5 percent interest to defeat the proposal. Continental was fully aware of this danger and was prepared to accept a voluntary delisting from the NYSE if necessary. In the event of a delisting, it would then approach the AMEX hoping that its regulations would be more lenient. Because the shares were already authorized, some legal advisors felt the NYSE might permit the issue without shareholder approval. Also helpful was the fact that Continental was incorporated in the State of Nevada, which did not require a shareholder vote prior to the establishment of an ESOP.

Texas International Responds

As expected, Texas International reacted harshly to the proposed ESOP. Philip Bakes, a former general counsel of the CAB, and legal vice-president of Texas Air Corporation, called the plan "flagrantly illegal" and not a valid ESOP. Lorenzo called the plan a blatant attempt at management entrenchment. He said the prior negotiations were nothing more than a charade. Moreover, he insisted that the merger was in the best interests of all involved and that no raid on assets or layoffs were planned. He further added that Feldman's comments represented an irresponsible attack and accused Continental management of using fear tactics in fostering the notion of extensive employee layoffs. Officials of Texas International vowed to fight the formation of the ESOP in every possible way.

Texas International also petitioned the CAB for the establishment of a "reverse trust" in order to assume control of Continental immediately. The essence of the reverse trust was to place Texas Air Corporation's 100 percent interest in Texas International into a trust that would be controlled by independent trustees. Texas Air would then be free to exercise full voting rights of its Continental shares. If the CAB later approved the merger, Texas Air would then dissolve the trust and complete the combination of the two airlines. If this trust were approved, Texas Air intended to use its voting interest to elect new directors at Continental's May 6 annual meeting and secure operating control of the airline. Texas International insisted that the reverse trust was necessary to protect the rights of current shareholders who would lose control of the company as well as equity if the new issue were approved. Continental claimed the ESOP was nothing more than a second bidder for the airline and that the reverse trust was an obvious attempt to circumvent the CAB process. Aware that CAB approval of the reverse trust was unlikely, Texas International submitted an alternative petition seeking an amendment to its current voting trust which would permit it to vote against the stock issue.

ESOP Gains Support

The ESOP gained support and momentum on April 30 when the CAB denied Texas International's request for a reverse trust, calling the idea a "sham." The CAB did give Texas International the right to request a shareholder vote on the establishment of the ESOP at the upcoming annual meeting. But the CAB did not give it the power to vote its shares independently on any proposal, including the election of new directors. It would be required to cast its votes in the same proportions as the remaining shareholders. The CAB also stated that this ruling did not force Continental to recognize any requests for a vote by Texas International. As expected, at the meeting Texas International did call for a vote on the proposed ESOP several times and each time Feldman ruled the request out of order to the cheers of approximately 1000 Continental employees and shareholders.

Frustrated by recent developments, on March 8, Texas International announced a $13 tender offer for the remaining 51.5 percent of Continental's shares. They requested that the Continental board review the offer and approve it for the benefit of all Continental shareholders. Continental replied that a special committee had been appointed to review the offer along with other alternatives, including the ESOP. On March 12, Texas International announced that it had arranged the necessary financing to purchase the remaining 51.5 percent and on March 20 it raised its offer to $14 per share. On March 21, Continental's board rejected the offer, calling it "inadequate." It stressed that the offer was not in the best interest of its shareholders because the viability of the combined airlines was still very questionable.

On June 3, the Continental board formally endorsed the ESOP. In rebuttal, Texas International requested that the CAB require approval of the ESOP before permitting issuance of the new shares. It contended that the Continental Employees Association as an entity was involved in the airline business and therefore should not be permitted to assume control without board approval. Continental dismissed this as a desperate move on Texas's part and a misrepresentation of the facts. The ESOP, according to Continental, was not a single entity, and therefore could not fall under CAB jurisdiction as any other airline would. This contention was further supported by the fact that the trustees and participants of the plan were not obligated to vote as a block. As a result, they could not be considered a controlling interest. On June 12, the federal appeals court denied an earlier injunction sought by Texas International to block the formation of the ESOP. Continental announced that the new issue would be distributed "shortly."

A Devastating Blow for ESOP

The New York Stock Exchange dealt the ESOP a devastating blow by requiring a shareholder vote before approving the new issue. In spite of the CAB ruling which restricted Texas International's voting rights, Continental still feared a vote on the ESOP. They suspected that shareholders would defeat the motion because they feared dilution of their stock value following such a large issue. The long battle had also attracted many speculators who were expected to vote against the measure. Further investigation indicated that the American Stock Exchange would be no more lenient than the New York Stock Exchange had been. Still confident, Continental was prepared to accept a voluntary delisting from the NYSE and petitioned the California Corporations Commission for a special stock issue just for the ESOP. The fact that no state or federal court would grant Texas International's requested injunctions against the ESOP gave Continental confidence that a special issue of this type could be arranged. Buoyed by this confidence, Continental hired two new executives, Michael Levine, a new executive vice-president, marketing, and George A. Warde to assume the office of president. Feldman was named chairman of the board and would direct his interest toward the ESOP formation while Warde would concern himself with the day-to-day operations of the airline.

Early in July there was considerable speculation that Texas International might be willing to abandon its bid for Continental. Momentum was heavily in Continental's favor and meetings were reportedly held between Lorenzo and Feldman at which details of a plan for Texas International to sell its holdings back to Continental were discussed. A feeling of cautious optimism was prevalent among officials at Continental.

On July 13, Continental's ESOP received what proved to be fatal news. Geraldine Green, California Corporations Commissioner, ruled that the requested stock issue could not be granted without shareholder approval. She further stated that she supported the principle involved but not this specific plan, calling it "unfair and misleading." Even if Continental could garner enough shareholder support it was not likely that the matter could be put to a vote prior to Texas International assuming control. Early indications from the CAB suggested that it would approve Texas International's request for control and that decision would be announced soon. In light of these developments, financial support for the ESOP began to erode. The investment market was very active at this time, and the banks began to withdraw their commitments in order to seek more secure profits in other areas. Without these financial commitments, the

ESOP appeared to be finished. Clearly, Texas International was back in control of the situation.

On July 20, the CAB gave preliminary approval to the merger of Texas International and Continental. Final approval was granted in early August, pending presidential review. Presidential review was still required because international routes were involved.

The Most Tragic Chapter

The most tragic chapter of this long battle was written on August 10 when Feldman was found dead in his office, the victim of a self-inflicted gunshot wound to the head. In addition to the myriad of business problems which plagued him at the time, he was also greatly depressed by the loss of his wife, Rosemily, to cancer in 1980. Shortly after Feldman's death, Warde assumed the duties of chairman. In September Texas International raised its interest to 50.3 percent and began to force the Continental board to recognize its majority interest. On October 13, following favorable review by President Reagan, Texas International assumed operating control of Continental Airlines.

In the end, despite its courageous and innovative efforts, Continental lost its bid to remain independent. The loss was magnified by the tragic death of its popular and widely respected chairman, Feldman. In assuming control of Continental, Texas International was at best a dubious winner. The battle had been costly and left it in a highly leveraged position. This, coupled with Continental's poor earnings history, prompted considerable speculation among industry analysts as to the value of this apparent "victory." Only time will tell whether these two airlines can fly together.

The Common Thread

In the past few years, companies facing unwanted tender offers or stock accumulation programs have resorted to using employee benefit plans as part of their defense strategy. Because of the percentage of stock held by employee plans, companies have endeavored to use their plans as a defense against takeovers. Four methods of defense stand out. One method involves the company using the ESOP to accomplish a leveraged buyout. A second calls for the employee plan to refuse to tender its shares, or to tender its shares to a firm with a friendly offer. In a third approach, the plan purchases the target company's stock, while a fourth entails using the plan's surplus assets. The target can use these strategies to help defend against an acquisition or, alternatively, to impose plan restrictions in order to prevent the acquirer from using the target's surplus assets in the event it gains control.

Many uncertainties are involved in using an employee plan as a defense against a takeover, not the least of which requires determining the many state and federal laws which apply to the situation. The question of fiduciary duty and responsibility is also raised. Additionally, such strategies are not always successful. The previous three cases have presented situations where companies sought to use employee plans to avoid mergers. This section explains the methods involved and the merits and dangers of such defenses. In particular, the first part of the common thread, entitled Deployment of Employee Benefit Plans, describes the use of defenses structured around alternative employee benefit plans, while the second part, Rules of the Game, discusses the structure of these plans and their application.

DEPLOYMENT OF EMPLOYEE BENEFIT PLANS
Buying Stock to Kill the Deal

In some cases an employee plan's funds are used to make defensive purchases to prevent a takeover. In this manner, stock is placed into friendly hands. Grumman succeeded in this effort when its pension plan bought an additional 1.2 million shares of Grumman stock to thwart LTV's takeover attempt. Continental Airlines also attempted a similar defensive strategy by forming an ESOP. With the ESOP, a company can quickly place a large block of stock into the plan. Financing comes through the target company. Unfortunately for Continental, the California Corporations Commissioner would not allow Continental to issue the stock to the ESOP without share-holder approval. In the case of Bendix–Martin Marietta, Bendix had assumed that the pension plan shares were safe from the tender offer, only to have Citibank attempt to tender the shares. Dan River had more success against Carl Icahn when its ESOP aided in buy-ing out all existing shareholders. Harper & Row had similar results when 1 million shares, representing approximately one third of its outstanding shares, were acquired by its profit-sharing plan from the Minneapolis Star and Tribune, which was trying to force a merger with Harper & Row.

Too Much of a Good Thing

When the assets of a defined benefit pension plan exceed all cur-rent, vested liabilities, the plan is said to be overfunded. The direct allocation and use of these excess funds can become a critical two-edged sword in potential merger situations. The availability of these funds can make a target company more attractive to the acquirer and conversely, the target may take steps to prevent these funds from reverting to the employer as a means of deterring takeover attempts. These funds can represent a low-cost source of capital which the target can use to defend against unfriendly advances.

According to the Employee Retirement Income Security Act (ER-ISA), when a pension plan is terminated, surplus assets can revert back to the employer provided this has been stipulated in the plan definition and such reversion does not violate any state laws. If either of these two conditions are not satisfied the surplus must be distributed to the participants and beneficiaries of the plan. Very often surplus assets can be generated by the act of termination. The Internal Revenue Code and ERISA state that the corporation must make contributions which are sufficient to provide all retirement benefits defined in the plan. The amount of these contributions must be consistent with sound actuarial principles and the as-sumed rate of earnings on these funds must be reasonable. Histori-cally, the assumed interest rate used to calculate these earnings has been in the 6 to 7 percent range. In the event that a plan is termi-nated, the assets are distributed to the participants and beneficiaries according to a specified termination plan. The interest rate used in compiling this termination plan is periodically set by ERISA and the Pension Benefit Guaranty Corporation and generally reflects current market conditions. Recently, this stated rate has been in the 9 to 12 percent range. This discrepency in interest rates means that on termination, fewer assets are required to fulfill the liabilities of the plan. The end result is that surplus assets are often "created" where none existed in the ongoing plan or, if there was a surplus in the ongoing plan, the amount becomes much larger at termination.

Faced with hostile overtures from potential acquirers, firms often view the surplus of a pension plan as a readily available, low-cost source of capital. Upon plan termination, this capital can be utilized to finance various defensive strategies. The establishment of ESOPs and the purchase of large volumes of stock from major shareholders are two common uses for these funds.

In summer 1981, Harper & Row terminated its pension plan and in the process recouped $9.8 million in surplus funds. As previously described, these funds were used to help finance the purchase of roughly one third of its shares from the Minneapolis Star and Tribune. A majority of these shares were deposited in the newly established ESOP. Periodically, shares were distributed to an employee's account and the employee became vested in these shares at a rate of 20 percent per annum. The voting rights of all nonvested shares were controlled by the trustees of the plan.

Subsequent to this action, a suit was brought against Harper & Row by several hundred of its employees. Prudential Insurance Company, which underwrote the benefit annuity at plan termination, was named as a codefendant in the suit. The claimants called for an immediate reinstatement of the pension plan, including return of all excess assets. They contended that Harper & Row's actions constituted a management entrenchment scheme and a violation of fiduciary duty under ERISA. They also denounced the action as "contrary to the best interest of shareholders" because Harper & Row retained the voting rights to nonvested shares. They also argued that management-held voting rights discouraged third party bidders for the company and diluted shareholders' interests. Prudential was charged with using an unreasonably high interest

rate, 15 percent, in establishing the annuity. The effect of this alleg-
edly excessive interest rate was to minimize the assets required for
the annuity and maximize the available excess funds at termination. Use of this rate was cited as a violation of ERISA and the bylaws of the retirement plan itself. As evident by this case, such
amendments to the plan are often associated with legal battles.

Similarly, Graniteville Company, a South Carolina textile manufacturer, terminated its two pension plans in 1983 in an attempt to
repel a tender offer from a group led by Victor Posner. Posner, a 64-
year-old financier from Miami Beach, controlled Southeastern
Public Service Company (SEPCO) and had accumulated a 26.1 percent interest in Graniteville on SEPCO's behalf. By terminating the
pension plans, Graniteville was able to fund an ESOP with the
plan's surplus assets which purchased 781,000 of previously authorized, unissued shares of its own stock. This represented approximately 15 percent of the total outstanding shares and reduced
SEPCO's holdings from 26.1 percent to 22.1 percent. Graniteville's
major concern was that although SEPCO was not seeking a merger,
it was attempting to obtain a majority interest. The Graniteville
board believed this action would greatly jeopardize the interests of
the remaining shareholders. SEPCO later changed its strategy, this
time agreeing to purchase all of the remaining 3.8 million Graniteville shares, contingent upon a successful tender offer for 2.3 million shares. Satisfied that all shareholders were assured a fair value
for their interests, Graniteville withdrew its self-tender offer and
the Posner group assumed control.

Surplus pension funds played a major role in the defensive strategies of both Harper & Row and Graniteville. The degree to which
these actions succeeded is, as yet, unclear. In the Harper & Row
case, independent of the final outcome, in the interim it was able
to fund the purchase of the stake held by the Minneapolis Star and
Tribune stock. If the court rules in favor of the employees, the disposition of the 1 million shares currently held by the ESOP will do
much to determine who ultimately will control the company. In
Graniteville's case, the use of the pension funds appears to have
been unsuccessful in warding off SEPCO's advances. However, the
strategy was effective in that it forced SEPCO to restructure its offer
such that all Graniteville shareholders were assured a fair price for

their stock. If the purpose of defensive strategies is to protect the shareholders' interests, Graniteville was indeed successful.

The once rarely used strategy of employing surplus pension funds as a defense strategy is becoming more common. In June 1985, United Airlines announced its plan to convert $962 million of surplus pension fund assets to general corporate use. UAL's executive vice-president, finance, John Cowan, described the preemptive defensive move and indicated that

> we are taking this step so that outsiders who might be tempted to try a takeover of the company to obtain those excess assets in our pension program will clearly understand that they are not available. Under-utilized assets like those in our pension plans might attract those who would see the excess as a source to pay off their own takeover of UAL.

The events surrounding the largest corporate pension draining program prior to UAL's may have stimulated it to act. For example, Occidental acquired $375 million from several Cities Service pension funds after it acquired the company. Seeing this example of an aggressor raiding the surplus of a target may have been sufficient motivation for UAL to reduce the available "free" funds in its own pension fund.

Deterring Unfriendly Advances

Acquiring companies often view a prospective target's overfunded pension plan as a source of capital which can be utilized to finance the acquisition. Because of this, target firms frequently take action to protect these funds in the event of hostile advances. By prohibiting the acquiring company from securing these assets they have limited the acquirer's available financing and made themselves a less attractive target.

Changes in the provisions of pension plans as a defensive strategy have a long history. In 1973, the Great Atlantic & Pacific Tea Company (A&P) was the subject of a hostile tender offer from Gulf & Western. In an attempt to repel these advances, A&P amended its pension plan, stating that if the plan were terminated, all excess assets would be distributed to plan participants and beneficiaries. The purpose of this amendment was to inform all potential acquirers, including Gulf & Western, that in the event of a takeover, A&P was prepared to terminate the plan and render the excess assets unavailable. If the plan was terminated prior to completion of any merger, the new company would be powerless to reverse this decision and recover the funds for its own use. The defensive strategy was successful and A&P was able to thwart Gulf & Western's advances.

Interestingly, in June 1981, A&P board of directors amended the plan again. This time, the original bylaws, which called for excess assets to revert to the employer in the event of plan termination, were reinstated. In October of the same year, the A&P board terminated the plan in an attempt to recoup the $200 million surplus that existed. In response to the board action, a former A&P executive filed a class suit claiming that the amendment was unlawful and requesting an order to direct the surplus funds to plan participants and beneficiaries. He contended that the participants were being denied funds that were rightfully theirs and that the board's action violated ERISA in that it did not act "solely in the interest" of the plan's members. The resulting settlement granted the participants of the plan $50 million with the remaining funds reverting to A&P. This settlement was approved by the courts in February 1983.

In another case, the ESOP was used as a multipronged defense. In February 1985, National Can, attempting to thwart takeover pro Victor Posner, used its ESOP in an innovative repurchase tactic. While it first resulted in the usual reduction in the number of shares available for the raider, it also had another effect. It enabled National Can to legally exclude Posner from the repurchase. Posner held 38 percent of National Can's stock. The ESOP's charter prohibited the purchase of shares from a holder with more than a 10 percent stake in the company. As a result, Posner, in a suit against National Can and its ESOP, charged that the directors disregarded shareholders' best interests by controlling the company "for the sole purpose of entrenching themselves." National Can's chairman responded that "We're going to defend our position very strongly. We think we've done the right thing for our shareholders." In the end, both sides got what they wanted. Posner got a nice fat profit by selling out to Triangle Industries, which made a white knight offer to National Can. And National Can, while preferring to remain independent, at least was not going to be controlled by their arch enemy, Victor Posner.

As a 1986 New Year's resolution, Union Carbide obviously decided to strengthen its ability to fight GAF. On the last day of 1985, it announced it had retrieved $509 million in surplus pension assets. Doing this, it no doubt felt it was in an improved position to mount a more effective defense to either remain independent or gain a better return for its shareholders.

Attracting Friendly Suitors

The availability of surplus pension funds can be used as bait by companies looking to attract friendly suitors. These funds enhance the attractiveness of the target and can be used by the acquirers as a low cost source of financing for the acquisition.

The GAF Corporation revised its pension plan in June 1982, calling for the revision of surplus assets to the employers in the event the plan was terminated. Shortly thereafter, the plan was terminated and the corporation recouped approximately $35 million in surplus funds. The original bylaws of the GAF plan, written in 1968, had called for reversion of surplus assets to the employer at termination. When the plan was rewritten in 1976 to comply with ERISA, no mention was made as to the disposition of surplus funds at termination. In December 1982 a former GAF employee brought suit against GAF. The plaintiff contended that the amendment and subsequent termination of the plan was unlawful and called for the return of the surplus assets to the participants of the plan. The suit also alleged that the purpose of the plan termination was to increase the liquidity of GAF in the interest of attracting a friendly acquirer. In August 1983, the courts ruled in favor of GAF, stating:

> This decision is consistent with the policies and purposes of the statute and the plan itself. The employee participants shall receive their respective defined benefits as the plan contemplates. The existence of a surplus at the time of termination and the amount thereof is purely fortuitous, and the extent to which it exists is due to the acts of the employers. If in an effort to be conservative, the plan is overfunded, surely the employer should not be deprived of that surplus,

which the statute specifically permits the employer to receive, if the plan so provides.

The courts, in this case, reinforced the original contention that, so long as no laws are violated and the plan so stipulates, surplus funds may revert back to the employer.

ESOP Leveraged Buyout

In recent years, the use of the ESOP leveraged buyouts has increased in frequency. Companies have discovered the benefits which ESOPs can provide and are including them in their corporate strategic planning. Managers consider utilizing ESOPs in leveraged buyouts to reap a number of advantages. They provide a financing tool, generate employee support, and could play an important role in the prevention of a takeover.

The ESOP is often preferable to debt financing because of the lower interest rates and the tax shields related to principal repayment. In addition, conventional financing may be undesirable to a company with a debt-laden capital structure. There is the implicit assumption that analysts do not consider off-balance sheet financing through the ESOP when predicting a company's performance. Restrictive covenants from existing loan agreements may also be in place. Furthermore, if an external market does not exist for additional company securities, then issuing new shares is not an alternative.

Generally, employees are inclined to support the creation of an ESOP because they would share in the ownership and, they hope, in the profits of the organization. Employees have been known to accept wage concessions to keep the company intact. Such was the case in Continental's battle against Texas International. Continental employees agreed to sacrifice 15 percent of their gross pay over a four to seven year period in order to repay the debt incurred in the ESOP leveraged buyout that was planned. Similarly, at Pan American World Airways and Rath Packing Co., employees agreed to large pay cuts in return for partial control of their respective companies. As strange as it may sound, sometimes willingness to take a pay cut may weaken management's defense. For example, in July

1985, while TWA's management fought Carl Icahn, the TWA pilots' union said it would accept pay cuts as great as 20 percent if TWA were taken over by Icahn. They feared the cost-cutting, union-busting white knight who was also bidding for TWA, Frank Lorenzo. He had used Chapter 11 bankruptcy laws to void union contracts and cut wages when he took over Continental.

In thwarting a takeover, the creation of an ESOP serves three purposes. First, through buying stocks in the market, the ESOP reduces the number of shares available to outsiders. Second, a company can effectively dilute the block of stock held by other shareholders by issuing additional shares to the ESOP. Third, employees will usually vote their shares with existing management because they are as concerned as management about their employment prospects in a hostile takeover.

A target company may face difficulties in finding a white knight as was evidenced in the case of Dan River defending against Carl Icahn. The financial advisors for Dan River engaged 34 companies in merger discussions without obtaining a single serious offer. Dan River's only viable option to surrendering to Icahn was to convert to an employee-owned company using the leveraged ESOP as the financing vehicle. But looking back with hindsight, many Dan River employees regret the creation of an overnight ESOP. The creation was so hurried that union officials decided against having a union attorney or accountant study the ESOP before it was set up. In a 1985 interview, the president of the local union expressed his dissatisfaction with the setup, stating "that was our big mistake. If you are going to get into an ESOP, you sure as hell don't want one like Dan River's." In Continental's case, the company considered the ESOP being planned by the Employee's Association as nothing more than a second bidder; it could be likened to an internal white knight.

RULES OF THE GAME

The Structure of ESOP

An ESOP works in the following way: the company sets up a trust into which it can contribute annually. It can contribute stock directly to the trust, or it can contribute cash to be used to buy company stock from outside investors or lenders. In either case, the contributions are deductible from taxable income. Basically, the employee accumulates stock and ownership in the company, and the company receives tax deductions. Additionally, benefits can be distributed in the form of company stock, or the employee can cash in the stock which has accumulated in his/her account. A major feature of the ESOP is that, unlike a profit-sharing plan, it is empowered to borrow from the company.

When a company develops an ESOP, it must follow certain requirements under both the Internal Revenue Code and ERISA. Foremost, the plan must be established and function solely for the benefit of the employee participants. In addition, contributions to the plan must be in proportion to wages. In other words, the company cannot discriminate in favor of employees who are members of management or who receive the highest salaries. Another important rule dictates that the plan must be designed to invest primarily in employer securities. Moreover, these securities must be properly valued through independent appraisal before they are contributed to the trust. The fiduciary or trustee of the plan must exercise prudence in managing the plan's assets. The Internal Revenue Code also establishes certain voting requirements for ESOPs. Plan participants must be allowed to vote the securities allocated to their accounts if the securities are registered. Securities required to be registered include shares of publicly traded companies with more than 300 employees in the ESOP or shares of companies dealing in interstate commerce. A small intrastate company does not have to register securities even if it is publicly traded. In this case, voting rights are provided only for matters which, by state law or charter, must be decided by a supermajority of the outstanding shares. Matters of such importance include issues of merger, liquidation, reorganization, and similar significant decisions. For issues involving company operations and election of board members, the trustee of the plan votes the block of shares for the employee participating in the ESOP. Additionally, the trustee votes the shares which have not yet been allocated to the employee accounts.

If the employer's stock is not publicly traded, voting rights must be passed onto employees when more than 10 percent of total ESOP assets are invested in employer securities. However, voting can be limited to matters, such as mergers, liquidation, and so forth, as in the case of the small intrastate public company. Employees do not vote directly for members of the board. Decision making for issues related to ordinary operations of the company rests with management. Furthermore, voting rights cannot be guaranteed because a privately held company is not regulated by the SEC. Indeed, a recent study shows that in 85 percent of all companies with ESOPs, worker-owners do not have voting rights.

ESOP as a Financing Tool

Typically, the ESOP is utilized as a financing vehicle for the employer corporation. Under the Internal Revenue Code, contributions to the plan, either as cash or stock, are tax deductible. For a regular or nonleveraged ESOP, deductions allowed for contributions are limited to 15 percent of the compensation of all employees in the plan. Increased cash flow from this tax shield is the primary source of funds for a nonleveraged ESOP.

In order to encourage adoption of ESOPs under the Economic Recovery Tax Act of 1981 (ERTA), Congress allowed a tax credit of 0.5 percent of the ESOP participants' wages if the employer contributes an equal amount to the plan. In addition to tax reductions, ESOPs are designed to have a real effect on the firm's operations. Some advocates of ESOP argue that as part of the new ownership, employees become more conscientious and productive. They realize that their future income depends on the success of their company. This increased productivity translates to greater profits and additional funds for the company.

In leveraged ESOPs, the plan essentially borrows money to buy employers stock. In one scenario, the ESOP borrows money from the lender and uses the funds to pay for the company's stock. Meanwhile, the lender holds the shares as collateral for the loan. Over time, the employer collects employee contributions and transfers them to the fund which uses these funds to repay the lender. Under the Internal Revenue Code, these contributions are payable in pretax dollars. Under another scenario, the ESOP borrows from the

company, which in turn borrows from the lender. With the passage
of ERTA, Congress liberalized the limits for contributions made under both scenarios. This act allows the employer to deduct contributions applied to the repayment of principal up to 25 percent of
the wages of plan participants. In addition, it provides for an un-
limited deduction for employer contributions to the ESOP to pay
the interest on the loan. As the loan is paid off, shares of stock are
transferred to the employees' accounts. In essence, the leveraged
ESOP enables companies to borrow large amounts of money and
obtain considerable tax deductions for payments of both principal
and interest.

Through the Tax Reform Act of 1984 (TRA), Congress provided
companies with additional incentives for creating ESOPs. Companies can borrow at an interest rate of about 80 percent of prime.
This is possible because the TRA makes 50 percent of the interest
paid tax exempt for the lender if the ESOP loan bought employer
stock. The lender passes some of these savings to the ESOP purchaser in the form of a lower interest rate. Though the tax incentive
is legitimate, the "no free lunch theory" implies that it is not cost-
less. Paul Samuelson, Nobel Lauriate Economist at MIT, represents
this school of thought by saying, "In the various ESOP utopias, the
alleged ability to mobilize new bank credit costlessly and with net
social advantage is illusory." In other words, he claims the bank
loans could be used for more productive alternatives. He went on
to say that "people would start using opium to produce cotton shirts
if [given] an economic incentive to do it." An additional incentive
is that cash dividends paid on stock held by an ESOP are tax deductible if the distributions are passed on to the employees.

Schizophrenic Dilemma–Shareholders or Employees?

The administrator of any employee plan is a fiduciary and, as such,
subject to both federal and state laws. His actions should be made
in the best interests of the participants and beneficiaries of the plan.
According to ERISA rules, a fiduciary is required to discharge his
duties with prudence. A fiduciary is prevented from using the assets of a plan in his own interest or acting in any transaction in-

volving the plan on behalf of a party whose interests oppose those of the plan's beneficiaries and participants. One question deals with the issue of who should serve as the trustee of an employee plan, a company official who faces a conflict of interest or an objective third party. Another question involves the purchasing or tendering of shares in a hostile takeover situation.

For example, in the Grumman–LTV case, the trustees of the pension plan were also officers of the corporation and faced a conflict of interest between their duties to the plan and their duties toward the company. The court ruled that by failing to tender shares to LTV, and by buying additional shares of Grumman stock, the trustees breached their fiduciary duties by not acting in the best interests of the plan.

In the Bendix–Martin Marietta case, the trustees of Bendix's employee plan, Citibank, felt that in order to live up to ERISA's definition of a "prudent man," it should tender the shares to Martin Marietta, despite the fact that such an action violated the trust documents. The courts upheld Citibank's decision.

When A&P again amended its pension plan after Gulf & Western's takeover attempt failed, surplus assets were to fall once more to A&P, not the plan participants. The trustees of the plan were charged with breaching their fiduciary duty by depriving the plan's beneficiaries of the assets.

Not Everyone Is Happy

Despite all of its positive aspects, the ESOP has received considerable criticism in recent years. One focus of criticism is the issue of employee control. Employees are given ownership via the allocation of stock to their individual accounts. However, if employee-owners are not given the right to vote for members of the board, they do not gain control of the operations of the company. This was the case in Dan River. The ESOP provided 70 percent of the funding for the buyout, received 70 percent of the stock, but was given no rights to vote directly for the board. Management, however, contributed 3 percent of the funding, received 25 percent of the stock, and received voting control of the company. This type of inequity has drawn the attention of the Labor Department in the cases of

Blue Bell, an apparel manufacturer, Raymond International, an engineering concern, Scott & Fetzer, a conglomerate, and others. The Labor Department intervened when the terms of the leveraged buyout in each company gave the managers a disproportionately large amount of stock for a very small investment. The ESOPs on the other hand, furnished large contributions in return for smaller stakes in the companies. Some argued that it was a transfer of wealth from the employees to the managers, with managers unduly enriched at the ESOP's expense. Both Blue Bell and Raymond Industries responded to the Labor Department's suggestion by reducing management's share and increasing the ESOP's stake in the company.

Another criticism of the ESOP is reflected in the statement of Morton Klevan, a deputy administrator in the Department of Labor's Office of Pension and Welfare Benefit Programs. In his opinion, "A lot of ESOPs are really MESOPs, management entrenchment or management enrichment stock ownership plans. If it looks like a MESOP, the odds are it violates the law." Creating an ESOP in the midst of a takeover battle usually provokes such a claim. In 1983, Southeastern Public Service Company (SEPCO) filed suit against Graniteville for forming an ESOP. SEPCO claimed that the ESOP was "part of a plan of managerial self-entrenchment" which "diluted existing shareholder interests, wasted corporate assets, . . . and precluded SEPCO from protecting its investment." In this particular instance, the charges did not hold. In Texas International's battle against Continental, similar claims were made which contributed to Continental's failed attempt to establish a leveraged ESOP. Charges were made that management failed to meet the business judgment standard by not acting in the best interests of the shareholders and presumably protecting themselves by creating an ESOP.

Pension advocates express concern that companies are replacing retirement plans with ESOPs. Traditional pension plans provide security but no real opportunity for significant growth. On the other hand, ESOPs provide the opportunity for capital appreciation but are riskier. What happens if the value of the stock drops or if the company fails? The Pension Benefit Guaranty Corporation, the federally sponsored pension insurance agency, does not cover ESOPs.

As a result, the participant is not insured against the loss. Advocates advise companies to retain their pension plans to coexist with the ESOP in order to guarantee that employees receive the benefits they have earned. In the case of Weirton Steel Corp., the company maintained its pension plan when the ESOP leveraged buyout occurred. However, Dan River and Raymond International both terminated their pension plans. Therefore, employees in these cases are extremely nondiversified and had to rely on the future of the company.

The Ingredients of Success

The three cases presented in this chapter raise the question of when employee funds can be used successfully to defend against an unwanted merger. Why did Grumman and Dan River succeed, while Continental's efforts fail?

One key ingredient of success seems to be the commitment of shareholders and employees to their company. Grumman employees, who constituted a major block of stock, feared an LTV takeover would cost them their jobs and so refused to tender their shares. Citizens of Danville, Virginia, many of whom were Dan River employees, joined the fight against Icahn by buying stock in Dan River. Even though Continental's defense failed because of a lack of other success factors, employees showed their support when 98 percent of them voted in favor of ESOP. Clearly, this commitment was an important factor.

The legal counsel received was another major key to success. Rules govern the establishment of plans, the conduct of fiduciaries, the termination of plans, and similar issues. In itself ERISA is an unusually complex law, difficult to understand even to those who work with it on a daily basis. In Grumman's defense against LTV, Grumman trustees were found guilty of breaching their fiduciary duty. The courts, however, found no violation of SEC laws, so the stock purchases were not rescinded. On the other hand, the potential for violating antitrust laws was a major reason for LTV's failure.

Icahn was caught in a classical "Catch 22" situation. If he voted on the selling of Dan River to its employees, he would have been required to disgorge profits on sales of shares held less than six months. If he didn't vote, he wouldn't violate any securities law, but he couldn't win. His decision: not to vote. Dan River, on the other hand, followed ERISA guidelines to the letter, thus meeting with success. The ability to juggle the myriad of state and federal laws was an important determinant of success. Amazingly, three years later in July 1985, Icahn found himself trapped by the jaws of the same laws. Icahn held 33 percent of TWA's common stock and he expected to benefit from the proposed Texas Air–TWA merger. But again, he couldn't vote his shares in support of this deal without incurring the possibility of forfeiting the profits as an insider trader. Luckily for Icahn, he found other avenues to profit from his holdings.

Gaining shareholder approval is another necessary element for success. For example, Continental's ESOP required shareholder approval before the stock could be issued. This approval was required by both California state law and NYSE regulations.

Being able to reduce the number of shares available to the acquirer aids the target company in avoiding a merger. The purchase of 1.3 million shares by Grumman's pension plan represented about 9 percent of Grumman's stock. Together with the employee investment plan's holding, Grumman succeeded in putting approximately 40 percent of the stock into friendly hands. Dan River's purchase of stock at a price above the tender offer severely hurt Icahn's efforts. Continental's ESOP would have had a similar effect on Texas International, had the ESOP been approved.

Sufficient funding to purchase additional shares was obviously a deciding factor in determining success. Grumman's pension plan had enough financing available to buy the additional shares. Dan River was able to acquire sufficient funds to purchase 900,000 additional shares. When Continental's financing commitments fell through, the company became an easy target for Texas International's takeover efforts.

Employee funds can play an important role in defending against an unwanted merger. As we have seen, the most important factors are likely to be support of employees and shareholders, knowledge and use of applicable laws, reduction in the number of shares available to the acquirer, and sufficient funding. Obviously, each will play an important role in a successful defense.

8
The Proxy Defense

The T. Boone Pickens Philosophy: The Most Fertile Oil Field Is The Floor Of The New York Stock Exchange

MESA PETROLEUM vs. GULF OIL

As the market for oil contracted, the entire oil industry came under pressure to reorganize its assets. The oil giants, those integrated companies that once seemed "inviolable," were no longer immune. The oil industry failed to participate significantly in the 1983 stock market rally and, as a result, stockholders in petroleum companies became restive.

As investors grew impatient with lagging returns, those companies that proved deficient at improving their performance risked having it done for them through takeover attempts, breakup of assets, or even liquidation. For one large oil company, Gulf Oil Corporation, this risk became reality on August 11, 1983.

Pickens Goes Fishing in the Gulf

By 1983, Gulf Oil seemed to be too large to be seriously threatened by a raider. With 1983 sales of $29 billion, Gulf was the fifth largest U.S. oil company. However, this oil giant was not trouble-free. In recent years, its sales were flat and its earnings were volatile. Mostly due to a series of oil discoveries, Gulf's exploration and production division looked strong. Unfortunately, its other divisions were not performing so well. Like the rest of the industry, Gulf's refining and marketing division was suffering from overcapacity. As a result, in 1981 it lost money and in the following year it barely earned 3 percent on sales. In an effort to streamline the division, Gulf sold most of its European refining and marketing facilities to Kuwait. It also closed heating oil and service station operations in upstate New York and parts of Vermont, Ohio, and Michigan. Another disappointing performance was reported by Gulf's chemical division. It suffered from depressed prices and in 1982 lost $328 million on revenues of $2 billion. To further compound the bleak outlook, Gulf's mineral division was limping along with earnings of just $13 million.

Gulf's weakness was not overlooked by oil pro T. Boone Pickens, Jr., the chairman of Mesa Petroleum Co. The thought of an encounter with Mesa, an oil and gas producer with 650 employees and 1983 sales of only $422 million, sent shivers up the spines of most major U.S. oil men.

Pickens, a native to the oil industry, was born within sight of working wells. He grew up in Holdenville, Oklahoma. After graduating from Oklahoma State with a degree in geology, Pickens joined Phillips Petroleum. Unhappy from the start, he left Phillips after only four years. Using part of the $1300 he received in severance pay from Phillip's profit-sharing plan, Pickens purchased a 1955 Ford station wagon. He loaded the wagon with his exploration gear and set out on his own.

The road was slow and bumpy but after a year of knocking around without financial backing, Pickens secured a $100,000 line of credit. This money was used to form Petroleum Exploration, his first company.

In 1964, Pickens formed Mesa Petroleum and by 1971 he was a millionaire. At the heart of his fortune were the energy finds and lucrative investments that had been made by Pickens. Some properties that he acquired rose staggeringly in value. For example, in 1959, Pickens invested $35,000 in Canadian drilling sites using the income to fund new wells. In 1979 he sold the Canadian operations for $600 million.

Pickens was quick to realize that oil company stocks were undervalued and began searching for riches on Wall Street in the early 1980s. He reasoned that it was both easier and smarter to get new oil reserves by taking over a company than by drilling for more oil. He said, "It has become cheaper to look for oil on the floor of the New York Stock Exchange than in the ground."

To determine a candidate, Pickens's analysts at Mesa study in depth every prospective target. "By the time my guys get through with the numbers," Pickens says, "we know those companies better than they know themselves." Over the years, Mesa accumulated an extensive library of the U.S. petroleum industry. Its analyst team spends months sifting through piles of public documents including annual reports and other sources describing possible target firms. The accumulated data, which usually focuses on a firm's domestic oil and gas reserves, is fed into a computer along with other data such as projected interest rates and energy prices. A company spotted by the Pickens computer filter would likely appear soon on the front page of *The Wall Street Journal*.

The Early Signs

Gulf's shares had risen a healthy $8 over the previous year to $35. However, that value represented only one-third of the company's oil and gas reserves. Chairman James E. Lee knew that despite its huge size, Gulf could become a takeover target unless its stock price firmed further.

Even after making valiant strides cutting costs, streamlining unprofitable refining, and marketing operations, and allotting $1 billion to buy back its own stock, Gulf's market capitalization was only 2.2 times cash flow. This figure was the lowest of any of the oil giants. Furthermore, given Gulf's oil reserves, it was equivalent to a price of about $4 per barrel compared with an average cost of more than $10 per barrel for finding new U.S. reserves.

On August 11, 1983, trading in Gulf stock was unusually heavy. The man behind the action was none other than T. Boone Pickens, Jr. who had started acquiring what would start off as an 8.75 percent stake of Gulf's 165 million shares. Pickens did not say he was trying to take over the company, nor did he say he planned on greenmailing it, but he did make it clear he believed stockholders could get more value if Gulf were restructured.

"Skunk Repellent Defense"

Under the assumption that Pickens intended to wage a proxy challenge at the annual meeting in May 1984, Gulf management called a special shareholder meeting for December 2 in Pittsburgh. The objective of the special meeting was to get enough votes to get rid of the present cumulative voting system for electing directors. Under the cumulative voting mandated by its Pennsylvania charter, with just 7.7 percent of Gulf's 165 million shares, a dissident holder could gain a seat on the company's board. The December 2 proposal called for a reorganization of Gulf into a Delaware chartered holding company. The advantage of being incorporated in Delaware was that under Delaware law, companies may pass bylaws prohibiting such cumulative voting practices. Gulf called the Delaware incorporation its "skunk repellent" defense.

In defense of the proposal to eliminate cumulative voting, Gulf's chairman said Gulf is "unequivocally committed to the principle that Gulf's shareholders are best served by directors who are responsible for representing all shareholders, not just a few."

Pickens Wages a Proxy Fight

On October 31, T. Boone Pickens announced that he was waging a proxy fight against the proposal by Gulf to reincorporate as a Delaware corporation, a move aimed at keeping him off its board.

The Pickens group consisted of Sunshine Mining Co. of Dallas, Harbert International of Birmingham, Alabama, Wagner and Brown of Midland, Texas, and the greenmailing pros of Canada, the Belzbergs. Since early August, when it started buying Gulf's shares, the group had spent a total of $800 million to increase its holdings to 10.8 percent. The group was seeking to persuade shareholders to reject the company's proposal at the December 2 special shareholder meeting. With 165.3 million shares outstanding, either party needed 82.7 million shares to win.

Gulf Wins the First Round

Gulf won a clear victory over the Pickens group at the December meeting, with 55.7 percent of the shares voting in favor of the Gulf-sponsored resolution to reincorporate in Delaware.

Before a breakdown of the voting was publicly available, sources from the Pickens group claimed the group won the majority of the votes it had courted most ardently, those of the institutional holders. This meant that the big players, the people whom Pickens had gone after and who most understood his proposal, had moved into his camp.

Gulf countered saying Pickens did not really get as much institutional support as he thought. It went on to say that many of the institutions which admitted voting against Gulf claimed they did so only because of their fiduciary responsibility to shareholders.

On January 13, Gulf announced the final result showing it had received 4 million shares beyond the minimum required to win the December 2 proxy battle. On the same date, Pickens sued in a U.S. district court to invalidate proxies covering nearly 6 million shares on the grounds that the proxies contained technical defects.

The Royalty Trust Proposal

The Pickens group continued to accumulate Gulf shares after its loss of the proxy battle. By early January, the group had accumulated 13.2 percent of Gulf's 165 million common shares.

On January 11 the group proposed a royalty trust that called for a spinoff of 40 percent of the company's oil and natural gas producing properties to be set aside in a trust, with profits paid to the shareholders. The proposal also contained a sweetening twist: a 5 percent royalty interest on future gross income from Gulf's improved properties, aimed at making the trust more attractive to shareholders.

Pickens viewed big oil companies as inefficient and their downstream investments as only marginally profitable. The Pickens group and its supporters argued that if oil company managements were forced to pay out more income to shareholders, they would have to allocate their capital more prudently. A royalty trust, they argued, would speed up the closure of marginal refineries and other obsolete assets, resulting in higher cash flow, part of which would go to the shareholders.

Gulf responded to the proposal with a letter from Chairman James E. Lee. In the letter he said, "We are satisfied that the royalty trust concept, as it might be applied to Gulf Oil Corp., has been thoroughly studied and thoroughly discredited, and that your [Pickens's] continuing public advocacy of it is a disservice to our shareholders."

Gulf argued that royalty trusts leave too little cash in the company to cover debt and other expenses, and negatively affect the amount available for discretionary investment. As much as 40 percent of any royalty trust would be taxable as a dividend at distribution. Gulf argued that as a result of this tax effect, many individuals would probably sell their shares to institutional investors. These investors were likely to be pension funds which are not subject to a dividend tax. Management believed such stock transfers would lead to radical shifts in ownership.

A Word on Royalty Trusts

The immediate reason for setting up a royalty trust was to avoid double taxation. In theory, under a royalty trust, income from oil and gas production properties would flow directly to shareholders instead of getting taxed once as corporate profits and again as shareholder's dividend income. The cash flow the shareholders collect would otherwise be used to search for new reserves or other investments.

Given that the oil industry's earnings were poor, royalties from trusts were advocated as a way to quiet restive shareholders who were dissatisfied with stagnating dividend growth. Couple that with the longstanding desire to avoid paying taxes and the idea becomes even more attractive.

However, even if management decided a royalty trust would be appropriate, there were some big problems involved in setting one up. When an oil company spins off a royalty trust, the first factor for the IRS to consider involves the specific properties to be spun off and whether the company has enjoyed tax benefits on the properties that the IRS can recapture.

The next question is whether the company has any accumulated profits on its tax books which have not been paid out as dividends. If so, the distribution is taxable as a dividend. The tax consequences vary, depending on who owns the shares. Individual shareholders get hit the hardest. Corporations, on the other hand, pay tax only on 15 percent of their dividends. Obviously, at the extreme, the most favorable tax treatment goes to tax exempt institutions, such as pension funds.

After the royalty trust is spun off, individual shareholders are in line for some nice tax treatment. The income from the trust after expenses is sent directly to them, and it counts as ordinary income for tax purposes. However, individual shareholders also get to deduct depletion. The result is that a big chunk of income is not taxed.

A Two-Pronged Defense

A ruling on the suit by the Pickens group, which was filed to reverse its apparent defeat in the proxy fight against Gulf, was handed down on January 16. A federal judge upheld the shareholder election that gave Gulf the authority to move its corporate charter from Pennsylvania to Delaware. Pickens said, "We paid the money for the special election and we don't want to just walk off on it."

Despite the fact that Pickens's legal challenge to the vote failed, Gulf's shares moved steadily higher on heavy volume to almost $50 a share, up $6 since the December 2 vote. The activity was based on expectations that the Pickens group was going to make a tender offer for an additional 25 million shares or roughly 15 percent of Gulf. This would give the group about 30 percent of Gulf's stock at its annual meeting, enabling Pickens to propose a full slate of directors to oppose Gulf's slate. Pickens had also rumored he might put the royalty trust before the stockholders at the meeting.

After discovering Pickens's detailed plan to acquire the company for $55 a share, Gulf management announced a two-pronged defense against the acquisition. The defense involved both legal and financial measures to sustain its independence.

Legally. Gulf sued the Pickens group in a Delaware court, charging the group with "market manipulation and other violations of the securities laws." The suit involved a request for an order which would block the Pickens group from continuing with the takeover plan.

Financially. The Gulf board authorized the company to increase its bank credit lines from $5 to $6 billion. The board also said the new credit lines, if used, would grant lenders "a security interest such that these lines would be senior to any obligation contemplated by the Pickens group." This would discourage potential lenders to the Pickens group by giving Gulf's lenders first call on the company's assets. Pickens's response to Gulf's actions was, "The same old thing, drilling dry holes, it just isn't going to work."

The Gradual Death Program

Drexel Burnham Lambert prepared a two-step takeover plan. The first step involved raising $3.66 billion to be used for a $55 a share tender offer for 61.3 million shares of Gulf stock. If successful, the purchase would give the Pickens group slightly more than 50 percent of the outstanding shares. The tender offer would be made by a new company formed for the purpose of acquiring Gulf. According to the document, the financing for the tender offer included investment units issued by the new company. These units would consist of common and preferred stock in the new concern. The remainder of the financing would come from bank borrowing and the Pickens group itself.

After the successful tender offer, the new company would propose a merger with Gulf. The remainder of Gulf stock would be exchanged for additional securities from the new company valued at $55 a share. These securities would include $3.07 billion in 20-year junior debentures often referred to as junk bonds paying 16 percent interest, and $1.5 billion of preferred stock of the new company paying a 15 percent annual dividend.

The second step in the plan would be the liquidation of Gulf over a period of as many as three years. Bank debt would be paid off and the securities issued in the merger would be redeemed using the proceeds from liquidating Gulf's U.S. non-oil assets. In contrast, the proceeds from liquidating Gulf's U.S. oil assets would be shared with holders of the new company's common stock. The document said the Pickens group would hold 75 percent of this stock, with the remaining 25 percent held by buyers of the investment units who received common stock in the first step of the takeover. The document estimated that the sale of the U.S. oil assets could result in "net proceeds" of $2 to $5 billion to holders of the common stock.

Wanted: White Knight for Rescue

Gulf stock, which had sold for as low as $29.25 a share in 1983, jumped to nearly $70 a share in early March and some said the bidding would not stop until it hit $80 a share.

The Pickens group, which had acquired over 13 percent of Gulf's stock, picked up a new partner, Carl Lidner of Penn Central Corporation, which conveniently provided the Mesa group with $300 million. With the help of the new financing, the group announced a bid of $65 a share for another block of stock. This was planned to raise the group's stake to 21 percent. Gulf's management, fearing Pickens could then capture another 30 percent of the votes at the May annual meeting, accelerated its search for a white knight.

The company opened its most secret documents for the perusal of several big corporations including some firms outside the oil industry. The conditions were simply that the information be kept confidential and not be used to make an unfriendly tender offer for Gulf shares.

A Basket of Alternatives

Gulf considered various alternatives prior to embracing the white knight rescue. These included buying another company in order to block a takeover or taking itself private. However, in the end, the white knight proposal prevailed. Gulf, in fact, had three white knight options:

1. A cash bid from Atlantic Richfield Company for $73 a share.
2. A leveraged buyout in cash and debt from LBO specialist Kohlberg, Kravis, Roberts & Co. for $87.50 a share.
3. A cash offer from Chevron for $80 a share.

The leveraged buyout was too tenuous in Gulf management's eyes, involving a $6 billion bank loan commitment for a deal that would have had a debt/equity ratio of 30 to 1.

In the resulting deal, Gulf was purchased by Chevron, the fourth largest U.S. oil company for $13 billion. At the time, it was the largest merger ever to take place. Even though T. Boone Pickens lost the battle, he became a hero to hundreds of speculators who shared in the $300 million windfall. New York City honored Pickens with a gala dinner to toast the $50 million that the Gulf fight brought the city through legal fees and other services. In the midst of the dinner, a chimpanzee on roller skates appeared dressed as a Gulf gas station attendant. As it sat down next to Pickens and started licking his face, the oil pro quipped, "James Lee was never this friendly."

Looking back on the deal, Pickens, a veteran of several unsuccessful but immensely profitable tender raids, deadpanned, "Shucks, I guess we lost another one."

Irwin Jacobs's Tavern: Everything You Ever Wanted In A Beer, And More

IRWIN JACOBS vs. PABST BREWING

Irv the Liquidator

Irwin Jacobs's battle against Pabst Brewing is one of the most fascinating and complex proxy contests to have ever taken place. It involved numerous tender offers, companies trying to swallow one another, allegations of organized crime, coalitions of former friends stabbing each other in the back, juicy name calling, and unbelievable wealth. The central figure in this complex affair was Irwin Jacobs.

Jacobs was the son of a Russian immigrant. He first worked in a slaughterhouse, then peddled junk and old clothes. Only later did his father develop collecting and reselling used burlap bags into the family business. After attending only two days, young Jacobs dropped out of the University of Minnesota. He decided to follow his father's streetwise example rather than fulfill his parent's wish that he go to college. Jacobs received his first taste of buying distressed goods and selling them for a profit when, at age 18, he bought 355 pairs of skis at $13 a pair at a U.S. Custom's Service auction. Minutes later, he sold them outside for $39 a pair. He became familiar with liquidation through a family business which liquidated the inventories of bankrupt retailers and wholesalers. But his full time job was at the business his father started, Northwestern Bag Corp., now a maker of burlap, cotton, and paper bags.

In 1975, at age 35, Jacobs made an unsuccessful try at running a troubled Minneapolis brewing company, Grain Belt Breweries. Though profitable operation eluded him, he managed to turn a $4 million profit by liquidating the breweries. His next major deal was also profitable: the purchase of W.T. Grant's receivables. With the money he made from these and other quick killings, he built a small empire of some 23 operating companies. They did everything from making steel bathroom sinks and pottery to selling real estate. Jacobs pointed to these companies as proof that he was more than just a liquidator. Detractors, however, countered that the poor performance of some of the companies provided evidence of Jacobs's lack of credibility as a manager of operating businesses. For instance, the value of Jacobs's quarter interest in Arctic Enterprises, Inc., a maker of snowmobiles and boats, declined to only about half what he had paid for it.

In subsequent years, Jacobs enhanced his reputation as a corporate raider and liquidator. His first foray into the purchase of large blocks of stock was his 9.8 percent stake in Holly Sugar. Soon after the purchase, he filed an SEC disclosure expressing dissatisfaction with the management of Holly. In it, he called for the sale or liquidation of the company. He also said he would consider the sale of his stock to a private investor. Jacobs made a $45 million offer for Holly, but later withdrew it, possibly because he lacked adequate financing. Still, Jacobs's talk of liquidation set off buying by professional arbitrageurs on Wall Street. As a result, Holly's price soared. In February 1980, Jacobs sold his stock for a $3.5 million profit.

Jacobs next used this profit to increase his holdings in Republic Airlines to 5 percent. But this investment proved unprofitable as Republic's stock price plummeted. Although the airline repurchased Jacobs's shares in May 1980, he lost more than a million dollars on the venture.

Undaunted, in July, Jacobs bought a 9.7 percent stake in American Distilling Co. It had just sold all of its assets and was looking for a company to buy. Jacobs threatened a tender offer or proxy solicitation and simultaneously announced he would petition the courts to force American to liquidate. In defense, the management group, which held 39 percent of the company's shares, revealed a plan to repurchase 16.7 percent of its outstanding stock. American Distilling ultimately paid Jacobs $21.50 for all the shares he had bought for $19.

During the same period, Jacobs and some friends at Mid America Bancorp ran afoul of the Federal Reserve Board. In November 1979, the Fed learned that Mid America intended to borrow money and repurchase its stock in order to help Jacobs increase his ownership to 30 percent. The Fed negotiated a reduction in the planned borrowing. It also secured Jacobs's personal guarantee for a portion of the debt and a pledge that Mid America would retire the debt over 10 years. The stock redemption was approved in March 1980 and took place in April. Later, the Fed learned that Jacobs was moving to liquidate the holding company by offering its subsidiary banks for sale. The Fed filed formal charges and issued a temporary order prohibiting the sales. Jacobs and his group challenged the Fed in court, but their case was dismissed in December 1980. Two months later, the Fed announced that Jacobs and specified Mid America officers would pay penalties of $50,000. This was arranged as part of an out-of-court settlement for providing false and misleading information in a stock redemption application.

Despite Jacobs's failure at operating Grain Belt Breweries, his thirst for breweries was not quenched. Back in November 1980, he and a group of investors bought a large stake in Pabst Brewing. The investors included Daniel Lindsay and Dennis Mathisen, president and chairman respectively of Mid America Bancorp, Wayne Olson, president of Watkins Corporation, and Gerald Schwalbach, executive vice-president of Jacobs's bag company, the Jacobs family business. The group filed the required information with the SEC, making known its intention to hold the stock as an equity investment. The amount of the stake was 8.3 percent of Pabst's 8.2 million shares. Since no member of the group held more than 5 percent of Pabst stock, the filing indicated the group would vote as a block.

Pabst, Another Perfect Jacobs Target

It is amusing to note that some of the financial press portrayed Jacobs's interest in Pabst as a midlife desire to successfully operate a brewing business. He remained fascinated with the industry, even after his unsuccessful attempt to run Grain Belt Breweries. These articles romanticize the cunning of the Jacobs raider group, and may have reflected Jacobs's own public relations posturing. Not coincidentally, Pabst represented to Jacobs a very desirable target. It had all the necessary ingredients for a successful takeover:

1. Low management stock holdings, less than 2 percent.
2. An unsettled management team, including discord among top management.
3. Poor operating performance. Pabst's income had dropped from $32.2 million in 1976 to $9.5 million in 1979, and its share of the market had fallen from 12 percent nationally to 9 percent. Worse yet, Pabst's market losses were in sales of its flagship brand "Blue Ribbon."
4. Low market value of $13 a share compared to book value of $34 a share. To many, this meant that the liquidated value of Pabst would likely exceed its market valuation.
5. Absence of antitakeover measures in the bylaws or articles of incorporation. Pabst's incorporation in Delaware made it particularly attractive since Delaware law allowed the takeover of a corporation through shareholder consents without waiting for an annual shareholder meeting at which to stage a formal proxy fight.

Schlitz might have been an alternative target for the Jacobs group. Schlitz was a similarly poor performer among major companies in the beer industry, and it had newer facilities. However, more than 50 percent of its stock was held by family members friendly to its management. Pabst, then, was the preferred target. It had recently fended off an attempted takeover, raising traders' interest in the possibility of another battle.

Consolidation in the Beer Industry

The beer industry was in a period of consolidation driven by the dominance of the two market leaders, Anheuser-Busch and Miller. Together, they controlled over 50 percent of the market. Some analysts speculated that consolidation would eventually lead to pricing stability and improved profits. Advising portfolio diversification, they also drew attention to the recession-proof character of beer revenues. An important development in the market was the growth of high profit premium and low calorie beers. These beers, such as Budweiser's Bud Light, rolled out in the spring and summer of 1982. Growth in such market segments implied further decline in the flagship brands of second rank brewers like Pabst. For these reasons, many analysts saw no reason to believe that mergers would improve the second rank brands. On the other hand, combination might allow company survival. The consolidated company may operate from a stronger financial and strategic regional base and be better able to deal with the giants.

Trouble at Pabst

In the face of the likelihood that Pabst would be acquired and possibly dismantled, the company was attempting to improve its performance. In April 1980, Pabst hired Anthony J. Amendola as president and chief operating officer. Formerly with Anheuser-Busch's advertising agency, he had been responsible for some of its most successful advertising campaigns. Amendola promptly initiated a new national TV campaign for Pabst, featuring takeoffs on movie heros and the slogan "Give that man a Blue Ribbon." The slogan differentiated Pabst beer from other beers by taking advantage of the Blue Ribbon name.

A major problem plaguing Pabst was the legacy of its 1960s strategy of cutting back on advertising and reducing the price of its beer. Pabst did not skimp on its beer formula. This strategy resulted in a slimmer contribution margin than the leaders enjoyed. Along with Pabst's lower volume, this market plan meant that Pabst had no hope of out-advertising the giants. Pabst's outlays for advertising in 1979 were $18.3 million versus Miller's $75 million and Anheuser-Busch's $87.1 million. Amendola, however, planned a 40 percent increase in 1980 and expected to match the larger brewers in key cities.

Although earnings for 1980 were up 33 percent to $12.6 million, Amendola apparently did not see eye to eye with Frank C. Deguire, Pabst's chairman. In February, Deguire forced Amendola out and assumed the title of president. Worse yet, Pabst reported an unexpected loss of $1.8 million in the first quarter. Management claimed this was due to a "temporary field inventory imbalance resulting from a scheduled overhaul of some packaging lines." Updating Pabst's packaging had been one of the objectives of Amendola's marketing plan. Although it was not clear whether this operational failure was the fault of Amendola or Deguire, Deguire was forced to resign in July 1981. Analysts agreed that although Deguire was well liked, he was not moving the company. Thomas McGowen, 53, an attorney and outside director of the company, was named interim CEO.

Jacobs Takes His First Shot

Jacobs saw an opportunity to make a power play for control while Pabst was experiencing poor results and a management upheaval. Having recently bought into the company, Jacobs said he viewed the situation with alarm. Concrete action followed swiftly. On July 12, the Jacobs group filed a new SEC report. The group now held about 9.5 percent of Pabst's stock, no longer claiming to hold it simply as an equity investment. The filing spoke of a lack of leadership and direction in the company's management and outlined the group's intention to demand five seats on the board and the installation of Jacobs as chairman under pain of a proxy fight if these demands were not met.

Jacobs a Pabst Director

At the July 28 meeting of the board, a compromise was reached. Jacobs agreed to drop his demand to become chairman with five seats on the board and to withdraw his threat of a proxy fight if the board elected him to a new, fifteenth seat on the board. It did. Jacobs immediately persuaded the board to make a bid for Schlitz, which had just accepted a $494 million offer from Heileman Brewing. Heileman had offered $17 in cash and stock with all Schlitz stockholders to be treated roughly equally. Jacobs convinced the Pabst board to offer Schlitz a deal Pabst valued at $588 million, or $20 a share. It included roughly the same amount of cash as the cash portion of the Heileman offer. The balance of Schlitz shares were to be exchanged for debentures bearing 15.5 percent interest and convertible into Pabst common at $27 a share.

Several weeks later, on August 16, Schlitz approved a definitive agreement to be acquired by Heileman, thus rejecting the Pabst offer. Schlitz apparently reasoned that the equity portion of Heileman's offer was worth more than the debt portion of Pabst's offer. With the conversion price of the Pabst debentures set at $27, they were unlikely to be converted soon and therefore were not expected to be traded at par. Meanwhile, the expected debt service on the debentures lowered the real value of the Pabst offer. As it turned out, the antitrust division of the Justice Department blocked Heileman's purchase of Schlitz. It undoubtedly would have blocked a Pabst purchase as well.

Jacobs did not attend the September board meeting but demanded in a letter that McGowen, the board's interim CEO, be removed for subverting the Schlitz takeover attempt. Jacobs wanted Pabst to make a better offer. He had persuaded the board to consider a cash offer of $20 a share, but Pabst couldn't raise the money. Jacobs announced he would revert to his plan to take over Pabst through a proxy fight. He hinted he would buy the company himself, but his claim that he had the resources to buy Pabst was disputed by two directors. Reviewing this episode, it is clear that Jacobs was demanding that Pabst take a high-risk gamble to move fast and acquire another company, or otherwise be acquired. Naturally, Jacobs hoped the result would produce profits for his group.

A New President at Pabst

At its September 15 board meeting, Pabst tapped 46-year-old William F. Smith, Jr. to become president and CEO, as well as a director. Smith's previous career was with a small regional brewer, Pittsburgh Brewing, where he had worked through the ranks to become president. In that capacity, he turned the company around by capitalizing on the popularity of Pittsburgh's winning sports teams and Pittsburgh's pride in local brand names. Smith became the focal point of the Pabst management's public relations campaign against the Jacobs group.

While the public relations campaigns of both sides were getting started, Smith tested the insurgent group's determination by refusing to give them a stockholder list. The laws of the State of Delaware, where Pabst was incorporated, are particularly liberal on the subject of a shareholder's access to the stockholder list. As a result, Jacobs won the list through a court order in November. He then announced he might seek to unseat the incumbent directors by soliciting shareholder consents. State law in Delaware permits shareholders to approve actions without holding a meeting if a sufficient number of them give consent in writing. Shareholder consents, under this law, are solicited according to the same rule as proxies. However, they may be solicited at any time chosen by the soliciting group. Under federal law the disclosure obligations for consent solicitations are the same as for proxy solicitations. In fact, it makes consents a specific form of proxy. There are pitfalls to the rarely used consents, including the right of the company to ask shareholders to rescind their consents. Indeed, Jacobs's attempt to control Pabst's board through shareholder consents ran afoul of both state and federal securities laws.

William Smith decided to get the company moving. He contrasted his solid business management experience with the image of Jacobs as "Irv the Liquidator." Smith was hamstrung, however, by Blue Ribbon's pricing structure and the difficulty of commanding premium prices for the beer. As a result, his management strategy was based primarily on reducing overhead costs and adjusting production capacity. Pabst's production capacity was 19 million barrels, but it shipped only 13.5 million. To cut costs, Smith restructured the marketing department, which was now reporting to him, and gained certain tax and wage concessions when he threatened to shut down the Newark plant. He also sought concessions from workers at the Peoria brewery using a similar threat. All this was designed to produce at least the image of a turnaround. In a

December 8, 1981 *Wall Street Journal* article, Smith was quoted as saying that he had not met Jacobs and had "more important things to worry about right now." He indicated, however, that the threat of an expensive proxy fight was not helping the company. A Pabst statement said, "At a time when our company needs harmony and cooperation, Irwin Jacobs has taken a separate course."

Jacobs and Smith at the OK Corral

When Smith finally did ask for a meeting with Jacobs, it took place on odd neutral ground in an airport hangar in Minneapolis. The meeting lasted less than an hour. Jacobs simply asked Smith what side he would take in a proxy battle. He did not get an answer until a week later, when Pabst filed a 65-page suit. It accused Jacobs and his group of securities law violations and impugned Jacobs's character and tactics. It charged him with illegally soliciting proxy votes by "massive publicity," and making repeated "false and misleading statements" to the press. It also accused him of "using press agentry without submitting the legal documentation and financial disclosures required by the SEC in formal proxy solicitation efforts." Smith had chosen his side, and Pabst had adopted the classic defense of questioning the insurgent's SEC filings in court. Pabst's suit was clearly part of management's continuing public relations campaign seeking to contrast Jacobs's financial chicanery with Smith's solid efforts to restore Pabst's profitability. The suit, filed in federal court in Minneapolis, asked for injunctions against further purchases by the Jacobs group and sought an order forcing the Jacobs group to divest itself of Pabst holdings.

For their part, the Jacobs group pursued the tactic of aggressively increasing its holdings to improve its voting position. In a new SEC filing on January 10, 1982, the group disclosed holdings in excess of 1.2 million or about 14 percent of Pabst's 8.2 million shares. The Jacobs group also established a shareholder's insurgent committee to broaden the influence of its group. On the committee were the widow of a popular former Pabst CEO as well as Fran Tarkenton, the well-known former professional football star. Three days later, the Jacobs group filed again with the SEC, disclosing that it had increased its stake to 1,254,555 shares, or 15.3 percent of the shares outstanding. The additional holdings, however, appeared to have been those of committee members who were now legal participants in the proxy fight and thus required to make disclosures to the SEC and to the solicited shareholders.

Pabst reported a loss for the fourth quarter of 1981, but Smith predicted profitability in 1982, claiming, "I need some time to save this company and I don't need Irwin Jacobs." Pabst also beefed up its board with the election of three new well-known outsiders.

In another tactical move, on February 2, Pabst announced an agreement to purchase Smith's former company, Pittsburgh Brewing. It was part of a strategy to grow through small but regional acquisitions. The board agreed to pay $7 a share for Pittsburgh, all in Pabst stock. When consummated, the deal was expected to dilute Jacobs's holdings. It was "coincidently" planned to take place after the April annual meeting.

The Fight Turns Nasty and a New Hunter Enters the Field

The proxy battle turned nasty and personal during the final months. Jacobs told reporters that he thought "of the Pabst board as an organ grinder and of Smith as its monkey." Smith was quoted as saying, "I was willing to listen to Mr. Jacobs's thoughts, and found out he didn't have any." On numerous occasions, Jacobs was referred to as "Irv the Liquidator." Jacobs called McGowen "an idiot," and he protested, "How can they call me a liquidator when they're the ones selling off capacity?"

In the midst of this squabble, a new party exhibited interest in Pabst. On February 22, Philadelphia-based Schmidt Brewing offered to buy Pabst for $128 million, or $16 a share. Schmidt apparently turned the tables when Pabst made inquiries about purchasing it. Pabst rejected Schmidt's offer, which some viewed as modest in light of Pabst's market price of around $13 a share and its book value of almost $34.

The Jacobs–Pabst legal and public relations battle continued. Pabst filed a legal motion demanding "corrective disclosure" from Jacobs on his statement that the purpose of the Pittsburgh Brewing deal was to dilute his group's voting power at the upcoming annual meeting. While this motion was denied, the court continued to consider an injunction against Jacobs for alleged "personal abuse" of Smith, especially for the monkey and organ grinder analogy. For its own part, Pabst's campaign was handled by a public relations agency. Through "a clerical error," it released to two newspapers a "privileged and confidential letter" from Pabst to the SEC, accusing Jacobs of making "seriously inaccurate statements."

The insurgents' formal proxy solicitation materials were mailed on March 16, 1982. The proxy materials were intended to develop the specifics of their program to restructure Pabst. They included page after page of proposals and complex textual discussion. The insurgents discussed their future plans for Pabst in the event they would be elected to the board. The group also made disclaimers which stressed the uncertainties involved in their proposal. Finally, it indicated their inability to commit themselves categorically to their plan of action. The plan laid out in the proxy solicitation was to have Pabst conduct a $20 per share self-tender offer for 2 million or 24.4 percent of its shares. The Jacobs group would not tender its shares under this repurchase offer. Not tendering had the effect of giving the Jacobs committee and nominees 21.3 percent of the remaining stock outstanding.

Pabst management responded by calling the repurchase plan a blatant effort to garner proxy support. It claimed that the actual value of the repurchase to remaining Pabst shareholders would be only around $16 a share. It also argued that the debt incurred to repurchase the shares would double Pabst's fixed charges. The plan, Pabst management said, was designed to conceal the Jacob group's lack of new ideas and lack of successful experience in the brewing industry. Moreover, it claimed the repurchase "wouldn't produce or sell a single barrel of beer."

Who Could Best Sell Pabst: Management or Jacobs?

Pabst's management acknowledged that its days as an independent brewer were numbered. It now admitted to be looking simply for the "maximum value for shareholders." Concurrently, Pabst's management was undertaking an interesting defense against Schmidt's attempt to buy Pabst. On March 26, Schmidt upped its offer to $20.50 a share or $167.8 million. Meanwhile, Pabst was conducting a public relations campaign against Schmidt, alleging the connections of its owner, William H. Pflaumer, to organized crime and his record of felonious misconduct as a Philadelphia area beer distributor. Pabst claimed, nonetheless, to be seeking a $25 a share offer from Schmidt or another buyer. Pabst's management hired Lehman Brothers Kuhn Loeb to seek a buyer.

The public relations campaigns of the proxy battle and the takeover fight intertwined. Pabst pointed out that Schmidt's $20.50 offer made Jacobs's $20 offer untenable. In another development, the Wisconsin Securities Commission ruled that Jacobs and other members of his group filed false and misleading statements when they acquired 13.1 percent of Pabst stock during the two previous years. Primarily for public relations, Pabst pursued this and many other challenges to the Jacobs group's SEC filings. While the filings were found deficient, they were merely slapped on the wrist. The group needed only to amend its filings to cure any inaccuracy or omission.

In the Pabst–Schmidt fight, Pabst publicly questioned Schmidt's financial ability to buy the Milwaukee company. Schmidt was a closely held company, its financial statements were not available publicly, and, as a hostile competitor, it had not shown financial statements to Pabst. Pabst discovered that a major financial backer of Schmidt, Crown Cork & Seal, was one of Pabst's own suppliers. They put pressure on the supplier to pull out of its deal with Schmidt. This produced countercharges from Schmidt that Pabst was trying to exert undue influence on Schmidt's backer. Meanwhile, Jacobs joined Schmidt in publicly criticizing Pabst's management over its handling of the Schmidt offers. Jacobs specifically accused Pabst management of not dealing with Schmidt in good faith and conducting a campaign against Schmidt through news releases. He further claimed that his group was "better able to negotiate a [merger] transaction than anyone else."

One could see that the date of the battle was getting close. Just before the April annual meeting, Pabst management rushed out first quarter results, showing earnings of $1.6 million versus the $1.8 million loss in 1981. Nevertheless, the outcome of the proxy battle was especially unpredictable because of the large number of shares (70 percent) that were held by institutions. These proxies were not expected to be submitted until the evening before the meeting.

Incumbent Management Victorious

The proxy fight results showed that management had won by a narrow margin, garnering 54 percent of the votes. After the meeting, Jacobs cried foul, claiming that Pabst used "illegal and unfair" tactics to solicit proxies by selectively disclosing inside information about its potential mergers. It was public knowledge that Pabst management had used the Schmidt offer to discredit Jacobs' proposed $20 offer. Jacobs also suggested some irregularities involving the submission of broker share proxies. Although the suit was later dismissed, the Jacobs group filed suit on April 20 in federal court in Delaware. It argued to enjoin the proxies of Torray, Clark & Co., a Washington, D.C. brokerage firm holding 15 percent of Pabst's shares in its accounts. The major factor against the Jacobs group seemed to have been a widespread suspicion that, given control of Pabst, Jacobs would seek to liquidate the company. In the process, he would line his own pockets.

While Pabst and Schmidt were busy exchanging charges, Schmidt's management was preparing its next moves. On May 11, it added $5 per share in debentures to its $20.50 offer for Pabst. Schmidt also agreed to share certain information with Pabst's investment bankers. Pabst rejected this offer as well, holding to its requirement of a $25 cash offer. Pabst also expressed concern that the continuation of Schmidt's takeover attempt without success might be too costly. It feared the attempt would result in Schmidt's benefiting from information disclosed even though the merger was not completed. With takeover rumors rampant, it also suggested distributors might fail to aggressively market Pabst's brands during the summer months. Continuing its public relations onslaught, Pabst questioned the value of the subordinated debentures Schmidt had offered.

At this point a new suitor entered the fray. Heileman offered $24 a share, or $196.8 million for Pabst. A member of the Jacobs group remarked, "I think Pabst ought to take the money and run." Pabst suggested that the Justice Department would oppose such a combination on antitrust grounds. Heileman and Pabst together controlled 50 percent of the beer market in Wisconsin and Minnesota.

Meanwhile, to make the situation even messier, Pabst's management decided to strike out on its own, bidding $28 a share for Olympia Brewing. It proposed a $356 million tender offer for 49 percent of Olympia's shares, to be followed by a merger proposal giving Olympia holders securities valued at $22 a share. At the same time, Pabst's management said it would not oppose the Heileman offer if Justice did not. Pabst's proposal for Olympia included a recapitalization plan for Pabst. If the merger was completed, Pabst holders would get shares in the merged company or debentures with a face value of $25. Since the debentures were expected to be traded near par, management announced this as a plan to give some shareholders a way to cash out of their investment. Obviously, management hoped the Jacobs group would take this opportunity to cash out.

On June 10, 1982 Olympia and Pabst agreed to merge. The only change in the deal was that the merger was to be accomplished with the remaining 51 percent of Olympia holders receiving securities valued at $26, up $4. The deal struck with Olympia included an interesting provision to defend against an insurgent stockholder takeover. Pabst promised that if it decided not to merge, it would pay Olympia enough to make a self-tender offer for its own remaining shares at $26 each. This provision would be triggered if there were a change in the majority of Pabst's board. Meanwhile, Pabst was ignoring the Heileman offer due to "insurmountable antitrust problems." As it turned out, expectations were realized. On June 14 the Justice Department announced its intention to oppose the Heileman bid for Pabst on antitrust grounds.

Cleaning Up the Mess

At this point, confusion reigned supreme. Offers were made, revised, rejected, coalitions were formed, numerous lawsuits were initiated, and a proxy battle was fought. With all the confusion, each of the combatants had to assess its present position and formulate strategies for the future. Taking inventory of their strategic positions was crucial. At this time:

- Jacobs's proxy solicitation for a $20 self-tender was defeated.
- Jacobs controlled 15.3 percent of Pabst.
- Pabst and Olympia had agreed to merge.
- Pabst agreed to compensate Olympia if the Pabst–Olympia merger was not completed.
- Heileman had offered $24 for Pabst.
- Schmidt had offered $25.50 for Pabst in cash and securities.

Jacobs Takes a Partner

A new wrinkle in the Pabst–Jacobs saga arose when Jacobs proposed splitting Pabst with Heileman. The deal included a tender offer for 39 percent of Pabst shares at $22 a share if the Olympia deal went through, or $24 a share if it did not. The offer was clearly intended to discourage consummation of the Pabst–Olympia merger, thus leaving Jacobs and Heileman a smaller catch to swallow. After gaining control of the corporation, the Jacobs group would then tender its own shares to a newly formed holding company for $24 a share. The Jacobs group entered into an agreement with Heileman whereby Jacobs had the option, valid until December 1983, to sell Pabst's Newark and Georgia breweries to Heileman. It also obtained an option to sell the marketing rights for the Pabst brands in a 27-state region mostly east of the Mississippi.

Jacobs's plan, through this agreement, was to obtain Pabst at a bargain basement price. If the plan worked, it would own approximately half of Pabst at a cost of only $60 million. Some argue that the bargain price is evident when one considers that Pabst's book value as of December 31, 1981 was $254.8 million. The tender offer was contingent on the deal being approved by the Justice Department. It was scheduled to start June 23 and expire July 28. If it worked, the Jacobs group was expected to pocket $12 million.

In defense, Pabst and Olympia agreed that Olympia would conduct a competing tender offer for Pabst to repel the Jacobs takeover: "Anything he can do, we can do better." The plan amounted to using a Pac-Man strategy as a defense against a takeover by a third party. Under the Pabst–Olympia agreement, Pabst shareholders tendering to Olympia by July 16 would receive $25 a share in cash.

Pabst's public relations efforts aimed to discourage stockholders from tendering shares to Jacobs. Pabst announced, "We are convinced Mr. Jacobs's offer is illegal under the antitrust laws and therefore highly unlikely of consummation." The Pabst offer for Olympia drew 49 percent of Olympia's shares. The Olympia offer drew 77 percent of Pabst common. Among those tendering Pabst shares to Olympia was August Pabst, the only remaining family member actively involved in the management of the company.

The defenses and counterdefenses were carried forward in the courts. On July 12, Pabst sued Jacobs and Heileman to prevent more purchases. Pabst alleged antitrust and securities law violations. The suit charged that Jacobs and Heileman worked together on a tender offer without fully disclosing their relationship. The suit also attacked Jacobs's character, charging that if Jacobs gained control of Pabst, "his plans for it would destroy the company and reduce industry competition." On July 14 Jacobs sued Pabst and Olympia to halt Olympia's bid for Pabst. He argued that rather than "a simple third-party offer to purchase Pabst stock," the Olympia bid was "one step in a fraudulent and unlawful scheme, contrived and controlled by the Pabst directors and financed by Pabst at the expense of its shareholders with its sole purpose to block any unwanted bids for Pabst." Jacobs also claimed that Pabst stockholders would be disenfranchised by the offer of preferred stock. This charge neatly disregarded the fact that the preferred stock was convertible to common in two years.

On July 22, both the Justice Department and the federal court intervened. Justice announced its intention to challenge the proposed purchase of Pabst by Jacobs on antitrust grounds. Justice determined that the proposed spinoff of breweries and marketing rights would hurt competition in the beer industry. It would also leave the remaining part of Pabst too weak to compete successfully. The federal district court of Delaware separately enjoined Jacobs's proposed acquisition of Pabst. Olympia was also enjoined from buying Pabst shares. As a result of these actions, Jacobs ended his offer but vowed to seek control. Similarly, Olympia canceled its bid for Pabst, claiming, however, that the court would have allowed it to go forward with its tender offer for Pabst if it had amended two easily corrected items of disclosure. In particular, it should have said the offer was partly to benefit Pabst, and it should have stated the effect of consummation of the offer on shareholders' voting rights.

Jacobs Solicits Consents

Jacobs decided to go at it alone again, planning to take Pabst private if he could win election of his "Shareholders Committee to Revitalize Pabst" through the solicitation of shareholder consents. On August 30, his committee and nominees filed with the SEC. The deal resembled that offered in the earlier proxy battle. If elected, the slate would make a tender offer for 49 percent of Pabst shares at $23 each, up by $3 from $20 in the proxy solicitation. After acquiring these shares, some combination of cash, debentures and equity securities worth $21 would be offered for the remaining shares. The total value of the deal was $187 million. Jacobs declined comment on the 49 percent stake in Olympia owned by Pabst and its intention to merge.

On September 6, Pabst sued the Jacobs group in Delaware's federal district court alleging that the consent forms violated Delaware and federal securities laws. Specifically, the complaint alleged both misleading information and violation of several federal securities laws. The complaint also charged that the defendants were guilty of misconduct in Pabst's business affairs and asked for compensatory and punitive damages of $25 million.

On September 20, 1982 the Jacobs committee reported having received consents for 50.7 percent of Pabst's shares. The committee, therefore, argued in Delaware federal court that the Pabst directors be declared invalid. On October 13, the court ruled that the committee consent forms and materials were in violation of securities laws, specifically that (1) consents are valid for only 60 days from the date the first consent is expressed, not the nearly seven months the committee had claimed, (2) revocations of consents are valid regardless of the soliciting party, (3) consents must permit shareholders to vote for any nominee and withhold authority to remove any director, and (4) the tender offer proposed in the consent materials violated the tender offer rules. The defendants appealed without success to the court of appeals.

Wounded but undaunted, on October 26, 1982, Irwin Jacobs announced a tender offer for Pabst, saying, "If I give up, that will be because I'm going to my funeral." A Pabst insider commented, "What's going on is a vendetta. He [Jacobs] refuses to accept the fact that he was turned down by shareholders in a fair proxy fight. This is enormously damaging to the company, despite his pious statements about helping the shareholders." Jacobs claimed to have turned down an offer by management to buy him out: "I've made a commitment to shareholders and feel an obligation that I shouldn't sell out for my own personal sake." He claimed to hold no grudge, but said victory would be "very sweet when that day comes."

Heileman's End Run

Heileman, Jacobs's former partner, made an end run around Jacobs at this point. On November 7, Heileman announced having struck a deal to buy Pabst, keeping breweries in Texas, Georgia, and the West Coast, and spinning off the leftovers to Pabst holders. The holders would receive $25 a share for 73 percent of current holdings or $150 million. Pabst would retain exclusive rights to Blue Ribbon, and Heileman also committed itself to supply beer to what remained of Pabst for five years. After selling 73 percent of its holdings, the Jacobs group was expected to become wealthier by $10 million. Alternatively, it could withhold shares and become the dominant holder of the spun-off Pabst assets. Heileman's offer was $25 per share for 6 million shares, conditioned on a minimum of 3.7 million shares. At the time of the offer, it had started accumulating Pabst stock, having already bought 400,000 shares.

Two days later, on November 9, 1982, in order to preempt the competition, Heileman raised its bid to $27.50 a share with the offer to begin November 10. The offer was conditioned on a maximum of 5.5 million shares and a minimum of 3.8 million. In contrast, Jacobs's offer was $24 per share, for 3 million shares, the remainder to be acquired for cash or debentures valued at $20 a share. Jacobs was tendered 5,340,000 shares before his November 12 deadline, but those shares could be withdrawn for at least another week.

On November 10, the Justice Department announced it would not delay the Jacobs tender offer but continued to study it. The reason for Justice's interest was that half of the group's holdings were controlled by Paul Kalmanovitz, a Polish immigrant with personal wealth valued at that time around $250 million, compared with Jacobs's personal net worth of around $20 million. Kalmanovitz owned breweries operating in some of the same markets as Pabst and Olympia. These included Falstaff, General Brewing, and Pearl Brewing Co.

On November 18, the Jacobs group raised its offer to $30 a share for 3 million shares. The remaining shares were to be purchased with cash or debentures at $20 a share. The Jacobs offer now averaged $25 a share, up from $22. Since Heileman had not set terms for the second step of its offer, no comparable average per share value was available. Holders had until November 27 to withdraw from the Jacobs offer. To reduce Jacobs's chances for success, Smith told the press, "We believe that what Jacobs has done in trying to defeat a $150 million transaction with a $90 million transaction is in violation of the federal securities laws, and we intend to promptly seek judicial relief against it." The Delaware federal court refused to stop the Jacobs offer, but it did require Jacobs to notify shareholders that Kalmanovitz was providing financing for his group's tender offer. The money required for Jacobs's new offer came almost entirely from Kalmanovitz. As things came down to the wire, a major arbitrageur entered the picture. A unit representing the ownership of Ivan Boesky tendered 7.7 percent of Pabst common stock to Jacobs. It included a block of 627,294 shares purchased at prices ranging from $23 to $25.

At this point, the fight was getting hot. Former collaborators Jacobs and Heileman were using all their ammunition to sink each other's plans and win the Pabst blue ribbon.

Impediments to the Bidding War Removed

The Justice Department planned an announcement of its position on the Heileman offer Friday, November 19, just before the deadline for withdrawing Pabst shares that were tendered under the Jacobs offer. Indeed, Heileman entered into a consent agreement with the

Justice Department to shed a part of Pabst. The consent agreement was filed simultaneously with the settlement of a civil antitrust suit filed in Delaware federal district court. Heileman would retain three breweries, eight Pabst brands, and Olympia. Justice waived a 1973 consent decree barring Heileman from acquiring any brewery making or selling beer in an eight state region of the upper Midwest. Now there were no legal impediments to the bidding war over Pabst.

At the close of business Monday, November 22, 48 percent of Pabst's shares had been tendered to Heileman. One day later, on November 23, the Jacobs organization raised its bid for the first three million shares of Pabst to $35. As a result of the Pabst suit, Jacobs notified shareholders that he was financed by Kalmanovitz, who provided all the financing to raise the bid to $35.

On November 24, motions by each side to enjoin the other failed in federal court in Delaware. Two days later, Heileman confused the issue. It lowered the number of shares it was willing to accept from 5.5 million to 4.25 million, but kept the offering price at $27.50. While this was lower than the first part of the Jacobs offer, tendered shares were expected to be accepted on a first-come, first-served basis, as opposed to the pro rata basis of the Jacobs offer.

Jacobs Throws in the Towel

On November 26, Jacobs agreed to endorse a further increased Heileman offer of $29 a share for as many as 5.6 million shares, up from $27.50 for 4.25 million shares. This represented a $162.4 million acquisition. The remaining shares held by Pabst stockholders were expected to be exchanged for 10-year notes at 15 percent interest with a face value of $24 each. The Jacobs group planned to tender its 1,140,305 Pabst shares to Heileman. Heileman would try to find a third party to purchase the notes owed to the Jacobs group. This way, Heileman would have the cash desired by Jacobs. Heileman also agreed to pay Jacobs $7.5 million in legal expenses. Analysts estimated that Jacobs's "sweet loss" would lead to a gain of about $18.2 million from the deal.

Kalmanovitz was offered $5 million to withdraw from the bidding, but he claimed to the press he was willing to keep up the fight. Indeed, on December 3, a Kalmanovitz company, 21-115 Inc., announced a tender offer for $32 a share, $3 more than Heileman's offer, conditioned on the tendering of at least 4.15 million shares. It would give him a controlling interest in Pabst. He offered to buy the remaining shares at $26 payable in notes.

The following week, on December 9, the Pabst board voted to support the Heileman offer. Then, on December 15, Heileman increased its bid once more. This time its bid was for $32 a share for 5.6 million shares. Since only 1 million shares had been tendered to Kalmanovitz, on December 22, 1982 Kalmanovitz raised his offer to $40 a share and increased the interest rate on the notes to be offered for the shares acquired in the second step of his planned takeover. This last-minute attempt to defeat the Heileman offer failed. On a first-come, first-served basis, Heileman's tender offer was still more attractive to most shareholders. As of December 22, Heileman had received 6.73 million of Pabst's 8.2 million shares. At last, on January 11, 1983, Pabst reached agreement with Heileman and Olympia to merge all three companies and spin off certain holdings of Pabst and Olympia.

Now that the battle was over, the players could reflect on the struggle. Indeed, it was told that in the middle of the war, Pabst president Smith posted a sign on his wall stating "Show me a good loser, and I'll show you a loser." Many would envy Jacobs's loss, especially when the loser walks away with a $18 million check.

———

What Did Odysseus Say Returning From Troy? "You're Going To Like Us, TWA"

ODYSSEY PARTNERS vs. TRANS WORLD CORPORATION

Is the Whole Worth Less Than the Sum of Its Parts?

Perhaps the most unconventional takeover battle in recent times was the proxy solicitation of Trans World Corporation's (TWC) shareholders by a dissident group, Odyssey Partners. This group attempted to force the separation of the company's five major divisions into independent publicly held entities. They felt that conglomerates in general were valued less than the worth of independently operated divisions. The ensuing battle was likely to catch the attention of the financial community because the general directors of Odyssey were thought by some to be among the shrewdest deal-makers on Wall Street.

Odyssey believed one possible reason for this "conglomerate discount" was that large blocks of most major companies are held by institutional investors. These investors base their portfolios on extrapolated economic models. If they anticipate a decrease in interest rates, they weigh their portfolios toward interest rate–sensitive stocks. Since many think diversified companies are not as sensitive to changes in interest rates, in 1982, Odyssey believed that this was reflected in a lower share price. At the time, they thought that the 1982 Trans World conglomerate discount was on the order of a staggering 50 percent.

Leon Levy, one of the principals of Odyssey Partners, along with some of his associates, began assessing conglomerate market values back in 1981, before Odyssey Partners was formed. At the time, he was a partner with Oppenheimer & Co., a Wall Street investment firm. Oppenheimer's research identified several candidates which it felt were trading well below breakup value and confirmed Levy's suspicions that there was potential for profits in breaking a company into its parts. However, Levy was intimidated by the enormous size of most of them. Outright purchase was impossible, but if a fair number of institutional investors could be brought in, the tactic might well succeed.

The company of choice would need to meet several criteria. Most important, the operating divisions had to be both operationally and financially independent, as well as in relatively good health. Little debt was also desirable. Finally, a large proportion of the company's shares needed to be controlled by institutional investors whom Odyssey felt would be most open to a sound business proposal.

TWC met all these criteria. Along with very little debt, 35 percent of the company was controlled by institutions. Headed by its 59-year-old chairman and CEO, L. Edwin Smart, TWC consisted of five operating divisions. Trans World Airlines accounted for the largest share of the revenues (65 percent). However, the airline was experiencing a downturn at the time, resulting in a significant decrease in the market value of TWC. Also included in TWC were Hilton International, the hotel chain; Canteen Corp., a food business involved with vending machines and meal service contracts; Spartan Food Systems, Inc., operating Quincy's and Hardee's restaurant chains; and Century 21, the large real estate broker operation. In 1982, all of the divisions, except the airline, were profitable.

According to Leon Levy, "The Hilton International subsidiary was intrinsically worth more by itself than the market was saying the entire corporation was worth. In 1982 Trans World Corporation's market value was around $500 million, just about the sum for which Pan Am had sold its Intercontinental Hotels. Hilton was much larger than Intercontinental in number of rooms and . . . more highly regarded as a business."

To Proxy or Not to Proxy

With a specific company in mind, Levy now began to consider how to go about the breakup of Trans World. Two main possibilities were apparent. First and preferable was a precatory proposal made directly to TWC management. A precatory proposal is essentially a recommendation of action made to a company, either to the management or to the shareholders. By making their proposal to management, the expenses associated with the second alternative, a shareholder proxy solicitation, would be avoided. Were management unreceptive to the proposal, a detailed plan could be presented to the shareholders, thereby forcing a breakup if approval were obtained. The proposal would simply be a suggestion to break up the company and reissue shares in the names of the five divisions.

Levy was optimistic that a proxy solicitation might not even be necessary. Perhaps Trans World's directors would appreciate the benefits of a breakup. His partners did not share in his optimism. In fact, they anticipated a response more akin to all-out war. Levy's optimism was already evident back in 1981. At that time Levy and his associates at Oppenheimer had already started buying TWC stock as an investment.

Although Odyssey had already performed a valuation of TWC, it wanted independent confirmation of the analysis. For this purpose, Booz, Allen & Hamilton was contacted and assigned a $500,000 study of the venture. A few months later, the consultants presented a conclusion which was in very close agreement with Odyssey's numbers.

Buoyed by this five-volume report, Levy and his friends began discussing their plan with investors in both the United States and Europe. For the next several months, Levy met with a large number of unenthusiastic responses, perhaps because of the proposal's novelty. Then on August 13 he lunched at a restaurant in Geneva with Sir Sigmund Warburg, a British investment banker. Warburg was not only somewhat familiar with the idea of conglomerate discounts but was also enthusiastic about entering into a partnership whose objective would be to force the disbanding of TWC. Warburg put his firm, Mercantile House Holdings, behind the deal and in November joined the Hepplewhite Limited Partnership. Hepplewhite had been formed in July 1982 specifically for this purpose of disbanding TWC. By November, the main partners were Warburg, Levy, and two of Levy's associates from Oppenheimer, Jack Nash and Lester Pollack.

It was not long before word of their intention leaked out. The first public notices came in two *Wall Street Journal* articles in November. Levy was no doubt upset that his card had been tipped. Shortly after that, Nash and Pollack received a call from Geoffrey Boisi, a partner at Goldman, Sachs, informing them that Goldman, Sachs had been retained as advisors by TWC. In addition, Boisi notified them that TWC would "fight off whatever you had in mind."

Levy, Nash, and Pollack, along with others, probably anticipated the dissolution of Hepplewhite in the face of a now obviously hostile proposal. Several of the investors were much less interested in light of the now less favorable prospects. So Odyssey Partners was formed by those partners still optimistic. It was headed by Levy, Nash, and Pollack. Whereas Hepplewhite had acquired 5.3 percent of TWC stock, Odyssey Partners had only 1.2 percent, holdings worth about $10 million. The Hepplewhite control of more than 5 percent had necessitated filing of a Schedule 13D with the SEC in which the Hepplewhite Group declared that it did not wish to take control of Trans World. The next day, Trans World issued a press release stating Odyssey should "seek its opportunities elsewhere and stop threatening to disrupt the business and affairs of TWC." Both partnerships coexisted briefly with Hepplewhite finally disbanding on December 1, 1982. On that day TWC shares dropped $3⅛ to 26⅜.

It's Time for a Smart Move

The time had come for Odyssey Partners to move. They began approaching institutional investors with their proposal. They pointed out how in the 1960s and 1970s management had been left to manage as it pleased. However, now in the 1980s the time was right for the large block owners to suggest policy as well. Odyssey claimed that institutions had traditionally taken a back seat because, since the late 1960s, there had been a lack of investment opportunities. With the August explosion of the stock market, institutions were becoming more open to new ideas. They also argued that the appetite for newly issued shares was greater than at any time since the 1920s and that investors would be hungry for the shares that would result from the TWC breakup. Interest was aroused. Within the next few months, institutional control of TWC rose from 35 to 60 percent, being distributed over about 50 major institutions.

Levy and Pollack, despite the phone call from Goldman, Sachs, managed to arrange a meeting with the Trans World chairman, L. Edwin Smart, for January 6, 1983. Levy tried to be optimistic at the meeting. He was careful to point out to Smart his awareness of the CEO's various tactical decisions which had preserved each division's operating independence. Pollack was impressed by Trans World's recent decision to sell some preferred stock backed by TWA's assets instead of issuing holding company preferred, which would have been possible at a lower dividend rate. It was a "courageous decision" according to Levy, a decision which "seemed to make sense only if he [Smart] ultimately intended to separate the companies."

On the surface it was a cordial meeting, with Smart being assured that Odyssey Partners was not interested in a hostile takeover or proxy contest. Smart said he recalled Levy saying that "the god-father responsible for putting together a company" should receive a stock interest in the new companies as they are taken apart.

As Pollack and Levy prepared to leave, Smart indicated that he would be in touch. "In other words," replied Levy, "don't call us, we'll call you." "That's right," replied Smart and they parted.

Lining Up the Ducks

Shortly thereafter, Odyssey Partners retained the public relations firm of Hill & Knowlton and also a firm specializing in stockholder solicitations, the Carter Organization. Strategies were discussed with both firms. Hill & Knowlton, which also handled the Century 21 account for Trans World, abruptly resigned the Odyssey account shortly after the initial meetings, explaining that it would other-wise lose its Century 21 business.

On March 9, 1983, a letter was sent to Smart requesting a stock-holder list. Four days later, Trans World responded by filing a 53-page complaint in New York federal district court claiming "the defendants have been conducting a widespread, unlawful solicita-tion that has never been truthfully disclosed." TWC justified its ac-cusation of unlawful solicitation by noting that Odyssey had been talking to other investors. The response came within two working days after receipt of the request. Under Delaware law, where TWC was incorporated, a full five days were permitted.

Odyssey denied TWC's charges and said it wanted the list "as a routine matter" and that Edwin Smart had been personally advised that Odyssey's proposal didn't involve any takeover bid, any at-tempt to take control of TWC, or any effort to change the composi-tion of the board or management. In addition, Odyssey countered by filing in the Delaware Court of Chancery to obtain the list. Over the following few weeks, hundreds of thousands of dollars were burnt up in legal maneuvering. At last, the Delaware judge awarded the list and the New York judge decided to permit Odyssey's proxy solicitation.

The New York suit wasn't without benefit to Trans World, how-ever. Lengthy depositions were taken from Levy, Pollack, and Nash and many other Odyssey and former Hepplewhite partners who had

little or no direct involvement in the current battle. The depositions served to prevent the partners from meeting and planning for
the approaching proxy solicitation itself. An artful delaying tactic
had been employed.

Odyssey's lack of open criticism of Trans World's management
was striking. The battle was termed a "white glove rather than bare
knuckles skirmish." Further indications of the low profile could be
seen in the relatively restrained newspaper ads issued by both sides.

Pollack conceded publicly that the TWC battle is "a test of the
Odyssey investment strategy," the development of which the press
attributed to Levy. As the first test of a major new strategy, the battle received good coverage from this point on.

As a prominent Wall Street takeover lawyer pointed out, "If Odyssey's proposal does do well, the flood of similar shareholder resolutions will be unbelievable. A majority vote would do for proxy
fighting what Inco's (1974) takeover of ESB did for hostile tender
offers." This refers to the tender offer made by International Nickel
of Canada to shareholders of ESB, the world's largest battery manufacturer. The battle is considered by many to have made hostile
tender offers "respectable." At the time Odyssey initiated the proxy
fight, it was unacceptable behavior in the eyes of a large number of
investors.

The annual meeting was scheduled for April 27, 1983, and, in
preparation, TWC had sent out its proxy to shareholders on March
24. It was only then that Levy realized TWC management had set
up golden parachutes and bylaw changes at a March 14 board meeting. The bylaw changes made it more difficult for dissidents to be
nominated at the annual meeting. They now required that nominees for director be named at a board meeting at least 30 days prior
to the meeting at which they are to be elected. Thus, director nominations from the floor were restricted.

Shortly before mailing its proxy, Trans World took the initiative
by placing the first of a series of full page ads oriented toward
investors. Theirs was the "stop, look, and listen" variety, warning
TWC's shareholders of Odyssey's intentions.

Odyssey mailed its 13-page proxy statement on April 1, in which
they disavowed any intent to take control of TWC. Along with it
was a 32-page booklet which summarized the findings of the Booz,

Allen study. In summary, they had valued TWC's major parts at: Hilton International, $1 billion; Spartan Foods, $490 million; Canteen Corp., $180 million; Century 21, $110 million; Trans World Airways, $813 million. The total was $2.59 billion. In addition, the study assigned a value of $77.7 million to TWA debentures held by the parent company, thus giving an overall estimated value of $2.67 billion to TWC's assets. Given the number of TWC common shares as well as all other securities which were convertible to common stock, the market value of a fully diluted TWC share was estimated at about $70. This estimate assumed that little or no taxes would be paid on the breakup. The $70 bottom line was also emphasized in a cover letter. Odyssey's proxy material also mentioned selling some of the primary subsidiaries as an alternative to spinning them off to current shareholders.

Critical to the Odyssey plan was the support of the institutions. Levy firmly believed that most of the New York banks and houses with substantial holdings would vote for "disaggregation," as Odyssey termed the strategy. Morgan Guaranty Trust and Forstmann-Leff, each of whom held over 9 percent of TWC, were of particular concern. Visits seemed to go well. Forstmann-Leff even said that there was no need to visit as they had already decided to vote with the Odyssey proposal.

However, Smart and Frank Salizzoni, TWC's financial manager, were also visiting interested parties. Word began filtering back to Levy that some of the fund advisors with whom he and Odyssey had been negotiating were beginning to feel pressure from higher up. As it turned out, TWC's management was talking not only to fund advisors, but to the various company heads who held the pension plans which the advisors managed. As Levy put it, "As a very big company with more than $5 billion a year in revenues, Trans World is an important customer for various companies. Top executives of many companies are friends of Trans World board members. All together, TWC's prestigious directors serve on the boards of more than 40 companies." Thus, Smart was attempting to alienate Odyssey in the eyes of many major company's directors, creating an "outsider vs. establishment" battleline. The pressure percolated down to the fund advisors despite their own intentions. Many directors were made uncomfortable by Smart's suggestions, "If it happens to us, you may be next."

Levy was also becoming frustrated by the effectiveness with which Salizzoni was arguing that the breakup of TWC would result in the loss of a standing $100 million tax benefit accrued by TWA. Levy had little doubt that a breakup would yield far more than a $100 million incremental in value.

In the final days institutions began changing their votes to the Trans World management. However, a few did stay with Odyssey. As Pollack recounts, he received a call from a money manager who wished to vote with Odyssey. When asked if he cared to discuss the plan further, the manager replied, "Oh, no, Goldman, Sachs put us into the stock on the basis of the breakup value." Interestingly, just six months earlier, a Goldman, Sachs research report said, "Separately, Trans World's non-airline assets are worth more than the corporation's total stock market value."

Is It a Safe Landing?

The annual meeting took place in Kansas City on April 27. TWA employee turnout was enormous. Odyssey's representatives spoke first. Pollack introduced the proposal and Levy followed with three main points:

1. Conglomerates, and particularly Trans World, sell at discounts.
2. Single industry businesses are usually more efficient.
3. Differences exist between the interests of managers and the interests of shareholders.

Then Edwin Smart spoke. He indicated that conglomerates offer advantages, such as being able to support each others' lines of business. He declared that an intact Trans World "will provide for the shareholders' greater value than will be provided if the company is split up into parts."

It was not until May 12 that the results were announced. Management won. Morgan Guaranty had voted mostly along with TWC and Forstmann-Leff had entered abstentions, perhaps indicating partial dissatisfaction with TWC management. Over 1 million proxy votes were changed in the last few weeks. Along with the announcement came mention of first quarter losses resulting in a stock drop of $1\,1/8$ to $31\,5/8$.

Several months later, on October 25, 1983, at a five-hour board meeting, Trans World Corp. directors decided to spin off the airline division. Earlier that year, on February 9, TWC had sold 5 million shares of TWA in a move seen by some as a first step toward divesting themselves of the financial drain imposed by the air carrier. The overwhelmingly affirmative approval which shareholders gave the board's proposal suggests Odyssey's strategy may have made an impression at Trans World.

_____

The Common Thread

We have just seen three examples of attempts to influence a firm's liquidation or divestiture through a proxy contest. Yet what exactly constitutes a proxy contest situation and how can a target successfully defend against it? There are really three variations of an aggressor's proxy strategy. The first is a formal solicitation of proxies, usually mailed separately from the firm's proxy materials. This is the most common form of proxy contest and it was used or threatened by dissident shareholders in all of our cases. The second is a shareholder resolution that is mailed with the firm's proxy materials. In late 1983, in a hard-fought family battle, Willametta Keck Day, the sole surviving daughter of Superior Oil's founder, used this variation of a proxy contest. She tried to force Superior to consider offers at a price matching or greater than the market price of Superior's stock. The third variation a proxy contest may take is the solicitation of shareholder consents. This is really a special case of the formal proxy solicitation. While proxies must be submitted at a shareholder meeting, consents can be solicited without having to wait for a meeting. The use of shareholder consents is less frequent. In our cases, Irwin Jacobs attempted to win control of Pabst through their use.

The Proxy Arena: A Bird's Eye View

Different opinions have surfaced regarding the benefits of shareholder advocacy. Some view the rise of proxy contests as the legitimate effort of shareholders to influence major decisions or initiate major actions affecting the value of their investments. Others view proxy contests as usurping the normal responsibilities of management and the board, with damaging effects on the firm's ability to operate or to protect itself in an environment of daily takeover announcements.

There are basically three types of situations in which proxy contests arise. The first involves elections to replace all or part of the present board. In the 1980s, a subcategory of this situation has become popular. Raiders have repeatedly adopted the tactic of threatening proxy fights as a means to force management to buy back their stock at a premium. In the cases presented here, Irwin Jacobs and T. Boone Pickens practiced this kind of greenmail.

The second situation arises from shareholder opposition to a merger or acquisition proposed by the board. For example, in early 1985, New York-based insurer Leucadia National Corp., a 7.2 percent owner of National Intergroup, objected to Intergroup's proposed merger with Bergen Brunswig. Intergroup was the sixth largest U.S. steel company and Bergen Brunswig was a major Los Angeles-based drug distributor. Leucadia waged a proxy war but management successfully defended its merger proposal. The irony of the battle resulted when Bergen Brunswig terminated the deal a month later, citing deteriorating business conditions. Not long afterward, Leucadia took on Intergroup again. This time it sought to reorganize Intergroup and place four directors on its 13-member board. Like its first proxy attempt, this one also failed. By August 1985, management decided to reduce Leucadia's now 9 percent stake in the company. To do so, it entered into a multipurpose deal with Wesray Corp., the investment company chaired by former Treasury boss Bill Simon. In the deal, Intergroup issued 3 million shares to purchase the Houston-based company, Permian Corp. A major result of the share issuance was the dilution of Leucadia's stake from 9 to 7.8 percent of the company. While dilution was accomplished, no one doubted that the mating dance between the two would continue. It did for one more month, after which an agreement was finally reached between the two combatants, leaving Intergroup an independent organization.

The third situation occurs when shareholders seek to reject management's shark repellants, suggesting that putting up a "not for sale" sign may lessen the market value of their shares. Proxy contests may also be viewed along a continuum from those that are issue oriented to those which are motivated by general dissatisfaction and focus on management's poor performance. Odyssey Partners' proposal to TWC shareholders was a key example of an issue oriented contest. Issue oriented contests tend to be more decorous. Contests focusing on management's performance, on the other hand, can be personal and vindictive. In the Jacobs–Pabst case, for instance, Jacobs referred to the Pabst board as an organ grinder and to Bill Smith, Pabst's president, as its monkey. Of course, in practice, contests tend to have elements of both extremes. Although the Superior Oil proxy battle was issue oriented, Willametta Day had personal objections to her brother Howard Keck's controlling the business. This was evidenced in depositions recounting his responsibility for the death of her childhood pet ostrich by stuffing an orange down its throat.

Life as a Dissident

For management to defend itself more effectively, it is important to understand the aggressor's remedies, limitations, and motives. The usual prerequisites for insurgents in all proxy contests may be summarized in four guidelines. The first is that, prior to the fight, the management of the firm usually does not control a significant proportion of the votes. Irwin Jacobs, for instance, probably chose to go after Pabst, and not Schlitz, because the latter brewer's family interests controlled more than 50 percent of the voting stock.

The second is that the insurgents typically communicate a good story about how a control change or the success of their proposal will lead to a prompt and/or lasting increase in shareholder value. Some dissidents choose to be specific in their plans for the company, while others avoid providing a detailed program. An example is Jacobs's complex and highly detailed description of his two-tiered Pabst takeover plan. Most others are less detailed. As described earlier, another "good story" that has become very popular for natural resource firms has been the "royalty trust." In theory, a royalty trust allows income from successful natural resources properties to flow directly to shareholders, instead of getting taxed once as corporate profits and again as shareholder dividend income. Pickens was the first to propose such a royalty trust at Mesa Petroleum and he advocated it for Gulf's shareholders.

A third prerequisite is for insurgent shareholders to have a sufficient stake in the firm such that their potential gain justifies risking the expense of a proxy contest. Occasionally, however, proxy fights are waged by insurgents holding extremely small stakes. This occurred in the highly issue oriented contest where Odyssey Partners waged a proxy fight against Trans World Corporation even though the partners controlled only 1.2 percent of Trans World's stock. Odyssey Partners depended on the appeal of their argument that Trans World was an undervalued conglomerate. A final prerequisite is that the participating insurgents believe they have adequate standing and credibility to win votes for their side. Suspicion of Irwin Jacobs, for instance, was a detriment to his ability to succeed in the Jacobs–Pabst case.

Proxy Repellents

Proxy contests allow a great amount of time for management to maneuver. Moreover, management fights with shareholders' dollars. Although if the insurgents succeed, they may be reimbursed by the firm. Management has available a large number of defenses against proxy contests. The most typical are the shark repellents commonly associated with takeover battles. Ordinarily, one of the target's first moves is to change the charter or bylaws of the firm. For example, it may adopt a staggered board so that control cannot be seized in one election. Management may also seek to eliminate cumulative voting. Such voting tends to grant minority holders seats on the board. Gulf undertook to reincorporate in the state of Delaware in order to eliminate cumulative voting from its charter. Management may also increase to well over 50 percent the proportion of shares needed to call a shareholder meeting at which a takeover bid might be considered. Such a supermajority requirement may be used to limit changes in the board and numerous other decisions affecting control of the firm. In states of incorporation allowing the use of shareholder consents, a firm may outlaw the use of such consents in its bylaws.

Management may concurrently employ other strategies to avoid takeovers. In many cases, management negotiates a lucrative severance agreement, or a golden parachute, which would be triggered by any hostile takeover. It is doubtful that this by itself would serve as a successful defense. Some companies pursue a "fatman" acquisition strategy designed to make the company too large to swallow and less attractive to potential purchasers. A key success factor in formulating management's strategy is understanding the aggressor's motives. In one type of situation, dissident shareholders claim that the company's performance is poor and therefore requires a radical change in direction or management. In other types, dissidents believe some acquisition, sale, or reorganization will lead to a prompt and lasting increase in shareholder value. There are two key considerations for management in mounting its defense against these claims. First, management might present stock market results for the company by detrending the effects of the market as a whole. In other words, this is a presentation of the firm's stock market performance net of the market effects which are out of management's control. For example, if the company's stock dropped 10 percent in the past year, yet the Standard & Poor's 500 fell 15 percent, the net result is an increase of 5 percent relative to the market. This increase would then be adjusted for the degree of risk undertaken by the company. In such a situation, management's presentation for each month or quarter would include only the stock's results over which management has some influence. Second, management often hires an outside consultant to evaluate the firm's future possibilities, rather than past performance. This report should be made available to all shareholders. The objective of this type of shareholder communication is to refocus attention from historical trends to an assessment of future opportunities.

Often the motivation for insurgents is the desire to break up or liquidate the company. In mounting a defense against such a strategy, management may want to emphasize the potential detrimental effect on the community and employees, thus gaining the support of these important groups. Since investor groups initiating proxies typically do not have the resources to analyze all prospective targets, a lengthy proxy fight aiming toward selling the firm can draw the attention of multiple prospective acquirers. In fact, both the

Pabst and Gulf fights produced multiple offers for these firms. However, in cases where management determines that the investor group is heavily leveraged and not well financed, time can be used as a weapon. Thus management may wish to extend its battle to the extent possible.

Another reason for the use of proxy contests as a takeover strategy is that acquiring companies through tender offers is more expensive. Once control of the board has been achieved, the acquiring group often offers to pay with junk bonds and other risky paper. For example, the plan Jacobs outlined in his proxy solicitation materials included both stock repurchases and swaps of stock for debt to enable him to purchase Pabst with a minimal cash investment. In such situations, the embattled management should refocus the proxy war on the value of the paper. The Jacobs–Pabst case also contained an unusual use of the Pac-Man strategy. While this strategy usually involves the protagonists attempting to take over each other, Pabst financed Olympia's self-tender while its own tender offer for Olympia was under way. The complex arrangement was designed to undercut Irwin Jacobs's tender offer for Pabst. Finally, management may simply seek to repurchase the dissidents' shares at a premium. But such a ransom, called greenmail, should be management's last resort.

The Three-Course Menu of Proxy Contests

Earlier, three variations of the proxy contest strategy used by insurgents were described. Each variation is associated with different laws, requirements, and federal regulations. The first was the formal solicitation of proxies mailed separately from the firm's proxy materials. In such a solicitation, the federal securities laws require extensive disclosure by all participants. The participants must divulge a 10-year history of employment, any proxy involvement in the past 10 years, any conviction, and complete information on ownership of the firm's stock, including any borrowing used to effectuate purchases during the preceeding two years. The laws also require disclosure of any trading in the firm's stock by relatives of 5 percent stockholders, directors, or nominees. Such detailed disclosure requirements are a clear disincentive to any shareholder wishing to start a proxy solicitation while maintaining privacy in his financial and personal affairs. This invasion of privacy occasionally leads to extreme business decisions. For example, the Bass brothers, known for their paranoia about their private lives being made public, gave up an estimated $7 million stake in Atlantic City's Sands Hotel and Casino. They preferred this to the alternative of submitting to a rigorous investigation by the New Jersey Division of Gaming Enforcement. When the contest is to replace the present board of directors, appropriate nominees must be found who will also submit themselves to these disclosure obligations. The disclosures themselves are a rich source of information from which management can fashion strong defensive lawsuits. Such legal maneuvering is common. Moreover, any substantive omission in the disclosures may provide grounds to overthrow a contest. Pabst sued Jacobs in a number of courts for providing such misinformation.

The power of the proxy solicitation is that there are very few limitations on what can be proposed. A proposed slate of directors and a new management team are the most frequently encountered threats to incumbents in proxy solicitations. It was atypical that the dissident's resolution against Trans World did not touch this issue. Rather, it focused on a breakdown of the conglomerate into separate public concerns while leaving the management team intact.

A formal solicitation by dissident shareholders is both time consuming and expensive. It is expensive due to the inevitable lawyers' fees, public relations activities and solicitation procedures. It is time consuming due to the ubiquitous battle for the shareholder list.

Time management in the face of delay tactics is a concern which the defense should never underestimate. The shareholder list is usually the first battleground over which time consuming litigation occurs. It is obviously in the defendant's best interest to delay the insurgents from contacting shareholders. As far as management is concerned, the less time an insurgent has to stir up discontent, the better. Thus a dissident's request for a proxy list is rarely granted without litigation.

By now, conservative Republican Senator Jesse Helms is fully aware of this defense. In 1985, his group, Fairness in the Media, disclosed in government documents that it intended to influence network news coverage at CBS. It charged that CBS reflects a "liberal bias in its news coverage of political events, personages, and views." It also filed with the SEC indicating its intention to start a proxy contest. Its plan was to elect one or two directors to the CBS board and possibly adopt shareholder resolutions. A New York state-based Fairness in Media supporter filed suit, requesting the CBS shareholder list. CBS initially refused. It crafted a time delay strategy to prevent the immediate release of the list. The strategy worked. CBS finally gave them the list, but it was too late for Fairness in Media to start a proxy fight for the upcoming regular shareholder meeting.

Another important issue is the state of incorporation. It bears directly on the ease with which a shareholder list may be obtained and whether consents may be solicited without waiting for a shareholder meeting. Since some state laws place impediments on obtaining a shareholder list, insurgents occasionally have attempted to rely on the laws of New York. Any New York resident that is a shareholder in a corporation doing business in that state may sue under its laws to obtain a list. Jesse Helms is not the only southerner to use New York. In 1983, when Delo Caspary, an oil man from Rockport, Texas, initiated a proxy battle with Louisiana Land and Exploration Company, he used it as well. Caspary was greatly inconvenienced when his request for a list from Louisiana Land was denied. Under Maryland law he had no legal right to obtain it because he owned less than 5 percent of the stock. It was therefore impossible for him to lobby the major shareholders. The Caspary group was finally able to secure the list just two weeks before the annual meeting with the assistance of a New York stockholder who volunteered to help the group obtain it using New York corporation law.

Since the proxy voting is generally concluded by the end of the annual meeting and management usually starts out with the upper hand, the incumbent's defense usually involves pressing for a rapid conclusion to the voting. The insurgents, however, usually benefit from added time to make their case. If they can afford it, they can usually be found suing to postpone the annual meeting.

The second variation of the proxy contest strategy is the shareholder resolution that is mailed with the firm's proxy materials before the annual shareholder meeting. Federal regulations provide procedures through which shareholder may include certain proposals with a corporation's proxy statement. The shareholder may submit only one proposal and a supporting statement of no more than 500 words. The most important substantive requirement is that the proposal not be related to an election to office. Thus, a shareholder resolution that is mailed with the firm's proxy statement cannot be a direct proposal to transfer control of the firm.

Of the three variations, the shareholder resolution requires the least commitment of resources. Unlike a formal proxy solicitation or a solicitation of consents, participants need not make financial or personal disclosures. Because the company mails the resolution, the dissidents need not obtain a shareholder list. On the other hand, since the regulations governing the proposal disallow any connection to an election to office, the shareholder resolution will not provide the insurgents immediate control of the firm. If control is the aim, however, the success of the resolution may position the insurgents to seize control.

The third variation of the proxy contest strategy is the solicitation of shareholder consents. A consent is simply a written authorization from one shareholder that another shareholder may vote his shares on a given issue. The corporate laws of several states permit stockholder action without a formal meeting and at any time if the insurgent group successfully solicits the required number of votes.

Consents, like proxies, may relate to an election to office, and therefore can be used in a contest to replace the board. However, a solicitation of shareholder consents must satisfy all the procedures and requirements of a formal proxy solicitation. The use of shareholder consents allows the insurgent shareholders to overcome management's usual control over the timing of the contest because consents may be solicited at any time. Dissidents soliciting consents require the same high calibre lawyers, agents, and advisors as those soliciting formal proxies. As a result, the expense of soliciting consents is comparable to that of soliciting proxies.

Depending on the state of incorporation, there are various guidelines that apply to solicitation of consents. For example, in the case of Irwin Jacobs's battle to control Pabst, the Jacobs committee solicited consents in an effort to remove the incumbent directors and elect the committee's nominees as directors. However, under Delaware law, a defense can be built around the fact that action on the consents must be taken within 60 days of the day the first consent is expressed. The Jacobs group's consents were in effect for some 7½ months. The courts, therefore, ruled that the consents were not legal and action could not be taken.

Institutional Holders

Certainly a major influence on the heightened activity of the takeover market has been the tremendous growth of institutional ownership. With the growth of tax-advantaged pension funds and ESOPs, this trend will continue. In the 1980s, institutional investment has accounted for 25 to 50 percent of the shares of publicly held corporations, compared with about 10 percent in the 1960s. By garnering the support of a few institutional investors, the dissident shareholder greatly increases the chance of winning the contest. Institutional investment advisors have evidenced increased sophistication and receptivity to siding against management. They recognize that this can enhance their portfolio values. Although in the three proxy contests we presented, none was immediately successful for the insurgents, the attempt to obtain institutional support of the insurgent proposal or slate was a major issue in each case. For example, Odyssey Partners appealed strictly to institutional investors in their attempt to reorganize Trans World Corp. A significant element in each successful defense was the courting of the institutional investors by management. The ability to convince such investors is a key success factor in virtually every proxy battle.

To Proxy or Not to Proxy

Proxy contests will continue to be an attractive takeover strategy for insurgents. As long as mergers and acquisitions are free to take place with relatively little intervention on the part of government, and as long as institutional holders continue to control large blocks of public corporations' voting stock, takeover activity will be high. Innovative defenses are likely to march lockstep with innovative proxy offensives. Standard shark repellents, good PR, combative legal counsel, and successful wooing of institutions are the key elements of the proxy defense. While the odds are usually on the side of the defense, proxy battles have been initiated at an increasing rate.

How do managements feel about the recent proliferation of proxy fights? A writer in *Barrons* summed up the situation with the following observation:

Managements of the companies embroiled in proxy fights generally view them as threats or, at best, nuisances. But democracy can be an annoying and exasperating process. And, after all, it is the shareholders who own the company and employ the managers. The examples of the current fights may serve as a reminder of that often forgotten fact.

9
The Shark Repellent Defense

"You can take us over as long as you can convince seven of us."

KEEPING THE SHARKS AT BAY

When tender offers began to gain popularity as a way to obtain corporate control, target companies found that they were often unprotected. In general, state legislatures were slow to react and often reluctant to intervene. As a result, companies started to respond by inserting provisions in their charters and bylaws designed to discourage unwanted takeovers. By 1986, these amendments, termed "shark repellents," were adopted by the vast majority of the Standard & Poor's 500, including such giants as Mobil and General Motors.

The initial amendments frequently dealt with an early form of the supermajority clause. They required a majority vote substantially higher than 50 percent on decisions involving a business combination. They were simpler and less aggressive than the elaborate and sometimes complex provisions that are now developed by companies.

In order to understand the remedies available to a target, different categories of shark repellents are discussed. In particular, their usefulness and limitations are described.

Staggered Board: You Own but You Don't Control

The implementation of a staggered board, sometimes referred to as a classified board, greatly limits the ability of a majority shareholder to effect a rapid change of management. Under a staggered board, the directors are usually divided into three classes. Each class comes up for election only once every three years. As a result, a majority shareholder can elect at most one-third of the directors each year, and therefore must often wait at least two annual meetings before gaining control of the board. Though some states permit a large number of classes, the NYSE limits listed companies to three classes of approximately equal size. Therefore, those contemplating a raid on an NYSE company with a staggered board provision should expect a hostile board for the first two years even though the raider has already obtained a majority of the voting shares.

Targets should be aware of differences across states with respect to this issue. For example, the state statutes of California and Illinois do not permit classification. In the case of Illinois, a state statute permitting a staggered board was ruled unconstitutional on the grounds that it conflicted with other state laws.

The staggered board provision has gained popularity in recent years. Corporate raider Sir James Goldsmith is familiar with its popularity. In mid-1984, Continental Group, a forest products, packaging, insurance, and energy concern, instituted a staggered board provision in its defense against Sir James. One year later, in a 1985 "media-focused" battle, Crown Zellerbach unsuccessfully applied the same measure as one of its repellents against raider Sir James. Similarly, other professional raiders have faced this type of repellent while attacking their targets. At the end of 1983, analysts speculated that Unocal would make a good takeover candidate because of its relatively low stock price and strong reserves. In response, its board approved a staggered board provision, preparing it for the upcoming T. Boone Pickens attack. Several months later, on April 11, 1985, Uniroyal rejected Carl Icahn's plan to make an $18 per share offer. At the same time, its board urged shareholders to approve a staggered board provision.

Frequently, management faces opposition in instituting shark repellents. Therefore, it should explain the proposed changes to its shareholders and be ready to provide them with a sound business justification for their implementation. The one reason most often cited to stockholders by management is that classification helps to assure continuity and stability of corporate management, since a majority of the directors at a given time have had prior experience as directors of the corporation. Obviously, if the amendments are proposed in the midst of the battle, management must be more direct in its justification. In such a case, it is often argued that a staggered board can better protect minority shareholders' rights. Specifically, when an acquirer wishes to force out minority shareholders in the second step of a two-tier merger, the continuing directors might be able to obtain a better price.

In fact, the main issue surrounding the staggered board amendment is not convincing shareholders to support it, but the real power of the provision. Indeed, some professionals doubt the effectiveness of the staggered board provision. For example, Wilbur Ross, managing director of Rothschild Inc. stated that "no serious raider is deterred by a staggered board, and the probability of outside directors being willing to devote a major portion of their time to legal or other forms of defensive warfare is zero." Ross's argument was supported by arbitrageur Asher Edelman. With only 12 percent of Datapoint's shares, he got himself elected chairman and won control of half of the board. The board was supposedly protected by a staggered board provision.

Changing the Board Is No Longer Easy

If a corporate charter permits its shareholders to remove its directors without cause, the intended benefits of a staggered board can be greatly undercut. Therefore, a staggered board is frequently supported by a special charter provision that permits stockholders to remove directors only with a specific cause, not simply by a majority vote. As is the case with many other provisions, the legal status of the removal of directors differs significantly across states. Under the frequently applied Delaware law, a director on a staggered board may be removed only for cause, unless the charter otherwise provides. However, this is an exception to the general Delaware laws. These laws state that a director may be removed without any specific cause. In contrast, in New York, stockholders may remove directors without cause only if it is explicitly supported by the charter or bylaws. In many states, where the concept is not part of the statute, potential targets wishing to battle hostile acquirers should amend their charters to prevent removal of directors without cause. Some corporations have adopted provisions under which removal without cause requires a supermajority vote, typically in the range of 75 to 95 percent. For example, such a repelling provision was included in the September 1982 proxy statement of Service Corporation International. Several years earlier, one was included in a proxy statement of Dennison Manufacturing Company, with the text of the latter amendment reading as follows: "No director may be removed from office except by vote of three fourths of the outstanding stock of the class or classes then entitled to ordinary voting power." In addition, targets might want to define the company's meaning of what is a valid "cause," either within its provisions or in the proxy statements. For example, a company can define an acceptable "cause" as a conviction of a felony by a court or misconduct in the performance of duty that resulted in a major loss of assets for the corporation.

Another desirable provision involves the manner in which vacancies are filled. Even with a staggered board provision, it might be possible for an insurgent group to gain control of the board in a single election if there are enough vacancies on the board and it can fill them. To avoid such a situation, when permissible under state law, a company should consider amending its charter, allowing vacancies to be filled by the remaining directors. Furthermore, to protect the operation of a staggered board, the newly elected director should serve for the remainder of the full term in which the vacancy occurred. Such an amendment was included in the April 1983 proxy statement of McDonald's.

The corporate charter should also fix the size of the board. This will help to prevent a majority stockholder from obtaining sudden control of a corporation by "packing" the board at a single annual meeting. For example, in a 1983 proxy statement of U.S. Industries, it proposed to fix the number of directors between 9 and 15. As usual, the "technicalities" concerning this type of amendment are fairly detailed. Nevertheless, it is important for a target to be aware of these details. In Delaware, for example, a certificate of incorporation can fix the number of directors. However, in New York, the number of directors may be fixed only in the bylaws. An alternative to fixing the size of the board is to require that new directors to a specific class be elected only by the incumbent directors of the same specific class. This might prevent an insurgent who elects directors of one class from seizing control of the board through the resignation of directors in other classes. An example of such a provision is found in the charter of PSA, Inc., which also adopted a detailed proposition regarding the mechanism for vacancies occurring as a result of an expansion of the board.

Directors' Qualifications: A Hidden Defense

Some state laws such as the New York law permit companies to adopt restrictive qualifications for directors in their charter or bylaws. These provisions require that a person fulfill certain conditions to be eligible as a director. For example, some companies require various qualifications such as residency. However, these restrictions are often contested in court by investors. For example, Joseph E. Seagram & Sons contested Conoco's restrictive bylaws which limited the number of shares that could be held by a foreign corporation. They won in court because the Delaware statute requires that a firm adopting such a provision obtain stockholders' approval.

Cumulative Voting: Trivial Arithmetic with Serious Implications

The term cumulative voting refers to a voting system in which each share entitles the holder to a number of votes equal to the number of directors. The most important implication of this voting system is that it gives minority shareholders the possibility of electing some directors. In general, however, cumulative voting is a two-edged sword. On one hand, when combined with a staggered board provision, it can further delay a majority stockholder or a proxy contestant from gaining control of the board, even if he already controls a majority of the outstanding stock. On the other hand, most corporate managements oppose cumulative voting since it allows raiders with minority holding of the stock to gain representation on the board. Therefore, targets in jurisdictions that require cumulative voting, in the absence of contrary charter or bylaw provisions, typically consider eliminating these voting rights as an antitakeover measure. Some states provide for mandatory cumulative voting. Such is the status in California and Illinois. Other states, such as Delaware and New York, permit cumulative voting if the charter so provides. As with all other charter and bylaw amendments, management has to "sell" the proposal to the stockholders. In proposing an amendment to eliminate cumulative voting, management often claims that each director should be responsible for representing the interests of all stockholders rather than the special interest of any single group. For example, in its April 1983 proxy statement, the management of McDonald's argued that the amendment is a measure against a potential greenmailer. Using its terminology, McDonald's management claimed that "cumulative voting might be utilized by sophisticated major investors as a means to induce the target to purchase their stock at a favorable price to the detriment of other stockholders." Similarly, as part of its 1985 defense against T. Boone Pickens, Unocal came to the battlefield with an amended charter. Sure enough, the cumulative voting provision was eliminated, a fact that made it more difficult for Pickens to gain a seat on Unocal's board. By now, one can assume that the leaders of the conservative group Fairness in Media are also familiar with the concept of cumulative voting. In their futile 1985 battle to control CBS's board, they needed to garner a majority of voting shares because CBS did not have a cumulative voting provision.

The issue of cumulative voting becomes more complex as the raider's holdings approach a majority of the shares outstanding. At some point in the takeover attempt, if the raider continues to accumulate shares, the other shareholders' holdings approach a minority position. At this point in the game, their interest is to institute a cumulative voting system. Some companies have inserted into their bylaws a provision letting all shareholders vote cumulatively for directors once a raiding group controls 40 percent of the shares. Recent adopters of such an automatic introduction of cumulative voting include International Minerals & Chemicals and Perkin-Elmer.

Special Shareholder Meetings Become Very Special

If the statutes or the charter provisions enable shareholders to call a special meeting, an insurgent can do so and remove directors, expand the board, have its slate elected to the new directorships, or initiate some other significant changes. This possibility is an obvious source of concern to a target's management. To determine a target's vulnerability, the first place to look is the bookshelf with the state laws. After doing so, a target will find itself in one of the following three categories:

1. In a state that mandatorily specifies that some percentage of shareholders may call a special meeting. Typically this requirement is in the range of 10 to 25 percent. An example of such a

state is California where mandatorily 10 percent of the shareholders can call a special meeting. In these states, the target's
goal may be reached by other means. Most importantly, these
include provisions regarding the removal of directors, the size
of the board, and the filling of a vacant seat on the board.

2. In a state where a specified percentage of shareholders may call
    a special meeting unless the charter provides otherwise. Ex-
    amples of such states are Louisiana and Ohio. It should be
    noted, however, that in many of the states in this category, there
    is a percentage ceiling set for calling a meeting. For example,
    Ohio General Corporation Law sets a maximum of 50 percent
    as the requisite percentage that in all events will be able to call
    a special meeting. In other words, Ohio corporate bylaws re-
    quire that the percentage for calling a meeting be at most 50
    percent and not a number such as 70 percent. However, many
    of the states in this category grant considerable flexibility about
    how soon the special meeting must be called. For example, if
    the statute calls for 10 to 50 days advance notice of shareholder
    meetings, it might be helpful to adopt a bylaw requiring at least
    a 40-day notice period. Furthermore, if the statute does not re-
    fer to the issue of how quickly a corporation must respond to a
    demand for a special meeting, a minimum waiting period of 60
    days and no more than 90 days may be sustainable.

3. In a state where shareholders have the right to call a special
    meeting only if the charter or bylaws so provide. Examples of
    this category are the important states of Delaware and New
    York. In such a state, the target's management in planning its
    defense should review the charter or bylaws and, if necessary,
    amend them to delete all provisions allowing shareholders to
    call a special meeting. The importance of this type of shark
    repellent is best evident by the extent of its usage. For example,
    in January 1983, Superior Oil Corporation, battling several
    shareholder groups, amended its bylaws and increased from 20
    to 50 percent the proportion of shares needed to call a share-
    holder meeting at which a takeover bid might be considered.
    Similarly, Jewel Company, a firm with supermarkets and drugs-
    tores in 25 states, amended its bylaws in preparing itself for the

attack by American Stores, a Salt Lake City-based drug and foodstore chain with operations in 28 states. Though the offer from American Stores was made on May 31, 1984, Jewel's management amended its bylaws in April of that year. Specifically, the changes forced shareholders to notify the company of planned nominations for directors and any other business to be discussed at the upcoming annual meeting. This notice must be given at least 60, but not more than 90 days before the meeting. Even when management does not fully anticipate the aggressor's moves, it usually does not take long to change the bylaws. For example, on February 14, 1985, T. Boone Pickens announced that a group led by him acquired 9.7 percent of Unocal common stock. On February 25, 11 days later, Unocal amended its bylaws by extending the notice period required for nomination of directors to 30 days. Previously nominations could be made as little as 24 hours before a shareholder meeting. In another example, the broadcasting giant CBS did not wait long to amend its bylaws concerning shareholder meetings. Threatened by political groups such as Fairness in Media and Atlanta investor Ted Turner, on March 5, 1985, the CBS board had a special "meeting" held over the telephone. It eliminated a provision mandating a special meeting if 10 percent or more of CBS shares requested one. The amended provision indicated that such a meeting may only be called jointly by the CBS chairman, the Executive Committee chairman, and by a vote of a majority of CBS directors. The bylaw amendment punched Fairness in Media right in the face. This shark was surprised by the quickness and effectiveness of CBS's "special meeting repellent."

Preventing the Deal by Not Consenting

Written consent refers to the right to vote without the need for an actual shareholder meeting. The threat of such a vote to a target company is obvious. If shareholders are able to act by consent, an insurgent may be able to solicit written consents for both the removal of incumbent directors and the election of new directors, thereby seizing control of the board without a shareholder meeting.

While contemplating a proposal for such a shark repellent, the management of a target company will find itself in one of the following two categories:

1. In a state that enables the use of consents unless the charter provides otherwise. An important example of such a state is Delaware, where it is obviously desirable to amend the charter to eliminate the written consent provision.

2. In a state such as Michigan, which authorizes the charter to include this type of provision.

In the case where amending the written consent provision is not feasible because the insurgent is already on the scene, it is still possible to make a raider's life miserable by adopting bylaws that regulate written consents. For example, in 1982, General American Oil Company of Texas used this approach to protect itself against major league player T. Boone Pickens. Its bylaws provided that any stockholder wanting to use written consents had to "request the board of directors to set a record date." This record date, which refers to when the shareholder list is constructed and submitted to the insurgents, was to be set 15 days after the request. This delay allowed General American Oil to better prepare its defensive strategy. The bylaws also provided that, whenever the consents are related to the removal or replacement of a member of the board, the secretary of the company decides on the validity of the consents. Alternatively, the secretary designates two persons outside the board to decide on the validity of the consents. One can guess that the secretary or the two designated outsiders would not enthusiastically support their validity.

Another case where the written consent provision was used as one of a set of repellents is the war between professional raider Carl Icahn and Uniroyal. The chemical, plastic, and rubber-products concern did not wait long before it struck back. On April 11, 1985, it rejected Icahn's plan to make an $18 per share offer. On May 2, two weeks after its annual meeting, Uniroyal announced that its shareholders narrowly approved antitakeover measures, including a provision requiring all stockholder action to be taken at a meeting, unless all eligible shareholders consented to the action in writing. The condition requiring that all shareholders consent obviously made it impractical for Icahn to consider the written consent alternative.

Supermajority as a Superdefense

The supermajority vote provision requires that shareholders approve a business combination by a vote substantially higher than normally required by the state law. The provision, which is one of the oldest and most popular shark repellents, usually requires the approval of 75 to 95 percent of the target's shareholders for a two-step merger. The required percentage is sometimes based on a sliding scale, depending on the percentage of the company already owned by the acquirer. For example, some companies require a 75 percent vote for a merger with a 20 percent shareholder and a 95 percent vote for a merger with a 40 percent shareholder. Other companies require a majority or supermajority vote of the minority shareholders which are unrelated to the acquirer in order to approve a merger. For example, if the raider owns 30 percent of the shares, this provision necessitates majority support of the shares which are not owned by the raider. Many corporations listed on the NYSE have adopted such a provision even though the exchange has indicated it did not favor this particular supermajority strategy.

As seen in cases throughout this book, as well as in many other situations, the supermajority provision is not only the most popular repellent, but also one that can be formulated in numerous different versions. For example, in the late 1982 poison pill scenario when El Paso played the role of the pill provider and Burlington Northern Industries tried to avoid swallowing the pill, an interesting supermajority provision was introduced. El Paso's amendment provided that a holder of 25 percent or more of El Paso common stock cannot effect a merger at a per-share price lower than the price paid for the original 25 percent interest, unless the holders of at least 90 percent of the preferred shares vote otherwise. A similar provision was included in the 1984 poison pill instituted by Enstar in its battle against Tesoro Petroleum Company, as well as by Mesa Petroleum in defending itself against the Pac-Man counterattack by Cities Service. More recently, the supermajority provision was applied in the 1985 battle between Uniroyal and Icahn. Uniroyal's shareholders passed an amendment that any acquisition must be approved by 80 percent of the shareholders, instead of the prior requirement of a two-thirds majority.

Often, in order to provide for more flexibility if needed, a double buffer is created. It consists of the requirement that a specified percentage of shareholders support a business combination as well as the requirement that a certain majority of the board support it. For example, Unocal amended its bylaws so that a merger with a group owning 10 percent or more of Unocal's common stock requires approval by at least 75 percent of the voting shares unless the transaction has been approved by three-fourths of the board.

As a final note, in order not to impede routine internal reorganization, the supermajority provision should exclude transactions approved by the board and transactions between the parent company and one of its wholly owned subsidiaries. However, a company should be cautious in drafting such provisions to avoid having an imaginative raider use these exceptions as loopholes to skirt the supermajority provisions.

A Fair Price: Equality for All

Fair price amendments are used to protect the shareholders that have not tendered their stock in the first step of a merger so that they can obtain a "fair price" in the second step. Practically, the fair-price can be defined in a number of ways. The most commonly applied definition is a requirement that the second step price equal or exceed the price paid in the first step of the tender offer.

These fair price amendments are designed specifically to prevent "front-loaded" transactions that put pressure on stockholders to tender at the time of the initial offer. For example, Bendix Corporation called a special meeting to adopt fair-price provisions after it received Martin Marietta's two-step offer. Martin Marietta was offering $75 in cash for 50.3 percent of the shares outstanding in the first step of its offer while in the second step it offered an exchange of stock valued at approximately $55. When Bendix drafted its fair price provision, it suspended the requirement of a supermajority conditioned on a "fair price" being paid to all shareholders.

In many cases, the fair price provision is added to the firm's by-laws significantly prior to the aggressor's active move. For example, in May 1984, Hook Drugs Inc. of Indianapolis approved a fair price amendment designed to thwart a two-tier tender offer. Only eight months later, in January 1985, was the threat perceived as real. Rite Aid Corp., a discount drugstore operator, began an unsolicited tender offer to acquire any-and-all of Hook Drugs' shares. In inducing the any-and-all offer, the fair-price provision, laying in wait for a hostile acquirer, did its job.

In order to "sell" this amendment to the shareholders, management often relates the supermajority provision to the fair-price provision. In such cases the fair-price provision is drafted as an exception to the supermajority voting requirement, so that when a "fair" price is paid, the requirement of a supermajority vote is suspended. For example, in 1985, Oscar Wyatt's Coastal acquired American Natural Resources (ANR) for $2.5 billion in cash. One of ANR's last defensive moves before the acquisition was the institution of a fair-price/supermajority amendment. The fact that ANR finally was acquired isn't proof of the ineffectiveness of the fair-price amendment. To the contrary, the fact that it was a one-price, all-cash acquisition should be taken as a victory for the company's shareholders.

Robbing the Treasury of the Hostile Acquirer

Compulsory redemption provisions provide the shareholders the right to require the corporation to repurchase their shares if an unwanted suitor becomes the holder of a specified percentage of shares. This "put" provision is costly for the acquirer because the repurchase price is typically defined as the "fair price," and therefore it removes the aggressor's alternative of proceeding with a lower cost second-tier transaction. However, it is also costly for the target company. It may require liquidation of a significant proportion of its assets in order to obtain the cash needed for redemption in the event of a takeover. The ability of companies in regulated industries, such as banking and insurance, to redeem part of their equity is limited. Their capitalization is closely watched by regulatory bodies such as the FDIC or state insurance commissioners. More importantly, a target company cannot know in advance what its available net assets to repurchase shares will be in the future, and therefore it cannot rely on a stock redemption provision to block an aggressor. Because of these reasons, it is not as frequently used as other shark repellents. In addition, the validity of the amendment has not yet been tested in court, and both New York and Delaware laws seem to prohibit the issuance of common stock redeemable at the option of the holder.

Golden Parachutes to Ensure a Safe Landing

Golden parachute agreements are aimed to protect top executives. They are most relevant when a company is merged or taken over. Given their objective, it is not a surprise that these benefits are more generous than ordinary employment contracts. In all cases, they are designed to assure an executive's safe landing. In light of the fact that these agreements are written by lawyers specializing in the field, one should not be surprised to learn that they are extremely long, very complex, and tailored specifically for each case.

While they are all custom-tailored, each agreement typically consists of three major elements. First, they include a definition of when a "change in control" has occurred. Second, they contain provisions protecting the executive from specific adverse consequences of a change in control. For example, the corporation's ability to terminate the executive is sharply limited for reasons "softly" defined as cause or disability. Third is a description of what happens when the executive loses his/her job. This is the section with all the dollar signs and the one that most obviously flags the potential raider's attention. Directors often argue that parachutes aid the target's stockholders by freeing the directors from any concerns about job security. According to this argument, they are now able, in free conscience, to weigh a raider's proposals.

No matter what a firm chooses on the menu of defense strategies, the golden parachute is nearly always selected as a side dish. For example, in the case of TWC battling a proxy fight, the golden parachutes were introduced to the menu in the last minutes. Its annual shareholder meeting was scheduled for April 27, 1983. In preparation, TWC sent out information to its shareholders four weeks earlier. The material included a statement informing shareholders about a golden parachute set up just 10 days prior to the mailing.

Trans World dissidents, led by Leon Levy, only then realized that Trans World management provided itself with monetary security. While TWC instituted its golden parachute at the very end of its battle with Odyssey, Texas Gas introduced one in the midst of its defense. Texas Gas used self-tender as its major weapon and used golden parachutes as one of its supporting pieces of artillery. The board issued parachutes to its top nine officials and accelerated stock options to 20 employees. The parachutes were payable to any of the executives leaving the firm within three years after a change in management not approved by the board. The amount of the parachute was four years' salary plus a bonus. For the chairman, it totaled $1,506,324 in addition to his bonus.

In another case, the golden parachute accompanied an LBO defense. The winning bidder, The Williams Companies, was willing to pay Northwest management some staggering sums. The chairman received $15.8 million and a secretary for two years, the president walked away with $9 million, and the vice-president pocketed a hefty $5 million.

Revlon spent nearly five months of 1985 trying to evade the clutches of Pantry Pride, a Florida supermarket chain. Finally in November, in a $2.7 billion transaction, Revlon succumbed. No doubt for Michael Bergerac, the ousted chairman of Revlon, the pain of the takeover was eased by a $36 million parting settlement.

Not only does target management protect itself with golden parachutes, the aggressor's management has also, on occasion, found it useful. To protect himself in his Pac-Man war with Cities Service, T. Boone Pickens managed to get the approval of Mesa's board for a parachute amounting to twice his annual pay along with consulting fees equal to his annual compensation for the following seven years. Ironically, several months later, Pickens was upset when the management team of one of his targets, General American Oil, was granted hefty parachutes. Pickens's Mesa went as far as questioning the legality of the parachutes, calling them a "silver wheelchair bonanza."

Despite their frequent use, many question their real impact as a shark repellent. For example, City Investing's 11 top officers were to receive golden parachutes in excess of $39 million in case of liquidation. However, in late 1984, when liquidation was considered, alternative evaluation methods determined City Investing's worth to be in the range of $1.39 billion and $2.05 billion. One might wonder whether the $39 million in parachutes were significant for a potential raider compared to the $600 million dollar difference in value estimates.

Moral Majority Standards

Another form of shark repellent authorizes the board of directors to consider nonmonetary factors while evaluating a tender offer. Most corporate bylaws require that, in addition to estimating the offer's fair-market value, the target company will also study (1) the legality of the offer, (2) the present and future financial condition of the aggressor, (3) the competence, experience and integrity of the acquirer, and (4) the social and economic impact of the acquisition on the target company, its employees, customers, vendors, and the community in which it operates.

Anyway, these provisions should be part of a standard procedure in the evaluation of every business combination and thus might not signal resistance. Nevertheless, they can protect the target's management from any subsequent shareholder suits if the target rejects a tender offer at what is perceived by some shareholders as an "attractive price."

Authorizing the Weapons to Prepare for Battle

By being able to quickly issue more common or preferred stock with special voting rights, a target company has the potential to reduce the relative size of a block of shares held by hostile hands. Many companies have amended their charters to increase the number of authorized shares. While this provision might seem simple to institute, it is often contested in court on the basis that it lacks a legitimate business purpose or that it is improperly undertaken without the approval of stockholders. For example, the NYSE requires a shareholder vote for issuance of shares to officers, directors, or significant shareholders or if the shares issued exceed 18.5 percent of the outstanding shares. Such stock exchange requirements are crucial for a wide range of defense strategies. The shark repellent is no exception.

The management can also be creative by authorizing a class of "blank check" preferred stock. This stock can have more than one vote per share, can be authorized to vote with common stock as a class, or have the right to vote separately. The sole purpose of their issuance is to dilute the aggressor's control and thereby deter it from consummating the takeover.

The poison pill, which is also referred to as the "exploding pre-ferred" is a special case of preferred stock issuance. These preferred shares are convertible into the shares of the acquirer's voting com-mon stock on a second tier of a business combination. The conver-sion is usually made in accordance with a prespecified formula which is extremely biased in favor of the target's shareholders. In its traditional form, the poison pill takes effect when the tender offer is completed. Its enactment has a significant dilutive effect on the aggressor's control and is one of the most feared weapons in the target's defensive arsenal.

Finally, corporations that contemplate the use of stock issuance as an antitakeover device should also eliminate preemptive rights, if possible, in order to increase their flexibility in the event of a takeover attempt. When shareholders have preemptive rights, they have the privilege to buy the stock of a new issue before it is offered to other investors. By eliminating these rights, a company will not have to first offer the new issue to existing shareholders, and will save time and expense along with gaining more flexibility. The tar-get is said to have more flexibility because it will be able to sell a new issue to a prospective white knight and thereby avoid an ag-gressor from utilizing its preemptive rights and maintaining its proportional ownership.

It is important for the target to review the corporate statutes of its state of incorporation. For example, in certain states such as New York, shares carry preemptive rights unless the certificate of incorporation provides to the contrary. Obviously, if the target's state falls into this category, it is important to propose an amend-ment to eliminate the preemptive rights. In contrast, Delaware law indicates that shares do not have preemptive rights unless other-wise provided for in the charter.

Bonding Up the Acquirer

Instead of authorizing more stock, some corporations have amended their charters to be in a position to issue bonds which are convertible into shares of common stock. The conversion will have a dilutive effect on the aggressor's holdings.

Other target corporations have authorized the issuance of common stock with different voting power including, in the extreme case, a one-tenth vote per share. In the 1985 Hook Drugs –Rite Aid case, Hook Drugs applied several shark repellents including the creation of two classes of preferred: Class A with full voting rights, and Class B with limited voting rights. Even though these provisions have been upheld in court, they have not always received the approval of shareholders. The use of two classes to concentrate control has been proliferating. Its adopters have included the well known Hershey Foods Corp. and the owner of *The Wall Street Journal*, Dow Jones & Co. A number of other companies have also become creative in fighting short-term profit takers. The Georgia insurer American Family Corp. designed two classes of shares with 10 votes assigned to shares held by existing shareholders and one vote to new ones. The classes were designed so that speculators and other takeover opportunists would have to cool their heels for four years before receiving 10 votes per share for their holdings. Among the recent converts recommending similar two-class provisions are the discount airline, People Express, and the Orville, Ohio jam producer, Smuckers.

Changing the Neighborhood–Changing the Rules

The shark repellent protection permitted under different corporate statutes varies remarkably. For example, Delaware is obviously the most popular state of reincorporation because its statutes permit corporations to adopt a wide variety of defensive weapons. Likewise, Maryland is popular because of certain takeover statutes, such as supermajority and fair price provisions. Similarly, Ohio is favored by shark repellent "seekers" because it has adopted a new statute that requires prior shareholder approval to all share acquisitions which give an acquirer voting power of 20 percent or more.

Often, reincorporation to a state with more favorable shark repellent statutes is easier than changing the company's charter and bylaws. Technically, shareholders are asked to vote on the issue of reincorporation rather than a set of specific shark repellents. However, full disclosure of the nature and effects of the move is still required, including a list of new provisions that will be automatically rendered ineffective as a result of the reincorporation. Nevertheless, this distinction is often ignored by many shareholders, and it still might be easier for management to "sell" the reincorporation amendment than specific shark repellents.

Some of the most widely publicized takeover battles included the reincorporation repellent. For example, Gulf Oil was incorporated in Pennsylvania, which provided a cumulative voting system for electing directors. Under its charter, a dissident holder with just 7.7 percent of Gulf's outstanding shares could gain a seat on the company's board. In late 1983, T. Boone Pickens had accumulated an 8.75 percent stake of Gulf's shares. In response, Gulf Oil reincorporated from Pennsylvania to Delaware and was able to eliminate the cumulative voting provision. About one year later, Pickens again observed the same reincorporation weapon used against him. The only difference was that this time it was used by Unocal rather than Gulf. Eliminating cumulative voting was also the main motivation for Carter Hawley Hale's reincorporation from California to Delaware. Carter Hawley Hale is a Los Angeles-based retailer threatened by Limited Co. By May 1985, Limited dropped its $35 per share tender offer after being stymied by some of Carter's defensive moves. However, it still held 698,805 of Carter's 18.9 million common shares, and said it would attempt to elect two directors to Carter Hawley's board. Carter Hawley Hale's reincorporation, resulting in the elimination of cumulative voting, made it nearly impossible for a minority holder to gain a seat on the board.

The Shark Fades into the Sunset

Some provisions assure that supermajority requirements can only be amended by a supermajority vote. This is particularly important to have in states such as New York where stockholders can amend the charter without board approval.

Sunset amendments provide that shark repellents provisions automatically lapse after a stipulated period of time if not extended by a vote of a simple majority of shareholders. The sunset provisions are designed to make antitakeover amendments more palatable to substantial shareholders. They do so by limiting any long-term entrenchment effect of the shark repellents and requiring a periodic review of their propriety and efficiency. However, sunset provisions can make the corporation vulnerable to takeover attempts if the amendments are not reapproved.

Shareholders and the Shark

Some state statutes permit the board to include important defensive bylaw provisions without obtaining stockholders' approval. However, having such provisions is not without its own detrimental effect. It is often preferred that the board submit such proposals to the shareholders in order to avoid claims that the provisions were only included to entrench management.

When shareholders' approval is necessary to enact defensive bylaw provisions, it is often advisable to submit them as a single set. The effectiveness of shark repellent amendments usually depends on their implementation as an overall package. For example, the implementation of a staggered board provision might be ineffective without the support of a limitation imposed on the size of the board. However, if a special provision is likely to be vulnerable to legal attack under state law, it might be better to separate it in order not to jeopardize the entire package of amendments.

Finally, the timing of the presentation of the proposal to the shareholders is also important. It might be preferable to call a special meeting to present shark repellent amendments which, for most stockholders, are complicated and need to be explained.

Institutions and the Shark

It is often advisable for a corporation to make informal inquiries of institutional shareholders prior to proposing a shark repellent provision in the proxy materials for an annual meeting. The passage of such a proposal often depends on the support of these shareholders.

Some institutions may routinely vote against antitakeover provisions as a matter of policy. However, they usually have different views on the types of amendments used. Institutional holders are likely to approve amendments aimed at preventing disruption or seizure of control of the board by a minority shareholder. However, the institutions might object to those amendments aimed at simply preventing the success of a tender offer by another corporation. Therefore, it is crucial that management carefully plan its shark repellent proposal. Also, after it decides to submit it to shareholders, management should devote sufficient time and energy to maximize the chance of obtaining shareholders' approval.

Future Repellents: Will Sharks Care?

Though shark repellents are now widespread, their effectiveness is open to question. Some ponder the shape they will take in the future. Takeover fights often resemble an electronic war game. One player designs a defense, and in response the aggressor develops an antidefense strategy. This, then, is followed by an "anti-anti defense." So the game continues. One of the merger defense specialists often involved in battle, Kidder, Peabody's Martin Siegel argued that "against a well-financed determined bidder, there's really nothing a company can do."

Others, however, argue that having no repellents is an invitation to sharks. For example, TWA was spun off by Trans World Corp. in early 1985. While the holding company, TWC, was armed with an array of repellents, the new independent corporation, TWA, was naked. Trans World executives wrongly assumed that only the hotel and food units would be highly desired by raiders. They never imagined that their ailing airline would be a target. It didn't take long for Carl Icahn to recognize TWA's lack of defense. After Icahn's attack, their lack of preparation caused one TWA executive to concede, "We were caught totally off guard."

Aside from management and raiders, there are several other key players who have a future stake in shark repellents. Two of the most important are institutions and the judicial system. During the past few years, institutions have been increasingly reluctant to support antitakeover bylaw changes. This attitude is reflected by Dean LeBaron, head of Batterymarch Financial Management, who suggested that "the whole range of antitakeover amendments . . . . is counterproductive." Also representative of this school of thought is Citicorp. Its investment division consistently votes against antitakeover amendments proposed by managements of companies in which it owns stock.

Another important player in the implementation of shark repellents is the judicial system. Managements are not likely to find an ally in the courts. According to defense specialist Arthur Fleischer, of the law firm Fried, Frank, Harris, Shriver & Jacobson, "The legal framework generally favors the offense . . . . The courts don't like to intervene in these transactions; the regulatory agencies are reluctant; and the states have been basically emasculated."

One state, however, that has come to the aid of its corporate residents is New York. In December 1985, the legislature passed a law which requires an unfriendly buyer of more than 20 percent of a target's shares to wait five years before merging with the target or selling its assets. The state instituted shark repellent was designed to protect firms which are both incorporated and headquartered in the state. However, Daniel J. Good, merger and acquisition head of E.F. Hutton argued that "it's a bad bill and it won't stop a takeover." Other merger experts argued similarly and indicated that the legality of the measure is likely to be tested in court.

The ultimate defense is a stock price high enough to repel an aggressive raider. Nonetheless, having shark repellents in the target's arsenal is likely to cause a raider to think twice before commencing the war.

10
The Antitrust Defense

THE ANTITRUST DEFENSE: A SMALL, BUT STORM-LADEN CLOUD

Antitrust arguments are one of the most frequently used forms of merger defense. Yet such arguments are rarely successful in warding off an aggressor. One might wonder why, in so many cases, the antitrust defense is implemented. Moreover, it has been used as a defense in cases where little reason seems to exist for its justification, cases such as St. Joe Mineral's battle against Seagram or Brunswick's attempt to stave off the aggressive pursuit of Whittaker. Not surprisingly, in these cases as well as most others, the defense has been denied by either the courts, the Department of Justice, or the FTC.

While several antitrust defenses merit further discussion, most have been used primarily for two reasons: (1) as a signal to the aggressor that pursuit of the target will be opposed vigorously and will result in a potentially long and costly courtship for the aggressor and (2) as a long-shot business decision with a potentially high return. In this case the odds of success in the courts may be small, but if the target should win, the target is able to maintain its independence, at least until the next aggressor arrives on its doorstep.

Fighting an aggressor using an antitrust argument is one of the more common defenses to keep a hostile raider at bay. Unfortunately for the target, the defense is usually not successful and often puts hardly a dent into the aggressor's timetable. For example, Buffalo Forge requested an injunction against Ampco-Pittsburgh Corp. (APC) on the grounds of antitrust violations. Within days, the request was denied and appealed. Two days following the Buffalo Forge appeal, the U.S. appeals court backed the lower court and refused to block APC's takeover attempt. In a Pac-Man case involving the two insurers, NLT and American General, NLT filed an antitrust suit against American General prior to American General's takeover attempt. As the signs of an imminent takeover attempt became clear, NLT decided legal action was necessary. NLT argued competition would be significantly reduced in the market for certain types of life insurance. The precipitating event was American General's request to the Tennessee Department of Insurance to increase its stake in NLT from 9.1 percent already held to 25 percent.

Subsequent events showed that the American General–NLT combination was really all right with NLT; it just wanted the deal on its terms. Several weeks later, NLT dropped the antitrust suit when it announced it would turn the tables and make a tender offer for American General. Obviously, regulators did not completely buy NLT's original antitrust argument because they permitted the deal to be consummated. In another Pac-Man case, Bendix left no stone unturned in its battle against Martin Marietta and United Technologies. Bendix filed an antitrust suit in Baltimore federal court to prevent a United Technologies acquisition. However, because United Technologies was primarily interested in the Bendix aerospace division, the more effective defense was the agreement by Bendix to sell the division, its crown jewel, to Allied. Not long afterward, United Technologies announced the withdrawal of its tender offer.

In several cases, however, the antitrust defense was the key to successfully thwarting the takeover. LTV dropped its bid for Grumman primarily on the basis of an antitrust ruling. Because the federal appeals court ruled that the antitrust violation was indeed significant, LTV expected a lengthy and costly court battle to win approval. The ruling was based on the fact that Grumman and LTV already held major shares in the market for parts of commercial planes, market shares which were expected to grow in the future.

Even if the antitrust defense is not the key defensive strategy, it can buy time for the target. It is particularly important when the hostile acquirer is not well financed. Although CBS used the poison pill, a variety of shark repellents, and a self-tender restructuring plan in its 1985 battle against Ted Turner, it did not fail to make use of the antitrust defense. In a filing with the FCC, CBS argued that the merger would lessen competition in the national advertising market. CBS's intentions were clear. The financial squeeze resulting from using antitrust delaying tactics against Turner was recognized by a number of market participants. For example, Joseph Fuchs, an analyst with Kidder, Peabody, recognized that Turner's financial resources would be stretched thin. He said, "He's paying legal and accounting fees. I imagine the meter is running at a fairly rapid clip."

Interestingly, a white knight was thwarted by antitrust arguments in one of the major oil industry merger attempts of the 1980s. Reacting to Mesa's hostile takeover attempt of Cities Service, Gulf emerged as a white knight to the rescue. A deal was struck, yet antitrust action caused the deal to fall through. As a result, Cities sued Gulf for $3 billion, alleging fraudulent misconduct.

In a different twist of the antitrust plot, government action seemed to loom over all the players in the Irwin Jacobs–Pabst battle like a storm-laden cloud. First, the antitrust storm fell on Heileman when the Department of Justice announced its intention to oppose its bid for Pabst. Later, to compete against Irwin Jacobs's offer for Pabst, Olympia agreed to conduct a competing tender offer for Pabst. However, by the date shareholders had to tender their shares, there was still uncertainty whether the Justice Department would approve the competing Jacobs transaction. In the end, Justice lowered the boom. It announced its intention to challenge the Jacobs purchase on antitrust grounds. It determined that the proposed spinoff of marketing rights and breweries would hurt competition in the beer industry.

As can be seen, antitrust can strike an acquirer in a number of ways. Yet, even with most antitrust defenses not yielding successful outcomes, its use is nearly always considered in the case of a large unfriendly merger attempt. What determines whether the defense will work? Are there any rules of thumb available to the target in considering its defense? We will consider guidelines issued by the Department of Justice (DOJ) to help firms determine the government's attitude toward acquisitions. In addition, to better understand the antitrust defense we will review the antitrust aspects of Marathon's feisty defense against Mobil and the reasons for its victory.

The Government Is Here to Help

Back in 1982, the DOJ issued its first merger guidelines in 14 years. It described government policy toward mergers and proved to be successful. For example, in 1983, less than 2 percent of the 1128 mergers that filed the premerger notification required by the Hart-Scott-Rodino Act were challenged by the enforcement agencies.

Assuming that the government agencies were faithfully applying the guidelines, these figures suggested that the business community was well acquainted with the DOJ merger policy.

Nevertheless, on June 14, 1984, Attorney General Smith announced the issuance of the 1984 guidelines. Although everyone admitted that the 1982 guidelines were a necessity, there was no unanimity over the publication of the 1984 version.

The 1984 guidelines had several differences compared with their recent predecessor. A much more formal treatment of foreign competition was established, and an attempt to further quantify the market definition tests was set. Additionally, efficiencies resulting from a merger became a relevant factor in the merger analysis process. Mergers that traditionally seemed to be anticompetitive because of the size of the firms involved relative to their industries would not necessarily be challenged by the DOJ if they could demonstrate that they would produce substantial economies.

The new guidelines stated that "although [the guidelines] should improve the predictability of the Department's merger enforcement policy, it is not possible to remove the exercise of judgment from the evaluation of mergers under the antitrust laws." Unfortunately, it seemed like the release of the third generation of guidelines had just the contrary effect, reducing, not increasing predictability. As an expert in the field put it following the 1984 release, "The net effect of the changes is to increase prosecutional discretion and decrease enforcement predictability." Some experts believed that the 1984 guidelines were the result of the desire of the DOJ to move further away from historically arbitrary rules.

However, some critics argued that the increasing complexity and decreasing predictability of the 1984 revisions was too high a price to pay. It is interesting to note the DOJ's perspective was that the 1984 guidelines were motivated by its desire to reduce ambiguity and further refine the merger analysis.

Regardless of whether corporate America is better off with the 1984 revisions, these guidelines clearly focused on (1) the definition and measurement of market, (2) the treatment of foreign competition, and (3) efficiency arguments. Let us take a closer look at each of these areas.

The Unexpected Debate: What Is the Market?

The DOJ believed that some people thought the 1982 market definition was too rigid to determine market power. The DOJ would establish a hypothetical market and hypothesize a 5 percent price increase. It would then estimate the number of buyers in the product market that would shift to substitute products within one year under that higher price. More substitute products would be added to the hypothetical market up to a point at which the percentage of buyers that shifted to substitutes was not "significant."

The "geographic market" was defined in a similar way. Specifically, the DOJ stated that it would define a provisional geographic market based on the shipment patterns of the merging firms. It would then assume a 5 percent price increase and would add more firms selling the product until it would become unprofitable for a firm to sell into the enlarged market at the higher price. In sum, the approach defined the market based on projected responses of demand and supply to hypothetical price changes. To prevent the perception of "unwarranted rigidity," the DOJ explicitly indicated in its revisions that in some cases it would be convenient to use a price increase that could be "much larger or smaller than 5 percent." Unfortunately, it did not specify the cases in which it would apply a specific value, claiming that it would "depend on the nature of the industry." For example, in reviewing a case involving retail outlets, retail prices would be the relevant figures. Moreover, whenever future prices could be predicted with an acceptable degree of confidence, the DOJ would use the projected prices, rather than current prices, in order to assess the impact of a merger.

In addition to concerns about the "5 percent rule," many players feared a "strict mathematical" interpretation of the 1982 measure of market concentration, the Herfindahl-Hirshman Index (HHI). The HHI was defined as the sum of the squared market shares of all the existing firms in the relevant market. Thus, the index has an upper bound value of 10,000, reaching it only in those markets with a unique monopolistic firm (100 percent share). Similarly, the index has a lower value of zero in those highly atomized and competitive markets where each firm has an almost negligible share.

The 1982 set of rules, like those of 14 years earlier (1968), identified three levels of market concentration. The 1982 specified: (1) "highly concentrated" markets where the postmerger HHI was above 1800; (2) "moderately concentrated" markets with a postmerger HHI between 1000 and 1800; and (3) "unconcentrated" markets where the postmerger HHI was below 1000.

The advantage of the HHI over the previously accepted measure of concentration which summed the market shares of the four firms with the largest market shares (four-firm concentration ratio) is obvious. When calculating concentration, the HHI not only considers the total size of the firms in the market, but it also gives weight to the size disparity of the firms. For example, the DOJ introduction to the 1982 guidelines provided a simple example that illustrated the difference between the two market concentration criteria. Consider a hypothetical market with 44 firms: four firms each having a 15 percent share, and 40 firms each having a 1 percent share; and a second market, also with 44 firms, where one firm has 57 percent of the market and the remainig 43 firms control 1 percent each. While the four-firm concentration ratio would be 60 percent for both markets, the HHI values would be 940 for the first market and 3292 for the second, more than three times as great.

Consider another example, a market with only six firms with measurable market shares distributed as follows: 20, 20, 20, 20, 8, and 8 percent. The four-firm concentration ratio would be 80 percent and according to the 1968 guidelines the market would fall in the highly concentrated category. Based on the 1982 rules, though, the HHI indicator would be 1728 points, and the market would be considered only as a moderately concentrated one. As a result, the merger would likely be challenged under the old rules, while permitted under the new ones. In contrast, if one considers another market, also with six firms with measurable market shares distributed as follows: 30, 20, 20, 10, 8, and 8 percent, the four largest firms would have the same 80 percent share of the market, but the HHI measure would be 1928 points. Based on the 1982 guidelines, the market would fall in the highly concentrated category this time. In this case the new rules would likely result in the same outcome as the old rules, a challenge by the DOJ.

In the 1982 guidelines, two factors were considered when evaluating the impact of a merger on market concentration: the post-merger HHI, as explained, and the amount by which the HHI differed from its value before the merger. Because of the perceived strictness of the index, the DOJ in 1984 introduced more flexibility when deciding on a particular merger. However, with the flexibility came increased ambiguity.

While DOJ's attitude toward the intermediate range of concentration remained unchanged, it introduced more discretionary power in the two extreme categories. This change, again, was a detriment to predictability, but increased the likelihood that an antitrust defense would be attempted by a takeover target.

The Invisible Threat: Foreign Competition

Following a "cautious position," foreign competition had not been included in the analysis in the 1982 guidelines. However, in the 1984 revisions the DOJ clearly stated that United States imports would formally be considered when calculating market concentration. In effect, foreign competitors would be assigned a share of the relevant market.

The DOJ conceded that import conditions were subject to frequent changes, which made it difficult to predict the impact of trade policy shifts. However, foreign imports would be assigned a share of the market "in the same way they are assigned to domestic firms." In the absence of an import quota, the share would be calculated based on the "production that is likely to be devoted to the relevant United States market." If a quota existed that limited imports of the relevant foreign good, then the amount used to calculate the foreign competitors' share would be the shipments allowed under the quota.

The inclusion of foreign products in the concentration computations will no doubt increase the number of future mergers in the sense that the merging firms' shares of the market will be reduced, thus reducing the chance of a successful antitrust defense employed by the target.

Increased Efficiency: Is It a Good Excuse?

The 1982 guidelines clearly stated that "except in extraordinary cases, the Department will not consider a claim of specific efficiencies as a mitigating factor for a merger that would otherwise be challenged." The reason for that, according to the 1982 document, was that even if economic advantages were evident in a merger, their magnitude was hard to quantify, and thus, it was difficult to determine the extent of the efficiencies.

In contrast, in the 1984 revisions, the DOJ explicitly mentioned all types of efficiencies that would be considered as mitigating factors: economies of scale, better integration of production facilities, plant specialization, and lower transportation costs. It would also consider reductions in selling and administrative and overhead expenses, even though it recognized that these last savings were difficult to demonstrate. Unfortunately for the target mounting a defense against a raider, the inclusion of these efficiencies was a clear signal to the business sector of a less intrusive policy by the DOJ.

In order to understand the dynamics of the antitrust defense, some key elements of the Mobil–Marathon battle will be described. For a more detailed description of the nonantitrust issues of that defense, a review of the Mobil–Marathon case is presented in the Lock-Up chapter. While the battle took place in 1981/82 under earlier antitrust guidelines, the arguments presented could well have taken place today. Although the quantitative measure of concentration today differs from the measure used then, the nature of the arguments remains unchanged.

THE ANTITRUST BATTLE BETWEEN MOBIL AND MARATHON

Setting: November 1, 1981, two days after Mobil announced an offer to purchase Marathon for $5.1 billion. If successful, it would be the second largest merger in history.

Marathon began to fight the takeover attempt by instituting a lawsuit against Mobil in the U.S. Court for the Northern District of

Ohio. It alleged that the effect of the proposed acquisition would substantially lessen competition in the exploration, production, and refining of crude. The lawsuit also argued that competition would be reduced in the transportation of crude and refining products and in the marketing of gasoline in certain regional, state, and local markets. Marathon also alleged that competition would be lessened because it would be eliminated as a major supplier of gasoline to independent marketers in the midwest. Mobil, on the other hand, argued that the relevant geographic market was nationwide, and the proposed acquisition wouldn't lessen competition since the increase in concentration in the petroleum industry nationwide would be de minimis. Mobil also argued that it would continue to supply gasoline to independents.

Mobil and Marathon had assets of $32.7 and $5 billion respectively. Ranked by sales, Mobil was the second largest industrial company in the country while Marathon was number 39. Federal Judge John M. Manos of the Ohio court said that the crucial question was whether "the relevant geographic market was nationwide or something else." Section 7 of the Clayton Act provides that "no person . . . shall acquire . . . stock . . . where, in any line of commerce . . . in any section of the country, the effect of such acquisition may be substantially to lessen competition."

The court concluded that Mobil was wrong in its definition of a nationwide market. Moreover, it found that in six states, a combined Mobil–Marathon would lead to the following sales percentages and rankings:

Geographic Market	Market Share %	Ranking by Sales
Illinois	17.80	Second
Indiana	17.13	First
Michigan	20.44	First
Ohio	16.70	Second
Tennessee	10.44	Second
Wisconsin	17.44	First

Additionally, in each of those regional markets, a combined Mobil–Marathon would result in the following four-firm concentration ratios:

Geographic Market	Without Merger %	With Merger %
Illinois	48.0	53.0
Indiana	47.1	49.6
Michigan	45.2	51.5
Ohio	53.0	55.8
Tennessee	40.4	44.0
Wisconsin	38.1	43.5

While these ratios showed an increase in the degree of concentration using the four-firm concentration ratio, the 1984 guidelines' HHI would also likely provide supporting evidence in an antitrust defense.

Mobil sold motor gasoline nationwide through Mobil brand outlets. Marathon, on the other hand, marketed gasoline in only 21 states, selling about 15 percent of its gasoline to independent branded jobbers, branded distributors, and branded dealers in the six states mentioned. Marathon sold the other 85 percent unbranded through its wholesale marketing division. About 60 percent of all the gasoline sold by Marathon was eventually sold at retail, several cents per gallon below that sold by Mobil in its branded outlets. Mobil admitted that if it acquired Marathon, it would become the largest marketer of gasoline in the United States with an estimated 10 percent market share.

Judge Manos referred to past cases similar to the Mobil–Marathon situation. In the 1962 case of Brown Shoe Company, the combined market share of Brown Shoe and G.R. Kinney Co. was found to exceed 5 percent nationwide, rising to 57 percent in some cities. In the 1966 case of Pabst Brewing Company, the merging firms would have had a combined market share of 4.49 percent in the United States, and up to 23.95 percent in Wisconsin. In both cases, the mergers were held to violate Section 7 of the Clayton Act in some markets. Referring to the Mobil–Marathon case, Judge Manos concluded that "[Marathon showed] a reasonable probability that it will succeed at trial on the merits of the issue of probable substantial lessening competition" in these six states where the combined company would rank first or second by sales.

Mobil was therefore temporarily restricted from taking any further action to implement the offer. On November 10, however, the order was modified, allowing Mobil to continue with its offer, but prohibiting it from actually purchasing any shares until the court made its decision on Marathon's preliminary injunction.

An Opportunity for Politics

In the meantime, Marathon got some spontaneous partners in its cause. The Ohio political machinery on Capitol Hill decided to join the action. On November 5, 23 Congressmen sent a letter to the FTC urging it to examine the proposed acquisition. The letter said that "[Marathon] had a tradition of commitment and service to Ohio whereas Mobil was a big multinational with no commitment at all."

Representative C.J. Brown (R-Ohio) introduced a bill to block the merger. The legislation, if successful, would be retroactive to October 1 and would prevent the acquisition of independent oil companies by large multinationals. It proposed that "no more than 5 percent of the stock could be acquired of a mid-sized" oil company. Governor James A. Rhodes, in Columbus, Ohio, signed a new antitakeover measure directed to bar the acquisition of an Ohio corporation that would cut competition in the sale of oil products in the state. Senator Howard M. Metzenbaum (D-Ohio) expected to introduce a bill similar to Brown's in the Senate, while Metzenbaum together with Senator John H. Glenn (D-Ohio) were pressing the FTC to intervene in the case.

On November 2, the Justice Department agreed to let the FTC handle the antitrust aspect of the case. Fearing the possibility of other potential acquirers, Mobil suggested to the FTC that it would be willing to acquire Marathon on a conditional basis. Specifically, it offered to keep Marathon independent in terms of its financial and business activity while the FTC conducted the investigation. The petition was denied.

Mobil Intercepted by the District Court

On December 1, the U.S. Court for the Northern District of Ohio issued a preliminary injunction prohibiting Mobil from acquiring shares because of the substantial likelihood of an antitrust violation.

Just before the issue of the preliminary injunction, Mobil had requested the court to modify the injunction on the condition that, after the acquisition, it would hold separate all of Marathon's refining, marketing, and transportation assets. The offer said that within 60 days following the acquisition of Marathon, Mobil would present a plan of divestiture of these assets. The modification, however, was rejected.

Then, on December 6, Mobil agreed to sell Amerada Hess all of Marathon's marketing, refining, and transportation assets if it gained control of Marathon. In view of this attempt to solve the antitrust violation, Mobil asked the court to reconsider its preliminary injunction. Two days later, however, the application was denied.

The FTC Dilemma: To Bar or Not to Bar?

On December 8, the FTC, whose decision was still pending on the Mobil–Marathon issue, said that it wouldn't attempt to bar Mobil from taking over Marathon under any circumstances. However, it would wait "until Mobil presents a plan to sell Marathon's transportation, storage, and marketing assets."

In spite of the divestiture plan proposed by Mobil with its friend Hess, on December 11 the FTC instituted an action against Mobil in the same Ohio court. The FTC preliminary injunction referred to Sections 7 and 11 of the Clayton Act, and said that the takeover would be barred:

> Unless and until such time as there is presented a transaction, subject to the approval of the Court, which would result in an immediate divestiture of the transportation, storage, and marketing assets of Marathon in such a manner as to maintain the divested entity a viable competitor in the relevant markets, and which divestiture would not violate any of the antitrust laws of the United States.

The Sixth Circuit's Six Commandments

The U.S. Court of Appeals for the Sixth Circuit supported the decision of the district court. It concluded that the district court was correct in finding likelihood of an antitrust violation, and it based its finding on the following factors:

Size of the Industry. The court argued that even if an industry is large with respect to the size of the nationwide economy, size per se does not imply less competition. However, it pointed out that size becomes important for antitrust issues when firms within an industry have the power to raise prices above or restrict output below levels that would occur in a competitive marketplace. It suggested that Mobil was already very big and an increase in its size by acquiring Marathon would increase its monopolistic power. It followed that the larger Mobil, the greater the likelihood that the welfare of the consumers would be threatened.

Industry Concentration. The court mentioned the figures that were previously pointed out by Judge Manos, and agreed that the market for motor gasoline was the most significant "line of commerce" affected under Section 7. The argument of Mobil's expert, Dr. Stigler, was that "gasoline prices in the nation tend to approach uniformity with due regard for transportation costs," and concluded therefore that the country as a whole was the relevant market. Marathon's economic expert, Dr. Scherer, said that the argument failed to explain differences in prices across various areas of the nation and "demonstrates that motor gasoline does not move from area to area in response to price changes easily or as readily as Mobil asserts."

Elasticity of Demand. It was determined by the court that the demand for motor gasoline was relatively inelastic with respect to price changes. In other words, increases in prices were followed by less than proportional reductions in demand. Specifically, it argued that the huge price increase since the Arab oil embargo in 1973 had been accompanied by only a small decrease in the demand for the product. It followed that it was risky to allow Mobil to increase its share in a market in which the demand for the product was rather price inelastic.

Barriers to Entry. Barriers to entry in the petroleum industry were found by the court to be very high, since it was extremely capital intensive. Thus, it found it unlikely that a new fully integrated oil company would enter the market and replace Marathon as a supplier for independent dealers.

Joint Operations in the Oil Industry. The court argued there were close relationships among the oil producers including joint ventures for exploration, production, operation of pipelines, and transportation. It also suggested that an increase in the size of Mobil would reinforce the occurrence of those joint operations and that it would therefore lessen competition.

Efficiency or Other Benefits. The court said that Mobil failed to convince it that the merger would help to increase efficiency in the operation of Marathon or that it would bring any other type of benefit.

And thus ended one of the most dramatic antitrust defenses mounted in the last decade. Marathon was able to successfully convince the court that the proposed merger would restrict competition sufficiently to warrant the court's intrusion. While it successfully thwarted Mobil's hostile takeover attempt, its independence was not long lasting. Soon after, Marathon announced its intention to merge with white knight U.S. Steel—thus concluding one of the fiercest boardroom merger battles ever witnessed.

THE ANTITRUST DEFENSE–ITS FUTURE

As seen in cases throughout this book, antitrust arguments are one of the most frequently used forms of merger defense. While it is usually unsuccessful in the courts or on the DOJ and FTC battlefield, the defense does signal the target's intent to do battle. Moreover, it often results in either a higher price paid to the target's shareholders or a white knight appearing on the scene.

The defense is rarely used alone. It is frequently used together with lock-ups, the poison pill, or other defense strategies. However, the adoption of Pac-Man has, on occasion, caused it to be

dropped only days or weeks after its initiation, sometimes resulting in egg on the target's face. How can the merger be anticompetitive one day, while beneficial for the marketplace the next, when
the only difference is the juxtaposition of target and aggressor?

The DOJ guidelines have changed, bit by bit, over the years. With
the implementation of the 1984 guidelines most merger participants would probably agree that the uncertainty associated with
the ultimate success in repelling an aggressor has increased. However, the inclusion of imports in the 1984 market definition has
caused the probability of a successful defense to significantly erode.
On the other hand, it is likely that the unmistakable signal a target's
court challenge entails will continue to cause targets to use antitrust as a first line of merger defense.

Above all, political considerations will continue to play a key
role in the use of the antitrust defense. To the chagrin of most targets, the administration has reduced the scope of mergers it has
tried to block. It has subordinated court-created antitrust rules to
economic analysis in determining which mergers reduce competition and warrant challenge. Attorney General Meese, in 1985, re-
assured the free market advocates by indicating that the unwilling-
ness of the Department of Justice to challenge mergers for the past
few years has been appropriately based on "sound economic analysis and a desire to avoid unnecessary government intervention."

While in previous administrations the proposed acquisitions of
part of MCI Communications by computer giant IBM and of Hughes
Aircraft by General Motors would likely have been stymied, the
trend in the Reagan administration toward such acquisitions is
more favorable. This trend toward a more merger-accommodating
administration has been detected by the marketplace. It is clearly
reflected in statements made by some of the key players. Consider
the 1985 transaction in which MCI would acquire IBM's Satellite
Business System, an MCI competitor in long distance communications. Long before the outcome of the proposed 1985 MCI–IBM
transaction became known, James Denvir, former head of the Justice Department's trial team, revealed his opinion. While measured
by the HHI, this transaction certainly reduces competition; nevertheless, Denvir said the department "probably wouldn't challenge
it" because of the small market shares of SBS and MCI.

Even the conservative *Wall Street Journal* adopted this feeling that more mergers would be approved by regulators. During the 1985 negotiations between Hughes Aircraft and General Motors, *The Wall Street Journal* speculated that "competing lines of business [wouldn't be a problem]" and "it seems likely that any overlaps can be fixed."

Obviously, if such an acceptance of mergers becomes prevalent, the antitrust argument as a defense against raiders would be substantially weakened. However, targets may take heart in the view of some influential members of Congress. Representative Peter Rodino, chairman of the House Judiciary Committee, complained that unfriendly raids "are focusing management's attention on short-term survival, not the productive, long-term planning and development that is vital for economic growth."

A Glossary of
MERGER BUZZWORDS

BLANK CHECK   Previously authorized issuance of a large block of preferred stock with no attached provisions. Such preauthorization enables the firm to quickly institute a poison pill defense.

CONGLOMERATE DISCOUNT   The theory that conglomerates are valued less than the combined value of their operating divisions if these divisions were operated independently.

COUNTER ACCUMULATION   A target's purchase of a raider's shares in the open market.

COUNTER TENDER OFFER   A tender offer by a target for some portion of the shares of a firm which is simultaneously trying to acquire it.

CUMULATIVE VOTING   Voting system in which each share entitles the holder to number of votes equal to the number of directors. It gives minority shareholders the possibility of electing some directors.

ESOP   An employee stock ownership plan qualified under the Internal Revenue Code. It must comply with various participation vesting and distribution rules established under the Employment Retirement Security Act (ERISA) to protect the interests of the employees. Often the target's plan is used to purchase securities of the target when it is attacked by a hostile raider.

FATMAN STRATEGY   Defensive strategy in which a target acquires poorly performing assets, often another company, in order to decrease its short-term value to a potential acquirer.

FLIP-OVER PROVISION   Provision enabling the target's convertible preferred stock to be converted into the raider's convertible preferred. The raider's convertible preferred is then convertible into its common stock. It is associated with the poison pill defense.

FORCED EQUITY PROVISION   Provision enabling the target's preferred shareholders to directly convert their stock into common stock of the acquirer. This provision is associated with the poison pill defense.

GOLDEN PARACHUTE   Guarantee that senior management will receive hefty compensation if they leave the firm as a result of a merger or takeover.

GREENMAIL   The target's repurchase of its own shares from a hostile acquirer. The raider, often extracting a high premium, is referred to as a greenmailer.

HOSTILE TENDER OFFER   Tender offer which the board has determined to be unfriendly.

IN PLAY   Company for which a tender offer has been made. The offer draws attention of other suitors, who may knock at its door. The increased attention increases the likelihood of an eventual takeover.

JUNK BONDS   Unsecured bonds, whose payment of interest and repayment of principal are potentially in doubt. As a result, interest rates are typically higher than those of high-grade bonds.

KAMIKAZE STRATEGY   Defensive strategy describing those defenses in which a firm makes itself less attractive to a potential acquirer. This term refers to the following strategies: fat-man, sale of crown jewels, and scorched earth.

LEVERAGED BUYOUT   Purchase, often by management, of a company in which the deal results in an unusually high debt-to-worth ratio for the purchased company. A large proportion of the assets of the bought out firm is typically used as collateral to secure the borrowed funds.

LEVERAGED ESOP   An ESOP which uses borrowed money to purchase securities.

LOCK-UP   A target's promised sale of stock or assets to a potential acquirer in order to dissuade others from purchasing it. The sale is usually contingent on the purchase of the target by a third party.

OFFERING CIRCULAR   Information describing details of a tender offer. It is required by the SEC.

PAC-MAN   A defensive strategy in which the target turns around and attempts to swallow the aggressor.

POISON PILL   A preferred stock dividend to the target's shareholders which has the special conversion feature enabling the shares to be converted to shares of the acquirer. In a broader context, the term poison pill refers to the defensive issuance of any securities that can be converted to cash, notes or stock of the acquirer.

PRECATORY PROPOSAL   A recommendation of an action made to a company, either to management or to shareholders.

PRORATION DEADLINE   Date before which tendered shares would be included in the proration pool. If the offer is oversubscribed, shares in the proration pool would be purchased on a pro rata basis.

PRORATION POOL   Pool of tendered shares from which shares will be purchased by the acquiring company. Shares may be withdrawn prior to the withdrawal deadline.

PROXY BATTLE   Battle between company and dissident shareholders. The battle is precipitated by the solicitation of proxies by dissident shareholders in order to obtain approval of a shareholder resolution.

SALE OF CROWN JEWELS   Target sells the assets which are most likely to interest a raider. These are often the most valuable assets of the corporation.

SELF-TENDER   A tender offer for a firm's shares by the company itself. The goal of the self-tender is to reduce the number of shares available for purchase by a hostile acquirer.

SCORCHED EARTH POLICY   Policy in which a company defends against a takeover by liquidating a significant proportion of its assets.

SHAREHOLDER CONSENTS   A special case of formal proxy solicitation. While proxies must be submitted at a shareholder meeting, consents can be solicited without having to wait for a meeting.

SHARK REPELLENT   Provisions in a corporate charter and bylaws designed to discourage unwanted takeovers.

STAGGERED BOARD   Arrangement of the board, whereby directors come up for election at staggered intervals. As a result, a hostile aggressor cannot gain control of a company immediately but must wait until the directors' terms of office expire.

SUPERMAJORITY PROVISION   Requirement of the bylaws related to certain decisions such as mergers and director selection. It requires a substantially higher proportion of votes than the state law mandates.

TENDER OFFER   Formal offer to buy some or all of the shares of a public company.

TWO-TIER OFFER   Sometimes called two-step offer. It consists of an initial offer, usually designed to gain control of a target firm, followed by a lower priced offer for the remainder of the firm.

WHITE KNIGHT   A corporation that comes to the aid of the target in a takeover battle.

WITHDRAWAL DEADLINE   Date after which tendered shares may not be withdrawn from the proration pool. Prior to this date shares may be withdrawn at will.

Corporate Players

Individual Players